From Management Education to Civic Reconstruction

From Management Education to Civic Reconstruction provides a unique analysis of how a combination of diverse, culturally based approaches are implicitly or explicitly built into the development of a business or organization. By addressing key issues at the forefront of developmental management, the authors demonstrate methods whereby principles of ecology can be applied to different stages of organizational development at both local and global level. Distinctive features of this work include:

- examination of management and organizational development from a post-modern perspective
- up-to-date case material from a wide range of organizations, spanning the public, private and civic sphere
- development of a transcultural approach to the study of management principles and practices, incorporating practical and theoretical insights from across the globe

This text will be of interest to students and practitioners in the fields of organizational behaviour, corporate strategy and management education.

Ronnie Lessem is Founder of the Four Worlds Institute. The inventor of the concept of the global businessphere, he is the author of over twenty books including *Management Development through Cultural Diversity* (1998).

Sudhanshu Palsule is Head of Learning and Knowledge Management at Anglia Water and co-founder of the Four Worlds Institute. He is the originator of the concept of a knowledge creating ecology and is co-author of *Managing in Four Worlds* (1997) with Ronnie Lessem.

Managing across cultures: developmental perspectives
Series Editors
Ronnie Lessem and Sudhanshu Palsule
Four Worlds Institute

This series is oriented towards the development of managerial and educational principles and practices from across the globe, focusing upon business in America, Europe, the Middle and Far East and southern Africa. It comprises three types of book – contextual, comparative and developmental – set within the context of transcultural management in general, surveying the development and dissemination of business principles and practices that draw upon diverse cultures of our global village. Each title will portray not only such transcultural concepts and their application, but also the way in which they can be cultivated and transferred from within businesses and business schools, as well as management consultancies.

From Management Education to Civic Reconstruction

The Emerging Ecology of Organizations

**Ronnie Lessem
with Sudhanshu Palsule**

London and New York

First published 1999
by Routledge
11 New Fetter Lane, London EC4P 4EE

Simultaneously published in the USA and Canada
by Routledge
29 West 35th Street, New York, NY 10001

© 1999 Ronnie Lessem

The right of Ronnie Lessem to be identified as the Author of this
Work has been asserted by him in accordance with the Copyright,
Designs and Patents Act 1988

Typeset in Baskerville by
The Florence Group, Stoodleigh, Devon
Printed and bound in Great Britain by
MPG Books Ltd, Bodmin

British Library Cataloguing in Publication Data
A catalogue record for this book is available from the British
Library

Library of Congress Cataloging in Publication Data
Lessem, Ronnie
    From management education to civic reconstruction: the
emerging ecology of organizations / Ronnie Lessem with
Sudhanshu Palsule
        p.   cm. — (Managing across cultures)
    Includes bibliographical references and index.
    1. Organizational change.   2. Corporate culture.
3. Organizational learning.   4. Management.
I. Title.   II. Series.
HD58.8.L473   1999
658.4′063—dc21
                                              98–35446
                                                  CIP

ISBN 0-415-18232-8 (hbk)
ISBN 0-415-18233-6 (pbk)

To all our students and organizations on City
University's Management MBA programme

Contents

Figures

Tables

Acknowledgements

This book represents an intimate partnership between business, consultancy and academia. From the 'business' world, we acknowledge our debt to CEO's Chris Mellor and Alan Smith, HR Director Clive Moreton as well as former Employee Development Manager David Taylor at Anglian Water; to Ray Mahoney at the Corporation of London; to Professor Ken Mortimore and to Geoff Johnson at Ford; to Mike Millikan and Brian Foss at IBM; to Heide and Makis Werlamis at the Idea Center in Austria, together with Eva Maria Rosenmayer; to Terry Heyday and Terry Webb at Lloyd's; to Barry Wilding and Duncan Hopper from the insurance industry; to Dr Nabil Nassar, co-founder of Medlabs in Jordan; to Chairman David Sainsbury and HR practitioners Howard Bentley, Judith Evans and Andrew Tanner at Sainsbury; to Chief Constable Ian Blair, Deputy Chief Constables Ian Beckett and Jim Hart, and Andy Thompson at Surrey Police; to Michael Page and Boyd Rodger at Thames Valley Police; and to MD Rowan Gormley and his Deputy Jane-Anne Gardia at Virgin Direct.

From the consultancy and academic worlds, within and adjacent to City University, we wish to acknowledge our educators Professors Chris Hendry, Clive Holtham, George Selim and Carole Vielba as well as Lakis Kaiounides at City University, together with visiting faculty, Professors V.S. Mahesh from Buckingham University, Ralph Stacey from the University of Hertfordshire and Paul Roberts from Roffey Park. We also want to acknowledge our debt to our facilitators Wendy Briner, Ann Brocksbank, Alan Clark, Jonathon Cowan, Romy Jenkins, Ann Leeming and Ian McGill. Moreover, the book stands on the shoulders of conceptual giants spread across the globe, i.e. America's Christopher Bartlett, Don Beck and Chris Cowan, Will McWhinney, Jim Moore, Emmett Murphy, William Strauss and Neil Howe, Margaret Wheatley and finally Ken Wilber; Anglo-Frenchman Max Boisot; Canada's William Randall; Englishmen Kevin Kingsland and David Whyte; India's Samantra Goshal; Japan's Ikijiro Nonaka and Hirotaka Takeuchi; and again South African Ralph Stacey.

Finally, we would like to thank Dr Helmi Salaam and Dr Mohammed Mikdashi, co-founders of TEAM in Cairo, our partners in the Arab Middle East, as well as Professor Hugh Murray and Keith Holland at Executive

Development in England, Cathy McSweeney, Catherine Butler and Melissa Fisher in the MMBA office, and my editor at Routledge, Stuart Hay, for his sponsorship, support and enthusiasm.

Part I
Orientation
Knowledge creating ecology

1 Knowledge creating ecology

Management education to civic reconstruction

Catalysation is a phenomenon through which a number of 'tag-on' processes undermine the existence of the previous 'conservative' order of stability and increasing equilibrium. Whether they are the invading bacteria, forest fires or typhoons, these catalysts alter the earlier structure and create new situations in which the energy blocks are removed. In contrast to the 'de-sensitized' state of the eco-system at the conservation stage, the system becomes highly sensitized at the catalytic one. Positive feedback loops amplify small changes and push them through the entire system, keeping it in a 'far-from-equilibrium' state. This is also the stage where life can take new directions and lead to the development of new species and behaviour.

Lessem and Palsule, *Managing in Four Worlds*

INTRODUCTION – CONTEXT

From education to civilization

Our purpose is to invite you as a manager, your organization and your society to journey through four worlds – from individually oriented education and training to organizationally oriented intellectual capital, and from inter-organizationally oriented knowledge creation to societally based civic reconstruction – mediated by our so-called 'knowledge creating ecology'. The journey begins at City University Business School, through its evolving Managment MBA programme. Alongside it first, as a strong force of political and economic tradition, the commercially and somewhat parochially based City Corporation and Lloyd's of London are individually evolving. Such an evolutionary development is from management training towards executive education and from didactic instruction towards action learning. Second, together with our programme, those Anglo-Saxon national symbols of modernity, Ford and IBM, based in the USA, and Sainsbury's, based in the UK, are converting, implicitly if not yet explicitly, physical and financial into intellectual capital.

Third, and now in transnational 'post-modern' guise, we illustrate for you how intellectual capital, or knowledge management, is evolving towards knowledge creation. Starting in the 'west' with the insurance industry in Britain, we journey transnationally towards the Austrian 'north' via the Internationales Designcenter, to the Palestinian middle 'east' through health oriented Medlabs, and to the indigenous 'south' via Thames Valley Police, drawing upon New Zealand's Maoris. In each case we cite our co-evolving relationship with knowledge intensive service industries. Finally, returning to our perennial source, that is civic society, where global knowledge creation and civic reconstruction meet, we take you to Surrey Police and to Virgin Direct, to the Body Shop and to Anglian Water.

For us at City University, then, the journey began ten years ago. In the late 1980s an entrepreneurial professor of Export Marketing at our Business School set out following the course of all pioneering ecosystems, to 'colonize' the MBA market in the UK. As such he established a project based masters programme, aimed exclusively at a largely untapped demand for accredited management education, that of practising managers. In the same period Anglian Water, one of the UK's leading water utilities, was set for the same pioneering course, through a programme of privatization. What any eco-system knows, as it were, but neither Prime Minister Thatcher nor our entrepreneurial professor did, is that such 'colonization' is only a first step along a richly varied 'fourfold' way, that is towards a fully fledged know-ledge creating ecology. Had each known this, their respectively ministerial and professorial regimes might have been even more enduring, reaching all the way to genuine civic reconstruction.

Three years later I met up with my ecologist colleague Sudhanshu Palsule in Goa, having teamed up with our pioneering professor to take the MMBA forward, at a symposium dedicated to a 'catalytic' process of turning busi-nesses into learning communities.[1] As an economist and psychologist, I had been focusing on business and economic development in Europe and Africa. Sudhanshu Palsule, a physicist and ecologist, had been orienting himself towards business and the physical environment, in Asia and America. Some five years later, though he was unaware of it at the time, Sudhanshu would arrive at Anglian Water in the UK, via Denmark.

From individual manager to civic society

Soon after Goa, that is in the early 1990s, I joined forces with Franz Neubauer, a German-born Professor of Strategic Management at IMD (the Institute for Management Development) in Lausanne, to focus on European business systems.[2] The connection between Neubauer and me had been made by another Indian colleague, Jagdish Parikh, who was also at the Goa conference, and who subsequently co-authored the book with Warren Bennis and me, on *Beyond Leadership: Balancing Economics, Ethics and Ecology*.[3] The plot was thickening! During the European project it came to my attention that management development generally, and the MBA specifically, were basically Anglo-Saxon inventions. In other words, while 'westerners' naturally focused on the individual, 'northerners' such as the Scandinavians were more naturally oriented towards the organization. Similarly, the more 'eastern' oriented, for example the Germans within Europe and the Japanese within Asia, tended to be focused on whole industries, while the more 'southerly' Latins or Africans tended to be communally oriented.

By now, with my responsibility for the development of our MMBA programme, I was pondering this discrepancy between such an individually oriented education promoted by the 'west', and the innate developmental requirements of the rest of the world. Sudhanshu had a parallel concern. Having become, in the early nineties, Professor of Learning Ecology at the International People's College in Denmark, he was reflecting upon the difference in emphasis between classical economics, with its explicit orientation towards individual enterprise, and the tacit connection of both economics and ecology with *oikos*.

Oikos was concerned with 'management of the household'. Whether it is an organisation, a society or any of the other myriads of forms that we forge, each of these, in one way or the other, is rooted in 'oikos'. An understanding of these indelible links is the singular act of understanding a universal system at work, through an array of complex relationships, chains, linkages, alliances, interdependencies that make us and our environment a fountain of energy flowing through a circuit of soils, rocks, microbes, plants, animals, the atmosphere, our societies, and our organisations. Consequently, it provides a powerful model and metaphor for the far-reaching changes we so badly need to create in our societies, organisations and lives, and thereby to return home.[4]

Sudhanshu Palsule had left India, where he had been a Professor of Physics and Ecology, soon after we had met one another, and took up his post in Denmark. At the same time the Management MBA, still patronized by its founder member, the leading UK food retailers Sainsbury's, had in the early nineties been joined by Anglian Water. Soon thereafter the renowned insurers Lloyd's, Ford Motors, IBM (Europe) and the Corporation of London came on board. The more we worked together the surer I became – duly influenced by Sudhanshu's ecosystemic orientation on the one hand and by my own transcultural orientation on the other – that we needed to catalyse the development of a worldwide 'knowledge creating ecology' rather than conserve a parochial masters in business administration. For the individuals who participated in our programme, implicitly and developmentally if not explicitly and educationally, were each part of a wider business ecosystem, and needed practically and theoretically to be considered as such. In effect, traditionally based management education needed to be developmentally set in a modern context of the enhancement of intellectual capital. Furthermore, such functionally oriented knowledge management needed to be set within the further reaches of organization-wide knowledge creation, if not also civic reconstruction.

From here to eternity

As much as I intuitively felt this to be so, it was difficult to find a coherent as well as practical way forward. If I was to be honest with myself my previous orientation towards 'total quality learning'[5] as well as 'business as a learning community' may have been attractive in theory, but both lacked practical application. As I looked around me for a solution I came across an intriguing *Harvard Business Review* article, by a certain Ikijiro Nonaka, on the so-called 'Knowledge Creating Company'.[6] What appealed to me about it was that the article was based on the practical business approaches of such Japanese giants as Canon, Honda, Sharp and Sony.

Soon afterwards, that is in the mid-nineties, I had been invited to join a group of management researchers from France and Germany, Italy and Spain, as well as – for control purposes – America and Japan. The topic we were to investigate was European/ness and Innovation.[7] The three-year project was sponsored by Germany's Roland Berger, Europe's largest group of management consultants, based in Munich. The Japanese representative within this European symposium turned out to be none other than Nonaka himself. Fate had evidently played its hand, and had added a Japanese (eastern) to my own southern African birthplace (southern), British place of residence (western) and continental European parentage (northern).

Very soon, then, I came to realize that our own 'four worlds' approach, and Nonaka's 'knowledge creating spiral' were macro–micro counterparts of each another. When he and his colleague Hirotama Takeuchi, now based at Harvard, published their book *The Knowledge Creating Company*,[8] I became convinced that it provided a practical key to unlock the door to the hitherto amorphous concept of business as a learning community. As a result, we reconstituted our MMBA programme accordingly. Three problems, however, remained.

First there were no knowledge creating companies to draw upon in our own part of the world, and we were hardly likely to turn our companies into Japanese ones! Second, I was unhappy with the engineering terminology underpinning Nonaka's work, and was keen to base our work upon ecological foundations rather than technological ones. Third, and most important, we were still focusing, in essence, on developing the individual MBA.

The first problem, through a remarkable piece of serendipity, was easily solved, for in 1996 the Surrey Police joined our MMBA programme. Much to my pleasant surprise, and as will be prolifically revealed in this book, I came to discover that this regional police force is a fully fledged knowledge creating organization. In fact it is the only one I have come across in this country. The second problem, which we began to address in our book

Managing in Four Worlds will be more concertedly dealt with here, by means of the organizational ecology that I shall be uncovering. Underlying such an ecology are what we have termed 'evolutionary grounds'. In fact, and as we shall see, while ecological succession forms the definitive basis for our organizational ecology, the stories of each of the participating organizations in our programme, coupled with the involvement of their participants on the MMBA, form the narrative backdrop. Ultimately, the ecological succession is paralleled by a developmental shift in orientation from education and training towards civic reconstruction, and by a historical and societal evolution from a traditional to a modern, and from a post-modern to what I have termed a 'perennial' outlook on work and life.

To make this fundamental shift in orientation real is the most fundamental challenge with which we are now faced. If we succeed, we shall have totally transformed the relationships between knowledge and practice, university and business, ecology and economics.

Catalysing development: towards a civic society

This book, then, starting off in America and the UK, and venturing out into continental Europe, the Middle East practically and the Far East theoretically, as well as to the worlds of indigenous peoples in general, will establish the processes through which such individual, organizational, inter-organizational and societal development can be 'catalysed' through our knowledge creating ecology. I shall therefore be taking up, practically, from where our recent book, *Managing in Four Worlds* (with Sudhanshu Palsule), has left off theoretically. As a result, whereas I have previously positioned myself as something of an academic observer of the business scene, in this case I shall become – through the words and deeds of significant managerial, organizational and societal others – a facilitator of a knowledge creating ecology. Such an ecology will have evolved somewhat, as we have now indicated, from a traditionally based commercial and training orientation (genesis) to a modern and industrial orientation towards intellectual capital (morphosis), and thereafter on to post-modern and service oriented organizational knowledge creation (metamorphosis), ultimately connecting with perennial civilization (homeostasis).

Accordingly, therefore, on our journey, we shall first draw upon such *traditionally* based commercial organizations as the insurers Lloyd's and the City Corporation, both based in the UK's capital city, London. Second, we incorporate those symbols of mass-producing *modernity*, Ford and IBM (the latter now bridging the modern and post-modern), each based in US industrial heartlands, alongside the mass marketeer based in England, the redoubtable retailer Sainsbury's. Third, we move from the UK to pursue a *post-modern* approach to the management of difference, through knowledge intensive service based enterprises. We visit Britain's emergent insurance industry via the Virgin Group along the 'western' way, thereafter incorporating

Northern
INTELLECTUAL CAPITAL
Organizational

Western	**KNOWLEDGE**	**Eastern**
MANAGEMENT	**CREATING**	KNOWLEDGE
EDUCATION	**ECOLOGY**	CREATION
Individual		*Inter-organizational*

Southern
CIVIC RECONSTRUCTION
Communal

Figure 1 Managing in four worlds

a 'northern' Idea Centre located in central Europe, and an 'eastern' set of private medical laboratories based in Palestine as well as visiting a 'southern' facing police force in England's Thames Valley; all of which, moreover, have become part of our knowledge creating ecology. As such we deliberately incorporate a holistically differentiated 'businessphere', as opposed to a rationally integrated 'global' orientation towards America, Europe, Japan and the so-called emerging markets.

Finally, we call upon our so-called *perennial* examples of enterprises enhancing civic society locally and also globally. While Anglian Water and Body Shop are profoundly rooted in ecology, the Surrey Police and the Virgin Group are deeply rooted in community. Between the four of them they represent the *oikos* of old in a 'civic economy' anew, Surrey Police in fact forming a knowledge creating bridge between the post-modern and the perennial. In thereby reconnecting the economic with the civic they transcend tradition and modernity, and even post-modernity, by reconnecting us with eternity.

From education and training to learning ecology

Organizations in our terms, then, across the globe, are undergoing a not too silent revolution, from the traditional to the perennial. As such, and on the one hand, the independent business enterprise and the dependable bureaucracy are giving way to an interdependent and ultimately transcendent community of organizations. As a result, and ultimately most important for our purposes here, 'western' training and education is being supplanted by the 'northern' enhancement of intellectual capital through knowledge management, which is in its turn transcended by 'eastern' organizational knowledge creation, and ultimately by 'southern' civic reconstruction. Taken as a whole, this represents a radical shift in our relationship between business and business school. In effect, a transactional relationship between independent business and independent academia is being replaced by a tranformative one. In this way the business school becomes the innovative centre of an interdependent business ecosystem.

All this is, moreover, being underpinned by a change in our theoretical foundations. Such a change in orientation is from economics to ecology, from education to catalysation, from classical science to the sciences of chaos and complexity, and indeed from exclusively masculine to inclusively feminine values. Ironically such a change in outlook is yet to impinge more generally upon the relationship between businesses and the very universities from which many of these ideas have emerged. In that context, perhaps unlike some fellow business schools, we are attempting to practise commercially what we preach intellectually.

In fact, and by way of contrast, the traditional MBA, which still remains the pride of business schools' offerings around the globe, remains locked into a Newtonian paradigm. In other words independent blocks of curricula, whether made up of business concepts or case studies, are parcelled up and delivered to blocks of individual students, usually disconnected from their organizations and often from their societies. Whether offered part-time or full-time, whether to Singaporeans or Americans, Chileans or Italians, an MBA is an MBA. Moreover, even when such programmes are project-based, or supposedly 'tailored' to fit a sponsoring company's needs, it is the individual student who 'does' the project, and not usually the organization.

As a result, even in the case of executive based, action centred programmes, the relationship between business and business school remains atomistic rather than holistic. As such a typical MBA programme is oriented towards individual learning rather than towards organizational knowlege creation. In shaping this prospect then, as a business/academic learning consortium, we hope to inaugurate a new era which serves to combine developmentally, the traditional and the modern, the post-modern and the perennial, within a composite learning ecology. In such a new era, a consortium of businesses and business school, interdependently, will not merely be helping to develop individual managers commercially through a 'preparatory' knowledge dissemination.

Nor will we merely be conserving and enhancing intellectual capital technologically, that is, through 'ordinary' and functionally based knowledge management. Rather, we will collectively be serving culturally as a knowledge creating catalyst, thereby fostering corporate as well as self-renewal transnationally, through an 'extraordinary' process of knowledge development. Ultimately, moreover, as a composite institutional and global force, we will be rebuilding the social foundations of civic societies, that is, engaging 'masterfully' in civic transformation.

Our aim, then, is to offer, by example, both businesses and business schools (or indeed consultancies) a newly ecosystemic relationship. Such a relationship is geared neither to delivering specific courses nor to undertaking reputable research, both in isolation, but to establishing a knowledge creating ecology. As such we shall be engaged in developing not only people and organizations but also new products and services, within the context of whole communities. This book is therefore aimed at four kinds of organizational ecologists around the world.

First we are addressing management developers, conventionally based in human resources, who want to amplify the nature of their service, and gain power and influence in the process. Second, we address knowledge managers, or chief knowledge officers, traditionally oriented towards IT, who wish to integrate more closely with the human side of the business, thereby enhancing intellectual capital as a whole. Third, we wish to communicate with those few genuine organizational knowledge creators, usually isolated within R&D rather than accessible to organization development as a whole. Finally we wish to pull so-called civic reconstruction out of what is usually a corporate affairs enclave, if it is not based in the chairman's favourite charity or foundation, so as to address the CEO responsible to make it more integral to the business as a whole. I now turn from this introduction to the overall context towards the book's specific content.

KNOWLEDGE CONTENT

Part I   Knowledge creating ecology: from colonization to co-creation

Our product – knowledge creating ecology

In this first chapter I have outlined the nature and scope of the journey we are undertaking together, identified with a *knowledge creating ecology* that has been built up through our MMBA consortium. We subsequently and specifically chart, in chapter 2, the progressive *metamorphosis of the MBA* at City University Business School, over the course of the last decade.

First I shall set it within the historical context of the evolution of management education and development, and more recently of intellectual capital and knowledge management, organizational learning and knowledge creation, and ultimately civic reconstruction. Second, I shall locate the programme's emergence within its current ecosystemic context, thereby incorporating its relationship with commerce and industry, local government and global business, as well as civically based organizations. Third, I illustrate how the transformation of the old-style MBA into a new-style knowledge creating ecology reflects both the demise of traditional education and also the advent of modern knowledge management. Furthermore, I shall illustrate how we supplement post-modern knowledge creation with the perennially located, prospective renewal of whole civilizations.

Our knowledge grounds – organizational ecology

In the third chapter, I shall focus even more specifically on our knowledge grounds, i.e. *organizational ecology* set within the 'four worlds' of what Sudhanshu Palsule and I have called the global businessphere.

These four epistemological worlds comprise pragmatism and rationalism, holism and humanism   in business and society   as I have continually illustrated over the past decade. These in turn are ecologically and organizationally lodged within processes of colonization and conservation, catalysation and co-creation, enabling you as academic – exemplified by me at City, or as a practitioner, as is, for example, the case for Sudhanshu Palsule at Anglian Water – to change mindset from enterprise to ecosystem, and from independent to interdependent operator. As such your activity base shifts from education and training to the development of a knowledge creating ecology. At such a point, moreover, the divide between business and academia is dissolved to the extent, for example, that 'knowledge management' has been further developed in companies than in universities. We start here, then, with the simple divide between individually oriented 'ordinary' training and 'extraordinary' education, at Lloyd's. Thereafter we distinguish between workmanlike instruction into ways of 'doing', and 'soulful' work based learning as a way of 'being', at the City Corporation of London. We thereby and initially establish the combined commercial grounds, and traditionally based individual training and educational foundations, upon which our programme is built.

Part II   The evolution of commercial tradition: from management training to executive education

Lloyd's of London – from management to leadership

When commercially based Lloyd's of London first joined forces with us, activated by link manager Terry Heyday, they were wedded to a traditionally based approach to professionally based training. This was their Accelerated Professional Examination programme, known as APEX. It did not take long for Terry to realize that such an 'ordinary' approach was to some extent out of tune with the stretching requirements of 'reconstruction and renewal' upon which Lloyd's had recently embarked.

Such a reconstruction demanded of people a somewhat more *extraordinary* process of management education, like the one Terry Heyday chose to undergo through our MMBA, rather than the *ordinary* programme of professional training he might, APEX-wise, have embarked upon. In chapter 4, through the work of Ralph Stacey, we distinguish between the ordinary requirements of management and of training on the one hand, and the extraordinary demands of leadership and of authentic executive education on the other. We then turn to the City Corporation.

The City Corporation: from instruction to work based learning

In the same way as Terry Heyday was trying to drag Lloyd's out of a traditional training orientation, so the Training and Development Manager at the City Corporation in London, Ray Mahoney, was embarking upon our MMBA with a similar struggle in mind, albeit in his case with a leaning towards action learning. While many of the City institutions, then, were pre-eminently hands-on in their approach, and thus oriented above all towards 'work' *per se*, Ray was trying to recognize the famous square mile's 800-year-old reflective 'soul'. His aim, therefore, was to combine activity and reflexivity through work based learning.

We draw then, interestingly, upon the British poet and consultant David Whyte. Through his *'work and soul'* (chapter 5) we portray, in both theory and practice, the basic divide between an individually oriented 'doing' approach to training and a 'being' oriented approach to learning. We locate such a divide within the evolutionary grounds of the City Corporation, home to London as a financial entity, and include its participants' involvement with our programme, most particularly drawing upon the Training and Development Manager, Ray Mahoney. While the 'City' undoubtedly 'works', as an active commercial centre, as we have said it forever runs the risk of losing its reflective 'soul', to the extent that long-standing traditions are not meaningfully renewed.

Our knowledge creating ecology however, as I have already indicated, has much more to it than these two contrasting, individually oriented elements. We next turn to three worlds of industrial modernity, starting out symbolically with Ford.

Part III   The development of modern industry: from material to intellectual capital

Ford Motors: rationalization, revitalization, regeneration

The City of London generally and Lloyd's in particular have played formative roles in the development of global commercial activity. Ford of Detroit has played a similarly global role in the spread of manufacturing based activities. Moreover, as we shall see, such modern large-scale manufacturing enterprises as Ford and IBM, in the US, and retailing enterprise Sainsbury's in the UK, have all undergone, in recent years, periods of crisis and renewal. All of these mighty enterprises, moreover, make up our knowledge creating ecology. In chapter 6, we first trace Ford's evolution through the eyes of one of the senior managers on our MMBA programme, Steve Harley. Such an evolution extends initially from its local and physically based craft oriented production to its nationally and financially based mass production. It subsequently culminates in 'Ford 2000', its most recently constituted local/global intellectual orientation. In that context, and as Ford develops from its traditional entrepreneurial and modern industrial grounds towards a glimmer of post-modernity, so – in the eyes of management experts Goshal and Bartlett – rationalizing turns to revitalizing, which turns to regenerating.

Sumantra Goshal – named by the *Economist* European business guru of 1997 – and Christopher Bartlett at Harvard are the most recent of the management thinkers to be drawn upon for our book, through their concept of the 'Individualized Corporation'.[9]

For them, rationalization first represents the embedding of traditional *entrepreneurial drive* in junior managers. We embody this approach ecologically in the traditionally based 'colonizing' of territory. Revitalization for them, second, represents the modern development of integrative synergies in middle managers. They represent this through the *leveraging of knowledge*, which we embody in an advanced form of modernity, reflected in 'conserving' resources. Post-modern regeneration, third, they depict in terms of continuous *self-renewal* or 'autopoiesis', whereby individuals and organizations 're-authorize' themselves individually and organizationally. This we embody, ecologically, in 'catalysing' activities.

Cycles in history: material crisis and intellectual awakening

IBM, like Ford before it and Sainsbury after it, has been through a period of material crisis, and is now emerging tentatively towards an intellectual awakening, which we locate here within its insurance based European solutions business. Through it IBM is, in effect, passing through the turbulent cycles of history. Such a fully fledged 'fourfold journey', as American economic historians Strauss and Howe[10] point out in chapter 7, is a recurring theme in the history of man and womankind.

Through their *Fourth Turning*, in portraying cycles of history based on successively changing generations, Strauss and Howe distinguish between respectively 'high', 'awakening', 'unravelling' and 'crisis' periods or societal turnings. Moreover, they depict the roles played by archetypal nomads and heroes, artists and prophets in the process. These roles are analogous to the hunters (individual students), herders (managers of intellectual capital), gardeners (organizational knowledge creators) and stewards (business leaders and management gurus) in our knowledge creating ecology. Moreover, these are all set in the context of IBM's historical evolution from industrially based modernity to knowledge and service oriented post-modernity.

Business ecosystems: material authority and intellectual renewal

In chapter 8 we turn from the cycles of history to forces of business and economic evolution, not unlike those of our organizational ecology. In the process we describe how Sainsbury's is prospectively becoming a 'business ecosystem', for the *age of business ecosystems* that is upon us leads to a reconfiguration of leadership and business strategy. Such a reconfiguration is provided through American James Moore's 'death of competition'.[11] The fact that such a co-evolutionary age is supplanting that of individually competitive firms is something with which Sainsbury's is gradually coming to terms. This is despite, rather than because of, its regressive tendency to look over its Tesco-facing shoulder. Within such an emerging business 'ecosystem' we thereby allude to a traditonal grocer, and subsequently modern mass marketer in food retailing, evolving intellectually and – together with MMBA participant Colin Rye – ecosystemically.

To the extent that this is taking place, in no small part facilitated by Sainsbury's participants on our MMBA programme, post-modern principles of catalysation supplant those of traditional colonization and modern conservation. We now turn from the 'western' US and the UK to the global businessphere.

Part IV   Post-modern knowledge intensive services: from knowledge management to knowledge creation

Insurance 2000: from protagonist to re-authorizer

Whereas the modern world of a Ford, an IBM or of a Sainsbury's in their heyday, was pre-engineered, a post-modern one is self-organizing, continually evolving and thereby knowledge creating. In that sense the post-modern manager, organization or society continually re-authorizes himself, herself or itself by renewing its knowledge and value base.

Moreover, whereas the aforementioned companies are quintessentially Anglo-Saxon, the post-modern ones we shall now meet are geographically and culturally diverse. Finally, while newly evolving modern industry, as opposed to economically based traditional commerce, conserves itself through lifeless technology, post-modern knowledge intensive services are catalysed by 'life-sustaining' biology and ecology.

We start our post-modern journey with two business entrepreneurs in the west, Barry Wilding and Duncan Hopper, set in the context of an emerging financial services industry. Here commerce and knowledge based services meet. In chapter 9, based on the work of Canada's William Randall, *The Stories We Are*,[12] we chart our entrepreneurial managers' development from so-called protagonist and narrator to reader and re-authorizer, thereby charting their own unique knowledge and value creating path.

Design spectrum: from vision to action

Turning north in chapter 10 – together with our Austrian associate Eva Maria Rosenmayr – we chart the development of the Internationales Designcenter in Schrems within north-west Austria. This design based enterprise, connected with us at City, is set in the evolving context of our involvement with Die Lichtung, a New Age conference centre in that area. In a knowledge intensive, service oriented world managers not only create themselves but also accommodate a wide spectrum of individualities, incorporated into the *management spectrum*[13] which developed out of the work of Anglo-Indian psychologist, Kevin Kingsland. The Internationales Designcenter and its founders Makis and Heide Werlamis not only design a wide range of products for export around the globe but accommodate a variety of managerial types. In the process they turn a centrifugally based vision into centripetal action.

From its northern vantage point, then, the Internationales Designcenter accommodates a wide range of post-modern intellectual and artistic perspectives.

Medlabs' information space: from centripetal to centrifugal

The post-modern organization is centrifugal, or multifaceted, rather than centripetal, or supposedly single-faceted. Turning to the Middle East, through Max Boisot's *Framework for an Information Society*,[14] we visit Medlabs in chapter 11, a company participating on our programme which operates private medical laboratories in the Jordanian and Palestinian region. Purposefully combining together the four worlds of fiefs and clans, markets and bureaucracies, it is set in a knowledge based service industry. To the extent that its four founders have been able to transcend the regional orientation towards overdone clannishness, so they are setting an example of how to run a post-modern operation within a traditional environment.

Thames Valley's organizational memes: spiral dynamics

Chapter 12, finally in this section, introduces the Thames Valley Police, another knowledge based service organization which has specifically drawn upon the south, that is the indigenous Maoris of New Zealand, for post-modern organizations draw upon esoteric cultures and feminine values alongside the prevailing culture and masculine values, incorporating a wide range of what Beck and Cowan have termed 'organizational memes'.[15]

Thames Valley in England is a knowledge based service organization, drawing upon a 'southern' communal approach. Such a Maori approach to 'restorative justice', where the wider community is involved in the judicial process, was first adopted and adapted by Thames Valley, and is poised to become more widely spread within the UK, duly championed by our MMBA, Boyd Rodger.

While a significant contribution to this development has been made by Boyd, duly championed by Thames' Chief Constable, the scheme as a whole has recently been recommended by Home Secretary Jack Straw to the country. The frame of reference deployed will be Don Beck's *Spiral Dynamics* (Beck was mentor to the victorious South African world cup rugby team in 1996) with its organizational 'memes'. From a post-modern world of branded services, we finally now enter the perennial realm of the civic society.

Part V   Perennial civilization: a free, peaceful, sustainable and healthy society

Fireborn – freeing up society

The bridge between the post-modern and perennial is formed by Richard Branson generally and by Virgin Direct specifically, symbol of free association in Great Britain. In chapter 13, we therefore review the birth, growth and development of Richard Branson's Virgin group in general as well as Jayne-Anne Gadhia's and Rowan Gormley's Virgin Direct – our newest MMBA recruits – in particular. Branson has embodied the spirit of enterprise, freedom and indeed individuality more visibly than any other business entrepreneur of our time. Through his service based, if not yet explicitly knowledge oriented, interests that range from railways to retailing and from airline transportation to actuarially based services, the Virgin Group stands for free expression, free enterprise, and free spiritedness all wrapped up into one. As such it lends itself to Margaret Wheatley's 'chaotically' inspired *Leadership and the New Science.*[16]

Richard Branson's, Rowan Gormley's and Jayne-Anne Gadhia's combined humanistic focus, alongside their rationally and pragmatically based financial activities, is that of free association. As a business and social nomad, in that respect, Branson represents the *fire* element of our perennial being.

Airborn – forging peace and reconciliation

Another civic organization in Britain, the Surrey Police force, which is also a fully fledged knowledge creation organization, is explicitly engaged in civic reconstruction. In chapter 14 we exemplify most clearly Nonaka and Takeuchi's Japanese concept of the *organizational knowledge creation.*[17] Citing the Surrey Police force, from whom we now have the largest contingent of participants on our programme, we allude most particularly to their knowledge based vision. This is set in the context of the police force's evolutionary grounds in Britain generally, and amongst the participants specifically. In the process we indicate how such a civic entity has developed its vision, and enabling conditions for knowledge creation, alongside processes of socialization, externalization, combination and internalization.

Ultimately, moreover, their civic role of building, making and keeping the peace is reflected in the second of our life sustaining elements, that is *air*, and is thereby embodied in the vision of societal hero, Deputy Chief Constable Dr Ian Beckett, alongside Chief Constable Ian Blair.

Waterborn – public health

Free association, peace and reconciliation, sustainable development and ultimately the public health of nations constitute our civic foundations, generally. Moreover, they comprise the origins and destination of mastery, on our programme specifically. In the penultimate chapter, together with California's authority on the management of change Will McWhinney, we revisit the process of ecological succession via his approach to *Paths of Change*,[18] analytical and participative, assertive and emergent. His work, in chapter 15, is set in the context of the story of Anglian Water and of its participants on our MMBA course.

Anglian's paths to change have been oriented participatively through empowerment, analytically through total quality management, assertively through a strategic systems review, and emergently through their so-called Transformation Journey. Overall their role in building a civic society is represented in enhancing life through water, is embodied in the artist-like harmoniser role played by chief executive Chris Mellor, and is reflected in *water* as one of life's four perennial elements.

Earthborn – sustainable development

In chapter 16, we draw upon the example of Body Shop, having cited Anita Roddick as the contemporary version of a business Artemis (equivalent to Diana in Greek mythology) in a previous book, *Total Quality Learning*.[19] Our close association with Body Shop, over the years, has led us to our belief that, more explicitly than most business enterprises, it exhibits not only body and mind but also heart and soul. As such the company draws upon the kind of traditional wisdom revealed by Emmett Murphy in his *Forging the Heroic Organization*.[20] Moreover, through its intricate linkages with the environment, it offers a strong base for the development of a learning ecology.

Anita Roddick herself ultimately, as an *earth* mother figure, is a *Prophet*-like personality, whose enterprise is engaged in its civic role of healing the planet.

Part VI   Re-building a nation

Reconstructing civic society

In chapter 17, finally, we revisit the organizational ecology that we have developed as a whole, and set it in the context of the individual, organization and society, helped along by the American social philosopher, Ken Wilber.[21]

A nation like Britain, first, has emerged through a 'traditional' – economically oriented – colonization, serving to build up its financial and insurance base. Second, though less concertedly than, say, our German or Scandinavian counterparts, it has undergone a 'modern' – technologically oriented – era of resource conservation. As such it has built up its transport, logistics and communications. Third, and currently, it has entered its 'post-modern', ecologically oriented, catalysation, thereby establishing its knowledge and service based industries. Britain's ultimate destiny, together with that of other nations, lies in a perennial role of civic co-creation, thereby enhancing peace, open society, sustainable development and public health, at home and abroad. Moreover, and in the process, it needs to transcend, but definitely not discard or bypass, its traditional, modern and post-modern heritage. In that integrated context, we shall hope to be making our own small contribution to the legacy of the late Princess Diana, that is in helping to *reconstruct civic society*.

Dancing in mountains, forests and marshes

In Roman religion Diana was originally a woodland goddess who later became identified with the Greek goddess Artemis. As such she had strong connections with wild animals, the hunt (thus in our terms 'huntress'), and with vegetation (thereby a 'gardener'), as well as with chastity (thus a 'conserver') and childbirth. She was in fact the most popular of the Greek goddesses with the ordinary worshipper. Her character and function varied greatly from place to place, but in all instances she retained the wild nature of one who danced in mountains, forests and marshes. Finally, she was considered to be the protector (hence in our terms 'steward') of the lower classes, particularly of slaves. As such she serves as a powerful symbol not only for organizational renewal, within an ecological context, but also for the rebuilding of our nation. With that in mind, perhaps surprisingly, we start with a business school, City University's!

BIBLIOGRAPHY

1   Lessem, R., *Business as a Learning Community*, McGraw-Hill, 1993.
2   Lessem, R. and Neubauer, F., *European Management Systems*, McGraw-Hill, 1993.
3   Bennis, W., Parikh, J. and Lessem, R., *Beyond Leadership: Balancing Economics, Ethics and Ecology*, Blackwell, 1994.

4 Lessem, R. and Palsule, S., *Managing in Four Worlds*, Blackwell, 1997.
5 Lessem, R., *Total Quality Learning*, Blackwell, 1991.
6 Nonaka, I., 'The Knowledge Creating Company', *Harvard Business Review*, Nov./Dec., 1991.
7 Kalthoff, O., Nueno, P. and Nonaka, I., *The Light and the Shadow*, Capstone, 1997.
8 Nonaka, I. and Takeuchi, H., *The Knowledge Creating Company*, Oxford University Press, 1995.
9 Goshal, S. and Bartlett, C., *The Individualized Corporation*, Butterworth Heinemann, 1998.
10 Strauss, W. and Howe, N., *The Fourth Turning*, Broadway Books, 1997.
11 Moore, J., *Leadership and Strategy in the Age of Business Ecosystems*, Wiley, 1997.
12 Randall, W., *The Stories We Are*, Toronto University Press, 1995.
13 Lessem, R., *Management Development and Cultural Diversity*, Routledge, 1998.
14 Boisot, M., *Information Space*, Routledge, 1995.
15 Beck, D. and Cowan, C., *Spiral Dynamics*, Blackwell, 1996.
16 Wheatley, M., *Leadership and the New Sciences*, Berrett Koehler, 1996.
17 Nonaka, I. and Takeuchi, H., *The Knowledge Creating Company*, Oxford University Press, 1995.
18 McWhinney, W., *Paths of Change*, Sage, 1997.
19 Lessem, R., *Total Quality Learning*, Blackwell, 1991.
20 Murphy, E., *Forging the Heroic Organization*, Prentice-Hall, 1994.
21 Wilber, K., *Sense and Soul*, Simon and Schuster, 1998.

2 From business school to learning society

Britain's role in the twenty-first century

INTRODUCTION: EDUCATION FOR WHOM?

As we have indicated in chapter 1, first – and specifically through our knowledge creating ecology – we want to enhance the relationship between our business school and the organizations it serves. Second, and more generally, we want to metamorphose the practice of management and indeed executive education, so that it adds organizational and societal value directly, rather than only indirectly through the individual's growth and development. In both cases, moreover, such pragmatically and rationally based management education and business administration will need to be altogether reconstituted.

As I have also indicated, in the course of uncovering 'European management systems', I came across an anomaly. For in uncovering major philosophical systems that have since become the hallmark of our 'Four Worlds Institute', it struck me, as a management educator and would-be organizational ecologist, that only one of these, that is 'western' pragmatism, was directly oriented towards the individual. In fact, I was taken aback, during my own postgraduate education, by the difference in emphasis between Harvard Business School and the London School of Economics. Whereas the educational orientation at the LSE was intensely individualistic, and thus thoroughly and pragmatically Anglo-Saxon, this was evidently not the case at Harvard, where the approach was much more group-focused and institutionally oriented. My own place of birth, to add a third businesspheric dimension, was an English colony, Southern Rhodesia, present-day Zimbabwe.

In an indigenous African setting, which we have termed in our recent work humanistic,[1] the community has primacy over the individual. In rural Africa, the pre-school education of the child takes place within a richly social setting. This in fact changes when the child goes to secondary school, but such schooling of course is based on a 'western' model.

Things should have been different in the 'east', at least amongst the Pacific Tigers where the colonial heritage was somewhat less obvious than was the case in Africa. Well not quite. We know that the Japanese approach to

Figure 2 Towards a learning society

education, for one thing, draws heavily on the French 'northern' tradition, that is, until the person graduates from school or university into business. In fact both Germany and Japan have been renowned, at least until recently, for their lack of business schools, and rather for the presence of the school-in-business. Seemingly, and particularly in Japanese organizations, the split between business consumer, with its collective orientation, and business school provider, with its individual one, had not taken place. In that sense, perhaps, the business institution was a more accurate reflection of indigenous culture than the school or university.

Fourth and finally, from my own 'northern' cultural perspective, I was born of central European parents, from Austria and from Lithuania. As will soon become apparent, this has been a significant influence on my intellectual outlook. It is time for us to go 'back to basics', though, with a view to subsequently uncovering the full trajectory of our programme.

GENESIS – TRADITIONAL – BUSINESS EDUCATION

David Wilson, a partner at the well-known firm of accountants Ernst and Young, is quoted by Thomas Stewart, the *Fortune Magazine* based author of *Intellectual Capital* as saying: 'It has been 500 years since Pacioli published his seminal work on accounting. Yet we have seen virtually no innovation in its practice, just more rules, none of which has changed the framework on measurement.'[2]

The balance sheet, took its present form in 1868, and the income statement appeared before the Second World War. For 400 out of the 500 years since Pacioli invented double-entry book-keeping, then, businessmen have been taught such accounting principles and practices. My very own father, when he decided to go into business on his own account, in Southern Rhodesia, did a course in book-keeping while running a rural bottle store. In fact such crafts of book-keeping, of merchandising and of selling, have been taught by trade schools for more than a century. Prior to the institution of that system, tradesmen, like craftsmen, were apprenticed to masters, both technical and commercial, to learn their skills. Skills were picked up in the traditional way, on the job, and reinforced by specific courses of instruction taught largely by rote. The Bachelor of Commerce degree, which I almost embarked upon for my first degree in South Africa, emerged out of this traditional orientation, with the economics of the firm, financial accounting, and the law of contract constituting its basic elements. Such constituents had been the stuff of 'western' business for a century and more.

MORPHOSIS – MODERN – INTELLECTUAL CAPITAL

Fayol on administration

Things began to change at the turn of the century, when sociologist Max Weber in Germany and engineer Henri Fayol in France started to develop a 'science of general administration'. Fayol, a mechanical engineer, not only newly conceived of the managerial functions of planning, organizing, command and control, but also of the business functions of accounting, production and sales.

Soon afterwards American business schools pioneered the masters in business administration so that, for the first time, management was advanced as a 'modern' profession in the same sense as engineering, medicine or the law. As such, it was disseminated to individual students.

Over the course of much of the twentieth century the supposedly 'modern' (though not really so, as we shall see) MBA curriculum, involving operations and marketing, finance and human resources, strategy and organizational behaviour, as well as now information technology, has remained essentially intact. While there have been some variations on this basic theme, it has remained remarkably enduring, whether the MBA programme is run in Hong Kong or Hawaii, Peking or Paris. While there has also been some shift in emphasis, over the course of this century, from a relatively economic and commercial to a more socio-technical orientation, the underlying morphology has remained undisturbed, both in substance and in form. Although there is some difference in emphasis between a case study or concept oriented programme, the basic Franco/Anglo-Saxon form remains. It involves, at core, delivering blocks of courses to batches of individuals – part- or full-time – in lecture, seminar or case study mode, with the odd project or business simulation thrown in at the periphery. Underlying such a form, the substantive content, like Pacioli's approach to book-keeping, has remained extraordinarily steadfast.

In our view, the transition from Bachelor of Commerce to Master in Business Administration represents therefore only half a step towards modernity, never mind the current further advance to post-modernity, for it remains focused on the individual, personally and pragmatically, rather than upon the organization, institutionally and rationally. In other words, and in Thomas Stewart's terms, the orientation is towards human capital in isolation from structural capital.

Structural capital

For Stewart such an individual and tangible orientation represents a traditional framework that fits the industrial enterprise, not the intelligent one. For at bottom, management accounting measures a company's accumulation and concentration of capital, and is based on costs. This conventional model falls apart when the assets in question are intangible. In fact, the cost of producing knowledge bears much less relationship to its value or price than the cost of producing, say, a ton of steel. In the nineteenth century an idea could not become valuable unless a measurable collection of physical assets was assembled around it to exploit it. Not so now, as we approach the post-modern age of knowledge based services, Stewart says. Unlike machinery or money, ideas have assumed power by themselves.

The complete transition from genesis to morphosis, from a traditional approach to modernity to a more post-modern orientation – or from individually based pragmatism to organizationally based rationality – has only recently taken place. However, it has not emerged from within the business schools, where the MBA remains firmly intent upon individual management development, but from within businesses themselves, and from management consultancies. Ironically though, if we go back to the origins of the university in medieval Europe, we find that the focus on the individual student or faculty member was in the background rather than the foreground. The American urban historian, Lewis Mumford, in *The City in History*, is quoted by Stewart as saying:

> In the university, the pursuit of knowledge was elevated into an enduring structure, which did not depend for its continuance on any single group of priests, scholars or texts. The system of knowledge was more important than the thing known. In the university, the functions of cultural storage, dissemination and interchange, and creative addition – perhaps the three most important functions of the City – were adequately performed.[3]

Thomas Stewart sees contemporary relevance in the medieval university. In effect, he substitutes the modern 'corporation' for the medieval 'city', and what he calls corporate 'structural capital' for 'university' based education. In this way he indicates how administrative systems, databases and other codified forms of organizational knowledge have superseded land, labour and capital. Such structural capital, then, Stewart aligns with human capital on the one hand, that is knowledge bearing fruit in works, and customer capital on the other, that is the level of retained customer goodwill. So we now have a twist in the tale. Not only, if we reach back into medieval history, do we find that the university in continental Europe served to enhance intellectual capital, but we find the same applying to progressive companies today, that is, through the way they maintain and enhance their human, structural and customer capital.

Universities in general, and business schools in particular, are thus falling markedly behind in the knowledge creating race. It therefore has been our intention that City University Business School – in co-operation with our commercial, industrial, service oriented and civic partners – should be the exception to the rule, both in word and in deed. Indeed, to give us a head start we have been standing on the shoulders of a historical giant who has served as a source of perennial wisdom embedded in his 'great instauration'.

The great instauration

The inspired source we have drawn upon has been that of Francis Bacon, inventor of scientific method and Chancellor of the Exchequer in Elizabethan England. For Bacon, on the one hand, knowledge had to bear fruit in works. On the other hand, he wanted to build his empire of hope from out of the common clay. Uppermost in Bacon's mind was the 'advancement of learning' in this first Elizabethan era, like the 'learning society' today.

In fact, Chancellor Bacon suggested in the 'device' of 1594 that royal assistance be enlisted to support a 'great instauration', or process of societal renewal. A library of books ancient and modern in all tongues was to be collected. There were also to be botanical gardens and a zoo on the grandest scale, fully accessible to observation. Such a museum was to contain, and classify inanimate natural objects and the products of man's ingenuity and skill. A laboratory was to be equipped with all materials required for experimental research. Bacon called such societal learning or re-learning 'instauration', that is, restoration or renewal. It was the sixteenth-century societal antecedent, in England, of what modern-day Thomas Stewart refers to, corporately, as structural capital.

Interestingly enough, a compatriot of Francis Bacon's, the venerable Sir Thomas Gresham, not only established the City of London's Royal Exchange, but left behind a legacy for educational purposes. Funded from that legacy was Gresham College, the birthplace of our City University Business School. In fact, in a perhaps inadvertent attempt to resurrect Gresham College in modern guise, our MMBA programme was created. However, at that time, that is some ten years ago, we were oblivious to the great instauration. It was to take a whole decade before we would practically realize what that sixteenth-century potential for the advancement of learning would represent in modern guise. Before we return to that theme, however, we need to take a bit of a detour, one that simultaneously takes us back to the traditional and the pragmatic and forward to the humanistic.

Mintzberg on management

The two most renowned dissenters from the conventionally and pseudo-rationally established MBA curriculum, in recent times, have been California's Tom Peters[4] and Canada's Henry Mintzberg. Both of them are overt pragmatists with covertly humanistic orientations.

However, while Peters has subsequently left the halls of academe, Mintzberg has tried to instigate such pragmatic-humanistic changes from within. Each of them, meanwhile, being in fact distinctly poised between the traditional and the perennial, has inveighed heavily against the prevailing 'modern' trends in the sixties and seventies, towards so called rational management. For Henry Mintzberg, then:

A good part of MBA training is devoted to drill in techniques, free of context, most of whose abilities have never been demonstrated in practice. Indeed if the success of the Japanese in practising management compared with their reluctance to teach it is any indication, then conventional MBA training should be considered part of the problem, not part of the solution.[5]

Mintzberg decries the lack of human context surrounding MBA-type training. I can readily identify with what he is saying, having been thrust from Harvard at the age of 26 into running the family clothing business in Johannesburg, supposedly rationally, without having had any practical background in the rag trade myself. I found the experience to be a profoundly daunting, and indeed alienating one, which in fact led me out of Africa and on to Europe, and out of the down-to-earth clothing business into the seemingly lofty heights of management education. Little did I know in the early seventies that I would later be dedicating myself to bringing those two micro and macro worlds together, twenty years later. For I was drawn in the late eighties to our own practically based Management MBA, which had been started by my marketing colleague, Professor Hugh Murray, very much in the Mintzberg mode. For commercially minded pragmatist Murray, like his illustrious counterpart Mintzberg, felt that theoretical training disconnected from practical context was a charade. So did I, but I was unable to discard my own heritages, as an African and a European, as well as a Middle Easterner (Jewish) and Anglo-Saxon.

I could no less easily forget that that Englishman Bacon wanted to build his empire of hope from out of the common clay as I could ignore the philosophy of Ubuntu – 'I am because you are' – which is generic to the indigenous African, or indeed the rational orientation towards organizations as systems, which was part of my Germanic heritage.

Pragmatic project-based education has its place, but I needed to remember that pure rationalism had not yet had its day, at least within the business schools, and that holism and humanism had their important and complementary parts to play. Moreover, and as we need to recognize when we approach the twenty-first century, the world is very rapidly, and globally, changing. In effect the modern world, in management as in life and work in general, is giving way to the post-modern, in the same way as the traditional needs to be replaced by what we have termed the perennial. Finally, and more to our particular point here, the knowledge intensive service sector, duly replacing traditional commerce and modern industry, is upon us.

METAMORPHOSIS – POST-MODERN – KNOWLEDGE CREATING ECOLOGY

From R&D to knowledge creation

Ever since the middle ages, universities have been the guardians of knowledge, of both its creation and its dissemination. In the twentieth century, however, initially in Europe and America as well as subsequently in the Far East, when it comes to the advance of scientific knowledge the business corporation has taken its place as equal creator, if not also disseminator, of such knowledge. In other words, while universities and technical colleges, alongside schools, have retained their primary role as disseminators, the creation of knowledge has also become the prerogative of businesses. This has taken place through research and development, often of course in conjunction with academe.

At the turn of this century, however, as we enter the next millennium, there has been a new twist. For now, and for the first time since the business schools were established in turn-of-the-century America, the development of intellectual capital on the one hand, and the creation of knowledge on the other, have become essential – rather than peripheral – to most progressive businesses. As a result, knowledge creation is no longer restricted to a specific 'research and development' department, nor is the enhancement of intellectual capital merely the responsibility of a training unit. For companies like Sony in Japan and Surrey Police in Britain, for Skandia Financial Services in Sweden and Anglian Water in the UK, the advance of knowledge and its conversion into products and processes has become all-pervasive within the business. In the process intellectual capital is overtaking financial capital as the primary source of competitive advantage. As a result, the learning organization, and more particularly the knowledge creating one, has become the institutional archetype of our post-modern 'information age'.

Firms of management consultants, including the globally based accounting firms like Andersen and Price Waterhouse, are now majoring on so-called 'knowledge management'. At the same time, 'corporate universities' are proliferating, extending all the way from McDonald's 'Hamburger

University' to more sophisticated versions such as Motorola University and indeed Anglian's University of Water. So where does this all leave the conventional MBA, as flagship programme of the allegedly – though not actually, as we have intimated – 'modern' business school?

Retracing our steps pragmatically

At the end of the eighties, when we established our Management MBA at City University Business School, we felt we had made a major breakthrough, towards practically based management education.

In fact, as we indicated in the previous chapter, our achievement was limited. We had merely shifted from the pragmatic/rationally based Euro-American orientation, modelled upon a prescribed MBA curriculum, to a more thoroughly traditional Anglo-Saxon, pragmatic approach. Moreover, while our project based programme was oriented towards realizing practical benefits for the company in which the manager worked, rather than relying on concepts or case studies, the predominating focus was still on the individual (western) rather than upon the organization (northern), the industry (eastern) or society (southern). Indeed, we were almost in danger of going back to a traditional skill-based orientation, rather than forward to a developmental one.

In the meantime, in the wings, the world around us was rapidly changing. The advent of knowledge work and of intellectual capital, of organizational learning and knowledge creation meant that the individual was being at least supplemented by the organizational and we were being left behind. While companies were building up what Thomas Stewart has called their 'structural capital', involving institutionally based activities ranging from 'hard' databases to 'soft' learning communities of practice, and the major consultancies were helping them organizationally to do just that, we remained lost in the individual backwoods.

Much of the conventional debate revolved around whether we should be identifying ourselves with 'executive development' or 'executive education', or whether or not we were a fully fledged MBA, or were more focused on organizational development. Whatever we were, in those limiting terms, we were aiming at the education and training of individuals. Locked up within a 'western', traditionally atomistic worldview, we were unable to see the organizational woods, and indeed the wider societal ecosystem, for the individual trees.

Out of the individual blockhole – forming action learning sets

All along at that time the individual student-manager on our programme was supported by a lone educator-academic supported by an individual course instructor supported by a single in-company coach supported by an individual corporate link manager. In other words, amongst our cast of characters, there were plenty of individual atoms but no combinations of molecules, never mind any fully integrated organisms. No wonder the projects completed had only limited impact in those early consortium days. Despite our trying to contextualize the work that individuals did in 'Business as a Learning Community', there was little evidence of it amongst such sponsoring enterprises as American Express, the International Stock Exchange, or J. Sainsbury. We remained locked into a traditional and trans-actional world, whereby sponsors paid so much per student, so that we served the interests of their management training functions, in anticipation of the individual manager's development. Benefit to the business was an added bonus, for which it was impossible to account properly!

The first step that we took in the early nineties, away from this individual pre-emphasis, was that of forming action learning 'sets', modelled on Reg Revans's approach to 'action learning'.[6] Although the managers continued to focus on their individual projects, duly enhancing their knowledge, skills and themselves in the process, they did so in the context of a small group of fellow learners. That helped to shift the programme's orientation from education and training, with instructors and educators taking the lead, to learning and development, with group facilitators playing a more critical role. Nevertheless, the focus on the individual as prior to the organization remained sacrosanct. The transactional relationship with the company, at least in explicit financial terms, remained unchanged. This shift in orientation therefore helped to con-solidate the implicit learning, through mutual challenge and support, but not the explicit relationship with the sponsoring client.

From action learner to knowledge engineer

Midway through the nineties I had the good fortune to join forces with Ikijiro Nonaka. I discovered specifically, as I have previously indicated, that our so called 'global businessphere' and Nonaka's 'knowledge spiral' both encompassed pragmatism (socialization), rationalism (combination), holism (externalization), and humanism (socialization) at a macro and micro level. Armed with this new insight we sought to develop it into a means of organi-zational knowledge creation. We introduced our participating managers to Nonaka's concept of a 'knowledge crew', incorporating knowledge officers, engineers and practitioners, duly positioning our MBA students in the middle, as such knowledge engineers. We also introduced his notion of a 'hyper-text' organization, where the conventional business system is accompanied by an unconventional 'project layer', aimed at product development. That certainly served to stir some of our managers into developmental action, but again to a limited degree, for the focus was still on the individual knowl-edge engineer rather than upon the knowledge creating organization.

In that respect we had not managed to step out of our traditional, individually oriented shoes. In fact we were not yet even 'modern' enough to market our product, as a consultant might well do, in terms of its enhancement of our client's human and structural capital, in organizational terms. Ironically, this was an orientation already adopted, in terms of its global 'solutions' provision, by one of our clients, IBM.

From ordinary to extraordinary management

It was at this point that a countryman of mine, Ralph Stacey, who originally hails from Johannesburg, came to our rescue, at least up to a point. In his seminal work on 'organizational dynamics', as we shall see in chapter 5, Stacey has distinguished between what he calls 'ordinary' and 'extraordinary' managers.[7]

The former deal with the predictable, set within stable situations of organizational and market equilibrium; the latter must cope with somewhat unpredictable situations, located within dynamic conditions that are far-from-equilibrium and that call upon group learning and political activities. We could now see our way towards not only ordinary projects, aimed at improved managerial and departmental performance, but also towards extraordinary ones. These were aimed at role evolution and business or organizational development. Moreover, we added a third 'mastery' project for good measure, one that was vision-driven, and drew upon leadership skills and more.[8] Stacey also drew our attention to 'learning communities of practice', to which Stewart has also referred:

> The relationship between individual learning and the organization's human capital – not just its stock of knowledge but its capacity to innovate – involves groups even more than it does individuals. Groups that learn, as so called communities of practice, have special characteristics. They emerge of their own accord. They are among the most important structures of any organization where thinking matters; but they are, almost inevitably, subversive of its formal structures and strictures. Such communities of practice, in fact, are the shop floor of human capital. Several traits define such. First they have history, they develop over time. Second they have an enterprise, but not an agenda; that is they form around a value-adding. Third the enterprise involves learning; as a result over time communities of practice develop customs, culture. Perhaps most intriguing, communities of practice are responsible only to themselves. People join and stay because they have something to learn and something to contribute. The work they do is the joint and several property of the group. A community of practice is voluntary, long-lived and has no specific deliverable, except knowledge transfer and innovation.[9]

What was becoming patently obvious to me by now was that in our sincere attempts to enable individuals and supposedly organizations to learn we were still keeping our eye on the wrong ball. We were still focusing, traditionally so to speak, on the individual student as immediate client rather than upon the immediate work group, if not also upon the organization as a whole. In proverbial terms, we were continually shooting our would-be group and organizational selves in the traditionally individual foot, notwithstanding our good 'modern' and even 'post-modern' intentions. Moreover, such a collective orientation needed to be towards emergent 'learning communities of practice' which had a shared developmental history, rather than merely upon pre-assigned individual projects. It was no wonder that we were becoming increasingly challenged by some of our clients to demonstrate the 'business benefits' of what we were doing, even though as we have indicated neither they nor we had any means of assessing these benefits.

Towards an organizational ecology

The breakthrough came in one sense gradually and in another respect suddenly. First of all gradually: ever since we had met in Goa in the early nineties, Sudhanhsu Palsule and I had been developing our ideas for linking together business and ecology. Between 1990 and 1996, the idea incubated, and fate played its hand, when we both arrived on the same European continent. The book we planned to write together was to integrate my psychologically and economically based 'global businessphere', which was already well developed, with Sudhanshu's physically and naturally laden notion of a learning ecology. Such a combination, moreover, was to be duly reinforced by MMBA graduate Stephen Gatley's biological orientation towards genesis and morphosis, metamorphosis and homeostasis.

While I was a management academic at City and Sudhanshu was an internal consultant to Anglian Water, Steve as the founder of the European Management Labaoratory was an innovator and business entrepreneur in his own right. After many false starts, the idea began to take concrete shape, after innumerable conversations into the night, and one particularly fruitful one on the plane back from Palestine to England. *Managing in Four Worlds*, which was published in the summer of 1997, laid out the initial conceptual framework. In Nonaka's terms it was the result of an enduring process of socialization between the two of us, aided and abetted by Steve,[10] and of subsequent externalization. The overarching metaphor of nature's network had led to the emergence of a new 'organizational ecology' that will be outlined in chapter 3. Interestingly enough, operating within the 'western' Anglo-Saxon environment as we do, we have access to the adjacent worlds of the 'north' and the 'south', as can be seen in the figure below, but we are somewhat blinded to the 'east'. Ironically, it is that very part of the world that has, at least until recently been dramatically in the ascendant (Figure 3, p.42).

This had been recognized at Anglian Water, where the three of us, together with a fourth colleague Terry Cook, who subsequently became its champion, had developed a 'Transformation Journey', aimed at all Anglian employees, to enhance team learning. Such learning, via what we now termed the 'Journey Compass' straddled the whole of the businessphere. Such a compass also became the basis for Anglian's University of Water's four faculties – commercial and technological, ecological and social.

What now came through to us, though, like a bolt from the blue, was that for ten years, on our MMBA programme, we had been barking up the wrong – or at least a misshapen – western tree. For while in 'ecological' terms our primary reward system, that is the MBA, had been reinforcing individual 'hunting', we had been vainly proclaiming the virtues of herding, gardening and stewardship.

While we were barking up that wrong individual tree, the City Corporation and Lloyd's, Ford and IBM and Sainsbury, as well as Anglian Water, all as would-be learning organizations, were, so to speak, getting lost in the forest! It was time, or so we came to realize in the late spring of 1997, for a genuine metamorphosis. In effect, we had to shift our attention simultaneously 'northwards', towards the 'herding' of intellectual capital, and 'eastwards' towards catalysation or – more proverbially – towards the gardening of knowledge. We were now ready to establish a genuine consortium, and so was born the idea of the 'link managers' forum', already referred to in chapter 1, encompassing a project database specifically and our organizations' 'evolutionary grounds' generally.

From individual to inter-organizational orientation

In June 1997 six of us sat down together representing, in turn, Anglian Water, IBM, Lloyd's, J. Sainsbury, Surrey Police force and City University Business School. Ostensibly we were there to review the workshop we had just run, for 100 of our MMBA community, on 'Organizations as Ecosystems'. Somehow the ecological overtone for which Sudhanshu Palsule was largely responsible struck a chord amongst many of our participants. Seemingly the time for metamorphosis was right. Conceptually our 'four worlds' book had served to bring the elements of the new ecosystemic argument together, in fact as a culmination of some ten years' prior thought, feeling and action. Practically we now also seemed ready to take up the challenge of turning from individual to organizational or even inter-organizational focus.

To begin with, Anglian Water had recently set up its University of Water and we were keen to turn this development to good ecosystemic effect. J. Sainsbury, meanwhile, was undergoing a process of midlife renewal, and as such was engaging in a series of joint ventures, the most prominent of these being in the banking field. IBM's insurance sector was beginning to explore opportunities for the City University Business School, IBM and insurance based corporate clients to work together on building up human and structural capital simultaneously. Lloyd's, meanwhile, was in the middle of a period of reconstruction and renewal, ripe for ecosystemic resolution.

Our regional police force, finally, was revealing itself to be a genuine knowledge creating organization, so that our MMBA needed to be positioned in this kind of context. The focus of attention, at least in the background if not yet in the foreground, was shifting from individual to organization to industry, and thereby from promoting management advancement to catalysing inter-organizational development. How was this to be fully achieved?

Colonizing – hunting – promoting management education

In our ecosystemically reconceived programme, in fact, emphasis was shifting away from 'colonially' based education, in which one student 'hunts' for knowledge, skills and self-development to secure 'territorial gains' within one subject or another. Such individually oriented 'hunting' has its place, duly supported by the university based instructor, but it has moved within the context of our MMBA from foreground to background. Acquiring such an MBA for the individual, like traditionally based management education and development for the organization, becomes a means not an end. Sponsoring organizations increasingly no longer 'put' people on to our programme, but use the programme to develop their intellectual capital, on the one hand, and to foster organizational and inter-organizational development, on the other. In that context each newly participating member builds on the 'project capital' built up by previous participants.

Conserving – herding – consolidating intellectual capital

Traditional management education and training has become subordinate to the modern build-up of intellectual capital. In Thomas Stewart's terms this incorporates structural (information technology), customer (client goodwill) and human capital.

> Unleashing the human capital already resident in the organization, firstly, requires minimizing mindless tasks, meaningless paperwork, and unproductive infighting. In the Information Age no one can afford to use human capital so inefficiently. The greater the human-capital-intensity of a business, that is the greater the percentage of high value added work performed by hard-to-replace people, the more the firm can charge for its services and the less vulnerable it is to its competitors. Smart organizations, moreover, will spend and invest as little as possible in work that customers do not value and whose workers' skills are easy to replace. Considering human capital in these terms, secondly, sheds new light on how to build it, and on the process of capitalizing human knowledge to create an organizational asset. In particular it tells you that training, in the traditional sense, is a waste of money.
>
> The false correlation of learning with training or education is one of the most costly errors in corporate management today. The relationship between individual learning and the organization's human capital – not just its stock of knowledge but its capacity to innovate –

involves groups even more than it does individuals. Such groups that learn are so called communities of practice. But smart individuals or even groups don't necessarily make smart companies. Structural capital, thirdly then, incorporates information systems, laboratories, or market intelligence. Fourthly and finally customer capital is the value of an organization's relationships with the people with whom it does business, that is depth (penetration), width (coverage) and attachment (loyalty) generated. It's in such relations with customers that intellectual capital turns to money.[11]

Conserving and enhancing intellectual capital, ultimately then, is what 'herding' is all about, and it should be the role of academically based educators on our newly constituted programme to work with the different organizational domains – economic and technological, social and cultural – to achieve this. To the extent that they are able to work with groups of managers from a given organization, rather than with individuals, this is all the more likely to be the case. Such a process, if it is successful, will involve optimizing the recruitment, development and deployment of human, structural and customer capital. However, stimulating the development of intellectual capital falls short of catalysing organizational development.

Catalysing – gardening – organizational knowledge creation

Ecological overview

Organizational learning generally and knowledge creation particularly, mediated through our holistic learning ecology, represents the truly post-modern orientation of our programme.

Moreover, it is to be supported rather than led by pragmatically based training and development, and by the rationally oriented conservation, including enhancement, of intellectual capital. Furthermore, whereas the colonizing and conserving outlooks were individual and group oriented, the focus is now altogether different, for now it is organizational and inter-organizational. Charles Hampden Turner illustrates how this works with Singapore's Economic Development Board:

> There is a clear difference between Western and Tiger approaches to government intervention. In Western economies, where state initiatives are permitted at all, these are all product or project specific. The Tennessee Valley Authority in America, Concorde or Ariane in Europe all had specific objectives.
>
> They were high risk in the sense that they visibly succeeded or failed. All efforts converge on a single aim. You win or you lose. But the interventions by Tiger economies are quite different. Initiatives are aimed

at improving 'seminal' technologies, in which a great many businesses need to be successful. The metaphors are biological, 'rice of industry', 'blood of business', 'food chain', 'seed corn', 'technology trees'. In such 'seminal' interventions clusters beget clusters, machine tools, robots and semi-conductors procreate successive generations of new products. Products have knowledge 'genes' which are passed on from one generation to the next. A consensus orientation, ultimately, is vital to the building of clusters, in which victory in one game contributes to victories in clusters of games or one Infinite Game. These are typically joined by horizontal technologies which act as catalysts. Targeting a technology common to a cluster develops the entire group. Clustering also greatly increases the chance of fortuitous and creative connections, combining competition with cooperation.[12]

How, then, might our programme evolve towards such a developmental point, given the fact that the starting point, in our 'western' world, is more likely to be the specific individual and the project rather than the more general organization and the 'seminal' technologies, around which project 'clusters' are formed? Let us paraphrase Hampden Turner, to see what may be the catalytic eventuality:

There is a clear difference between pragmatic and holistic approaches to management and organizational development. In our originally pragmatic MMBA programme, where alignment with the sponsoring organization existed at all, it was participant or project specific. First, second or third projects all had specific, and separate, objectives. Each individual student or project fared well or badly, each on their own individual merits.

But our holistically oriented programmme, in prospect if not yet in actuality, is quite different. Projects are aimed at improving 'seminal' forms of intellectual capital, upon which many aspects of the business depend. The metaphors underlying these project clusters are the biological ones that Hampden Turner has pointed out as typical of the Tiger economies. In such 'seminal' projects clusters beget clusters, each preparatory, ordinary, extraordinary or mastery project procreating successive generations of new projects. Such projects have knowledge 'genes' which are passed on from one generation, or group of MMBA participants, to the next. A consensus orientation, ultimately, is vital to the building of clusters, in which success in one project contributes to successes in clusters of other projects, thereby constituting one Infinite Game. These projects, moreover, are typically recognized by organizational ecologists who act as catalysts. Targeting a product or process, service or system common to a project cluster develops the entire group. Clustering also greatly increases the chance of fortuitous and creative connections, combining competition with cooperation.

We now need to summarize how the programme as a whole, duly incorporating the full breadth and depth of the learning ecology, would work.

From colonization to co-creation

Phase 1 – genesis – education and training

Table 1 illustrates the fairly traditional starting point of our original MMBA programme, in which the independent business school is separate from the individual client, both being duly focused on the individual student. Emphasis is upon the training and development of the manager, thereby laying the preparatory ground for further development.

The focus remains traditional to the extent that a skill orientation prevails, the individual remains supreme, the relationship between client and university is transactional, and the student 'hunts' for particular morsels of knowledge and skill. We now turn to phase 2.

Phase 2 – morphosis – intellectual capital

The individual and transactional nature of our client relationship, in phase 2 (see Table 2), is transformed. Rather than paying for the education of individual students, the City University – in partnership prospectively with a knowledge based business like IBM – would be reimbursed for a composite service.

Such a service would duly incorporate management development and also the enhancement of a client's intellectual capital, reinforced to begin with through the 'ordinary' projects. Moreover, a database of prior projects would be constructed so that forthcoming ones could cluster around pre-existing contributions. Finally, to ensure that structural and customer capital is enhanced alongside human capital, the business school would need to operate continually in close liaison with the appropriate IT based solutions provider. We now turn to phase 3.

Table 1 MMBA as management education

ORIENTATION	Educate the **individual** manager
RELATIONSHIP	**Transactional** – business vs. academia
METHOD	In-company **project** based programme
CHARACTERS	Instructor, **educator**, coach, link
GROUNDS	**Economic** orientation
PHILOSOPHY	Pragmatic – **practical** – experiential
PHILSOPHER-KING	Revans – **action** learning
COMPETENCE	**Skill** oriented
CURRICULUM	Modular based **conventional** MBA
PROGRESSION	**Preparatory**, ordinary, extraordinary
FOCUS	TRADITIONAL, **colonization**, commercial

Phase 3 – metamorphosis – organizational knowledge creation

In an Anglo-Saxon context such as ours, there is little chance of our establishing a collectively oriented Economic Development Board such as that in Singapore, for our resistance to catalytical government 'intervention' is too strongly ingrained. However, concepts of organizational development, learning and renewal have generally emerged from within our 'western' and 'northern' midst rather than from the East Asians. As a result, we should be looking towards our business schools, together with the organizations they serve, to play such a catalytic role. To such a challenge, in fact, we have been eager to rise. How might it manifest itself?

As we can see in Table 3, in the course of the 'extraordinary' cluster of projects, the orientation shifts from the education and development of the individual manager to the ultimate metamorphosis of the organization, duly mediated through our knowledge creating ecology. With that end in mind, business and academia need to work as a cross-catalytic partnership, rather than as transactionally based customer and supplier. Moreover, and as will be elaborated upon in chapter 3, what was, just like a particle, a discrete and individual project becomes like a wave, that is an integral and cata-lytical cycle. To that extent, while we continue to draw on Revans and Stewart, Stacey and Nonaka – alongside our knowledge creating ecology – now occupy pride of place. As a result, while the economic and techno-logical, social and cultural domains remain differentiated, ecology becomes the force of integration.

While, after a preparatory stage, the ordinary, extraordinary and masterly progression continues to characterize the individual's developmental trajectory, these individual project parts are subsumed by the organizational whole. For this reason, we have now constituted a link managers' forum, to help build up the evolutionary grounds established by previous participants on the programme. Finally, it is now organizational knowledge creation rather than management development which constitutes the holistic business that

Table 2 MMBA as knowledge management

ORIENTATION	Develop the **group**
RELATIONSHIP	**Relational** academe/solutions/business
METHOD	In-company **project** based programme
CHARACTERS	Instructor, **facilitator**, coach, link
GROUNDS	**Socio-technical** orientation
PHILOSOPHY	Developmental-**rational**-pragmatic
PHILOSOPHER-KING	Stewart – **intellectual capital**
COMPETENCE	**Knowledge**, skill and **self** oriented
CURRICULUM	Economic, **technical**, **social**, cultural
PROGRESSION	**Ordinary**, extraordinary, mastery
FOCUS	MODERN, **conservation**, industrial

Table 3 MMBA as knowledge creation

ORIENTATION	**Organizational** metamorphosis
RELATIONSHIP	**Developmental** – business and academia
METHOD	Natural and catalytic **cycles**
CHARACTERS	Hunter, herder, **gardener**, steward
GROUNDS	**Ecology** and the life sciences
PHILOSOPHY	**Holistic**-rational-pragmatic
PHILOSOPHER-KING	Lessem and Palsule – **Learning Ecology**
COMPETENCE	Compete/conserve/**catalyse**/co-create
CURRICULUM	**Eco**-economic/technical/social/cultural
PROGRESSION	Morphosis, **metamorphosis**, homeostasis
FRAMEWORK	**Autopoiesis** – self-making
FOCUS	Organizational **knowledge creation**

we are now in. The client paymaster, in this respect then, should be an innovation or development directorate, rather than the training unit or human resources directorate. We now turn to phase 4.

CONCLUSION – CULTURAL HOMEOSTASIS – PERENNIAL

Civic reconstruction

There is still one more stage (see Table 4) to go before we reach the end of our fourfold journey, remembering that in the end is a new beginning. Such a stage is embodied in what the new South Africa has termed a *reconstruction and development* programmme, oriented towards nothing short of civic renewal.

At this ultimate point in our MMBA programme, which is the focus of participants' 'mastery' projects, the horizons are lifted towards civic reconstruction. In other words, when the programme is functioning at its best, participants see themselves, for example, not as Ford or Sainsbury, but as providers of transportation and logistics locally and globally. To that extent they become concerned with the realization of those ultimate values – such as truth, beauty and goodness – embodied in the perennial wisdom of the ages. As a result, for example, a participating manager from Anglian Water, based during the latter part of our programme in New Zealand, saw his role, and his company's, to be that of acting as 'guardians of the water world' in that land, following the line adopted by the native Maoris. Similarly, a group of managers from the City Corporation had concerned themselves with enhancing the role to be played by financial capital in fostering sustainable development. The philosophical underpinning for this part of the programme, therefore, is humanistic, drawing, for example, upon Francis Fukuyama's[13] approach to building civic trust. What then are the specific

Table 4 Civic reconstruction

ORIENTATION	**Sustainable** development
RELATIONSHIP	**Transformative** – business and society
METHOD	Natural and catalytic **cycles**
CHARACTERS	Hunter, herder, gardener, **steward**
GROUNDS	**Cultural** anthropology
PHILOSOPHY	**Humanistic**-holistic-rational-pragmatic
PHILOSOPHER-KING	**Fukuyama** – Trust
COMPETENCE	Compete/conserve/catalyse/**co-create**
CURRICULUM	Economic/technical/sociological/**cultural**
PROGRESSION	Morphosis, metamorphosis, **homeostasis**
FRAMEWORK	**Perennial** wisdom
FOCUS	**Civic** reconstruction

implications for the different roles played by the wide-ranging cast of characters on our programme?

The cast of supporting characters

In the final analysis, then, the cast of supporting characters, for our project based MMBA, changes (see Table 5). Such change occurs according to the stage the participants, individually and collectively, have reached over the course of their 'ecological succession'.

Education and training – colonizing academic terrain

The first 'preparatory project', arising out of a process of training and education and in fact constituting coursework, is aimed at furthering individual understanding of management, of managing and of the manager him or herself. It is primarily supported by an academic *instructor*, who helps the participant tackle each of the MBA subjects at hand. Literally, therefore, and at the final viva, the manager is therefore required to 'defend' his or her work, as if it is new territory that has been captured, or indeed colonized.

Intellectual capital – herding knowledge and skill

The second set of 'ordinary' projects is aimed at upgrading intellectual capital, thereby enhancing the performance of both managers and also their departments. The managers are primarily supported by academic and in-company *supervisors*, whose joint responsibility is to ensure that intellectual capital is individually and departmentally enhanced, with a view to improving the performance of both. The verifying of such an enhancement – that is the upgrading of human, structural and customer capital – is the responsibility of the *link manager*.

Table 5 Stages of ecological development

Focus	Trajectory	Succession	Support	Orientation
Individual	Preparatory	Colonization	Hunter/ instruct	Training and education
Department	Ordinary	Conservation	Herder/ supervise	Intellectual capital
Organization	Extra-ordinary	Catalysation	Gardener/ facilitate	Knowledge creation
Society	Mastery	Co-creation	Steward/ mentor	Civic reconstruction

Organizational knowledge creation – catalysing development

The third cluster of 'extraordinary' projects is aimed at organizational learning and knowledge creation, thereby allowing managers' roles and the organization's development to evolve. This results in the evolution of new products or processes, and indeed vice versa, through recurring self-organizing networks.

It is the role of the university based *facilitator*, then, in conjunction with the client organization's *organizational ecologist* – responsible as a would-be gardener individually or jointly for organization development – jointly to catalyse such individual and institutional evolution.

Civic reconstruction – co-creating civic society

The final 'mastery' phase of our programme involves a process of co-creation whereby, under the joint stewardship of the sponsoring organizations and the MMBA *executive board*, projects of civic reconstruction are 'masterminded', locally and globally. In that context, and as we saw in chapter 1, a focus such as that of advancing public health, promoting sustainable development, resolving social conflict and promoting an open society all have their place. We now turn from our MMBA programme, specifically, to the generic notion of a knowledge creating ecology.

BIBLIOGRAPHY

1 Lessem, R. and Nussbaum, B., *Sawubona Africa: Embracing Four Worlds*, Struik, 1996.
2 Stewart, T., *Intellectual Capital*, NB Publishers, 1997.
3 Ibid.
4 Peters, T. and Waterman, R., *In Search of Excellence*, Harper and Row, 1982.
5 Mintzberg, H., *Mintzberg on Management*, Free Press, 1989.

6   Revans, R., *Action Learning*, Blond Briggs, 1980.
7   Stacey, R., *Strategic Management and Organization Dynamics*, Pitman, 1995.
8   Nonaka, I. and Takeuchi, H., *The Knowledge Creating Company*, Oxford University Press, 1995.
9   Stewart, T., *Intellectual Capital.*
10 Gatley, S., Lessem, R. and Altman, J., *Comparative Management: a Transcultural Odyssey*, McGraw-Hill, 1996.
11 Stewart, T., *Intellectual Capital.*
12 Hampden Turner, C., *Mastering the Infinite Game*, Capstone, 1997.
13 Fukuyama, F., *Trust – Social Virtues and Wealth Creation*, Hamish Hamilton, 1995.

3 Organizational ecology
The dynamics of ecological succession

INTRODUCTION

Beyond stability and equilibrium

In this key chapter I shall be laying out the general approach to organizational ecology, that Sudhanshu Palsule and I have developed and that provides the overall conceptual architecture for this book. To begin with I shall reveal how the search for stability and equilibrium has been the management equivalent of the holy grail for most organizations. Thereafter, in chapters 4 and 5, I shall align such stability with everyday 'work' and with 'ordinary' management, and instability with 'soul' force, and with 'extraordinary' leadership. Subsequently I shall unravel the four worlds that underpin our organizational ecology as a whole. To substantiate it, I shall turn to the so-called 'cycles of history', to a 'framework for societal learning', to the 'age of business ecosystems' and to 'transforming organizations', as different manifestations of this fourfold rhythm in business and organizational life.

In terms of organizational dynamics, as we shall see in chapter 5, this need for stability has given rise to four 'navigational principles'.[1] These, in effect, are a spin-off from classical science and the laws of Newtonian physics and Darwinian biology. The outcomes of such stability (see Table 6) have been traditionally associated with results such as return on investment, earnings per share and total quality.

Table 6 Stability seeking navigational principles

Orientation	Attributes
Control	Always control your organization through a concrete vision, long-term plans and systems of rules and regulations.
Uniformity	Maintain a common and unified culture and make sure that all managers adhere to it.
Profit	Always focus on the bottom line first and everything else later.
Adaptability	Adapt as closely as possible to your business environment and deliver what the customers want.

NORTH : MODERN
Conserve
Organizational/Socio-technical
Herder

WEST : TRADITIONAL   EAST : POST-MODERN
Colonize   **Catalyse**
Individual/Economic   Inter-organizational/Ecological
Hunter   *Gardener*

SOUTH : PERENNIAL
Co-create
Communal/Cultural
Steward

Figure 3 The knowledge creating ecology

However, in a rapidly changing environment, these principles that are geared towards 'reaching equilibrium' are fast becoming obsolete. Business enterprises, like Anglian Water, that could once use these strategies successfully are suddenly no longer sustainable in their traditional organizational form. On the other hand, those – like the Virgin Group or the Surrey Police in the UK or like INTEL or Microsoft in America – that are prepared to drop the 'mindset' described above are proving to be successful.

Control and stability are useful as far as they lead to identifying solutions to problems and applying systematic, formalized types of planning, implementation and control. But what is not often understood is that opting exclusively for stability results in brittle structures that ossify over time. In that context, the reason for the decline and eventual failure of the traditional General Motors-type American organizational form was rooted, paradoxically enough, in the very factors that made it successful. If organizations do not alternate and 'cycle through' between stability and instability, they are apt to run down. A stable structure, what Ikijiro Nonaka[2] in his knowledge creating company terms the 'business system' (see chapter 12), has to be complemented by unstable processes (Nonaka's project layer) that undermine the very structures that epitomize stability. It is this paradoxical tension between the formal structure and genuine process – often confused with business 'process' re-engineering – that we shall explore here.

Towards an organizational ecology

'To shake a tree is to shake the earth' goes an ancient East African saying, vividly evoking an image of nature as an interconnected whole. In a world of networked, global markets, financial systems that transcend national boundaries, and satellite based communication, the notion of interconnectedness acquires an even deeper significance. This is something that Lloyd's, as we shall see in chapter 5, has reactively come to realize, so far more to its cost than to its proactively based benefit!

Yet, while the world in which we do business and manage our organizations has altered radically, the mental and physical models that we use, the IBM insurance sector apart (see chapter 7), still have not. In other words, depending on mechanical models that arise out of the atomistic worldview of classical physics is ultimately counter-productive. The same truth holds for classical biology. However, in spite of all scientific evidence about interconnectedness that is around us, we continue to hang on to outdated biological models of absolute competition and survival of the fittest. Lloyd's of old, and privatized Anglian Water anew, are cases in point to the extent that our MBAs from these organizations are now running counter to the prevailing competitive wisdom. In this chapter I shall enter the world of the new ecology, and seek out a coherent model of 'organizational ecology' based on it that will provide an apt metaphor for transforming our organizations.

As we shall see when we look deeper into the organization and dynamics of ecosystems, the 'navigational principles' of stability, control and adaptability do apply to them, but in a limited sense. Ecosystems do seek stability and equilibrium. But that is only one-fourth of the story of nature: one world out of four. The need for equilibrium and stability is held together in a larger network of four worlds[3] in which stability and instability co-exist. When we deal with an interconnected system such as a lake or a forest in which every part (or sub-whole) is in unbroken contact with every other part of the system, the system as a whole needs to be simultaneously stable and in a state of instability. This is something that even the most traditional of organizations, the City Corporation (see chapter 5), is beginning to realize, as it searches tentatively for its own organizational ecology.

Business as a state of non-equilibrium

What we see repeated time and again in business organizations is the failure of success, which has been called the 'Icarus paradox' by Danny Miller.[4] Successful companies become highly specialized over time, basing their strategy upon a single asset. Seduced into following the 'done thing', they start seeking equilibrium at the expense of innovation and creativity. Very soon, they become ossified and the very factors that made them successful now lead to their downfall, as was the case for Icarus, who flew too near the sun and melted the wax on his wings. Sainsbury's, as we shall see, is today a classic case in point, which is why our people on the MMBA programme are trying to do something about it. If our earth's ecosystems, the coral reefs, the rainforests, the atmosphere had followed the dictates of seeking equilibrium alone, life would have stopped evolving. The story of evolution is one of continual tension between stability and instability.

From an ecosystemic perspective, equilibrium can be defined as a state of stability from which *no more energy can be extracted*, like a brick lying on its long side. Ecologically, a state of complete equilibrium is closer to a state of death since it is reached only when all energy is used up. Organizations that are in a state of equilibrium are therefore those that are traditionally waiting to be bailed out, taken over by a new management, or have simply declared themselves bankrupt. Many Lloyd's syndicates, during the dark days of the early nineties prior to the Society's so-called 'reconstruction and renewal', found themselves in such a situation.

Nothing on our planet is in a state of equilibrium. Contrast that with, say, Mars, whose atmosphere is in perfect chemical equilibrium. Rather than equilibrium, it is disequilibrium that suggests the presence of life, and Virgin Direct, as we can see later (see chapter 13) is a living testimony to that! The Earth's atmosphere is an extraordinary and unstable mixture of gases, but at the same time this composition has remained the same over quite long periods of time. For instance, the air we breathe is an impossible mixture of reactive oxidizing and reducing gases. There is 21 per cent of oxygen in the atmosphere and 1.7 ppm of methane. Oxygen reacts with methane in sunlight to form carbon dioxide and water. In an equilibrium state, the methane would soon be used up. That has never happened because methane is being continually replenished by methane producing organisms at the rate of 500 million tons a year. Organizations, too, are like complex ecosystems that need to be sustained in states of non-equilibrium. The strategy for success is in being able to maintain a *contradiction* within an organization, where one part tends towards stability and the other towards instability.

America's Richard Pascale explains the continuing success of Honda along similar lines.[5] On the one hand, Honda management is all about traditional Darwinian and Newtonian principles: coherence, centralization, tight controls and, most importantly, adaptation to the environment. But on the other hand, these traditional perspectives are continually being shattered through individual and counter-cultural freedom to seek out instability. Through this meeting of opposites, Honda has been able to move to a higher order state of '*bounded instability*' which is the hallmark of all ecosystems. Also called an 'autopoietic' state, an organization in bounded instability, or an *autopoietic organization,* is like a living system whose true identity is derived from the paradoxically simultaneous existence of instability and stability.

The late German-Swiss systems theorist Erich Jantsch defines it as the state reached once a structure has gone through the turmoils and turbulences of youth and adolescence and established its identity in the 'far-from-equilibrium' environment.[6] Autopoiesis, as we shall see again in chapter 8 based on *The Stories We Are,* literally means 'self-productive'. An autopoietic structure is able to resonate between using new inputs to dissolve itself and move into higher orders, and being stable in the presence of a rapidly fluctuating environment. Whereas Lloyd's in recent years had remained stable, in the face of rapid market fluctuations, it failed to dissolve its prevailing self to ascend to a higher order of complexity, and thereby ran into environmental and commercial trouble. Of what kind of parallel dissipation and progression might we then be talking?

ORGANIZATIONAL ECOLOGY

Organizational life phases

Youth to maturity

The classical principles of straightforward competition, adaptation and control are geared towards a start-up, *youthful* organization that has kept Lloyd's syndicates (see chapter 5) forever young. James Moore refers to this stage as 'pioneering', typical of Anglo-Saxon business enterprises like Microsoft or Netscape, Body Shop or Virgin. In the beginning, for organism and organization alike, there is a need for bodily growth and higher use of energy. Managers have to be alert, quick to seek out new opportuities, cashing in on quick returns, similar to organisms that *exploit* the environment and struggle to survive on their own.

At a second – in James Moore's terms 'expansive' – stage, successful strategies become genetically and behaviourally adapted and organizations develop their own formulae and systems. This was Sainsbury's in the seventies and eighties, in its expansive heyday, guided by the somewhat autocratic Sir John Sainsbury. A new order evolves, one of stability based on successful strategy. Resources are used at a lower rate, and the organization, now in its *adult* stage, acquires *control* of itself and the environment. It 'settles down' and stops exploring, seeking instead to reap the benefits of the stability it has acquired. Scandinavian organizations, like the Swedish IKEA or Danish Lego, excel at this point.

Around *midlife*, there is the onset of turbulence and a dissolution of the old identity. Instability appears in the nature of end-of-the-line product cycles, diminished sales, various problems that cannot be fixed in the same way as before, and conflict. The organization is in a state of dissonance and old structures come down, to be replaced by new processes. As in life, the organization seeks out a return to a state resembling the youthful stage through a new identity, and *letting go* of old mental and physical models, thus changing the course of the organization. The tight order that was established is replaced by a loose structure.

If, however, it is to engage in a genuine process of midlife renewal, as our MBAs at IBM (see chapter 7) are interdependently attempting to do, then an authentic organizational ecology needs to be established. Moore, in citing INTEL as an ecosystemic case in point, somewhat inappropriately uses 'authority' to represent this loosely integrated phase.

Finally, in the last stage, the organization becomes *mature* and evolves to become a *legacy*. It is stable once more, but in contrast to the control mode, its stability is the result of spreading out its resources and gains macroscopically. This is precisely what the Surrey Police force (see chapter 12) is attempting to do, as it engages reciprocally with its communal environment to co-create the conditions for peace.

The organization, ultimately, is indistinguishable from the society it is in, and it works towards the benefit of a larger whole. It is this fourth stage that Moore terms that of 'renewal', perhaps because he has an incomplete, somewhat Newtonian grasp of the third one. This developmental process as a whole is illustrated in Figure 4.

As is evident, the area of 'bounded instability' or autopoiesis is one that is contained in the centre of the four worlds, the overlapping area in the middle of the two axes. When we say that ecosystems are in a state of bounded instability or autopoiesis, it means that they are able to maintain themselves in a state of perpetual resonance within the four worlds of exploring, settling down, letting go and leaving a legacy. While they continue a pioneering, exploratory existence, they are equally well tuned into unpredictable, catalytic modes of being. Similarly, while they are highly stable as individual units, they are simultaneously responsible for maintaining the overall system of the earth.

Positive and negative feedback

What is important from the point of view of formulating new management strategies that are not based on the old models of stability and equilibrium is an understanding of how exactly these four worlds operate in an ecosystem. First, a prerequisite for stability is that of perceiving the organization as abstracted out of its environment. It then becomes an autonomous entity with a deep need for control and stability. It has a definite physical structure, it utilizes specific mechanisms that are structured into various hierarchical orders within itself, and it has a need for accumulating energy to its advantage. To gain and consolidate its stability, it has to compete with the other organizations and adapt to changes in the external environment.

New policies have to be agreed, new laws followed and new deadlines adhered to. Fixing targets for profits and then preparing annual budgets, setting time paths for product development, frequent monitoring, as well as corrective action are all aimed at keeping the business on a stable, predetermined equilibrium path. This is known as the path of *negative feedback*, a stability seeking mechanism which dampens any deviation from the norm.

A frequently quoted example of negative feedback is the central heating system in a house. A desired temperature is pre-set in the control mechanism, which also contains a mechanism to sense room temperature. The control system turns the heat on when room temperature falls below the pre-set mark, and does the opposite when the temperature rises above the level. By responding to the deviation away from the standard, the control

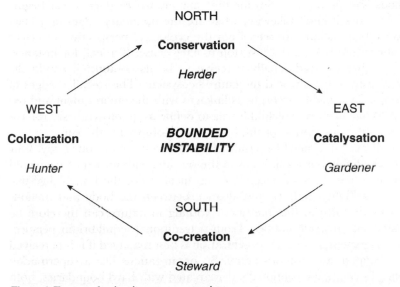

NORTH

Conservation

Herder

WEST

Colonization

Hunter

***BOUNDED
INSTABILITY***

EAST

Catalysation

Gardener

SOUTH

Co-creation

Steward

Figure 4 From colonization to co-creation

system dampens any deviant movement. In other words, the emphasis is on maintaining a pre-set condition of stability.

In ways similar to those observed in natural systems, an organization is simultaneously open to external and internal fluctuations and develops by being permeable to its environment. To counterbalance such negative feedback, it has to remain continually unstable. This goes against conventional wisdom, which says that instability is bad for the organization. Without instability, as we said before, the organization is apt to fall into decay. The thermodynamic balance that prevents the running down of a closed, stable system is generated by instability and loops of positive feedback that create vicious and virtuous cycles that amplify small changes. Life creates conditions for life that creates more life, which is an example of positive feedback. Similarly, organizations must continually create, through change and instability, conditions for organizational evolution. The organization is a set of open-ended interdependencies that link it to suppliers, financiers, retailers, consumers, the community that it serves and the natural environment through vicious and virtuous cycles.

These relationships flow in and through the company, identical to the chemical processes and cycles that flow in and through all ecosystems. The open-endedness demands instability through continual change. As a result, an ecosystem is a highly sensitized system. This means that if there is the slightest change taking place in any one part or aspect of the system, the change gets amplified over the whole. Later on in this chapter, we shall be calling this a '*far-from-equilibrium*' stage. Second, interconnectedness is only possible when the lines and boundaries that divide 'individual' systems turn amorphous and permeable. So, for that matter, where does a leaf begin? And where does it end? Likewise, what are the boundary edges of a lake, or a sea? When systems are seen from the ecological perspective, clear-cut demarcations and boundaries just stop making sense. If a leaf, for instance, 'ended' at what we traditionally perceive to be its contour, it would die instantaneously. And so would the entire ecosystem. The so-called edges of leaves are, in fact, highly amorphous linkages with the environment and the sun itself. What every schoolchild learns to define as 'photosynthesis' is basically a scientific description of the leaf's relationship with the sun.

Where do we end, then? Certainly not at the contours of our body. Our skins too are highly porous linkages to the outside, without which we would not survive. What digests a recently eaten meal is not the body's digestive system, but a highly sophisticated alliance between the body and millions of microbes that live in the intestines. Nothing in nature can therefore be demarcated into discrete entities. From a traditional, equilibrium perspective of management, in fact, an organization is best managed if it is perceived to be an isolated, autonomous entity. So organizations like a supermarket or a police force are conventionally demarcated with hard boundaries, both inside and outside, under the impression that a cartographed organization provides for stability.

In reality, such an organization is no more stable than the map of a country, or a stuffed animal in a museum. All three are examples of complex systems that exist only in continual interaction with the external environment. While the animal depends on sun, water, plants and other life-forms for its development, nations depend on the free flow of information, social, economic and political institutions, while organizations depend on managing the linkages with suppliers, retailers and consumers.

From this perspective, a state of complete equilibrium is simply unsustainable; stability has to be counterbalanced by instability and it is in the dynamic tension between the two that organisms and organizations alike survive, grow and develop. A plant, for instance, is able to respond immediately to a change in the acid level of the soil it is in, by changing its own pH value. This response is the outcome of an inherent instability in the plant that makes it open to fluctuation. Similarly, the very existence of the plant is the outcome of its permeability, its lack of clear boundaries. This is, however, not to ignore the fact that ecosystems and living organisms are also highly stable entities. The same plant that has an inherent instability about it is also highly stable in the sense that it is able to withstand a great deal of external perturbation. Trees in a forest are able to expand their size and numbers precisely because of a need for greater stability. Similarly, ecosystems are able to conserve themselves by being individualistic, or non-permeable. An organiztion cannot be permanently unstable. Rather it has to balance itself between phases of stability and instability. What may strike you as being a paradox, the co-existence of stability and instability, is, in fact, a generative ecological principle. Moreover, as we shall see, it also becomes the generative principle for our 'four world' approach to what we have termed, in this book, an 'organizational ecology'.

Transformation phases in ecosystems

Competition to co-creation

According to such an emergent organizational ecology (see Figure 5), to manage a supposedly stable and isolated entity that competes with other such entities, witness Lloyd's, simply does not work any more.

There is no absolute stability in the natural world. Rather stability goes hand in hand with instability. On a closer look at nature, it appears that the dynamic state of 'hanging on' between stable structures and destabilizng processes takes place at the centre of 'four worlds'. These worlds respectively comprise competition, conservation, catalysation and co-creation. These together constitute the 'four Cs' of our organizational ecology. Let us take an example from an ecosystem, first, and work this model through. After that, we can apply this model specifically to organizations and their management.

Four natural worlds

A handful of soil, for example, from your garden reveals the extraordinary life-support systems of the earth. Beneath the thin layer of topsoil covering the continents of our world lies the ecosystem that governs the existence of every species on earth. It houses the bacterial and the microbial power-house, containing billions of microscopic organisms. This same handful of soil also contains the strands of the four worlds of ecology.

The first world of colonization: pioneering and exploration

At first glance, the topsoil provides nutrition for plants and trees and consequently to all the other species. A 'good' patch of soil allows plants and trees to colonize it. It provides the ecological milieu for the pioneering stage of bodily growth in which plants, trees, shrubs and weeds increase their body mass. In their growth phase, all plants and animals use resources from their environment to build their tissues. They increase in size through a high intake of energy. This leads to a build-up of biomass in the system, characterized by a factor known as gross production.

Gross production is a bit like the Gross National Product that measures the financial well-being of a nation. Like the GNP, this factor only measures the expansion of biomass and the number of species. It does not take into account the overall qualitative well-being of the entire system, very much in the same way that the GNP does not take into account the quality of living in societies. The world of competition is the world of survival. It is

NORTH

Conservation

WEST		EAST
Colonization	**THE FOUR WORLDS**	**Catalysation**
	OF	
	ORGANIZATIONAL ECOLOGY	
High stability		Low stability
positive feedback		negative feedback

SOUTH

Co-creation

Figure 5 Four worlds of organizational ecology

all about individual plants, trees and animals trying to get maximum access to the initially plentiful resources available. Lloyd's of London and its constituent enterprises have been ingenious in this 'colonizing' respect.

The second world of conservation: settling down and organization

Left to itself, the pioneering, competitive aspect of life would completely overrun the soil and very soon it would be reduced to rubble. Not unlike the economics of societies and countries, where the pioneering spirit and competition have to be balanced by some kind of conservation of resources, the soil needs to be kept going by some built-in system. Northern European societies in Scandinavia, for example, have a built-in high taxation system for a welfare state in which all citizens receive the benefits of subsidized housing, hospitalization and an education for life. Similarly, the Idea Centre in northern Austria (see chapter 10), has resourcefully recycled the physical, financial and intellectual capital of its immediate Silesian region. In conservation, something is put back into the pool of resources for the benefit of all, whether Austrians, Scandinavians or indeed Greeks or Palestinians.

In the case of soil, this northern world is kept operable through millions of nitrogen-fixing bacteria in the soil. This mechanism of nitrogen fixation, transforms free nitrogen, which is otherwise useless in the life-cycles of plants and animal species, into ingestible nitrogen compounds. There are two types of nitrogen-fixing bacteria: (1) symbiotic bacteria, those that attach themselves to the roots of plants and (2) non-symbiotic bacteria, those that live free in the soil. (In the case of the Idea Centre, for example in its manufacture of table lamps, while local granite 'comes free' from the local area, the roots of its inspiration lie in Makis Werlamis' (one of the founders) classical Greek heritage.) It has been estimated that in a single season, in an acre of soil, the symbiotic (productive) bacteria which form small nodules on the roots of plants may add about 150 pounds of nitrogen to that acre. The asymbiotic (reproductive) bacteria, on the other hand, remain ceaselessly active in breaking down dead organic matter, to release again the nitrogen and the other nutrients of life into the soil and the atmosphere. The soil is thus able to conserve its nutrients and maintain its life-cycle over a longer time.

The third world of catalysation – creative destruction

The symbiotic and asymbiotic nitrogen-fixing bacteria prevent the pioneering stage from completely depleting the soil of its nutrients. As we saw, the ecosystem is thus better able to sustain the demands made on it by the pioneer stage. But over time, conservation of the soil through nitrogen fixation (mass production or mass consumption) alone is not enough. Conservation by itself is akin to a bureaucratic structure which, although necessary at a certain stage in the development of an organization or a society, becomes an impediment to further evolution. By becoming desensitized to the real needs and demands of the environment, bureaucratic structures become ossified.

If it were left only to the conservation world of the ecosystem, life would, over time, settle into predictable, highly organized structures, like Sainsbury's supermarkets. In the case of a forest, after having passed through the tribulations of the pioneer stage, it settles into maximum homogeneity and becomes specially adapted to specific niches.

This is also true of the Scandinavian societies which over time have become so highly homogenized that it is diffiult for them to adjust to the emergent multiculturalism that is sweeping the world. The effect of conservation, then, is to build up the entropy level in an ecosystem. Entropy is like life-energy which is either accumulated and stored, as regentropy, or dissipated. In the pioneering mode, energy is spent on exploration and the system is loosely bound in the sense that resources can flow in a diversity of ways through the system, just as has been the case in Lloyd's. In the conservation mode, energy is conserved and entropy thus accumulates in the system as a result of homogeneity and organization, as has been the case for Britain's hitherto leading food retailers J. Sainsbury's. But excessive entropy build-up, which is another word for equilibrium, is fatal for any living system. Under these conditions, the system simply buckles and collapses. What usually happens in nature is that this tendency to accumulate entropy and move towards full equilibrium is offset by certain processes that engage in what can be termed catalytic destruction. To prevent entropy from building up, ecosystems 'discover' another level of order, in which the structures that have been built up are destroyed to prevent ossification.

In the case of the soil ecosystem, other bacteria invade the plants and trees and start causing disease. The more homogeneous a forest becomes, the more susceptible it is to disease-causing bacteria, as is currently and metaphorically the case for Sainsbury's. The plants and trees that the bacteria invade are called the 'host species'. The association between bacteria and the host results in an abnormal condition in the host which causes blight and rot. Interestingly, these bacteria are carried from one tree to another by the very mechanisms that are part of the tightly bound structure – bees, pollinating insects and rain.

Hurst, writing in *Crisis and Renewal*,[7] uses the forest fire phenomenon as another example of 'creative destruction'. In the case of a fire, a system is not destroyed completely; it is partially destroyed in order to be renewed. Catalysation then is a phenomenon through which a number of 'tag-on' processes undermine the existence of the previous 'conservative' order of stability and increasing equilibrium. Whether they are the invading bacteria, forest fires or typhoons, these catalysts alter the earlier structure and create new situations in which the energy blocks are removed. For the British police force, as chapter 14 will reveal, the Brixton riots of 1981 served as such a 'forest fire'. In contrast to the 'desensitized' state of the ecosystem at the conservation stage, the system becomes highly sensitized at the catalytic one. As we shall see later, positive feedback loops amplify small changes and push them through the entire system, keeping it in a 'far-from-equilibrium' state. This is also the stage where life can take new directions and lead to the development of new species and behaviour, as has been the case for Surrey Police through its so-called 'neighbourhood policing'. Our own evolution from our anaerobic bacterial ancestors to oxygen-breathing ones was the result of a similar far-from-equilibrium development. Chaos and creativity seem to form a partnership in the ecosystemic model. It goes without saying that, as far as our organizations are concerned, this is the part that we have most trouble with!

In fact, as is the temptation in a company like Sainsbury's, the tendency is to go back to the world of colonization that it knew.

The fourth world of co-creation: social transformation

Whereas catalysation disrupts the ecosystem in order to shift it to another level of order, co-creation is the re-ordering of the system. In the Surrey Police case, for example, this would be represented by 'civic society' as a whole. As such the 'civilian' part of the force's organizational whole would be 're-authorized'. Such a re-authorization, through 're-storying who we are' (see chapter 14) lies at the very basis of life's, and organizational, evolution. Like a mountain spring from which a river keeps being eternally born, co-creation is a spring-source of the patterns, relationships, structures and processes in life.

From the point of view of the old biology, life evolved by adapting to the environment. But this is only one fourth of the truth, applicable to the competitive, pioneering aspect of ecosystems. What we now know is that life does not merely adapt to the environment, as would be the case, for example, in 'reactive' policing. Rather, life conserves, as in the case of 'problem solving' policing. It also plays its part in catalysing, or in undoing what went before, and finally becomes a partner with its environment in co-creation, that is in re-authorizing what went before, as in the process of 'peace building'. So, for instance, in our example of the soil ecosystem, we saw that the soil sustains life on earth. We also saw how the nutrients are recycled back into the soil with the help of certain bacteria. But where does the soil itself come from? In the old biology, it was taken as a given, something that exists as part of the environment. What we now know is that the soil, like civic society, is continually being created by the plant and animal (or economic and social) life that lives off the soil (or community). So carbon dioxide is pumped down by life on the surface after dissolution in water near the rock surface. The water may have come from rainwater or been fed by nearby spring and rivers. This solution now causes rocks to weather. The micro-organisms aid this process and more soil is created. Without life there would be no soil, but only regolith, the rock rubble of dead planets.

The emergence and the maintenance of life then, like peace building and peace keeping, is an ongoing transformative process. While life emerges from its environment, the environment needs to be continually transformed by living organisms to remain life-supportive. Moreover, this is achieved by life being in a state of continual change itself, not opposing the forces of the environment, but flowing with them. Life and the environment, like civilians and civic society, can be said to be partners in co-creation. To take another example of this co-creation, aquatic blades of grass reduce stream velocity, thereby forcing the waters to drop their silt load and the decaying plant material they carry along. Both these effects increase channel deposition, which creates more soil and nutrients for plant roots. Plants grow stronger, denser. This reduces velocity further, creating further deposition. Deposition displaces water. The stream overflows its banks and spreads out, greatly expanding its surface area. The water's energy drops drastically. Nourishing water and silt are spread over a broad channel, nourishing more lush growth. This growth creates greater accumulations of spongy, absorbent, plant material, spreading the slowing water even wider.

The interaction between natural energy and life's energy system is the chief principle of co-creation. This is the route to self-renewal that Sainsbury's should be seeking, as a food (natural energy) retailer (life's energy) rather than in seeking to be the 'customer's preferred supplier'. The interaction is often so subtle, so insignificant that we don't even see it. Each small shift in equilibrium creates another small shift. Each new equilibrium covers the tracks of the previous change. The power lies in the cumulative consistency with which these changes shift equilibrium in life's favour. Life creates conditions for more life, which in turn creates conditions for more life. These loops create change, not stability.

By shaping the development of its food producing environment, life, and in this case Sainsbury's, allows itself to be shaped by its food consuming one. Likewise, the purpose of business from this fourth world perspective is to co-create a common future in which resources and benefits transcend the four walls of the organization and encompass as wide an area as possible.

Organizations – like Surrey Police, as we shall see – that do so, develop; the ones that do not eventually die out. From a co-creative perspective, on the one hand your business depends on the external environment for its growth and development. But curiously enough, on the other hand, it must participate in the creation of an environment that is sustainable and conducive to doing business.

FROM ECOSPHERE TO BUSINESSPHERE

Organizations are like blades of grass, trees, coral reefs, forests. They stream-line the flow of resources and make them available to people in the form of goods and services. They too are contained within the four directions of competition (western), conservation (northern), catalysation (eastern) and co-creation (southern). Each of these four ecological worlds that iso-morphically pervade our organizational ecology therefore requires different eco-strategies on the part of the manager. We now consider each of these four eco-worlds in turn, and outline how such different eco-strategies need to be adopted by the manager within the context of an organizational ecology.

The 'western' territorial management: manager-as-hunter

The conventional hands-on management that is so much a characteristic of Anglo-Saxon business or communal enterprises is one that favours freedom and individuality over collective behaviour. The emphasis is on structured yet autonomous organizations that are able to adapt to the environment and create maximum profit, or detect the most crimes, through a dissemin-ation of products and services that sell or that work. The archetypal western world is fundamentally, therefore, a pioneering 'colonizing' one, of which an Edward Lloyd, on the one hand, or an Agatha Christie, on the other, would be proud. It is exemplified by rapid commercial growth and a spirit of action centred leadership as well as business entrepreneurship. As such it demands an empirical, hands-on approach that is more than comfortable experimenting in trial-and-error situations. The manager or leader here is clearly the hunter-gatherer like Richard Branson who stakes claims to unoc-cupied territory and the market or 'catch' that it offers. The attitude is highly competitive and the learning process is a *reactive* one, just as in, for example, 'reactive' policing.

The aim of the hunter-gatherer manager, or indeed police sergeant is to try and build structures that can strengthen the organizations' hold on the territory, the product or service, be it represented by consumer goods or by crime detection. Change is not welcome unless it is predictable change for which the hunter is prepared. Such a hunter uses business instinct and common sense, as either business entrepreneur or police detective, to advantage. Rationalization is often retrospective and is used only to build a succesful recipe. But the action, be it that of a Hercule Poirot or of Sir John Sainsbury, is primarily instinctive and based on a sensory reading of the situation.

The strategy of such a hunter-gatherer manager, inspector or surveyor is to try and cash in on the recipe by using it to exploit as many situations as possible. The recipe can involve a product like Coke, which is then marketed successfully across the globe.

Such a management or police strategy, or menu, involves a person sensing out emergent territories in the market and then quickly moving in to occupy them. Territorial management depends on physical resistance to opposing forces, and is therefore better attuned, for example, to peace making than to peace building. The strength of this mode is its extraordinary ability to venture into difficult market or social conditions by working or playing hard and using one's natural instincts. The disadvantage of this mode is that it works best when the organization is at a youthful stage. Entrepreneurship, the stronghold of western organizations, is all about going 'against the wind' and erecting strong structures that can take the impact. The pragmatic, hands-on model of the west searches for identity in the world of structure. Like pitching one's tent or putting up a flag, the identity of such youthful organizations as Lloyd's comes from territorial advantage and competition.

This mode works efficiently as long as the organization does not become 'over-adapted' like Sainsbury. Texas Instruments in their field, like Sainsbury's in food retailing, once set the standards for semiconductors and were packleaders in consumer electronics. But TI kept selling on price alone, as Sainsbury's did on product value, having adapted to a market notion that low prices meant maximum consumption. This adaptive mindset that was once the cause of their success, became the cause of their decline. TI was slow to move into the more sophisticated chip market, as Sainsbury's has been to move into knowledge intensive services, and faster rivals moved into the niche. What happened with IBM, and indeed with Sainsbury's, is a similar story. Hunting-gathering management is based on the premise that once the fences are erected around a territory, the company can coast along in a predictable world. But as both Sainsbury's and Texas Instruments cases tell us, the real world of private, if not also public, enterprise is anything but that.

A territorial organization is a *structural* organization, composed of one-to-one correspondences, strict linearity and 'for every effect there is a cause' logic. The bottom line, be it represented in financial performance or in crime records, is the deciding factor for all structures. For all practical purposes the organization has no connectedness with the outside world except in terms of goods sold and services rendered. The balance sheet is all about profit and loss, criminals detected or undetected, the core values of the territorial organization. The environment of such a business is restricted to commercial parties or individual perpetrators of crime, interested purely in the quantitatively based performance of the organization. Correspondingly, the balance sheet of the territorial organization makes explicit the singularly financial or statistical relationship of the firm to the world outside.

'Northern' world of niche management: manager-as-herder

The northern management ethos of the Scandinavians, unlike that of the typical Anglo-Saxons, is highly rational. In contrast to the hunter who is essentially a manager who relies on instinct and trial and error more than reason, the northern manager is a herder or 'problem-solver' who operates entirely through reason. Whereas the western organization adapts to the environment, the northern organization depends on the environment adapting to it. Rather than capturing territories, the emphasis is on developing and implementing systems that find a specialized niche in the market or community. It is not immediate profit that is the main concern now as the survival of the system is ensured. Rather it is to specialize in function and conserve resources as much as possible through a standardization of policies, procedures and species types. For instance, two of Denmark's biggest national dailies, *Politiken* and *Berlingske Tidende,* share a common spare parts inventory.

They also have a system whereby in case of shortage of staff in either newspapaper, they 'borrow' human resources from the other for the day. On all other counts, the two papers are competitors: they compete on price, quality, layout, readership. But at the same time, being associates involved in a common business, they 'herd' together and conserve resources. Herding organizations invest in technology and formal organizations procedure, as has traditionally been the case at Ford and IBM, as a way of increasing specialization. Unlike the recipe method of the hunter manager, the herder manager works with a formulated theory that is applied to solve problem situations. Hence IBM's new emphasis on providing solutions, which is not one that Ford (would-be transport solutions) has yet evolved towards. This is the world of the 'formula'. In the seventies and eighties the Sainsbury's formula for the development of supermarkets and hypermarkets in England was second to none. It was a formula, however, that became so 'niche-specific' that it seemingly could not be applied to Scotland, never mind to Austria or to Argentina!

The computer industry is an excellent example of how companies that were hunting successes were forced in the eighties to adopt a herding policy.

David Hurst, in his *Crisis and Renewal*, refers to the story of Compaq. In 1987 it made it into 'Fortune 500' after only four years of operation. Very much like Texas Instruments, Compaq was fairly and squarely a hunting organization with a closely guarded territory. Prices were kept high as the territory was relatively safe. But in the beginning of the nineties, sales started falling and the first losses began to register at Compaq. For the first time since its inception, there were lay-offs. What was once a unique Compaq territory had been invaded by many other competitors, who were selling similar products at much cheaper prices. What was clearly needed was a niche formation and a conservation of resources. Costs were cut drastically, the workforce was cut by 25 per cent and procedures made more efficient. In two years, Compaq quadrupled its output and improved sales growth.

The danger with herder organizations is that like homogeneous forests and other ecosystems, they are highly susceptible to catastrophe. Efficiency for the Sainsburys of this world is bought at the expense of flexibility and resilience, which are the characteristics of the territorial organizations. The herder manager therefore needs to be able constantly to upgrade existing systems to offset the brittleness of the northern organization. Such northern, niche organizations are *systematized* organizations, constructed on rational lines. The herder manager is a methodical and deliberative learner, a fully fledged executive who is able to conceptualize the organizational process better than the hunter manager. On the other hand, the herder manager lacks the instinct, the individuality and the sensory acumen of the hunter. He or she also lacks the insight into patterns of behaviour, and the appreciation of developmental processes of our 'gardener'.

'Eastern' symbiotic management: the manager as gardener

In stark contrast to the highly stable niche organization of the north, the eastern organization operates best in conditions of instability. The approach is neither to resist the flux of matter and energy in the environment nor to submit to it. The middle-path principle is that of the aquatic blade of grass, which prevents run-off not through direct opposition but by allowing the water to split and flow around it. The emphasis here is on maintaining a highly fluid organization that is able to create changes both within itself and in the environment. This model tends to rely exclusively on generating processes that result in loops of positive feedback. The assumption that the gardener manager of the east makes is that turbulence cannot and should not be controlled. Moreover, unlike in the niche organization, turbulence is perceived in positive terms, as a precursor to creativity.

Thus Ian Beckett, Deputy Chief Constable at Surrey Police, perceives his organization as being poised between chaos and complexity. Similarly Honda, for instance, purposely provokes instability by hiring large groups of managers in mid-career from other organizations. The aim is to prevent the crystallization of one corporate culture. Rather, counter-cultures – as for example between the so-called 'uniformed police' and the 'civilian police' – are encouraged to provoke instability and, consequently, innovative management. So, while the hunter manager within an organization such as Lloyd's syndicate adapts the territorial organization to the environment, the herder manager within the earlier structures at IBM or Sainsbury's created a fit for the organization within the environment. This takes the form of a specialized niche.

The gardener manager – as illustrated in chapter 7 through our group of managers within the IBM (Europe) insurance sector – perceives both the organization and the environment as dynamic phenomena, incapable of being abstracted into a condition of stability. Eastern organizations generate conditions for their sustenance by 'losing themselves', letting go of previously held boundaries of 'in here' and 'out there' and the strict hierarchies within. Our IBMers are poised to become such 'nonentities', but are not yet quite ready to take the actual and existential plunge into IBM oblivion! The development of a living system, as is the case with IBM and its insurance based clients, arises out of the interaction between life and the environment. To illustrate this, we use a term coined by C.H. Waddington: the epigenetic landscape, which is a multidimensional world of valleys and hills. This landscape is a picture of both the individual organism and the external environment it develops in. The epigenetic landscape consists of what Waddington called 'chreodes', well-worn pathways that represent previously used genetic tracks. Like a sphere rolling over a landscape, the developing organism is set in motion. It tends to follow the old chreodes. But the landscape itself is a dynamic one, it is alive, full of perturbations, and the organism may be influenced by the landscape to make a detour. The detour, however, etches out a new chreode on the epigenetic landscape, so that, when other organisms use this new chreode later, the eventual result is the formation of a new order of organisms. One organism therefore cycles-in the other through an interactive relationship between the organism and the environment, as was originally the case for Norwich Union and Virgin, resulting in the birth and growth of Virgin Direct (chapter 13).

Open-ended, eastern organizations, as in the IBM insurance case, maintain themselves in a state of development through a similar cycling-in process. The tendency in the territorial and the niche organizations is to resist perturbations and the demand for detours, and depend exclusively on negative feedback loops. Such feedback loops, in the Sainsbury's case for example, are constraining it to become more environmentally oriented, as opposed to product/market focused – thereby sticking to the old 'colonizing' territory. But what is vital to the eastern organization, as for our IBMers working with partner organizations, is to invite in the detours and allow new chreodes to develop. Sony's success with the Walkman and the Camcorder are examples of how product-chreodes develop through spontaneity and perturbation in the system. Crucial to the gardener manager's approach to management, then, is a phenomenon called symbiosis. It can be defined as an association of two or more living systems (for example Sainsbury and the Royal Bank of Scotland) within a larger ecosystem that creates a situation of mutual advantage for themselves and for the larger whole. Hence Surrey Police is prolifically engaged in partnership schemes with adjacent local authorities, as is IBM's insurance sector with its global clients.

Japan's legendary relationships between producers and suppliers are an excellent example of such symbiosis. At the Toyota plant in Takaoka, no worker has more than one hour's worth of inventory at the work station. When a defective part is discovered, it is immediately tagged and sent to a quality control area for replacement. The 'Just-in-Time' inventory system of Japanese corporations is possible only because of a symbiotic link of trust and mutual benefit between the parties involved. As Lynn Margulis points out,

> symbiotic co-operation is at least as important as 'survival of the fittest' competition; in order to compete – in order to get in the game in the first place – you have to co-operate. We now believe that the doctrinaire Darwinian view of 'Nature red in tooth and claw' is naive and incomplete. Symbiosis means survival.[8]

Symbiosis then means that competetitors are able to enter into harmony with each other. In natural systems, there are innumerable examples of microbes that have evolved amazingly complex symbiotic relationships. While some microbes lower hydrogen sulphide concentrations for others, the others in turn provide organic compounds.

Some microbes can eat but are anaerobic, which means they are not capable of breathing, but they exist in symbiosis with others who can breathe but cannot eat. Margulis extended microbial symbiosis further to what she refers to as 'endosymbiosis'. When two or more species co-operate closely enough, eventually qualities that have become obsolete no longer appear in the offspring. Margulis writes: 'The consortial quality of the individual preempts the notion of independence.'[9] That is something we are after within our own consortium based programme, though we still have a long way to go in order to reach it.

Once again, the Japanese organizational model seems to be directed towards what Margulis refers to as 'endosymbiosis'. Similar to the dropping off of redundant qualities as an evolutionary pattern, Japanese corporations place premium value on continually refining existing systems by eliminating those aspects that have become obsolete.

This dynamic state of continually evolving products towards higher forms of order is achieved through symbiotic interplay between competitors (like Australia's AMP and Virgin) and a deep interconnectedness between the organization and the consumer. An endosymbiotic organization thrives and profits from being part of an interconnected whole. The symbiotic interplay, both within the individual company and within the bigger organizational network, is the result of the gardener manager participating in the interconnection instead of being the objective observer. This is precisely the role we are attempting to play with our clients.

'Southern' homeostatic management: the manager as steward

The southern world is characterized by being able to maintain itself in a state of dynamic equilibrium. In biological terms, it seeks to maintain a state of *homeostasis*. The earth, for instance, is bounded on the outside by space with which it exchanges energy, sunlight coming in and heat radiation going out. It is bounded on the inside by inner space, the vast volume of plastic hot rock that supports the crust and with which the earth exchanges matter. Within this boundedness, it maintains itself through the presence of life.

All ecosystems are endowed with the necessary mechanisms for homeostasis; they include energy flows, material cycles and invisible information networks that connect all parts and regulate the system as a whole. Homeostatic management involves treating the organization as a macroscopic entity, like the self-regulating earth itself. On a macroscopic scale, boundaries become unimportant and the steward manager both draws in resources from as wide an area as possible and spreads services out in an equally wide area.

Such a steward manager's starting point, embodied within Surrey Police's orientation towards preventive *neighbourhood policing*, implies that the organization can never exist as an isolated entity. Like all ecological phenomena, it stays alive and healthy only as long as it maintains a web of relationships, both internally and with its environment. For the steward manager like Anglian Water's CEO Chris Mellor (see chapter 15), unlike the hunter or the herder, organizational operation is not a matter of formulae or theories. Rather, it flows in and through a web of relationships that bind the organization to society and the environment. The bond is a porous one, similar to the kind of amorphous link-edges that characterize a leaf or a lake. Products and services have to be developed and improved through a constant interlinking of people, ideas, skills and resources, and they have to reach the market, or community, through a network of processes. Resources enter the organization through link-edges, as in Surrey Police through the linkages between the police, the Probation Service, health and education as well as the public at large. Waste – in the Surrey case 'antisocial' behaviour – has to be disposed of through other links.

This runs contrary to the old organizational logic which still prevails in the traditional approach to, for example, policing, that we go about our jobs as managers or police officers convinced that the organization functions best when perceived as a fragmented entity. According to the new biology and indeed economics, rather than competing for survival, early chemical matter structures evolved through co-operation. What then was the reason for the co-operation? These early non-living micro structures were part of a very large macro structure, the chemical system of the whole earth. As the micro structures, or analogously 'local' neighbourhoods, evolved, they changed the chemistry of the macro 'global' system. This in turn produced more fluctuations and new micro structures emerged. Co-evolution is a holistic unfolding towards a future, not a random interaction of parts. Later, when bacteria appeared as the dominant life form on earth, there was no free oxygen. It was as if the whole neighbourhood was crime-ridden, as in parts of Soho or Toxteth, South Africa or Russia today. Some of the bacteria created fluctuations in their own (micro) structures and subsequently in the macro structure of the earth's atmosphere and restructured into forms capable of photosynthesis. This would be the case if such a social pathology as crime and destruction was turned into such 'prosocial' behaviour as the intensification of civic society. In fact that is precisely what Anglian Water have been focusing upon in their 'Transition Management' project (chapter 15) in Buffalo, New York, as is generically the case for the Body Shop (chapter 16), wherever it is based.

For the next 2,000 million years the bacteria went about totally transforming the earth's atmosphere by filling it with free oxygen! According to Erich Jantsch, there was a curious selflessness and vision in the way they went about it, just as is the case for Deputy Chief Constable Ian Beckett in Surrey today. Already adapted to the oxygenless (or analogously crime-ridden) environment, how did the bacteria 'know' that they had to restructure themselves to becoming oxygen-dependent, so that life could evolve further? According to Jantsch, the goal was the extraordinary intensification of life, as is the extraordinary intensification of 'civic society' for Anglian Water. In Jantsch's scenario, the universe as a whole is an autopoietic structure. 'Life appears no longer a phenomenon unfolding in the universe; the universe itself becomes increasingly alive.' A business or communal organization, then, as a micro neighbourhood structure which might be based in Surrey or Seattle, is enfolded within a macro worldwide structure of societies, cultures, the earth and life itself. Micro and macro structures are reflections of each other. The organization participates in the intensification of life, as pathological or poverty induced behaviours dissolve into prosocial and richly endowed ones. From the homeostatic perspective, the organization has no beginning and no end. A business organization is like a biological organism which thrives on being a part of a larger interconnectedness.

In this way policing becomes woven into peace building, in the same way as the Japanese American social historian Francis Fukuyama has woven trust, as a social virtue, into the creation of prosperity[10] From the ecological perspective, homeostasis is the natural path of the universe.

The southern homeostatic pole provides a sense of direction to the organisation by rooting it in a universal legacy of shared value, such as peace and reconciliation, or environment and sustainability. The southernness explicitly manifests itself through a 'mission' and a visionary need to express deeply rooted values and desires to change the world, locally and globally, through products and services. The business world still awaits a fully developed manifestation of the southern value mode, though Body Shop certainly comes close. Let us now conclude.

CONCLUSION

The legacy of '*Oikos*'

The term 'ecology' originates from an ancient Greek word, *oikos*, that simply meant home. Ecology (*oikos* + *logos*) thus became the 'study of one's home' and consequently of one's relationship to all that constitutes 'home'. Interestingly, the word 'economics' has also been derived from the same root. Since 'nomics' means management, economics translates as the 'management of the household', which involves an increase in 'value' for the benefit of the household. Accordingly, ecology and economics originate from a common ground and as such are intrinsically linked in their meaning. While economics without ecological value would make for unsustainability, ecology bereft of economics would lack structure and consistency. Each is enfolded within the other. This is ironic considering that the situation as we have traditionally known it has been precisely the opposite.

The generally widespread notion – both within the business community and outside it – that ecological considerations violate the very basis of economic well-being, and vice versa, is familiar rhetoric. In the mechanical worldview, success is measured in economic terms and not ecological ones, although the two are intrinsically connected. In effect, we are supposed to 'manage' our organizational household without 'valuing' it.

The dysfunctional organizational form of today, struggling to retain a foothold in the slippery world of contextual change is a consequence of precisely the same problem: managing without valuing. The first effect of this is to alienate the manager from the 'ecology' of the organization: the systemic networks and invisible processes that hold the company together. Second, the organization itself becomes isolated from its environment. Economic progress becomes a pendulum-like movement between production and consumption, within a completely closed system, governed exclusively by its own laws, rather than within the systemic pattern and processes that govern value in nature.

In the turbulence that is shaking up old structures of thought and beginning to produce unprecedented changes in our organizations and societies, a transformation of the traditional dualism between ecology and economics is imminent. Any new understanding must necessarily provide a framework that articulates a new coherent system in which ecology and economics return to being complementary forces. The return to one's home: the *oikos*, is simultaneously emotional and pragmatic. For to return is to renew, to gather sustenance for the future; it is to reach deeply into one's roots and tap the wellspring of belonging.

From the primeval carbon atoms that continue to exist and sustain our individual bodies, to the natural fossil resources and the elemental energy that we utilize and mould in every part of our organizational systems, our links with *oikos* are undeniable and irrevocable. Whether it is an organization, a society or any of the other myriads of forms that we forge, each of these, in one way or the other, is rooted in *oikos*. An understanding of these indestructible links is the singular act of understanding a universal system at work through an array of complex relationships, chains, linkages, alliances, interdependencies that make us and our environment a fountain of energy flowing through a circuit of soils, rocks, microbes, plants, animals, the atmosphere, our societies and our organizations. Consequently, it provides a powerful model and metaphor for the alternative we so badly need to create far-reaching changes in our societies, organizations and lives. And in the return to one's home, there is a genuine possibility for change.

Towards Gaia

As we move into the closing years of this century, the need for a new, coherent worldview for businesses and societies becomes more and more important. We believe that our organizational ecology, inclusive of its four interconnected worlds, is able to provide such a worldview. From the pioneering spirit that marks the human need to explore and further existing knowledge to the spirit of value that creates a context in which all can benefit, our evolutionary record carries the imprint of both ventures. Gaia, the name given by scientist James Lovelock to the planet earth is an embodiment of the four worlds that prevail in our organizations and the four cultural corners of our globe. It is also an embodiment of ultrastability. We now turn from 'Gaia' to the allied world of chaos and complexity, starting out our organizational journey with the commercially oriented Lloyd's. We consider two different worlds before accommodating four.

BIBLIOGRAPHY

1 Stacey, R., *Managing the Unknowable*, Jossey Bass, 1992.
2 Nonaka, I. and Takeuchi, H., *The Knowledge Creating Company*, Oxford University Press, 1995.
3 Lessem, R. and Palsule, S., *Managing in Four worlds*, Blackwell, 1997.
4 Miller, D., *The Icarus Paradox: How Excellent Companies Can Bring about their own Downfall*, Harper Business, 1991.
5 Pascale, R., *Managing on the Edge*, Penguin, 1990.
6 Jantsch, E., *The Self Organizing Universe*, Pergamon Press, 1980.
7 Hurst, D., *Crisis and Renewal*, HBS Press, 1993.
8 Joseph, L., *Gaia: the Growth of an Idea*, Arkana, 1991.
9 Ibid.
10 Fukuyama, F., *Trust: the Social Virtues and Wealth Creation*, Hamish Hamilton, 1995.

Part II

Traditional

From training to learning

4   Ordinary and extraordinary management

Reconstruction and renewal at Lloyd's

THE ORGANIZATION

In the latter part of 1997, more than three hundred years after Lloyd's had been founded, Terry Heyday, who had spent all his working life within the Lloyd's Society, was contemplating its further development in the context of a prospective University of Risk. In fact, Terry had first been involved in our MMBA in the context of APEX, an Accelerated Programme of Education and Examination. Such an overtly training oriented programme, inclusive of two years of study for insurance based professional qualifications, our insurance specific MBA, and a so called 'study tour' to Katie School of Insurance in Illinois, was an attempt to redress the Lloyd's balance in favour of professionalism. It had emerged in the aftermath of the Society's recent 'reconstruction and renewal', which had in fact saved it from imminent destruction. Terry Heyday, then, had decided to sample our MMBA, while at the same time recommending it to aspiring Lloyd's others. Little did he know at the time, in 1995, what would happen to him in the process. The result, for him if not also for Lloyd's, would be truly 'extraordinary', and as such a fully fledged education. By the end of it, in early 1998, he was considering how such an extraordinary personal experience could become the same for Lloyd's in general and for the participating companies – rather than merely individuals – on the MMBA.

Edward Lloyd – poetry in motion

The history of Lloyd's has been one of continuous growth and change, based on cumulative experience, but no step forward has ever been made until some crisis made it necessary. It all began with Edward Lloyd, formerly a journeyman framework stocking knitter, who established his Tower Street coffee-house in 1688. This became the meeting place of the forerunners of underwriters and brokers. At no stage was Lloyd himself concerned with the actual business of insuring ships. His role was simply to provide a coffee-house. The historian Lawrence Green, in his *History of the English People*, saw in the early coffee-houses the birthplace of modern English prose. It was in them that men discovered 'the new-found pleasure of talk'. We may therefore claim that Lloyd's and the modern English language have a common ancestor. From the outset, therefore, Lloyd's was socially as well as economically embedded within the community, albeit with an emphasis on matters maritime, which befitted an outgoing, seafaring nation. Within this risk-laden economic and social context, right from the start, information at Lloyd's was all. Gossip or 'intelligence' as it was then known, was the name of the game and inside information was the hardest maritime currency to obtain. All coffee-houses saw it as their duty to supply their customers with pens and ink, but Edward Lloyd went further. He supplied them with news. In 1696 Lloyd brought out his own newspaper of shipping movements. Under the title *Lloyd's News* it was printed for Edward Lloyd – coffee man. The coffee room at Lloyd's was therefore a centre for marine intelligence, extracted over coffee from returning seafarers.

John Julius Angerstein – intelligent enterprise

Standing on the shoulders of his predecessor Edward Lloyd, for whom already information was power, the Russian-born John Julius Angerstein represented the spirit of Lloyd's continued buccaneering ascent. Very often the kind of insurance underwritten would be something new, tailored to a special need, hacked out in endless discussions between underwriter and broker. It is this spirit of enterprise which is at the heart of Lloyd's, and through the centuries has been carried forward by a very few people. Angerstein was one of them. He was a nationally known figure, a financial adviser to William Pitt and patron of the arts, whose private collection would later become the nucleus of the National Gallery.

By 1829 Lloyd's had appointed over 350 agents in the world's ports, mostly shipping brokers or traders whose day-to-day work put them in touch with shipping matters. Lloyd's Intelligence Department has become, for the world's press and for a host of safety services, the most comprehensive and authoritative bureau of shipping information. Because Lloyd's insured ships it had an obligation to those who risked their lives in them. The first expression of this obligation goes back to 1782 when the members of Lloyd's raised £2,000 for the dependants of seamen lost in the *Royal George*. In 1794, during the Napoleonic Wars, a series of funds was set up to help those wounded in particular battles.

To take another example of the way the social and economic overlapped, in the early days of Lloyd's, a certain Mr Greathead had all his life been working on a plan for what he called a safety-boat or lifeboat. Now that he needed, in the 1780s, help to complete his designs, he approached the underwriters he had previously helped by disclosing to them the pathological lies of a ship's captain who had deliberately run the vessel aground. He sent these underwriters his designs. They subsequently wrote back not merely praising them but sending him money, and an introduction to the

Duke of Northumberland, who visited Greathead's workshop. In 1802, on Angerstein's initiative, the underwriters of Lloyd's voted £2,000 to encourage the institution of lifeboats at different places along the coast. 'We are obliged by your humane attention to us seamen,' wrote Nelson to Angerstein.

Henry Hozier – wireless telegraphy

The Secretary of Lloyd's at the turn of the century was Henry Hozier, a man in the buccaneering Lloyd/Angerst mould. An explosive, imaginative autocrat and technocrat, he had studied medicine in Paris, served with the Royal Artillery in the China War, and covered the Franco-Prussian War as a correspondent. After witnessing the siege of Paris and serving in the Intelligence Department of the War Office, he became Secretary of Lloyd's in 1874. Henry Hozier was an archetypal Victorian. He established a network of signals around the world over the course of the next three decades, until Lloyd's held a practical monopoly in the collection and distribution of shipping intelligence. In other words, Lloyd's at the turn of the twentieth century had become an 'intelligent enterprise'. Marconi's invention of wireless telegraphy in the 1890s, however, threatened Lloyd's monopoly. So, with characteristic energy, Hozier teamed up with the famous magician Maskelyn to conduct experiments with the recent inventions. Two years after the first patent had been filed, in the 1890s, Lloyd's started emitting signals. Marconi was sufficiently impressed to enter into an agreement for Lloyd's to handle ship-to-shore messages on behalf of the new company. The deal sadly ended in a row five years later. Hozier's great achievement, though, was to predict the importance of merchant naval intelligence in the early twentieth century and to set up a string of signal stations from the Lizard to the Suez Canal, all linked to Lloyd's in London. To this end he travelled the world, running up vast expenses, setting up his signal stations and a network of local Lloyd's agents. By 1906 he had seen these stations superseded by those of Marconi, but the network of Lloyd's agents would be an enduring legacy.

Cuthbert Heath – my creative word is my enduring bond

Cuthbert Eden Heath, who outlived Hozier by some thirty years, was elected to Lloyd's at the age of 21. In 1906, when the San Francisco earthquake struck and did $300 million worth of damage to property, Heath's was a leading syndicate involved. Other insurance companies collapsed or reneged on their obligations. But Heath cabled his San Francisco agent with words that established the reputation of Lloyd's in the USA: 'Pay all our policy holders in full irrespective of the terms of their policies.' Heath, moreover, fuelled by his deep service commitment, was a genuinely innovative underwriter. He was responsible for many innovations, for example workmen's compensation, bankers' insurance as well as insurance against burglary and theft. Within a few years of Heath's arrival at Lloyd's, the market was insuring things which, in the 1700s, would have been unheard of. They were insuring factories in Chicago and Baltimore against fire, they were insuring farmers in southern Europe against hail damage. In the story of the modern Lloyd's two things stand out. One was Heath's invention of a non-marine market. The other was America's discovery of Lloyd's. For example, Lloyd's has specialized in the reinsurance of major windstorm damage in the US since the days of Heath, who based his own rates on his research into windstorm records and statistics going back 600 years. These, of course, were social as well as economic innovations. Heath, in effect, helped the organization of Lloyd's evolve into a Society, formally established by an 1871 Act of Parliament thirty years before.

Enterprise and community

The growing size of the risks accepted had led by then to the creation of the syndicate system, whereby the underwriter no longer wrote part or all of the risk by himself, but acted on behalf of a syndicate of 'Names' or members. The preamble to Lloyd's policy statements stated: 'Individually we are underwriters; collectively we are Lloyd's.' In the words of Cuthbert Heath in the 1931 edition of *Siren and Shipping*:

> there is one thing which is still with us and shines as brightly as ever. It is the honourable feeling that, privileged as we are among traders in that our contracts are those of *uberimae fides*, our good faith must also be the supreme law of our existence. I feel quite certain that underwriters generally are still as determined as ever to do what is fair rather than insist on legal rights.

When Cuthbert Heath wrote the first burglary insurance, he was starting a tradition. The incident took place when a broker was renewing a fire insurance and half jokingly asked Heath if he would cover the house for burglary since there was a spate of thefts in London at the time. 'Why not?', he said. Cuthbert Heath's 'Why not?' has passed into legend. More than that, it has become almost a precept of Lloyd's underwriters to look out for new forms of insurance.

In the 1930s the working underwriters such as Heath still dominated Lloyd's. Not only did they lead the business but their syndicates also provided the capital base for the market. The brokers brought in business, but not new members, for the underwriters recruited their juniors and members from among their families and closest friends, and the great Names in Lloyd's were dynastic. By the mid-1950s, nevertheless, Lloyd's unique asset base and expertise meant it enjoyed an influence out of all proportion to its share of the world's insurance market. As a result, there were few calamities on the planet, ranging from a sudden shower on an English tea party to a catastrophic fire in a Burmese teak factory, that did not concern the policy underwriters in London. 'Its agents', quoted *Esquire*, 'are stationed in the four quarters of the globe, from Zanzibar to Zululand.' Forty years later, though, the tides had begun to turn.

Trapped in gilded cages

In an age of satellite technology, Jonathan Mantle maintains, even the most successful underwriters at Lloyd's were beginning to look trapped, by 1963, in their 'gilded cages'. The underwriters were resistant to change. It was the brokers who were offering innovative insurance programmes to international industrial companies. To work for Lloyd's was more of a passion than a profession. Young men grow up in the very special atmosphere of the Room, learning the traditions, unwritten rules, Lloyd's *esprit de corps* and code of decency. But behind the marble facade some young members were privately voicing misgivings. What Lloyd's presented as a desirable form of continuity seemed to them a collective inertia at odds with the outside world. The most successful brokers were the boldest salesmen. Even the best of them had few financial or managerial skills; and yet because the insurance business was booming they were becoming more and more powerful all the time. In 1968 a Commission of Inquiry was set up by the former Governer of the Bank of England, Lord Cromer. His conclusions were clear and simple. First, Lloyd's had to admit foreigners. Second, it had to admit women. Third, it had to admit a mini-Name. There were simply not enough new members to be found amongst the British rich. The admission of foreigners and women, interestingly enough then, were forced upon Lloyd's by commercial pressures rather than by an innate urge of the Society to move with the times. With hindsight this influx of new capital had its disadvantages as well as advantages, forcing down the rates. Moreover, Cromer's preoccupation was with practical and structural rather than with conceptual and systemic changes.

The reputation of Lloyd's for insurance innovation – whether it involved insuring an oil rig, a satellite or an earthquake – was not matched by the latest technology. The wooden underwriting boxes were positively Dickensian, and however much money they were making the furthest the underwriters travelled during the course of duty was to Lloyd's and back from their homes in the suburbs and shires. The brokers, on the other hand, were living a life of travel and adventure on an increasingly glamorous scale. There were experts, moreover, who specialized in anything from oceanology to bloodstock. Among the major risks that the broker Sedgwick is currently handling is the reinsurance for China's first nuclear power station at Daya Bay – so vast a project that three Sedgwick technical experts have spent over two years working on it.

Passive underwriting

By the 1980s, it is remarkable to note, only 6 per cent of profits came from underwriting income; 94 per cent came from investment income and from capital appreciation on syndicate funds. Without Lloyd's realizing it, its major source of creative enterprise, that of underwriting, was slowly atrophying, alongside the proactivity of its members. As a prominent such 'passive' member in the 1980s, a certain Geoffrey Rickman concluded that he knew too little about the market. He sensed, at the same time, that the underwriters knew too little about the risks they were insuring and reinsuring. Hamilton, Ontario, professional people were typical of such 'passive investors'. The closest they came to taking a risk was letting the fund manager choose the stocks. Little did they know what they were letting themselves in for. *Piper Alpha* was a good case in point.

There had been a great deal of activity on the *Piper Alpha* platform for weeks; midsummer was the maintenance period and new construction work was taking place as well as the usual oil and gas production. *Piper Alpha* was old and badly equipped and the men who lived and worked there were cynical about the cost-cutting and penny-pinching that kept it that way. A total of 167 men died on the night of 6 July 1988, in a massive and violent explosion. For this terrible eventuality Occidental Petroleum, the owners and operators, had made suitable provision. Like many oil rigs and gas platforms around the world, *Piper Alpha* was insured at Lloyd's. Like *Piper Alpha*, Lloyd's lacked the management controls and above all the safety equipment. Instead of reinsuring and making proper reserves, underwriters had passed the problem on in a reinsurance spiral in which the principal motives were the broker's commission and underwriter's capacity and income. It was high time for change.

Reconstruction and renewal

In the year leading up to, and during the 1990s, two parallel developments accompanied Lloyd's crisis of transition. The first kind of reconstruction and renewal, rooted in product and process rather than in finance and structure, had been going on for twenty years. It involved a certain Julian Radcliffe of the brokers Hogg Robinson. Radcliffe, who had studied terrorism in Beirut in 1970 while he was on a travel scholarship from Oxford, produced a paper outlining the possibilities and problems. Most kidnap business was led by one speciality syndicate, Cassidy Davis. Radcliffe put up the idea to Anthony Cassidy, the leading underwriter, that the chances of a loss could be reduced by teaching a potential victim to take precautions. The insurance industry might even go further. Staff could be provided to help in the negotiations with kidnappers. This was an extension of Radcliffe's guiding principle, the idea that along with a policy the market itself should provide some form of loss prevention. By the end of 1974 he had set up, within Hogg Robinson, a new company called Control Risks, recruited from former SAS officers.

Today Control Risks staff have become so internationally recognized as experts in their field that they are asked to train many police forces in anti-kidnap methods. Though the Cassidy syndicate does not insist that clients commission Control Risks' services, it will rebate up to 10 per cent of an assured's first premium if such clients consult them and use their precautionary measures. If Control Risks hadn't existed people would have paid more money more readily. Radcliffe is now moving into areas where the interests of the insurance market coincide with those of social usefulness. In the area of what Lloyd's calls fine arts, for instance, he is currently developing the idea of a registry of stolen works. But Radcliffe's most startling and creative idea is for a scheme for swifter and more efficient settlement of serious bodily injury claims. The new idea is that the initial emphasis should be on rehabilitation.

As soon as someone has been injured, the expert loss adjustment team will see his solicitor and try to put together some suitable package for getting him back to work. In many ways, Radcliffe has taken on from where Mr Greathead, with his lifeboats, left off some 200 years ago, whereby – and in both instances – the socio-political and economic activities of Lloyd's were closely interlinked.

The financial and economic process of 'reconstruction and renewal', second, spearheaded by David Rowland and his task force, followed upon the disastrous losses that were suffered in the early nineties. Once again, in Lloyd's historical evolution, it only responded when there was an external crisis. The major features of this reconstruction were to provide Lloyd's with more bureaucratic power and managerial influence, including the reinforcement of its regulatory powers, the introduction of corporate capital into the market, and the creation of a new financial entity, Equitas, to refinance historically based debts. The task force, reporting in 1992, intimated that the criteria for success for Lloyd's, over the medium term, would be a superior reputation for capital strength and security; the skills to compete in increasingly complex risk areas; a competitive cost position to maximize profitability out of tight margins; and an effective distribution system. The need to upgrade professional and management skills led to the establishment of the so-called APEX programme, as part of the Lloyd's Training Centre, for which Terry Heyday had significant responsibility, while remaining a Director of Owen and Wilby Underwriting Agency.

From Lloyd's Training Centre to the University of Risk

Launching APEX

Terry Heyday, who had himself been caught up in Lloyd's recent troubles, was looking to build on the task force's plans to raise standards of professionalism in the market. The route first chosen, as we shall see, was, in Ralph Stacey's terms, an 'ordinary' or traditional training oriented one. Along with Terry

Webb, Director of Training at Lloyd's, Heyday designed a five-year 'fast track' programme encompassing tuition from the Associated Chartered Insurance Institute (ACII), participation in our own project based MMBA and further study that would lead to FCII designation. Furthermore, it would involve a 'study tour' to the Katie Insurance School at Illinois State University, through which familiarity with the US insurance scene would be acquired. The whole APEX programme, moreover, was aimed at individuals based within Lloyd's, in their mid to late twenties.

Contingency planning

The current Managing Director of Cassidy Davis, Edward Creasy, was the first Lloyd's based participant on our programme. His three projects, in effect, were linked together by his interest in Information Technology, by his desire to organize and motivate better the underwriting teams within Cassidy Davis, and by a need to confront the future positively through what he saw as enhanced contingency planning. Central to Edward's thinking was the notion that he wanted to effect improvements in both his own managerial abilities and in the management team with whom he was working. Even more importantly, he wanted to create a positive corporate environment that would embrace even greater change within his own firm, though Cassidy Davis already had a considerable reputation as an innovative agency. Following in Edward's footsteps, Mark Cassidy, the son of the Cassidy who had worked with Julian Radcliffe on Control Risk, has chosen to enhance the finely tuned commercial relationships between the Cassidy syndicate and their insurers for his first MMBA project, by empowering those within his syndicate's own reinsurance department to find ways and means of improving the quality of the service they offered to clients. For his second one, and picking up directly from where Edward Creasey had left off, Mark was taking the risk of 'reinventing' himself as a developmental manager, duly advancing Edward's interest in risk management.

From Lloyd's to LIMNET

Creasey's interests in information technology and in risk management were matched by Tony Gregory's, albeit from a different angle. Building upon his experience as a former consultant to LIMNET (the London Insurance Market Network) Gregory's first project concentrated on the implementation of electronic trading and sought to push back both the frontiers of technology and the commercial relationships that it facilitated. LIMNET had been developed by Lloyd's together with IBM's insurance based business, which will be discussed further below.

Because of his interest in education, Tony used his second project for the marketing of insurance related conferences, which he had been pursuing on a part-time basis, entrepreneurially, before being recruited full-time into the

Lloyd's Training Centre. Through their joint involvement with the Katie Insurance School, Gregory and Heyday have developed a programme, in the UK, for senior managers from the US insurance industry, which will also involve the City University Business School. The programme will cover, among other topics, risk-based capital and new forms of risk transfer and electronic commerce.

Whither the Corporation?

Electronic commerce is a business that Centrewrite is in, as a subsidiary of the Lloyd's Corporation, the bureaucratic side of the Society's operations. James Maudsley and Dennis Vangelotis have both joined the MMBA from within Centrewrite, and are working on redefining the future of the enterprise, based respectively on social and economic reviews of their company. A similar review is also being undertaken by Simon Squires, but from an outside-in perspective. Simon had originally been at Sun Alliance, where his first project was based on the work he was doing for the company in Japan, thereby dealing with cross-cultural management. When he moved over to Neville Russell, in the wake of the Sun–Royal merger, he switched his orientation, for he was now engaged in a strategic repositioning of his new firm in the consultancy based market. Finally, for his third mastery project, he is reviewing the communal bases of both his own form and that of Lloyd's, in this way intending to renew its societal impulse. In that context he will be revisiting grounds previously established by Mr Greathead and by Julian Radcliffe before him, if not also by Edward Lloyd and by Cuthbert Heath themselves.

From commercial to intelligent enteprise

It was Edward Lloyd, through the 'intelligence' that tacitly worked its way through his coffee-house, and explicitly through *Lloyd's List*, who initially laid the foundations for the intelligent enterprise that Terry Heyday's proposed University of Risk would herald.

Vital to this was the work of Lindsey Roberts, a senior manager at Lloyd's of London Publishing (LLP), which had taken over *Lloyd's List* and other insurance related publications. Through her MMBA projects she was involved in planning a management buyout of LLP from Lloyd's, in integrating a former competitor from the world of financial journalism, and in devising a corporate strategy for her company.

Towards the University of Risk

The development of Lloyd's into an 'intelligent enterprise', thereby dragging it out of a traditional and commercial focus into not merely a modern and industrial one but a post-modern knowledge intensive, service orientation is indeed a tall order. For it would in the first place involve not only a renewal of Lloyd's original coffee-house based 'intelligence' – thereafter tele-graphically amplified by Henry Hozier via Marconi and subsequently incorporated by Lindsey Roberts and others into LLP – but also a signifi-cant upgrading of LIMNET and electronic commerce, taking on from where the two MMBAs from Centrewrite, James Maudsley and Dennis Vangelotis, Tony Gregory and IBM have left off. Second, and from another angle, it would incorporate the kind of knowledge intensive services incorporated into Control Risks by Julian Radcliffe, and further developed at Cassidy Davis into risk management *per se*. In other words, and in that composite respect, the APEX programme was only a training oriented drop in the ocean of reconstruction and renewal. Conversely the kind of University of Risk that Terry Heyday and his colleagues at the Katie Insurance School are talking about would aim to facilitate research and development within the Lloyd's market, leading to product innovation, to the establishment of a more profound link between the leaders in the world of education and those in the insurance industry. It is envisaged, moreover, that through this kind of development the wider social as well as economic benefits that Lloyd's provided, and which men like Cuthbert Heath understood so well, would be revitalized. The move from narrowly based professional training to fully fledged business education spanning commercial, socio-technical and psycho-logical risk, would thus be complete.

INTRODUCTION

From managerial economics to organizational dynamics

As I indicated in chapters 2 and 3, Ralph Stacey has played a seminal part in our work and lives. Just like one of us, Ralph is a southern African and originally an economist who in his midlife has turned to psychodynamic psychology. What makes his work utterly distinct is the way he has applied the sciences of chaos and complexity, along with psychodynamic psychology, to the fields of business and economics. Now based in the UK, and as head of the Centre for the Study of Complexity, he has carved out a unique niche for himself in strategic management and organizational dynamics. Moreover, he has clearly distinguished between what he terms 'ordinary' and 'extraordinary' strategy and management. In our Lloyd's context here, we thereby distinguish between ordinary training or instruction, and extra-ordinary education or learning.

Ordinary and extraordinary management

Stacey has taken on, in the world of business and management, from where Thomas Kuhn left off in his *Structure of Scientific Revolutions*.[1] For it was the

NORTH

ORDINARY   EXTRAORDINARY

WEST   **EAST**

PREPARATORY   MASTERY

SOUTH

Figure 6 Lloyd's organizational dynamics

American Kuhn who, some twenty years ago, distinguished between 'ordinary' and 'extraordinary' physical science. While the former merely served to extend the reach of what was already known, it was 'extraordinary' science that ventured into the unknown. All the great scientists of current and former times, ranging from Newton and Einstein, to Prigogine and Lovelock, were and are extraordinary. What, then, is the difference between the two, in a managerial if not also in a scientific context?

Ordinary management

Effective top executives, according to Stacey, that is 'ordinary' senior managers, are in control of their organizations and their strategies because of their vision, long-term plans, systems of rules and regulations.[2] For them, as for Terry Heyday when he was a senior manager at broker's Sedgwicks, an organization should have a common and unified culture. Any business, such as a brokers or managing agency, should identify what it is good at and deliver what its customers want. The standard curriculum of a conventional MBA programme in fact conforms to these ordinary standards, whether in relation to operations or marketing, financial or human resource management, organizational behaviour or corporate strategy. In this respect it is more to do, as we shall see in the next chapter, with 'work' than with 'soul'!

Extraordinary management

The trouble with standard maps and traditional organizational principles for Stacey, though, is that they can be used only to identify routes that others have travelled before. Such is the nature of training. Yet no one, Stacey argues, can know the future destination of an innovative organization; rather, that organization's managers, as is the case for genuine educators, must create, invent and discover their students' destinations as they go. There are echoes again, here, of David Whyte's distinction (see the next chapter) between the predictability of work and the unpredictability of the soul. To engage in soulful activity, managers must drop the old stable equilibrium mindset and develop a new one that recognizes the positive role of instability and the fact that long-term futures are unknowable. An extraordinary manager or educator will use instability and crisis in a positive way to provoke the continual questioning and organizational learning through which unknowable futures are discovered and created.

The resulting form of self-organizing control, moreover, is a group rather than an individual phenomenon, thereby transcending the bounds of an individually oriented traditional MBA. It occurs, for Stacey, when political interactions and dialogues between members of a group produce coherent behaviour. These interactions develop over time by passing through periods of instability, crisis or chaos. Thereafter they spontaneously lead to the making of choices at critical points, producing new forms of order. This is indeed a far cry from the 'ordinary' and predictable Accelerated Professional Examinations programme that Lloyd's envisaged might follow from its reconstruction and renewal. However, starting out in a place which is very different from where you eventually arrive is par for the extraordinary course, both from a strategic and also from an organizational perspective.

STRATEGIC MANAGEMENT AND ORGANIZATIONAL DYNAMICS

Managing the dynamic organization

Top executives or educators, Stacey argues in his seminal text *Strategic Management and Organizational Dynamics*,[3] do not drive and control new strategic directions. Instead, they create favourable conditions for, and participate in, complex learning and effective politics. Instead of well-laid visions and ready-to-work action plans, such operators focus on ever changing agendas of strategic issues, challenges and 'soulful' aspirations. Multiple, contradictory cultures therefore need to be developed to foster different perspectives and provoke the complex learning that is necessary for handling changing developmental agendas. This is a far cry from what we have in Lloyd's Society in general or in its Training Centre in particular, dominated by pragmatic, market-oriented free enterprise Anglo-Saxon culture on the one business hand, and by a 'civil service' orientation on the other institutional hand.

Learning groups, for Stacey, work in spontaneously self-organizing networks that encourage open conflict, engage in dialogue and publicly test assertions. Self-organizing political networks function to undermine the hierarchically based status quo. Without the consequent tension between control and freedom there could be no change. Unfortunately, within Lloyd's the upbeat nature of the market stands in the vibrant foreground, while the downbeat Corporation seemingly stands in the inert background. There is, in that imbalanced respect, less creative tension between free enterprise and controlled organization than destructive tension or, at best, passive accommodation.

Creating rather than adapting

The most important learning we do, Stacey maintains, flows from the trial-and-error actions we take in real time and especially from the way we reflect on these actions as we take them. How well people learn under these circumstances depends on the way they interact with each other in groups. Continuing success flows from creative interaction with the market environment, not simply building on existing strengths but intentionally steering away from equilibrium. The result is organizational tension, paradox and never-ending contradiction, and this provokes conflict and learning, the source of creativity.

The only route to long-term success, educationally or commercially, is through innovation and accelerated organizational learning, for no competitive advantage is inherently sustainable. Such accelerated learning, a far cry from accelerated examinations, is what enduring reconstruction and renewal is about. Such a view of organizational development, is a dialectical one in which contradictory forces – like those of the French Huguenot and the Romance side of Terry Heyday's dual heritage, or like Munich Re and Lloyd's – produce, through dynamic learning, a new synthesis of complex strategies and structures.

Success here lies away from equilibrium in a state of contradiction between stability and instability, formal and informal training, tight and informal education, tight constraints and flexible controls, centralized and decentralized structures, the market and the corporation. Adapting to the environment is thus replaced by creative interaction with other actors in the environment. Comprehensive control systems and culture change programmes are replaced by organizations as complex systems where all managers and facilitators can do is intervene at sensitive leverage points. Terry Heyday's role, therefore, having broken out of the 'ordinary' constraints of APEX, is to find such points of leverage, and intervene accordingly, to promote accelerated individual and group learning.

Far from equilibrium

The border area between equilibrium and disequilibrium, for Stacey, is a state of paradox in which stability and instability pull the system in different directions. Lloyd's should therefore be aiming to attract not only corporate capital and individual initiative, but also simultaneously to strengthen the power of a new centre while weakening the power of the old. Such a new centre would be global rather than local in its reach, enabling rather than restrictive in its systems and processes. At the same time, from a developmental perspective, both the Lloyd's Training Centre and the University of Risk would have important roles to play.

Scientists have called this combination of specific unpredictability and qualitative pattern a chaos, fractal or change state. Only when a system operates in this 'far-from-equilibrium' state is it continually creative. Chaotic behaviour, in this paradoxical respect, has an overall pattern. In other words, such 'chaos' is not utter confusion but bounded, rather than explosive, instability, a combination of order and disorder continually unfolding in irregular but similar forms.

'Chaotic' managers or facilitators seize on small differences in customer requirements and perceptions and build these into significant differentiators for their products – amplifying feedback. For example, Terry Heyday woud be taking due note of the fact that a fellow participant on the MMBA programme from the Lloyd's Corporation, James Maudsley, was overtaken by the course of recent events in Great Britain. James had connections with the British monarchy, through his family. In the wake of the death of Princess Diana, and because of his closeness to Prince Charles, he began to connect Lloyd's, the emergence of a new style in the royal family, and City University with the global evolution towards a post-modern, multicultural, multi-faith society. Such a cosmopolitain Britain is liable to function, because of the push and pull of diverse elements, in a nonlinear as well as far-from-equilibrium as opposed to linear fashion.

Creativity and chaos

When nonlinear feedback systems are pushed far from equilibrium, they follow a common sequence of steps in which they move from one state, through chaos, to unpredictable states of new order. Such a new order is emerging willy-nilly within Lloyd's, as corporate capital makes ever greater inroads into the financial fabric of the market. However, such a new economic order is not being matched by a progressive technological, cultural and social evolution. In other words, to the extent that Terry Heyday is able to rediscover the gypsy in his soul, juxtaposed against the spirit of Descartes, so Lloyd's may be able to renew its own romantic as well as classical orientation. These new states of order are known as 'dissipative structures'. In other words they are difficult to sustain because they require continual inputs of energy to survive. Functional politics involves continual dialogue around contentious issues. It is the mechanism for attracting organizational attention to open-ended issues. Its function is to spread instability, within boundaries. Such instability is necessary to shatter existing patterns of behaviour and perceptions so that the new may emerge. At each point of transition, systems driven far from equilibrium move through patterns of instability in which symmetry is broken, confronting the system with choices at critical points. Through a process of spontaneous self-organization, as Margaret Wheatley also intimates in the next chapter, involving a form of communication and co-operation among the components of the system, new order may be produced. This leads to a different perspective on strategic management, or indeed on training and education. Such a perspective starts with the detecting and selecting issues that need to be dealt with.

STRATEGIC MANAGEMENT

'Chaotic' strategy formulation

For Stacey, strategic management is an emergent rather than a rational process, and long-term strategy or development in particular is 'extraordinary' rather than 'ordinary' in character. As such it involves:

1   Detecting and selecting issues
    Open-ended change, the kind that strategic management or extraordinary facilitation is concerned with, is typically the result of many accumulated small events and actions.
2   Gaining attention and building support
    The birth of business strategy or organization development, for Stacey, involves some individual, at some level of the hierarchy, detecting some potential issue and beginning to push for organizational attention to be paid to it.
3   Interpreting and handling the emerging agenda
    That issue becomes part of the individual's, group's or organization's strategic issue agenda. It becomes the focus of the personal, interpersonal or institutional learning through which an enterprise develops new strategic agendas.
4   Clarifying preferences
    At some critical point, pressure arising from personality or group interaction forces a choice, whose outcome is unpredictable because it depends on the power play and group dynamics.
5   Taking experimental action
    Action will usually be experimental at first, thus providing a vehicle for further learning; task forces may be set up to carry out experimental actions in such areas as new product development.
6   Gaining legitimacy and backing
    Before such informal action is built into a strategy, formal bodies and procedures are required to legitimize choices being made and to allocate resources.

7   Incorporating outcomes into organizational memory
    In sharing memories of what has worked or failed to work in the past, managers or educators build up a philosophy; these recipes, taken together, become the enterprise culture. They provide another boundary around the instability of the political and learning processes through which strategic issues are handled.

In the context of all of the above, then, and to the extent that Terry Heyday is determined to create a University of Risk, if not also authentic business renewal at Lloyd's as well as academic renewal at City University and at the Katie School, he would be pushing his programme of activities forward. Obviously, to the extent that it became part of the Corporation's ultimate agenda, he would need to convince the newly appointed Chairman. Thereafter, and through his links within and outside Lloyd's, once a self-organizing group had been formed, it would be activated to foster learning experimentally, before seeking legitimization for its efforts.

Complex learning activities

Trying to predict the future is, for Stacey, a pointless exercise for an innovative group or institution. Strategic or developmental thinking in such a group requires anticipation and participation. It must be based firmly, moreover, on the qualitative nature of what is happening now and what has happened in the past, focusing particularly on the anomalies in the current situation. In the Lloyd's case, for example, the fact that the constituent enterprises claim to be global in their scope, and yet remain so parochially Anglo-Saxon, is one such anomaly.

Such an approach to strategic or developmental management means generating new perspectives on what has been going on. It means framing problems and opportunities. It means noticing potential and possibility. Lloyd's, of course, has the potential, because of its worldwide reputation, and indeed cultural influence, to attract resources from around the globe. By going into partnership with IBM, for example, it could greatly improve its technology based systems, and by aligning itself with the MMBA team it may overcome some of its anti-intellectual predispositions.

It means, additionally, creating group dynamics amongst, for example, our MMBA students that encourage participation in complex learning activities, making explicit and exploring not only issues themselves but also the group's learning behaviours. Such an analysis of group dynamics is anathema to an outward looking, market oriented set of underwriters or brokers, but may yield some powerful insights, and strategic ways forward. Moreover, and in a similar context, trying to identify the mental models that have led to the way problems and opportunities are being framed – with a view to developing a different learning model and changing mindsets – could lead to a much more thoroughgoing process of reconstruction and renewal.

Complex group learning occurs far from equilibrium, in the final analysis then, when individuals are in conflict and confusion, and search for a newly shared meaning. At this point they are willing to engage in dialogue.

Patterns of learning and innovation

The role of extraordinary management or facilitation, strategically or developmentally speaking, is not to invent and preach simple, clear aspirations or instructions but rather to create a context favourable to complex learning, from which challenges may emerge. People interacting in a business or academic enterprise, Stacey maintains, may produce a pattern in their actions through self-organization, provided that the context in which they work enables them to discover and learn. The focus will be on detecting anomalies in what is going on now, like the one I pointed out in Lloyd's above, using intuition and analogy to develop responses. While still placing boundaries around sequences of choices, it will examine and try to improve the group dynamics upon which the processes in organizations depend. Finally, the concern for developing common cultures and cohesive teams will be replaced by actions designed to promote different cultures in order to generate new perspectives.

Self-organization

Overall, then, such an extraordinary approach leads us away from a concern with the individual expert or visionary towards focus on the effects of the personalities, group dynamics and learning behaviours of managers in groups. Second, it discourages the stability of continuing consensus based on 'rational' reasoning and encourages the creative instability of contention and dialogue. Third, rather than condemning the messiness of real business and academic decisions it leads us towards examining, understanding and dealing with the organizational defence mechanisms and game playing that underlie such inevitable messiness. Fourth, rather than viewing group learning as a simple 'ordinary' process relating to outcomes, it leads us towards an understanding of group learning as a complex process affecting *how* people are learning. Fifth, instead of focusing upon the closure of problem solving, it is oriented towards the opening up of contentious and ambiguous issues. Finally, rather than trying to apply prescriptive models to many specific situations, extraordinary management or education leads in the direction of developing new mental models to design actions for each new strategic situation.

Hierarchy and network

Paradoxically, a dynamic, systems perspective such as the one Stacey proposes here recognizes the great importance of hierarchy, unequal power and clear role definitions in the short-term control of a business. It also recognizes the importance of self-organizing political networks in managing the unknowable long term and the necessary constraints on their operation provided by clear hierarchies. In fact both strong sharing and the failure to share culture at all have the effect of creating boundaries that are too tight or too loose, contexts inappropriate for complex learning.

Loosely shared multiple cultures, on the other hand, both generate instability and provide a boundary around that instability. The more effective the interacting multiple cultures are at complex learning, Stacey argues, the more they will be able to contain the instability that their learning inevitably generates.

Self-organizing networks

Self-organization, as we have seen, is a fluid process in which informal, temporary teams form spontaneously around issues, in contrast to self-managed teams which are permanent and formally established. Top managers or educators, whether at Lloyd's Corporation or City University or Katie School, cannot control self-organizing networks. They can only intervene to influence the boundary conditions around them, which is what Terry Heyday may be seeking to do through his University of Risk. Participants decide who takes part in self-organizing networks and what the boundaries of their activities are, whereas top managers or management 'gurus' make these decisions with regard to even self-managing teams.

Self-organizing networks operate in conflict with and are constrained by the hierarchy, but such self-managing teams replace the business or academic hierarchy. Unequal power energizes self-organizing networks through conflict but also operates as a constraint, but dispersed powers in self-managing teams are supposed to lead to consensus. Managers or students in self-organizing networks empower themselves but in self-managing teams people are empowered from the top. The self-organizing process is both provoked and constrained by cultural difference whereas the self-managing process is based on strongly shared culture. The Lloyd's market based culture is indeed strongly shared amongst its constituent enterprises, which is both its ordinary strength and its extraordinary weakness.

Managing the unknowable

Top managers or academics viewing politics and group learning as forms of control devoid of organization-wide intent operate on the boundaries of strategy, not directly on the process or the outcome. Where the organization faces an ambiguous, open ended future, the application of force, or the obligation to do conventional examinations, is disastrous. Groups in a state of submission or rebellion are incapable of complex learning. The most powerful managers or educators, according to Stacey, should sometimes withdraw and allow conflict, sometimes intervene with suggestions and influence, and sometimes impose authority, using power variably. If power is unequal but distributed and applied according to circumstances, we find a flexible, fluctuating boundary around the political process that enables complex learning. The heart of 'chaotic' management or education, then, is a flexible, ever changing agenda of open ended issues that are identified, clarified and advanced by the self-organizing networks of the organization. Group members should be chosen on the basis of personality rather than their position in the formal hierarchy, drawing membership from a number of different functions, units and levels. A team can only be self-organizing if it discovers its own goals and objectives. This means that top management or educators must limit themselves to presenting the group with some ambiguous challenge. In the Lloyd's case such a challenge may involve the prospect of being simultaneously global and local; in the City University case it could involve doing individual and group projects in parallel.

In the process top management and educators would do well to promote cross-cultural learning by moving people around between groups, functions, companies, countries. Brokers and underwriters, agents and corporation administrators, staff and students, would continually interchange roles and indeed countries.

New perspectives tend to appear when the same culture and unconscious mental models are diverse. The resulting learning is complex because it is not simply the absorption of existing knowledge, techniques or recipes, but the continual questioning of deeply held belief.

The creative work needed to deal with open-ended issues takes time and resources, but without this investment new strategic and developmental directions will not emerge. When the future is unknowable, managers or academics cannot install techniques, procedures, structures and technologies to control long-term outcomes. They can manage boundary conditions, thereby pushing the individual, group or organization far from equilibrium so that spontaneous self-organization may occur and new strategic or developmental directions may emerge. The key question extraordinary managers or facilitators face, then, is not how to maintain stable equilibrium but how to establish sufficient sustained instability to provoke complex learning. This then might be the responsibility of the University of Risk, thus instilling psychological as well technical, economic and political risk into the very fabric of the institution. In the final analysis, it is through such political interaction and complex learning that business and academia alike create and manage their unknowable futures. In the process, moreover, they enter the space for creativity.

CREATIVITY AND COMPLEXITY IN ORGANIZATIONS

Organizations as components in a system

Creativity and innovation at an organizational level are actualized when the institution concerned can engage the creative and innovative processes of other organizations. To accomplish this they need to involve an organization in both competitive and also co-operative processes and so amplify the schema changes across industries, economies and societies.

Each complex adaptive system is thereby a component of an even larger one, perhaps incorporating in this case Lloyd's, City University, Katie School and associated US insurers. Behaviour at each level is ultimately affecting and being affected by behaviour at all other levels. Again, to the extent that such a systemic process becomes a reality at Lloyd's, so it will have enaged in a profound reconstruction and renewal, accommodating a higher degree of complexity than its constituent enterprises have done hitherto. Such a phase transition occurs when institutional, industrial, economic or societal control parameters are set at critical points. Such parameters involve, most particularly for Stacey,[4] first the speed of information flow, second the extent of differences expressed and worked with and, third, the richness of interconnections between agents in the system. Fourth, they involve the levels of contained anxiety and fifth the degree of power differences as well as the way in which power is used.

The most critical of these, in times of rapid change, is the level of contained – as opposed to suppressed or manifest – anxiety. To contain anxiety, Stacey asserts, an individual requires a strong ego structure and a good enough 'holding' environment, which is to be found in the groups to which the individual feels a real sense of belonging. The space for creativity, therefore, cannot be located simply at the individual level: an individual mind is a nonlinear feedback network of interacting minds. Indeed, this has traditionally been the case amongst Lloyd's underwriters to the extent that they jointly underwrote large-scale risk, not to mention the role of the re-insurers in this respect. Such a network is made up of a set of minds co-evolving competitively and co-operatively with each other.

Evolution and predictability in the creative space

As managers, academics or indeed underwriters go around the 'ordinary' loop, they uncover puzzles that must be solved if their enterprise or module of instruction is to survive. The puzzles are posed by and soluble within the current paradigm, but anomalies and contradictions are not. This was indeed the case for individual Lloyd's operators in the early nineties, which is why the Corporation stepped in. Because such ordinary rationality is embodied in the dominant schema, contradictions within this schema cannot be dealt with in a technically rational way. The contradiction, at Lloyd's, between the market operators and the corporate centre is a prominent case in point.

Anomalies always expose the fundamentally paradoxical nature of the organization and raise pressures for synthesis. If these anomalies are missed, then no fundamental synthesis, or process of genuine renewal, ensues. This need for synthesis, in fact, is the driving force of the creative play within what Stacey terms the 'recessive schema', or our subconscious. It eventually leads to replacement of the dominant schema or parts of it, and thus to what is known as 'double-loop learning'. This is where we learn to monitor our patterns of thought and behaviour, with a view to fundamentally (or paradigmatically) revising them.

Organizations occupy the space for creativity when their members are fully engaged in the fundamental paradoxes that are so characteristic of that space, and only then are they in the phase transition, in which the recessive and dominant systems operate in tension with each other. What does this all imply, then, for strategic management, for a developmental approach to education, and for organizational dynamics?

Freedom and control in the space for creativity

Authentic managerial or academic authority, Stacey maintains, lies in two locations, in the task itself and in our own humanity. Establishing our own authority means taking the steps necessary to accomplish the task, as dictated by the task itself rather than by some figure in an authority role. The constraints to such authority then lie in what we believe to be right and in the need we will have to retain the support of those with whom we interact. Mature organizational members therefore who establish their own authority for performing the tasks of the organization – who self-organize – will not produce anarchy but may well produce creative new strategic or developmental directions. Such an orientation to managing, or educating, leads to approaches in which we are free to establish our own authority, constrained only by the nature of the task, the need to retain support, and the imperative to behave ethically. The new science of complexity, for Stacey, offers a hopeful preparation.

Leading in the space for creativity

The dominant schema that drives 'ordinary' managerial or educational thinking leads to the belief that organizational joint actions must be selected according to how likely they are to achieve desirable outcomes. The desirability of such an outcome is to be determined by those who occupy authority roles; such views lead to particular notions of business and educational leadership. In this ordinary context leaders in both spheres determine and articulate the direction in which a group or organization is to develop and then employ a number of motivational methods, ranging from force to inspiration, encouragement and facilitation to persuade others to move in the right direction. A complex adaptive systems theory of organization does not reject such notions of leadership; rather it puts them into a context that enables us to see that they are special-case notions, like that of the Lloyd's task force.

Its activities are applied to ordinary management, or training, through the medium of the legitimate system. They are confined to so-called single-loop learning (corrective action) and to making more efficient what an individual or organization already does well. However, far from certainty and equilibrium, leadership has a rather different meaning. In these circumstances leaders of the legitimate system cannot know, any more than anyone else can, the direction in which the organization is going. It is extraordinary management or facilitation, the self-organizing process of double-loop learning pursued in the shadow system, that determines creative new directions. In that context it becomes apparent that the formal process of reconstruction at Lloyd's, including the programmes of professional training duly authorized by the Corporation, has been at best a partial solution to its problems. The other part of the solution, the 'extraordinary' one, needs to emerge subversively out of a shadow system. For this we are still waiting for the University of Risk!

A business or academic leader's importance, in such an extraordinary context, then, is in relating to the shadow system. How he or she copes has a profound effect on the degree to which the anxieties of creative learning are contained rather than avoided. Such leaders, therefore, do not determine direction when they take up their roles in the shadow system. They become important participants whose primary function has to do with the containment of anxiety. They need to be involved in the group processes in the shadows, but from a position on the boundary, where thay can understand the processes but not get sucked into them. As people operate in the shadow system, leadership roles emerge spontaneously from the interaction. When the creative space is participatively occupied, then, the role of leadership shifts around the system according to which people have a contribution to make, and according to how effectively they are able to attract the attention of others to that contribution.

The kind of leadership required includes the capacity to contain anxiety for others, on the one hand, and the ability to provoke and contribute to double-loop learning on the other. An anxiety-containing capacity is a function of the leader that has to do with the manner in which power is used and with the compassion he or she has for the feelings and fears of others in the group. Leaders contain anxiety, when they are able to empathize with others and articulate or interpret what others are experiencing by playing with metaphor and images, and by posing stretching challenges.

CONCLUSION

In summary, extraordinary management or education, as opposed to ordinary management or training, for Stacey, is not a new process. It is what people in business and academic establishments are already doing in an automatic way without much awareness or reflection. What is new is a coherent overall framework for people to use in reflecting on what they are doing so that they can make sense of it for themselves. It involves true dialogue in which people engage with each other, not to be in control, but to provoke and be provoked, to learn and contribute to the learning of others. This process is like play in that it invites operation in the transitional zone of the mind, where reality and fantasy come together in the form of metaphors, analogies and images. 'Extraordinary' experience-based intuition, rather than 'ordinary' sequential, logical analysis leads to creative insight. Efficiency and creativity are therefore enemies, for the latter requires slack resources and the former demands that there is no slack. Efficiency requires that there be no redundancy, while creativity requires it. If we are to contain the anxiety of greater activity in the midst of such complexity, we must find a way of making sense of our experience of life in organizations. Stacey suggests that the science of complexity provides us with just such a framework.

This complexity oriented framework, in contrast to a simplistically based one, like, as we shall see next, Whyte's division between 'soul' and 'work' or between being and doing, reinforces the distinction between the so-called ordinary and the extraordinary. For the purposes of our book this is a revealing starting point, in enabling us to move from statics to dynamics. In the terms used by Margaret Wheatley and David Whyte, respectively the artist and scientist whom we shall now meet, it serves to distinguish training that works from education that is 'good for the soul', organizing from 'self-organizing', Lloyd's Training Centre from the University of Risk. We now turn from Lloyd's of London to its sister institution, the City Corporation.

BIBLIOGRAPHY

1   Kuhn, T., *The Structure of Scientific Revolutions*, University of Chicago Press, 1970.
2   Stacey, R., *Managing Chaos*, Kogan Page, 1994.
3   Stacey, R., *Strategic Management and Organizational Dynamics*, Pitman, 1995.
4   Stacey, R., *Creativity and Complexity in Organizations*, Berrett Koehler, 1996.

5 Work and soul

Rounding out the City's square mile

THE ORGANIZATION

The 'square mile' of the City of London, within which both Lloyd's and our Business School are lodged, has been long recognized as the financial hub of Europe, if not also of the whole world. As such, and as defined by America's Robert Reich in his seminal book *The Work of Nations*,[1] it is a 'symbolic analytical zone'. Within the context of our knowledge era, however, its business scope has been inhibited by the conventional divide between trading and learning. While the City has therefore gained international recognition for its commercial enterprise, its more rounded economic development, in our information age, has been restricted by an overly pragmatic, commercial orientation.

That having been said, the City of London Corporation, the local authority within which the commercial City is situated, has been taking a newly reflective, educational lead. Under the influence of Ray Mahoney, their Training and Development Manager who is a native of London's East End, the Corporation has become actively engaged in a wide variety of schemes for developing work based learning, including our project based MBA. Ray Mahoney is both a link manager and a participant in our action centred MBA. As a long-time champion of action learning Ray has been a major force in helping Reg Revans, the founder of such action learning in Britain, to gain the freedom of the City. In that capacity, symbolically then as well as materially, Ray has brought together trading and learning under the overarching banner of individual freedom.

In that respect the orientation towards both action learning and also action research, with which Professors Chris Hendry and Allan Williams at our Centre for Personnel Research and Enterprise Development have long been associated, is now alive and well both formerly within the Business School and latterly within the City of London Corporation.

This latter-day coming together, then, of the implicit commercial nous, for which the City has been famous, and the explicit learning acumen, for which it has not hitherto been noted, is very well illustrated in the case of MBA student Alan Gartrell. Alan is a surveyor within the Corporation, working within a department which is well known for its wheeling and dealing, and Alan was no exception when he joined us. It so happened, though, that he already had a master's degree in English literature, which I, as his academic facilitator, regarded as particularly significant.

As Alan entered our programme, and particularly once he has exposed to chaos and complexity theory, he realized that post-modern literature had much in common with contemporary management theory and, indeed, practice. As he began to integrate the actively commercial and reflectively artistic sides of himself, Alan discovered that he was able to make much more happen as such a reflective practitioner than had previously been the case for him as a surveyor-entrepreneur. In fact, Alan set about democratically establishing quality circles amongst the estates that he managed in a way that had never been done before within the hitherto hierarchical Corporation, thereby leading to major financial savings.

The way in which Alan had begun to integrate trading and learning, moreover, augured well for the Corporation as a whole, for these were auspicious times. In 1998 New Labour was in the process of installing a new, democratically elected mayor for London as a city. As a result the parochial and indeed national position of the financial City's Lord Mayor, set within an increasingly global-local City, was being called into question. MBA student Aidan Lines, who was in the same learning set as Alan, had become involved with a select group – as he was assistant at the time to the private secretary of the incumbent Lord Mayor – in reviewing the latter's role. In the process he was very well aware of the need to change the profile of the City of London from a traditionally commercial centre into a much more explicitly post-modern 'symbolical analytical zone', duly combining trading and learning. In that sense, Aidan was taking on from where Ray Mahoney and Alan Gartrell had left off, giving their work a new strategic and political focus. Such a renewed focus, moreover, was highly germane to the new positioning that our new Dean, the business historian Professor Leslie Hannah, was giving the Business School.

Interestingly, the Dean happened to live in the Barbican Estates, which was run by Sue Benjamins, the most recent participant from the Corporation on our MMBA, who was intent on combining her prodigious background as trader and community activist with learning and development.

INTRODUCTION: IDENTITY AND ENVIRONMENT

The Corporation of London, like Lloyd's the insurers or indeed like Lloyd's Bank, is a living system, capable of both ordinary and extraordinary behaviour. Ralph Stacey, is by no means a voice in the wilderness. He is one of a group of evolutionary biologists, depth ecologists and students of chaos and complexity – though he may be the most business oriented – who are revolutionizing our understanding of the world of living systems. Drawing

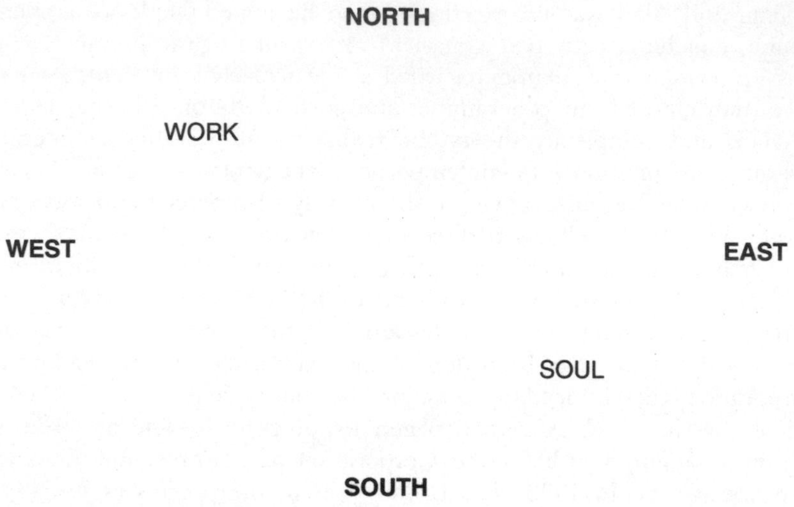

NORTH

WORK

WEST   EAST

SOUL

SOUTH

Figure 7 The City of London's work and soul

on the earlier scientific breakthroughs of such geniuses as the physicist Heisenberg in Germany, the chemist Prigogine in Belgium, and the geophysicist Lovelock in Britain, they have evolved a new approach to life and work that has been encapsulated in management by such people as Ralph Stacey and, as we shall see much later on in the book (see chapter 13), by America's Margaret Wheatley.

Such a division between the 'ordinary' and the 'extraordinary' is not exclusive to scientists, however. Artists, even in the context of management, have a say in this matter too.

PRESERVING OUR SOULS AT WORK

Work and soul

David Whyte is based in America but comes originally from Yorkshire in England. His unique claim to fame is that he is a poet by profession, who has spent the greater part of his recent working life as a business consultant to the great Boeing Aircaft Company in Seattle.

The combined fruits of poetry and consultancy have been recorded in his book published by Britain's Industrial Society, entitled *The Aroused Heart*.[2] Like Makis and Heide Werlamis, with whom we shall become acquainted in chapter 10, Whyte has fused together art and enterprise. His preoccupation is with the 'great art' of working in order to live, of remembering what place we occupy in a much greater story than the one our job description defines. This is precisely what Ray Mahoney and his fellow action learners are preoccupied with as they approach managerial mastery. Work for Whyte is drama. Our inability to live vitally upon its stage has much to do with the modern loss of dramatic sensibility, the lost sense that we play out our lives as part of a greater story. If work, is about doing, then soul is about being at home in the world, melding work life with soul life, the inner ocean of longing and belonging with the outer ground of strategy and control. This was the challenge that Ray Mahoney faced when, having first joined the City Corporation he then linked up with our Management MBA.

Work, then, on the one hand involves controlling conscious life. It organizes. In the process it aims at concrete goals, loving the linear and defined. Such is the lot of many a financial man, or indeed woman. Soul, on the other hand, finds its existence through loss of control to powers greater than human experience. It self-organizes. Whereas the Corporation wanted Ray to work materially, our developmental programme, and the spirit of London, called upon his soul, to which his work then responded! Work therefore belongs to the individual personality, whereas for Whyte the soul is governed by no one, not even by the personality formed around it. We stumble into a new sense of soulful belonging by realizing how desperately out of place we feel. Ray, Aidan and fellow MBA Ade – a Nigerian woman lodged within a male-led Anglo-Saxon City – often felt that way. This sense of loss has a natural way of drawing us inside ourselves.

It is not so much depression as the cry for a forgotten courage. To find the real path we have to go off the path. This applies as much to an organization or a society as it does to an individual. It certainly applied to most of the MBA participants from the Corporation. Work can both embolden, through self-organization, and strangle soul life, through organization, revealing how much we can do as part of a larger body, and how the wellsprings of our creativity are stopped at source by smothering organization. We learn that we do have a place in the world, but one which for Whyte is constantly shape-shifting, like the weather and the seasons, into something at once new and beautiful, tantalizing and terrible.

Towards a grounded creativity

Loyalty in a soulful organization is based on two ends of the creative spectrum: security in the form of money and power, and creative engagement by way of excitement and innovation. Ray's training establishment, at the time he was recruited, had plenty of the former and virtually none of the latter. By the time he had been there for a few years the security was beginning to disappear as well, foundering in the changing environment.

A soulful approach to work over the long term, Whyte maintains, is probably the only way an individual can respond creatively to the high-temperature stress of modern work life without burning to a crisp in the heat. It takes the soul's ability to elicit texture, colour, story and meaning from the tumult of events, to meet fire with fire and still have a fairly restful existence that is capable of wise policy somewhere at the centre of it all. The Corporation, calling for a little more creative fire from its people, must make room for the source of that fire and the hearth where it burns, that is the heart and the soul of the individual. On our Management MBA we do our best to make that room, and bring panic as well as inspiration to people like Ray, Aidan and Ade in the process.

For the more true we are to our creative gifts, Whyte asserts, the less there is any outer assurance at the beginning; the more we are on the path, the deeper the silence and confusion in the first stages of the process. Following our path therefore – individually or organizationally – involves first going off the path, through open country. There is an early stage when we are left to camp out in the wilderness, alone, with few supporting voices. Out there in the silence we must build a hearth, gather the twigs and strike the flint for the fire ourselves. In fact we can see the path ahead, but there is a good chance that it is not our path. In Ralph Stacey's terms, as we shall see, it is too 'ordinary' to constitute our longer-term direction. It is probably someone else's path that we have substituted for our own, as was initially the case for Ray, such as that prescribed by family or profession, company or culture. Our own path, by way of contrast, must be meaningfully and retro-spectively deciphered every step of the way. The soul, then, in knitting together experience out of the events of our lives, to our bafflement and distress, is as protective of its trials and failures as of its personal victories.

Our interior fire

We cannot neglect our interior fire, then, without damaging ourselves in the process. A certain vitality smoulders inside us irrespective of whether it has an outlet or not. If Ade had not faced up to the self-selected turmoil that she was presented with as a 'black' Nigerian stranger in this 'white' England, another kind of turmoil, such as severe problems at home or at work, might have been visited upon her, whether she liked it or not.

If we fail to create, or respond to, our own dramas in life, ones that arise out of our awakened soul force, then such drama will surround us in alter-native ways. When, moreover, the fire remains unlit, Whyte tells us, the body fills with dense smoke. The longer we neglect the fire the more we are overcome by the smoke. Yet we have the comfort of remembering that there is 'no smoke without fire'. So if we are suffering the consequences of asphyxiation from the smouldering fuel inside us, we are at least aware, as Ade became, that there is a fire and fuel there to find and choke on. Ironically, and at the time of writing this chapter in the autumn of 1997, East Asia is being engulfed by smoke stemming from the brushwood fires in Sumatra. The dreadful physical and human damage being wreaked serves to remind us forcibly of the fragile nature of our planet, calling upon our natural souls to respond.

According to Whyte, then, we must make a hearth and home at the very place where the life we feel we are stuck with (overly polluted in this context) and the life we desire (fresh country air) meet and overlap. Without the fiery embrace of everything from which we demand immunity, including depression and failure, our individual, institutional or societal personalities seek organized power over life rather than self-organized power through the experience of life.

In this way we throw the precious metal of our own experience away, exchanging it for the fool's gold of a superimposed image of 'success' or 'growth', of what our experiences should be rather than what they actually are. If Indonesia or Thailand, or Malaysia or Singapore, are to find their own integral way to a fulfilling future, arising out of the experience of asphyxiation, it will have to be environmentally as well as economically sustainable.

In fact, while these Pacific Tigers may, in James Moore's terms, be still at the 'hardworking' expansionary stage of their country's economic development, or to some extent still pioneering, the planet as a whole is in a state of 'soulful' midlife, where – above all – it is balance or ultrastability which is called for.

Within the context of the knowledge creating ecology that we are advocating here, then, an ecosystemic view of the world needs to prevail both economically and also environmentally, both individually and institutionally, for example, within both Ray Mahoney himself as an 'East End' lad, and also within his traditionally based 'western' City establishment.

The soul at midlife

Whether for profession or organization, industry or society, we initially apprentice ourselves to something seemingly greater, wealthier, older and much more knowledgeable than ourselves. Ray Mahoney, for example, had originally been serving not only the City Corporation, but London itself as a city. He was now being invited to transfer his loyalties from the East End of London, from which he orginally hailed, to the West End, and from global diplomacy to local ingenuity, and back again.

Our security gains us time and space until we can ground ourselves more solidly into our own identity. However, at midlife, as was the case for Ray, a man or woman feels an inner siren call like an old memory. Having spent years building and consolidating a business, career or family, at the zenith of midlife we want to find out who was at the centre of this attempt and for what we were building. In ecological terms, this is a time of catalysation, or metamorphosis, rather than conservation or morphosis. For every man and woman, therefore, midlife is a pivotal time of internal rebirth. Such a period in our lives, characteristically in our forties, calls upon us to experience in a new way, to birth ourselves into a new kind of usefulness.

Facing up to complexity

In focusing then on economic and technological – to the exclusion of social and cultural – realities, we hold at bay any romantic view of life, while scientific literature today uncovers a universe more astonishing than we could draw from myth or fairy story. Our worklife, reduced to ashes without the fuel of our deeper personal desires, becomes in Whyte's view an unconscious way of committing suicide. The soul, bereft of meaningful experience, begins to engineer its escape from the structures holding it in check, by dying to itself. The very act of making a primary soulful engagement with the world, by really giving it our attention, is a radical and revolutionary step. Ray's struggle to renew himself, and indeed his organization, was in these terms a life and death one, psychologically if not also economically and physically. Having an elemental and intimate relationship with the things of the world, instead of wishing to possess them, gives us a home at the centre of life that is already furnished and paid for, as it were.

CONCLUSION

The soul of the world

There is for Whyte a core delusion at the centre of our struggles in all organizations, a core delusion that narrows our sense of self and ignores the greater world beyond the organization. It is a world that can inform us of our personal destiny, but also a world that we have lost the time and inclination to investigate thoroughly. Trying to ignore this greater world, we forge a small identity held within the narrow corridors of the building in which we work. We have a job, or at best a role, but in no sense do we have what we might call a calling or a lifelong vocation.

Rather than breathing life and vitality into work from the greater perspective which is our birthright, we allow our dreams and desires to be constricted and replaced by those of the organization, and then wonder why it has such a stranglehold on our lives.

The first step to preserving the soul in our individual lives is therefore to admit that the world has a soul also, and is somehow participating with us in our soul and in our destiny. In that context, and through the smoke-ridden haze that filled up the East Asian skies in September 1997, the world's soul was being choked up, suffering chronically from the misdeeds of man locally and globally. The financial speculators in Malaysia and Thailand, at one and the same time, were both tearing the world's soul apart and also paradoxically signalling that that very soul was losing its integrity. Despite our best attempts to anchor ourselves in the concrete foundations of profitability and permanence, we remain forever at the whim, mercy and pleasure of the windblown world.

The ecology of learning

We have put our sense of self out of business, as it were, because much of our education has been bent towards raising us not as an intricate ecology of qualities but as a monoculture of, in our case, business administrators. In this way, Whyte maintains, our own internal leaf-moulds are eradicated from our self-identity in the name of drying us out, tidying us up and making us presentable for the global economy, not the global businessphere, that awaits.

Preserving the soul, in contrast, means that we come out of hiding at last and bring more of ourselves into the workplace, especially the parts that do not belong to the company or corporation.

That, arguably, is the distinctively soulful part that our knowledge creating ecology plays, to provide that wholesome middle ground between self and society that the manager can then revisit in the process of renewing his or her organization. In a sense, the very part of us that doesn't have the least interest in the organization is our greatest offering to it. The new organization that honours the soul, and the soul of the world, is as much concerned with what it serves as with what it is, as much trying to learn from the exquisite patterns that inform the greater world as trying to impose its own pattern on something already complete.

The organization that has made room for the soul learns slowly and painfully that clinging to premature, constricted identities, as is at least to some degree the case at the Corporation, restricts the flow of energy from outside the system it creates. Work and soul, for artist-consultant David Whyte, in the final analysis, represent for the developing individual what 'ordinary' and 'extraordinary' management, for economist-complexity theorist Ralph Stacey, represent for the developing organization. It is also the polarity between organization and self-organization with which Margaret Wheatley is so intimately concerned. We now turn from the basic duality between the ordinary and the extraordinary to the more complex threefold reality embodied in Goshal and Bartlett's 'Individualized Corporation', and in the Ford Motor company. In the process we turn from tradition vying with modernity, to modernity vying with post-modernity.

BIBLIOGRAPHY

1   Reich, R., *The Work of Nations*, Random House, 1993.
2   Whyte, D., *The Aroused Heart*, Industrial Society, 1997.

Part III

Modern

Upgrading intellectual capital

6 Towards the Individualized Corporation

Ford – from rationalization to regeneration

THE ORGANIZATION

In the early part of this century Ford Motors was an icon of modern industrialism. Ford's automatic assembly line represented the ultimate in centralization, standardization and mechanization. Arising out of it, as Henry Ford is so often quoted to have said: 'you can have any car as long as it is black'. Supportive of Ford, as a modern industrialist, was F.W. Taylor, an industrial engineer and apostle of such modernism. 'In the past man has been first,' declared Taylor; 'in the future the system must be first. Scientific management seeks to pre-process out of industrial operations the personal idiosyncrasies that distinguished workers as individuals.'[1] A lot has changed at Ford over the course of the last hundred years, and most particularly in the last ten, as it has revitalized and – to a lesser extent – regenerated itself as a business corporation, but a lot has stayed the same!

Henry Ford started out in adult life as a craftsman, building bespoke models. That was his traditional orientation. As he burst into modernity, in his midlife, he created a new industry. At the turn of the century, though, Ford was merely one of over thirty companies all fighting for a slice of the emerging car market. His vision from the outset was 'to democratize the automobile'. That all-consuming vision drove his design team on. Over time General Motors' share of the market had been eroded from 20 per cent to 10 per cent, while Ford rose to be number one in America.

As he matured, however, Ford became increasingly embittered and tyrannical, the company failed to renew itself, and its founder almost succeeded in ruining what he had himself created. Having, however, ultimately been rescued by posterity, his primary legacy as a modernizer and as a scientific manager has lived on. However, his secondary legacy as a liberator, as a creative innovator and as a humanist has faded into an ever more obscure background. Hence Ford's current difficulties in regenerating itself.

The management that took over from their founding father became the ultimate in rationally based, scientific management. That worked well for some fifty years. That was until the crisis in the American automobile industry of the early eighties. Over a three-year period Ford lost no less than

$3.3 billion. It was at that point, duly learning from the Japanese, that Ford joined the quality revolution, and began to move away from some of its ultra-rational modernist dogma. As a result, the pre-orientation towards the system and the machine was somewhat countermanded by a renewed focus on the person and the product, if not also upon purpose and process. Don Peterson, in fact, who was CEO at the time, was involved in developing a new mission, values and guiding principles: 'There was a great deal of talk about the sequence of the three P's – people, products and profits. It was decided that people should absolutely come first, and profits and products second.' This served to renew an original aspiration that Henry Ford himself had in 1916:

> I don't believe we should make such an awful profit on our cars. A reasonable profit is right, but not too much. I hold that it is better to sell a large number of cars at a reasonably small profit. . . I hold this because it enables a larger number of people to buy and enjoy the use of a car, and because it gives a larger number of men employment at good wages. These are the two aims I have in life.
>
> (*Detroit News*, 14 November 1916)

More than eighty years on, Ford's is undergoing a third process in its evolution, after the first managerially based rationalization instigated by Henry Ford's successors, and the second quality based revitalization instigated recently by Don Peterson. While the company has returned to profitability the industry as a whole is suffering from major overcapacity. Competition is intensifying on all fronts. In Europe now there are some fifty brand names selling around 300 basic models of car. To deliver what customers want, Ford has decided that it needs to drive down costs and drive up quality simultaneously. In other words, it is once again revitalizing its operation. The result is the 'Ford 2000' programme, whose goal is to leverage resources from around the world to create economies of scale, and to spread best practices throughout the organization. There are, seven key operating strategies:

1 *Empowerment* is the first one, involving the build-up of a team-oriented, supportive culture to inspire commitment and creativity;
2 *Process leadership* follows, i.e. finding new and better ways of working, thereby reducing complexity, abolishing waste and improving efficiencies, leveraging global resources to eliminate redundancies, and also becoming more responsive to customers' changing needs;
3 *World-wide product excellence* follows next, working concertedly to improve quality; if the quality is right the intention is to
4 *Keep production costs low* – with the cost reductions proposed, Ford intends to spend $11 billion less on products over the next five years;

5   *Corporate citizenship* remains important, though: a commitment to creating products and processes that are safe and environmentally friendly, while being both a good neighbour and employer, whereas

6.   *Customer satisfaction* is oriented towards Ford staying specifically focused on its customers, thereby improving the match between offering and expectations, so that, arising out of all these strategies is anticipated

7   *Worldwide growth*, with a particular emphasis on joint ventures both in the Far East and also within Eastern Europe.

It was with this 'Ford 2000' process of revitalization in mind that the company, at least within the UK, has engaged with us on the MMBA programme. While Steve Harley, a senior production manager from Britain, now posted to America, has been intimately involved with the Ford 2000 programme, Ian Twinley, a marketing manager from the UK also now based in Detroit, is now involved with the global branding team there. Both, moreover, as participants on our MMBA programme, were joined by Dennis Rycroft and Tony Mullins, Peter George, John Faragher and Keith Santon, all from the Dagenham manufacturing plant in Britain.

At the time when they got involved with us at City University, Ford – like Lloyd's – was also engaged in a process of corporate renewal, with a view to globalizing their production and thereby heralding a revolution in the way they organized their manufacturing and their marketing. Steve Harley, then in charge of 3,000 people in Dagenham, became the first person in Britain to comprehensively to document the nature and scope of this technological and organizational change, for his mastery project. Steve's colleague Dennis Rycroft spent the most formative part of his MBA in South Africa, where he masterminded a logistics programme which ultimately saved the company some £20 million. Dennis has subsequently sponsored two more of his production people on our MBA, and has in turn become their coach. One of them, John Faragher, has convinced his senior management that he should go to America to research the way they go about managing cultural diversity, picking up some of his ideas from Steven Harley who is now based over there, and applying the lessons learned back at home.

It was around this time, in the latter part of the nineties, that Ford's link manager, in discussion with us at CUBS, decided that there should be a more purposeful focus on the development of intellectual capital in the Dagenham plant in East London. This notion was reinforced by John Faragher, who felt that if the plant's intellectual capital was not purposefully upgraded, there would be no long-term future for it.

Ian Twinley, meanwhile, joined our programme, unusually, from the sales side of the business. Ian, who is at present, like Steve, based in Detroit, has been devoting all three of his projects to helping Ford reposition itself as a European brand within Europe. Having devoted his first project to repositioning the brand, in the eyes of the European dealers, the second 'extraordinary' project will be dedicated to reinventing Ford (Europe) by enabling it to enter wholeheartedly into the emerging European culture. In so doing, and uncharacteristically from a historical perspective, it will be aiming to link itself more purposefully with Europe's intellectual history as well as its physical geography. Finally, in his third mastery project Ian will be dealing with the manufacturing and logistic issues raised by this strategic European reorientation. Following in the footsteps of Steve, Dennis and Ian were Peter George and Tony Mullin, each of them from the Dagenham plant, in London's East End. Whereas Tony devoted his projects to transforming Ford quality, Peter worked on picking up multiple languages, not in a linguistic but in a managerial sense. Both transformed themselves from autocratic leaders into knowledge managers, and changed their organizations in the process. Most recently production manager Keith Stanton has been carrying the Ford torch forward, pursuing further the cultural and commercial changes, in the light of globalization, that their MBA colleagues had inaugurated.

While these 'students', or frontline managers in terms of the 'individualized corporation', are the initiative taking, responsive entrepreneurs, their so-called 'coaches', as middle managers, are the developmental *integrators* of their diverse project based activities. Finally, the 'link manager' has the role of linking the regenerative vision coming from the top, in this case from Alex Trotman in America, with these entrepreneurial and integrative activities. We now turn from Ford specifically to Goshal and Bartlett's 'Individualized Corporation' generally, without losing sight of the specific business application, set in the context of our programme.

INTRODUCTION: BIRTH OF A NEW CORPORATE MODEL

From mechanized operation to Individualized Corporation

Bartlett and Goshal's 'Individualized Corporation' of today and tomorrow, is the antithesis of Ford's and Taylor's mechanized operation of an earlier era, though it represents something of what the company is reaching towards, in the present, and is aspiring towards for the future. Christopher Bartlett from Harvard Business School and Samantra Goshal from London Business School between them represent the emerging 'post-modern' Anglo-Saxon business school establishment. They have taken on from where their predecessors, first Henry Ford of Ford Motors and subsequently Alfred Sloan of General Motors have left off. For lodged between modernity and postmodernity has been the multi-divisional, multi-product form of organization pioneered by Alfred Sloan at GM and by Pierre Dupont at Dupont's that has dominated the business scene for some fifty years, since the 1930s.

REVITALIZATION

Integration

INDIVIDUALIZED
CORPORATION

MMBA

RATIONALIZATION   REGENERATION

Entrepreneurship   *Renewal*

Figure 8 Ford 2000

Outstanding post-modern business leaders like Jack Welsh of GE and Percy
Barnevik of ABB have recently emerged to overtake Alfred Sloan and Pierre
Dupont practically, in the same way as Goshal and Bartlett have done theoretically. Ford and F.W. Taylor, Sloan and Peter Drucker, Barnevik and
Goshal between them, therefore, represent a process of business evolution,
from the traditional and the modern to the modern and the post-modern,
and in the process from the west to the north (Bartlett) and the east (Goshal).

Indeed, while both Sloane and Dupont were American, today's such post-
industrial icons are spread around the globe. In a dynamic global
environment in which competition is increasingly service based and knowledge intensive, such post-modern business leaders, according to Goshal and
Bartlett, have recognized that human creativity and individual initiative are
far more important as sources of competitive advantage than homogeneity
and conformity. Rather than forcing employees into a corporate mould
defined by policies, systems and constraints, they appear to see the core task
in almost exactly opposite terms. Their challenge is not to force employees
to fit the corporate model of the 'organization man' but to build an organization flexible enough to exploit the idiosyncratic knowledge and unique
skills of every individual employee. How does such an 'Individualized
Corporation'[2] work, and where does the newly emerging Ford fit in?

ORGANIZATION MAN TO INDIVIDUALIZED CORPORATION

Rationalize, revitalize, regenerate

For Bartlett and Goshal the 'Individualized Corporation' is characterized by three major 'processes' rather than by any particular structure. In this way it continually fosters individual initiative, it creates and leverages knowledge and it continually renews itself. These three attributes, which the authors associate with 'rationalizing', 'revitalizing' and 'regenerating', are also developmental phases. Let us consider each of these processes in turn. The role models that they draw upon, are GE, INTEL and 3M in America, ABB as well as Scandia Financial Services in northern Europe, Kao as well as Canon in Japan. Most favoured of them, by Goshal and Bartlett, is ABB, which serves to set each of the three processes in context.

Inspiring individual initiative: phase 1 – rationalization – embedded entrepreneurial drive

In the first phase of his business transformation, Barnevik at ABB stripped away much of the old bureaucratic superstructure to focus attention on the task of realigning the organization around the efficient operations of 1,200 frontline companies. It was at this stage that ABB energized hundreds of frontline entrepreneurs and gave them the mandate to build their businesses as if they owned them. This involved institutional entrepreneurship, a sense of ownership, developed self-discipline and a supportive environment.

Institutional entrepreneurship

Inspiring individual initiative, in the way that Barnevik did, requires that individuals feel a sense of ownership in what they do; this is achieved in smaller organizational units more easily than in large ones. Management therefore needs to reflect its respect for the individual in a supportive culture that is open to questioning from below and tolerant of failure. Only in such an environment can individuals feel empowered. Empowerment, moreover, only occurs when it grows out of a reciprocal system of faith. Those deep in the company must have faith in their company and its leadership, and senior management must have faith in the people in the organization. Why is it then, Goshal and Bartlett ask, that so few companies have been able to inspire individual initiative and entrepreneurial activity? They believe that the missing ingredient lies in the general lack of belief in the individual that lies at the heart of the individualized corporation.

Ford, though it has come a long way in that respect, over the course of the last decade, still has some considerable way to go if it is to develop as empowered a culture as 3M, INTEL or indeed ABB.

Creating a sense of ownership

According to Goshal and Bartlett, ABB and thousands of other companies like it are trying to re-energize individuals who have become isolated, disengaged and alienated within an impersonal and unresponsive modern corporate entity. As they do so, they have begun to discover truths that 3M, for example, based in America, has understood and practised for decades. They have begun to refocus on people, recognizing that the first step towards re-engaging individuals is to give them a sense of ownership. They need to become associated with much smaller units to which individuals can feel a greater sense of belonging and on which they can make a visible impact. Ford, in fact, subsequent to its total quality revolution, has significantly enhanced the sense of group autonomy, and hence the sense of ownership, amongst much of its workforce.

Developing self-discipline

At the same time, the companies Goshal and Bartlett have described as Individualized Corporations, like GE or 3M in America, ABB or Skandia in Europe and Canon or Kao in Japan, are far from organizational anarchies. ABB did not grow to dominate the highly competitive power equipment industry through the random activities of its 1,200 companies; 3M would not be able to maintain its ability to create hundreds of new businesses a year if its product development initiatives operated in unbounded chaos.

Yet focus, direction and performance in these companies are achieved not by retaining tight control over the strategic plans and operating budgets of the entrepreneurial entities but by embedding a sense of discipline in their ongoing routines and everyday behaviours. The most powerful means of building discipline into an organization, according to Goshal and Bartlett, is to establish clear performance standards, democratize information and continuously challenge people through internal peer comparisons. Ford has still a long way to go in instilling such an internalized, as opposed to externalized, sense of discipline in its manufacturing operations.

Providing a supportive environment

The changes referred to already in such companies as 3M and ABB can go a long way in creating an organizational environment that fosters entrepreneurial activity. The problem is that, after decades serving as loyal implementers in a classical hierarchy, most employees do not have the attitudes, knowledge or skills to allow them to take advantage of the new freedom made possible by such changes in structures and systems. To allow these individuals to become real frontline entrepreneurs, therefore, companies need to create a nurturing and supportive environment that develops the skills and builds the confidence of those being asked to take on this new role.

In the radical decentralization of assets and resources that has accompanied delayering and destaffing of so many companies in the past decade, the structural changes have generally been the easy part. The major difficulties typically followed later as management tried to redefine the roles of managers and realign the relationships between them and their employees. As control over key resources and responsibility for vital activities moved to the frontline units, many of these managers – classically supervisors in the Ford case – felt they had become irrelevant. For them the empowerment of some roles led to the evisceration of others. Such middle managers therefore became 'the layer of clay', blocking effective transfer of power down to the front lines and preventing the blossoming of initiatives from below. ABB, ever aware of this stifling tendency, defines the key role of its middle managers as being that of coaching and supporting new managers. This includes creating an environment that is tolerant of 'well-intentioned failure'.

Ford, in fact, in recent years, has put a lot of effort into developing such a coaching orientation amongst its middle managers. We now turn from so-called rationalization to revitalization, with ABB again setting the stage.

Creating and leveraging knowledge: phase 2 – revitalization – developing integrative strategies

As the entrepreneurial regime of frontline units began to restart growth, ABB's CEO Percy Barnevik motivated the company into the next stage of its transformation process, thereby creating an integrated learning organization. In this phase, he focused the organization more intensively on the task of linking and leveraging the valuable resources and expertise that had been developed in pockets of entrepreneurial initiative throughout the company. Through such initiatives, therefore, according to Goshal and Bartlett, ABB was able to combine products and technologies from dozens of its operating companies in Europe, Asia and the United States and deliver the final turnkey power plant project in India or China. How, then, has this come about in ABB specifically, and amongst 'Individualized Corporations' generally?

From individual expertise to organizational learning

People, according to Goshal and Bartlett, are innately curious and, as social animals, are naturally motivated to interact with and learn from one another. This is therefore the second key assumption that shapes the philosophy of the Individualized Corporation, supplementing the fundamental belief in the power of individual initiative that provides the bedrock of entrepreneurial activity. Over thousands of years, families, clans and communities have evolved as teaching and learning groups, with individuals sharing information and synthesizing knowledge as a central part of their binding social interchange and as a key engine of their collective progress. Yet somehow, modern corporations established in the original Ford mould have been constructed in a way that constrains, impedes and sometimes kills this natural instinct in people. The Individualized Corporation reverses the focus from such value extraction to that of value creation by establishing the continuous learning of individuals as a cornerstone of its organization, that is, not just as a means of achieving its business objectives but as an end in itself. As it enters the twenty-first century, if not in the twentieth Ford, is very much shaping up in this way of looking at learning, at least individually if not yet organizationally. Beyond a commitment to developing people's involvement and expertise, the Individualized Corporation must be able to link dispersed initiatives and leverage distributed expertise, embedding the resulting relationships in a continuous process of organizational learning and action. In fact this is the essence of Ford's Manufacturing 2000 programme in which Steve Harley has been seminally engaged. Managers worldwide, moreover, have begun to focus less on the task of forecasting and planning for the future and more on the challenge of being highly sensitive to emerging changes. How does this occur?

Developing horizontal information flows

As one example, Kao, the Japanese consumer packaged-goods company, sees itself not as a soap and detergent company but, above all, as an educational institution. And it is clear to all within it that the two most important responsibilities of any manager are to teach and to learn. Skandia Financial Services' 'Future Centre', as another example, is a virtual organization initially built around five 'future teams' designed to stretch, change and develop the high-potential employees assigned to them. Each team is assigned an issue of great importance to Skandia's future, such as the impact of changing demographics on the insurance market, or the future use of IT in the company's organization and strategy. Only then, when it develops the ability to transfer-share and leverage fragmented knowledge as well as expertise, will the company be able to exploit the benefits of organizational learning.

For such learning to occur, individual expertise in isolated units must be linked in rich horizontal flows of information and knowledge that can routinely diffuse critical expertise and transfer best practice throughout an organization. This is something with which the traditionally vertically segemented Ford is currently struggling, for while products might belong to a division, technology belongs to the organization as a whole. Jan Carendi, chief executive of Skandia Financial Services, through his own boundary spanning role, has become an active cross-pollinator of ideas. More important, he represents a role model and a catalyst, leading others to reach out beyond the parochial perspectives of their own job descriptions to embrace people and ideas from the other side of the organization.

Ingvar Kamprad, founder of Sweden's globally oriented furniture retailer IKEA, also recognized the power of personal networks and the cross-pollination of ideas. By the early nineties, the company had assigned 300 'ambassadors' to key positions worldwide, creating a dense personal network that could collect, interpret and transmit information without the distortions that formal systems could produce. Such a network may stand Ford in good stead, as it globalizes its production, while at the same time taking account of local needs.

The organization as an integrated network

According to Goshal and Bartlett, then, companies like IKEA, Skandia Financial Services, 3M and ABB have created organizations based on a framework that could be called an integrated network. This is an organizational model that allows companies to develop distributed capabilities and expertise, link those capabilities through rich horizontal flows of information, knowledge and other resources, and develop the trust that is required as a glue to hold together their distributed, integrated organizations. It is a form of organization that is built on two principles that are vital to the development of an embedded learning capability – a structural configuration based on distributed, specialized activities, and a set of relationships based more on interdependence than on independence or dependence. Ford still has some way to go in that respect, given its mechanistic and adversarial heritage. In the integrated network organization, the benefits of efficiency are obtained through specialization rather than centralization. Through such specialization, these companies are not only able to capture required economies of scale or critical mass, they are also able to develop focused expertise within each of the specialized units.

Thus, McKinsey leads its financial institutions practice from its office in New York, not only because that is where its largest client base is but also because that is where its consultants can become immersed in the most advanced practice and develop knowledge and expertise that can become an asset to other firms' offices. This has traditionally, of course, been the case in Detroit, though this is very much less the case today than in the American auto industry's heyday in the fifties and sixties.

Integrated interdependence

Today's complex and dynamic competitive environment, then, demands collaborative problem solving, co-operative resource sharing and collective implementation, as epitomized in the seventies and eighties by the Japanese rather than the American automobile manufacturers. That is why companies need to build their inter-unit relationships on interdependence. Only when a few senior partners at McKinsey recognized that the company had to compete on the basis of 'thought leadership' as well as 'client relationships' did the firm launch its two-decade-long effort to build a truly integrated and interdependent organization able to develop and diffuse knowledge rapidly.

Skandia achieved a similar management breakthrough in the late 1980s, when Jan Carendi, rather than treat each new market entry as a fresh challenge, decided to focus his organization's attention on capturing its learning, embodying it in a prototypic model, and transferring it from country to country. Vital to this effort was his ability to create an organization in which information, knowledge and expertise flowed freely: 'we must think of ourselves less as insurance specialists and more as specialists in collaboration,' he said.

Finally, then, Goshal and Bartlett turn from so-called rationalization and revitalization to regeneration, starting once again with the example of ABB.

Ensuring continuous renewal: phase 3 – regeneration – achieving continuous self-renewal

By the mid-nineties, according to Goshal and Bartlett, Barnevik was pleased with the progress that ABB had made, but knew the process was incomplete. As it headed into the closing years of the century, ABB was entering the self-regeneration phase of its transformation process. This was the stage in which the organization would have to learn how to balance the tensions and manage the paradoxes implicit in the new corporate model. It required managers to strive for superior individual unit performance while capturing the corporate-wide benefits of cross-unit integration. Moreover, they had to do so in an organizational environment in which the hard-edge demands for operational efficiency were offset by the uplifting challenge of innovative expansion, a management model our two authors describe as 'cooking sweet and sour'. Like the first two stages, the regeneration stage would rest on the achievement of profound changes in the perceptions and behaviours of the people in ABB, as was the case for Kao, once Maruta took over the helm.

From refinement to regeneration

When he assumed the presidency of Kao in 1971, Dr Yoshiro Maruta brought with him a management approach that reflected his deep involvement in Buddhist philosophy. Indeed, he always introduced himself first as a Buddhist scholar and only second as president of Kao. Starting from this philosophy Maruta introduced a radical concept. He insisted, as we have already indicated, that his managers view Kao not as a soap and detergent company but as an educational institution. He convinced them that the most basic responsibility of every member of the organization was to teach and to learn. And he replaced Kao's old emphasis on imitation and adaptation with a new emphasis on creativity and innovation. In the first half of the eighties, the

company therefore expanded into disposable nappies, cosmetics, and even –
by stretching itself – into floppy disks, a product that leveraged the company's
expertise in surface science, polymer chemicals and microfine powder technologies. Such an expansion, over the course of half a century, has not been
evident in Ford's case, to the extent that it has not drawn on its knowledge
base to review its business fundamentally. In that sense it has not kept up its
founder's visionary orientation towards serving mankind.

Creating a sense of stretch

Maruta in fact believed that the company's remarkable record of diversification and growth was due not to some clear-sighted product-market analysis
or competitive strategy but to his untiring sense of ambition to harness Kao's
technology to improve people's lives. 'As a company, we do not spend our
time chasing after our rivals', Goshal and Bartlett have quoted Maruta as
saying. 'Rather by mastering our knowledge, wisdom and ingenuity to understand how to supply the consumer with surprise products, we free ourselves
of the need to care about the moves of our competitors.' Kao's open and
mutually supportive learning environment, framed by Maruta's concept of
the company as an educational institution, has therefore created a collective commitment to the company's technology and new product development
ambitions. While Kao's commitment in Japan in that respect has been
eminently collective, INTEL's in America has been relentlessly personal. Its
ability to renew itself and to make the right choices in an industry where
changes in technological development and industry standards were extremely
unpredictable, was highly dependent on the willingness of individuals to
question existing company strategy and practice and push the organization
beyond its comfortable, linear development path. In that respect Ford
has fallen between the eastern and western stools, neither engaging in a
collective process of fundamental product renewal nor fostering a relentless
personal quest for transformation amongst its individual people, in the face
of ever-increasing environmental turbulence and complexity.

Building structural multidimensionality

Like INTEL, Kao and ABB, according to Goshal and Bartlett, most companies today cannot afford to ignore the fact that they are now operating in
extremely complex environments where survival depends on the ability to
understand and respond to multiple demands and opportunities. Maruta's
strong belief in the individual, they say, led him to reject the authoritari-
anism of hierarchy, preferring instead to represent his organization as a
series of concentric circles. Like King Arthur and his round table, the circular
model reflected the egalitarianism upon which the Kao philosophy was
based. Gathered around the board of directors at the centre of the circle,
business groupings, corporate projects and geographic units could emerge,

taking their place alongside the R&D laboratories and sales divisions that had previously monopolized the top levels of Kao's hierarchy. This perhaps represents the ultimate in quality circles, something to which Ford might well aspire.

Creating dynamic processes

Having downplayed the importance of hierarchical structure in Kao, therefore, Maruta preferred to concentrate on developing an organization 'designed to run as a flowing system'. In fact it may well be argued that a thoroughgoing renewal of the original assembly line based manufacturing process might have led in this organic direction. In what Maruta termed 'biological self-control', he described an adaptive model in which ideas, abilities and resources flowed freely through the organization to where they were most needed. INTEL's model of emergency relief teams, meanwhile, captured – for Goshal and Bartlett – many of the same elements of speed, flexibility and responsiveness that could also be seen at Kao. 'When problems arose, the right experts spontaneously went into action like a bunch of antibodies fighting a foreign substance in the bloodstream.'

Employees at Kao were regarded as the company's key strategic resource, and management's task was to 'link them with each other in a union of individual wisdom from which emerges the group's strategy'. This deep-seated belief that capable individuals with free access to information provided the best source of creative ideas and healthy debate was reflected in the company's design of what it termed 'decision spaces'.

These were large, open areas at the centre of an office floor or research lab, where people gathered to discuss and decide on critical issues. While somewhat more structured, INTEL's meetings were equally democratic. Young engineers often found themselves alongside senior managers in key decision making meetings. Those with 'knowledge power' had to deal as equals with those with 'position power'. Careers advance at INTEL, our two authors maintain, not by moving up or down the organization but by meeting company needs. In many ways, through our MMBA programme, this is the kind of role evolution we are encouraging at Ford in the UK, thereby inviting its senior management to take up the strategic challenge for the global company to renew itself. Inevitably this causes individual and organizational angst.

Creating dynamic disequilibrium

Going beyond the task of ensuring strategic alignment to providing strategic challenge, managers at Kao and INTEL complemented their responsibility to maintain organizational fit with a willingness to create organizational disequilibrium. This was a manifestation of CEO Andy Grove's permanent state of mild paranoia at INTEL, a quality that prevented him from ever becoming content with being a classic 'strategic aligner'. He realized that his much larger role was to become a 'strategic challenger'. Because it was often difficult to assess the viability of most of the emerging forces, let alone predict their likely impact, INTEL's top management learned to back the judgement of those with 'knowledge power', people closest to the customers or most familiar with current technology that had 'knowledge power'.

Maruta too, Goshal and Bartlett maintain, saw his role at Kao more as a strategic challenger than as a strategic aligner. It began with his broad challenge to the organization to stop thinking of itself only as a manufacturer and marketer of household cleaning products and aspire to be an educational institution that developed and applied technology to improve lives and contribute to society. Perhaps in that respect Alex Trotman at Ford could take a leaf out of Maruta's book. Maruta became an active cheerleader for an initiative that began to explore how Kao could employ its knowledge base in oil science, surface technology and liquid crystal emulsification processes to develop a cosmetics line. As a result, Kao's cosmetics were the first to be developed and marketed on the basis of functionality rather than image. Emphasizing dermatologically appropriate skin care, ultraviolet sun protection and other such functional benefits, the products were a huge success. The analogy for Ford, of course, might be one of relating their evolved line of transportation services to an ever more populous and ecologically unstable planet.

Managing sweet and sour

Continuous self-renewal, for Goshal and Bartlett, is built, finally, on the tension that develops between two symbiotic forces. These consist of the need for continual improvement in operational performance provided by continuous rationalization, and the need for growth and expansion generated by continuous revitalization. In self-renewing companies, moreover, these two processes are seen as symbiotic. The continuous rationalization process provides the resources and legitimacy for revitalization.

This, in turn, generates the hope and energy required to sustain the gruelling rationalization process yet again. In effect, such companies have learnt the recipes for mixing sweet and sour, structure and process. Arguably Ford, alongside many other automobile manufacturers, has been more successful at the first structural change than at the second processual one, which is why there is so much overcapacity in the industry.

From structure to process

Anatomy, physiology, psychology

Overall, then, what became clear to Goshal and Bartlett as they examined companies like INTEL, Kao and ABB is that management's obsession with structure is misplaced. What the managers of 'Individualized Corporations' were focused on – consciously or unconsciously – was a set of core processes supported by a different set of management roles and relationships. These two authors think of structure in terms of the organism's anatomy, an important but insufficient model for understanding how the living organism works. Equally vital is a thorough understanding of the organizational physiology, the processes and relationships that ensure the financial and informational resources that are the organization's lifeblood.

Finally, management must understand the organization's psychology, the culture and values that shape the attitudes and beliefs of organization members.

ABB, INTEL and Kao could not be satisfactorily understood in terms of their very different, and often quite ungainly, formal structures. As a result, Goshal and Bartlett began to conceive of them as a portfolio of 'processes', and through that lens they saw distinct commonalities that characterized these three companies and others that were becoming 'individualized'. Such 'processes', the authors assert, are neither the day-to-day ones like order entry or inventory control that have been the focus of 'business process re engineering', nor even the strategic processes like new product development or the integrated logistics chain. What they refer to are the processes that operate one level above – the core organizational processes that overlie and often dominate the vertical, authority-based processes of the hierarchical structure.

At the heart of ABB, INTEL and Kao lie the three organizational processes that underpin the Individualized Corporation. The first one which, Goshal and Bartlett call the *entrepreneurial process*, produces and supports the opportunity-seeking, externally focused entrepreneurship of frontline managers. The *integration process* for which middle management is primarily responsible, brings together the advantages of bigness – of size, scale and diversity – with the advantages of smallness – flexibility, responsiveness, creativity – by linking the dispersed resources, competencies and businesses of the company.

And the third process, for which top management should take prime responsibility, the renewal process, creates and sustains the capacity to continually challenge the organization's own beliefs and practices, thereby revitalizing the strategies that drive businesses. In summary, then:

- Frontline managers head small, disaggregated and interdependent units focused on specific opportunities, as the company's entrepreneurs. They are the builders of the company's business competencies and take full responsibility for both the short-term and long-term performances of their units. Importantly, they face out to an external environment with which they build strong contacts and relationships, rather than upward into a hierarchy from which they expect direction and control.

- Like coaches who use the strengths of individual players to build a winning team, middle managers link these separate businesses and leverage the resources and capabilities developed in each of them. Overall, they play the role of capability developers – developing both the skills and the competencies of the individual frontline managers through monitoring and guidance, and also the overall capabilities of the organization by integrating the diverse capabilities of the frontline units across diverse businesses, functions and countries.
- Top management provides the foundation of this activity by infusing the company with an energizing purpose – a sense of ambition, a set of values, an overall identity – so as to develop it as an institution that can outlive its existing operations, opportunities and executives. Like social leaders, top management creates the challenge and commitment necessary to drive change and ensure that the company continually renews itself. Rather than trying to control strategic content, top management focuses much more on shaping organizational context.

What overall, according to Goshal and Bartlett, does this imply for our new corporate era in general, and for Ford in particular, as we evolve from value-exploiting modernism to value-creating post-modernism?

CONCLUSION: TOWARDS A NEW CORPORATE ERA

Companies as value-creating institutions

At relatively unsuccessful Norton and Westinghouse, Goshal and Bartlett maintain, in contrast to their more successful American counterparts 3M and GE, managers thought of their companies in market terms. They bought and sold businesses, created internal markets whenever they could, and dealt with their people according to market rules. Through the power of sharp, market-like incentives, they got what they wanted. People began to behave as they would in a market, with a strong sense of self-interest.

What happens, however, when each individual acts only in his or her own self-interest is that a company loses its particular quality as an institution in modern society. It loses what distinguishes it from a market and which therefore endows it with the ability to create new value in a way that a market cannot. In a market, people carry out economic exchanges only when each of the parties involved can clearly see how he or she, individually, gains from such a transaction. Because markets have no purpose or vision of their own, they can ruthlessly weed out inefficiencies by reallocating resources among the best available options. But, for the same reason, markets are not very good at creating innovations that require new combinations of resources.

By thinking of their companies in market terms, then, Norton and Westinghouse, and to a lesser degree Ford, have become the victims of market logic. All they could do was strive to squeeze more efficiencies out of everything they did. Their strategy focussed entirely on productivity improvement and cost cutting, which is in effect a major justification for Ford's globalizing manufacturing strategy. They were unable to innovate not because they were physically incapable of doing so but because the logic of market they adopted internally did not allow for creation beyond the efficiency of existing activities. To create innovations and new value, a company must typically allow a level of slack – that is, it must sacrifice some efficiencies – by allocating resources to things that do not yield the highest immediate returns. This is because even path-breaking innovations often begin at a disadvantage to existing alternatives and reach their potential only over time.

Visions like ABB's purpose 'to make economic growth and improved living standards a reality for all nations throughout the world'; values such as Kao's espoused belief that 'we are, first of all, an educational institution'; and norms like 3M's acceptance that 'products belong to divisions but technologies belong to the company' all emphasize the non-marketlike nature of the Individualized Corporation. In these ways, for Goshal and Bartlett, they encourage people to work collectively towards shared goals and values rather than restrictively, within their narrow self-interests. Interestingly enough, through the vision of its founder, Ford had from its outset such an ulterior motive: to make individualized transportation accessible to the man, if not also woman, in the street. However, partly as a result of Henry Ford's own vagaries in later life, this visionary impulse has not been fundamentally renewed and applied to the forthcoming twenty-first global century.

Companies like 3M, Kao and ABB, and to some degree Ford, therefore offer their employees a temporary respite from market forces by actually modifying the market's sharp incentives and creating an atmosphere more supportive of collaboration and sharing. In so doing, they create (temporarily) protected environments in which individuals can work together to challenge market forces and generate new combinations of resources, thereby creating new value for society. This is precisely what 3M does, for example, by allowing people 15 per cent 'bootleg' time to pursue their own projects. A company's ability constantly to create new value for society, then, is a product of a management philosophy that views the company not just as an economic entity, but also as a social institution that allows individuals to behave more co-operatively and less selfishly than they would in the economist's free market. This has significant implications for employment practices.

The new moral contract

The same forces of global competition and turbulent change that make employment guarantees unfeasible, according to Goshal and Bartlett, also enhance the need for trust and teamwork that cannot thrive in a sterile environment of reciprocal opportunism and continuous spot contracting.

While they may maximize the economic returns by continuously hiring themselves out as commercial mercenaries, most people also long for the sense of fulfilment that comes from belonging to an organizational family.

To resolve this tension, the two authors' concept of the 'Individualized Corporation' is grounded in a very different moral contract with people from that which has hitherto been the traditional or indeed modern case. In this new contract, each employee takes responsibility for his or her 'best-in-class' performance and undertakes to engage in the continuous process of learning that is necessary to support such performance and constant change. In exchange, the company undertakes to ensure not the dependence of employment security but the freedom of each individual's employability. No longer are people seen as a corporate asset from which to appropriate value. Under the new contract, they are a responsibility and a resource to which value is added. Its adoption requires a rejection of the paternalism, even arrogance, that underlies life-long employment contracts. It recognizes that only the market can guarantee employment and that market performance flows not from the omnipotent wisdom of top management but from the initiative, creativity and skills of all employees.

At the same time, however, it acknowledges that companies have a moral responsibility for the long-term security and well-being of the people they employ, and for helping them become the best they can be in what they choose to do. By building the new company–employee relationship on a platform of value adding and continuous choice rather than on a degrading acceptance of one-way dependence, the new contract, in Goshal and Bartlett's view, is not just functional, it is moral. How does such a moral standpoint, finally, reflect itself in top management practice?

A changing top management orientation

From strategy, structure and system to purpose, process and people

The companies that were successful, Goshal and Bartlett conclude, adopt a particular top management philosophy. They place less emphasis on following a carefully analysed strategic plan than on building an energizing corporate purpose. They have developed their organization less through changes in formal structure and more through developing effective management processes. And they have become less focused on managing the systems to control employees' collective behaviour than on working directly to develop their capabilities and broaden their perspectives as individuals. In short, they have moved beyond the old 'modern' doctrine of strategy, structure and systems to embrace a more organic philosophy built on the 'post-modern' development of purpose, process and people. Arguably, Ford Motors, globally, is halfway between its modern origins and its post-modern destination.

Beyond strategy to purpose

Today the corporate leader's greatest challenge is to create a sense of meaning within the company, which its members can identify with, in which they share a feeling of pride, and to which they are willing to commit themselves. In short, top management must convert the contractual employee of an economic entity into a committed member of a purposeful organization. The concept of strategy, both as it has evolved in academic thinking and as it has come to be adopted in corporate practice, reflects and reinforces the notion of companies as profit-maximizing agents of economic exchange in a large and complex environment. This minimalist and self-serving definition, according to Goshal and Bartlett, grossly underestimates the institutional role of corporations in modern society. As key repositories of resources and knowledge, corporations have become one of society's principal agents of change with a unique responsibility for creating and distributing wealth by continuously improving their productivity and innovativeness.

Equally important is the role they play as the most important forums for social interactions and personal fulfilment for many in society. It is this fundamental philosophical distinction that differentiates those top executives who see themselves simply as designers of corporate strategy from those who define their task more broadly as the shapers of institutional purpose. To the extent, for example, that Ford recontextualizes some of the work of the Ford Foundation within the company, it might evolve more wholeheartedly in such a direction.

Beyond structure to process

By the early eighties, the weight of increasing bureaucracy in the highly developed multidivisional business model was crushing any sense of entrepreneurial initiative, according to Goshal and Bartlett. Its fragmentation and compartmentalization of resources was inhibiting knowledge diffusion and organizational learning, and the hierarchical relationships so perfectly designed to ensure the efficiency and provide the controls necessary to refine existing operations proved incapable of creating and building new businesses internally. In fact Ford's total quality reorientation, in the nineties, has gone some of the way to right these wrongs, but it still has a long way to go from here.

As they began to reshape their greatly simplified organizations, many top-level executives began to focus their attention on building integrative processes that would contribute more directly to the company's strategic value – often knowledge and service oriented – that was to be added.

Beyond systems to people

In a service based economy in the midst of an economic revolution, the old assumption that top management could define priorities and monitor operations through sophisticated information, planning and control systems has become an illusion. The old-style corporate employer, according to Goshal and Bartlett, has no clothes. At the same time, the creation of initiative, the encouragement of learning, and the assurance of continuous self-renewal is rarely achieved through a faddish programmatic change.

More often, it is rooted in an organizational approach and management style that rejects the isolationism of systems based management and replaces it with a model that works by building stronger relationships with those best able to make particular decisions and take specific actions, thereby developing their capabilities and actively supporting their initiatives. What it means is that, instead of the historical reliance on planning systems for setting direction, they rely on the deployment of key people to specific jobs to influence the company's evolution. Similarly, instead of depending primarily on formal information systems to influence the nature of information processing in the company, top management communicates complex ideas, senses subtle signals and fosters the transfer of knowledge through its personal relationships with people. Finally, instead of depending exclusively or even primarily on the traditional control systems, managers find more effective ways of influencing people's behaviours by shaping the context in which people work. In this area, over the last five years, Ford has made a lot of strides, as it has moved ever closer towards semi-autonomous work groups.

A rebirth of professional management

In summary, then, for Goshal and Bartlett, today's 'Individualized Corporations' have become the principal repositories of much of society's scarcest resources and knowledge. They are the creators of substantial amounts of social capital through their role as forums for human interaction and personal fulfilment, and through their vital contributions to the development of people. As those who shape and guide these great institutions, managers have an awesome responsibility but also a great privilege.

In a way few others do, managers are in a position to make a major difference to society. While this is particularly the case for a global company like Ford, it will need a thoroughgoing process of revitalization and indeed regeneration before this takes place to any significant degree. We now turn from the turn-of-the-century symbol of industrial modernity in America, Ford, to its post-war equivalent, IBM. In so doing, moreover, we turn from physical transportation to electronic communications.

BIBLIOGRAPHY

1 Beniger, J., *The Control Revolution*, Harvard University Press, 1986.
2 Goshal, S. and Bartlett, C., *The Individualized Corporation*, Butterworth Heinemann, 1998.

7 From crisis to awakening

IBM's cycles of history

THE ORGANIZATION

The awakening

Liz Machtynger, based in IBM's European insurance solutions business, was faced with a dilemma. On the one hand she could see that her company was 'awakening', certainly on the insurance side. In fact, it was patently obvious to her that the focus on business solutions generally, and on knowledge management specifically, was the way her part of IBM was going. In that capacity, moreover, she was building upon foundations set in place by earlier IBM participants on our MMBA programme, such as Sam Manning, Henry Blythe and Brian Foss, who had between them established and marketed a highly successful database product. At the same time she was working very closely with current programme participants Graham Sumner and John Moon, who were actively and explicitly engaged in knowledge management, as were her colleagues in an adjacent learning set, Gavin Brown and Graham Parry. All of them, moreover, were working interdependently with their clients, taking a leaf, as we shall see, out of the old Thomas Watson's book. Catherine Boardman, one of the first MMBA graduates, was closely involved with Lloyd's in London, and Axel Kock, one of the most recent ones, with Allianz in Germany.

On the other hand, all was not rosy in the IBM garden, for Sam and Henry, together with another fellow learning set member of Graham's, Julia Samways, had left the company. While some would argue that that is par for the MBA course Liz and her close senior colleague Brian Foss felt otherwise, particularly given the project based focus – on both IBM and on client companies – of this particular programme. For her, it was as if one part of IBM, the internally facing one, was still in crisis.

Meanwhile, the other externally facing part was awakening, while quite evidently the 'high' lifetime employment period that had obtained in IBM's recent history had been left behind. To that extent she wondered whether, in Lew Gerstner, IBM had found a new prophet to take it into a promised land, or whether it was more of a corporate architect that was required, to

put all the new pieces harmoniously together. She also wondered, anticipating our next chapter, whether the new IBM had to shed its old separate
identity completely and embrace the new age of 'business ecosystems',
thereby taking its proper place at the innovative centre.

One thing she was sure of was that IBM had to recognize itself from the
inside-out as well as outside-in, if not in the world in general at least within
the European insurance sector. In order to make a start herself, Liz needed
to revisit IBM's history, to return to its genesis and initial morphosis, before
perhaps – herself and others – helping it further along the way towards an
ultimately successful metamorphosis. At the turn of the century, IBM was
in effect born out of crisis.

Out of crisis

'The verdict and sentence were handed down on February 13, 1913. All
the defendants were found guilty and Patterson and Watson were sentenced
to fines of $5,000 and one year in jail.'[1]

Thomas Watson, the founder of what was to become IBM, and his
powerful mentor John Patterson from NCR, never served their sentences
for sharp business practices. Nature intervened in the form of the worst
floods that had hit Dayton, Ohio, in American history. As 90,000 people
were rendered homeless the autocratic Patterson took charge of the rescue
effort, converting National Cash Register's assembly lines into a manufacturing centre for robots. Watson, by now an ace salesman of tabulating
machines, made a hurried departure from his previous and troubled
employer.

Out of the ashes of this unsavoury situation arose Watson's phoenix, first
becoming a composite computing-tabulating-recording corporation, and
subsequently consolidated into International Business Machines. Watson's
objectives in 1915 were very simple. He hoped to create a sales force in
the NCR mould, produce advanced machines superior to those of any rival,
and, by wedding the two, become the prime mover in office machinery.
Along the way he would develop new devices and additional markets,
and eventually transform the company into an industrial giant larger than
NCR. In 1924, offering an indication of where he intended to lead the hitherto diversified firm, Watson turned CTR into the now focused IBM.

IBM on high

From the outset of the new business, the IBM salesman would contact a
manager and offer to analyse his operations without seeking any business
commitment from him. If the salesman was invited through the door he
would attempt to show how the use of IBM machines would speed the gathering and processing of data, increase efficiencies and cut costs. Watson's
men – he employed no women in prominent positions at the time – would

make a tailor-made system for each business from existing components. If all went well, the main office would be called upon to arrange leasing terms, and these were fitted to each individual need. IBM-trained technicians would install the equipment, accompanied by a service representative who would be on call if anything went wrong, and would offer advice on how best to alter or add machines as the business changed. Over the course of twenty-five years, by 1939, Thomas Watson Senior had created a superb research and production organization and a world-famous sales force.

Both of these had become models of their kind not only for business and machine producers but for much of American and even world industry. The company itself was in excellent financial shape, its patent positions secure, and its reputation unmatched. Moreover, by the forties, it had 'awakened'.

A time of awakening

The first Thomas Watson, who had a near-puritanical approach to business, nevertheless became an ardent and intelligent art collector, and a contributor of time and money to educational institutions. More significantly, he was one of the first American industrialists to realize that the right kind of connections with institutions of higher learning would stand his company in good stead. He came to appreciate, in fact, that university professors could become valuable members of IBM's research establishment. Ben Wood, a psychology professor at Columbia and a personal friend of Watson's, was one such. As a leading educational researcher, he was searching for a machine that could score tests that were being devised at Columbia University. Duly subsidizing such research there and at other universities, IBM and Wood had developed such a test scorer by the forties. At the same time, Watson sponsored the establishment of the school's Astronomical Computing Bureau, led by Wallace Eckhart, who subsequently came up with one of the world's first electronic calculators. In the forties, IBM then promoted the work of a group at Harvard led by Howard Aitken, which stood on the shoulders of Pascal and Kepler, Liebniz and Babbage. This group would, by 1945, produce the forerunner of the modern computer.

In the 1950s, once Thomas Watson Junior had taken over the IBM helm, the computer was still perceived as a highly specialized scientific and industrial machine. Yet some twenty years later, by which time America was employing up to 70,000 computers of many sizes and for a multitude of business purposes – the great majority of which were produced and sold by IBM – Columbia University's political scientist Zbigniew Brzezinski was led to write:

A far-reaching technologically induced revolution is now upon us. Symbolized by the new complexes of learning, research and development

it links institutions of higher education with society. As such it has created unprecedented opportunities for innovation and experimentation,
through what we may call techtronic America, with IBM at its head.[2]

In the sixties and seventies IBM equipment helped direct every one of
the space shots, and its machines were used in hospitals, oil and natural gas
fields, schools, banks, libraries, retail establishments and government agencies. In fact, they were used in every field in which quantification was possible
and information could be processed. Yet the times in the seventies were
changing.

Come the unravelling

In 1980 IBM reported gross revenues of more than $24 billion. It employed
340,000 people and had 65 per cent of the world's market for mainframe
computers. By most yardsticks this would have been considered impressive,
yet no longer by those usually employed in the data processing industry.
Not only was the company's growth rate far lower than those of small new
companies in the industry, like Wang and Apple, but it was also below each
of its old mainframe rivals such as Burroughs and indeed NCR. There were
other signs of trouble. IBM had blundered in the pricing of new products
and made costly financial errors. Wall Street's once premier growth and
glamour issue was badly tarnished. In the early eighties, moreover, three
related forces were beginning to play what would become a devastating
part: lower computation costs, simpler and more flexible software, and a
much more informed information processing public, both within large-scale
organizations and without. This was serving to bring about a new relationship between office and home that Apple Computers was beginning to
exploit. By 1981 IBM had therefore announced that it would be producing
its own new, small machine, for the first time breaking out of the mainframe market, and that, again for the first time, it would be encouraging
independents to produce software for it. Bill Gates was notably one such.
Don Estridge, moreover, a software expert rather than a hardware man and
a southerner rather than a member of the north-eastern establishment, came
to head up IBM's new personal computer project. He was a round peg
within the IBM culture.

> Estridge's personality wasn't doing him any favours in the mid-1970's
> in IBM. He walked around in lizard-skin cowboy boots while every-
> body else was wearing wing tips. Occasionally Estridge tried to fit the
> IBM mould, but he usually couldn't pull it off. In fact he showed a
> magical touch that has eluded IBM ever since he was pulled from the
> PC job. He seemed to understand intuitively the new counterculture
> that Steve Jobs and Apple had helped usher in, that you shouldn't trust
> a computer you couldn't lift.[3]

When Estridge took the PC project on in 1980 he immediately brought in Bill Gates and his small band from Microsoft. In fact, he went outside the company to buy almost all the parts for the PC. In Boca Raton, thousands of miles away from the headquarters in Armonk, his team had grown to several hundred in 1981. As things progressed that year, the hardware and software came together, and the DOS operating system that Microsoft had developed was finished. By August came the great launch of the new little machine in midtown Manhattan. While it was an enormous success there was one ominous note for the future.

IBMers resisted Microsoft's attempts to get involved with the launch. It was treated as just one of many subcontractors on a project whose most important feature was the Big Blue logo. Meanwhile, Estridge's high profile as the father of the new industry rankled with other IBM executives, whose concern evolved into a fierce jealousy that guaranteed that Estridge would eventually fall. Under quiet assault on all fronts from other parts of IBM, Estridge soon found himself spending most of his time fighting the internal bureaucracy. It ultimately convinced IBM's management that the PC business should be taken back into the corporate bureaucracy. The move not only ultimately inhibited the development of the company's PC business, according to IBM biographer Paul Carroll, but the bureaucracy also eventually put Don Estridge on a plane that cost him his life.

> IBM didn't start out being this bureaucratic. The politicking just sort of happened over the years as IBM vanquished its competitors so completely that the only way for its executives to measure its success was to see how far they could advance within the company. Besides, the IBM culture taught them to fight one another as hard as they could. For decades the calculated infighting kept people on their toes; it was only later that the debating turned into bickering.[4]

Instead of adapting, as the industry fundamentally changed, IBM settled into cultural gridlock, accordingly to Carroll. In fact, since its inception, IBM had produced most of the key technologies that had propelled the whole computer industry forward. IBM researchers had brought the industry two Nobel Prize winners and had spent one whole tenth of corporate America's research and development budget, leading to all sorts of innovations. The company had also become the nation's largest contributor to non-profit and educational institutions. Yet in the period 1986 to 1993 it reduced its workforce from 406,000 to 260,000 worldwide. Whole towns that sprang up in New York's Hudson Valley to service IBM were devastated.

By the mid-nineties, the company had lost $75 billion of stock market value before Lew Gestner's new regime began to turn things round somewhat. 'IBM's troubles raise questions about whether big companies can work any more. General Motors messed up. So did Sears. If IBM, once the managerial model for big companies can't hack it, then who can?'[5]

Anticipating crisis

Sam Manning, Henry Blythe and Brian Foss, who were based in Britain, all from IBM's insurance oriented sector in the mid-nineties, joined our MBA programme at an auspicious time. Their business for IBM was not that of selling hardware, or even software in isolation, but of selling insurance solutions. In fact Sam, whose original role in IBM was to construct robots, opted, during the MBA, to leave the company. He felt they were not supporting the new database product he had developed in the way he would have wished. At the same time his sales colleague Henry Blythe also departed, joining the German software house SAP, which had strong links with IBM. Brian Foss, the third of our IBM based MBA triumvirate, has stayed on with the company to develop the database product that Sam and his colleagues had originated – drawing upon seventeenth-century French mathematics – and has done so very successfully. While Sam, Henry and Brian continue to meet as colleagues and friends, in 1996 Brian recruited Liz Machtynger from BP to join his product group, which was now focusing on generating business in Europe and South Africa. Together with Graham Sumner, she also joined the MBA, and they immediately focused their efforts on Independent Insurers and Legal and General, two UK insurers who were doing business with IBM. In fact, Liz and Graham, like Brian, seemed to spend much more time with their clients than within IBM. It was thus increasingly difficult to distinguish where the boundary lay between their so-called customers, IBM and themselves. This boundary-crossing relationship included the likes of Sam Manning and Henry Blythe who were supposedly outside the company.

IBM then, as we saw it through the words and deeds of the IBMers on our programme, was – at least in the solutions oriented part of the business – becoming the 'non-entity' that the current unravelling was inviting them to be. In that guise, they were merely extending the bounds of what had originally been imprinted upon IBM: 'From the outset of the new business, then, the IBM salesman would contact a manager and offer to analyse his operations without seeking any business commitment from him.' But in the nineties, as opposed to the thirties, such a salesman had a much larger range of offerings – including hardware, software and consultancy based solutions – than was the case in the thirties. Moreover, and as we enter ever further into the age of interdependence, the distinction between customer and supplier, both individually and institutionally, is becoming ever more blurred.

Moreover, whereas in the thirties IBM could already be considered to be a leading player in the knowledge business, today it is more purposefully engaged in knowledge management. As a result, Liz Machtynger and the company's chief knowledge officer have set up a knowledge forum in the UK, with other interested companies including some associated with our programme. Such then, as the high turns from the awakening to an unravelling, duly anticipating a transformative crisis, are the cycles of history. The question that Liz Machtynger and her MMBA colleagues – past, present and future – now faced was how to stimulate a new awakening at one and the same time as CEO Lew Gerstner in America was trying to regain the 'high' ground that IBM had once occupied.

INTRODUCTION

American prophecy

So far we have drawn upon economics and psychology, ecology and complexity, in formulating our organizational ecology. We now turn to the lessons of history. William Strauss and Neil Howe are two of a distinctive breed of American philosophers, historians and indeed management thinkers who have a prophetic outlook on organizations and societies. In their *Fourth Turning*,[6] they have on the one hand gone back into five hundred years of Anglo-Saxon history, and on the other hand projected fifty years forward, to predict our likely futures. Whereas their orientation has been towards society as a whole, albeit angled particularly towards the Anglo-Saxon world, their notion of 'cycles of history' has inevitable implications for organizations in general and for IBM in particular.

Whereas societies unfold however, at least in Strauss and Howe's view, in regular hundred-year cycles, organizations are capable of 'forcing the pace', depending on the nature of the industry in which they are based. Moreover, while the two historians refer to four discrete 'turnings', set within each full cycle, in the corporate world such turnings are liable to be overlapping ones, as in the case of IBM that we have illustrated here, with a simultaneous crisis–high–awakening nestled against each other.

Patterns of history

Turnings

What are known as 'turnings' to these American historians come in cycles of four. They have discovered this through their review of the past five hundred years of Anglo-Saxon history. Each full cycle spans the length of a long human life. Such a life is roughly eighty to one hundred years, a unit of time the Romans called a *saeculum*. The four turnings of the *saeculum* together comprise history's seasonal rhythm of growth, maturation, entropy and destruction or indeed re-creation. The first turning they term a *high*, an upbeat era of strengthening of institutions and weakening of individualism, when a new civic order is implanted and the old values regime decays. In our own ecological terms, such a 'high' is lodged midway between colonization and conservation, when genesis turns towards morphosis. Thus in

HERO

High   Awakening

NOMAD   **ARTIST**

Crisis   Unravelling

PROPHET

Figure 9 IBM's crisis and awakening

the twenties and thirties Thomas Watson cast off his soiled NCR heritage and created a new moral order in what was to become IBM. The second turning is an *awakening*, a passionate era of spiritual upheaval, when the institutional order comes under attack from a regime with new values. In this case Watson himself countered his pragmatic, commercial sense with a rational belief in the power of thought and the university based world which embodied it. Through such an 'awakening' IBM produced not only Nobel Prize winning physicists but also successive generations of ever more powerful computers. This is the period, ecologically, when conservation of morphosis turns towards catalysation or metamorphosis.

The third turning is an *unravelling*, an era of strengthening individualism and weakening institutions, when the old order decays and the new values regime is implanted. Bill Gates' entrepreneurial Microsoft, lacking the idealism of an Apple but abounding with a new sense of twenty-first-century realism, symbolizes such an 'unravelling'. 'Big Blue' and its mainframe based hardware is supplanted by that new 'Window on the World', represented by the proliferation of software. In the process the stock market value of a 25,000-person software builder, Microsoft, overtakes that of a former 400,000-person hardware manufacturer, IBM. Catalysation and metamorphosis get caught up in a new wave, working its way towards co-creation and homeostasis.

The fourth turning is a *crisis*, a decisive era of saecular upheaval, when the values regime drives a new civic order to replace an old one. Such a crisis, which began to affect IBM in the early nineties, has been nominally dealt with by the deftness of a CEO like Lew Gerstner, newly installed at IBM's helm. The old style of co-creation gives way to a new style of colonization, and the crisis of rebirth ensues, between the two. However, and as anticipated by the newly evolved organizational ecology embedded in the work of our insurance based IBMers on the MMBA, the fully fledged crisis – leading to fundamental renewal – is yet to come. In other words, IBM as a knowledge based entity has not yet unravelled into a complete 'non-entity', with a view to establishing a new kind of knowledge creating community, lodged perhaps in the age of ecosystems.

Seasons in time

Each cycle of time, according to Strauss and Howe, is full of discontinuities. A new round does not emerge gradually from the last but only when the circle experiences a complete break. Such a break was apparent when the old IBM collapsed dramatically, in the early nineties. First rituals of 'emptying' purify the community of sins committed, in the wake of which former CEO John Akers was dismissed, and the new man Lew Gerstner was brought in, for the first time in IBM's history from outside. Second, a chaotic phase occurs in which all rules are breakable, including lifelong employment and an exclusive focus on mainframes. Third rituals of 'filling' which have not yet happened at IBM, propel the new circle to a creative beginning, perhaps filling IBMers with an eastern awe arising out of genuine undoing. While a crisis rearranges the outer world of politics and power, an awakening rearranges the inner world of spirit and culture. In the IBM case, today as distinct from yesterday, the outer world predominates over the inner one, to the extent that politics and power play are more in evidence than spirit and culture.

The result of the present-day imbalance, arguably, is the rate of the loss of individuals from the organization, though the fact that we are currently, from a societal perspective, living in an age of 'unravelling' also has its part to play.

While a crisis reinvents public space, i.e. the organizational space of IBM in general, an awakening also elevates the consciousness of the individual and reinvents his or her private space or prevailing mindset. Instead of serving the 'Think' god, he or she goes out in pursuit of an individual version of the truth, and hence helps to establish a 'knowledge creating company', as we shall see with the Surrey Police in chapter 14. Interestingly enough, the police force in Britain still offers lifelong employment.

The fourfold journey

These seasonal turnings, as we have shown here, have underpinned IBM's growth in the 1920s/30s/40s; maturation in the 1950s/60s/70s; entropy in the 1980s and 1990s as well as prospective destruction or indeed renewal in the twenty-first century. Such turnings, moreover, have prevailed societally in prehistory as well as in more contemporary business and civilization. To North American Native societies, for example, life was experienced as four 'hills' (childhood, youth, maturity, old age), each possessing its own challenge, climax and resolution. To the Hindus, second, it was a journey through four *ashranas*, four phases of social and spiritual growth. Pythagoras was amongst the first 'western' thinkers to interpret life as a cycle of four phases, incorporating the spring of childhood, the summer of youth, the harvest of midlife and the winter of old age. The Romans likewise divided the *saeculum* into four phases: *pueretia* (childhood), *iuventus* (young adulthood), *virilitas* (maturity) and *senectus* (old age).

From youth to maturity

The first phase is childhood, the spring of life, the time for growing and learning, acquiring competence, accepting protection and absorbing traditions from elders. This phase was represented in the pioneering NCR days, when Thomas Watson Senior was apprenticed to John Patterson, becoming a sales supremo who had learnt the ropes by selling adding machines. Adulthood, the second phase, is the summer of life, when Watson converted his initial dreams and ideas into projects and plans, launching careers and families, providing the muscle and energy of business and society. This was the time when 'Think' became the watchword of International Business Machines. Next comes midlife, the period of the greatest harvest, Jung's phase of individuation, a time when people's values tend to change towards their opposite.

Arguably, despite the seeming shift in orientation from hardware to software, and from mainframes to distributed networks, IBM is yet to enter wholeheartedly into its midlife phase, thereby changing its orientation from independence and dependence to one of interdependence. That having been said, our group of MBAs within the insurance sector, as we have seen, seem to be leading the interdependent way, tacitly if not yet explicitly. Old age, the winter of life, is a time for engaging in leisure and reflection, and also for setting standards, passing on wisdom, making endowments, taking on society's highest leadership posts. Liberated from the grinding burden of work and family, many elders are able to step back and provide the strategic wisdom every society needs. Such a role is more evidently being played, despite his being still in his early forties, by Bill Gates at Microsoft than by anyone at IBM today. Such maturity, in its corporate context, is more readily associated with such Japanese business leaders as Honda and Kaku (of Canon) than with their Anglo-Saxon counterparts, who tend to remain active and youthful and to hang on.

We now move from the four turnings to the archetypal characters who cause things to turn.

Archetypes in history

From prophets to artists

Prophets first, for Strauss and Howe embody vision, values and religion. We liken them, in our learning ecology, to our stewards. They are principled moralists like Ian Beckett at Surrey Police and Anita Roddick at Body Shop, summoners of human sacrifice and wagers of righteous wars, who are revered for their inspiring words. The 'born again' Thomas Watson, post-NCR, certainly possessed some of these attributes, if not all of them. Nomads, second, embody liberty, survival and honour. They tend to be astute, hands-on realists, such as Don Estridge who led the way towards IBM's PC revolution in the eighties, or Graham Sumner at IBM in the nineties. Within our own learning ecology these are the hunters. Heroes, third – our herders – embody community, affluence and technology, being aggressive advocates of economic prosperity and public optimism, carrying a reputation for civic energy and competence. Thomas Watson Junior would be representative of them, together with several more of the IBM senior executives who both accompanied and succeeded him. Finally, artists are oriented towards pluralism, expertise and due process, as sensitive and complex social technicians, like Sam Manning who left the company, advocates of fair play, geared towards political inclusiveness. Such 'artists', fourth – in our terms gardeners – or indeed maverick scientists, like the inventor of fractals Benoit Mandelbrot, were never as comfortable in IBM as they might have been in Apple; as a result the company has been inevitably inhibited from realizing its full potential. The cycles and the archetypal characters who play their parts in them change over the course of each generation, as we shall see later. The four turnings taken together are both structure building, like the 'high', and structure changing, like the 'awakening'.

The four turnings

From high to crisis

An awakening first begins, for Strauss and Howe, when events *trigger a revolution* in the organizational or societal culture; a crisis similarly begins when events trigger one in corporate or public activity. In that respect IBM experienced more of a technological than a cultural 'awakening', although it has had at least a strong glimpse of a crisis. As a result, as the IBMers on our programme experience things in the company today, the economic and technological (corporate) issues are being addressed much more wholeheartedly than the social and cultural (organizational) ones.

Both a so-called high or an unravelling, second then, *consolidate a new direction*. Such a high begins when a society or a corporation perceives that the basic issues of the prior crisis have been resolved, leaving a new civic or commercial regime firmly in place. In IBM's case such a prior crisis would have been associated with Thomas Watson Senior's NCR based sharp practices and imminent imprisonment. The new 'high' that it established not only built up its technology based reputation as the leading supplier of mainframe computers around the world but also its moral tone as a lifetime employer and a noted contributor to the societies in which each of its operations was based.

An unravelling begins with the perception that an awakening has been resolved, not entirely the case then in IBM, leaving a new cultural mindset in place. The gateway to such a new turning can be sudden and dramatic or subtle and gradual. In IBM's case the unravelling was gradual, on the one hand, and sudden on the other. The gradual part of the unravelling was the steady encroachment of PCs onto the market, establishing a new mindset. The computer was no longer part of an exclusive IT establishment but instead became part of a newly emancipated age. Such an age IBM has yet wholeheartedly to embrace.

Steve Jobs hailed from Silicon Valley, a direct descendent of the hippy generation on America's west coast; Thomas Watson Senior, on the other hand, had been part of the establishment north-eastern seaboard. The sudden part of the unravelling was the way in which, almost overnight, 'Big Blue' was overtaken by the Microsofts of this world. Today, this unravelling, that began with the challenging of established companies like IBM and Control Data by such fledgling enterprises as Compaq and Dell, Microsoft and now Netscape, is still in full swing. At one and the same time, however, and as we have seen, there are signs of a renewed awakening, although it stands in the shadows of the previous 'high', the recent 'crisis', and the current societal 'unravelling' that we associate with post-modernity.

The four turnings, then, as we have indicated, together comprise a quaternal social cycle of growth, maturation, entropy and death (or rebirth). The jury is still out on IBM as to whether it will ultimately suffer death or renewal; the company currently seems to be in a kind of positive limbo. Tracking back, we can recall that in a springlike high a society like America or an enterprise like IBM in the fifties fortified, built and converged in an era of promise. In a summerlike awakening, like the US or IBM in the sixties and seventies, both dreams and play exulted in an era of euphoria. In an autumnal unravelling, as we have seen in the eighties and nineties, each has been harvesting, consuming and diverging in an era of anxiety. Finally, as a hibernal crisis may be breaking out, the focus is upon struggle and sacrifice in an era of survival. When the full *saeculum* is in motion, no long human lifetime can go by without an ultimately sustainable society or enduring enterprise confronting its deepest spiritual and worldly needs. IBM accomplished this much more evidently in its high than in its unravelling.

We now move on to consider each of the turnings in more detail.

The first turning – high

A 'high', for Strauss and Howe, brings a renaissance to business or community life. With the new civic or economic, technological or social order in place, people want to put the crisis of transition behind them, as was experienced in America both during the pre-war Depression and during the Second World War, and feel content about what they have now (post-war) all achieved. Any social or organizational issues left unresolved by the crisis must now remain so, such as the gap between the rich and the poor or between the levels in the bureaucratic hierarchy. Meanwhile, the recent fear for group survival, both physically and economically, as was the case for IBM's precursors in Ohio at the turn of the century, transmutes into a desire for investment, growth and strength. This in turn produces an era of commercial prosperity, institutional solidarity and political stability such as was very much the case in Eisenhower's America, and during the regimes of both father and son Watson. The big arguments, in both enterprise and society, are over means not ends, so that institutional life seems increasingly under control while perhaps distressingly spiritually dead. As Strauss and Howe put it, 'it can do (or even Think) everything but no longer feel anything'.

The second turning – awakening

An awakening arrives with a dramatic challenge against the high's assumptions about benevolent reason and congenial institutions. The outer world now feels trivial compared to the inner world, as it did for example for the hippies of the sixties. New spiritual ideals and social agendas burst forth along with utopian experiments seeking to reconcile total fellowship with total autonomy. The prosperity and security of a high are overtly disdained though covertly taken for granted. Business or society searches for soul – as Whyte has intimated – over science, meaning over things.

While such a business outlook could be readily identified with an Apple, and to a lesser degree with a Microsoft, IBM's first awakening in the sixties was a partial one, reflecting its broader role in society externally but retaining its bureaucratic outlook internally. Indirectly, though, of course, the personal computer on the one hand, and horizontal as opposed to vertical organizational structures on the other, owe their origins to the 'consciousness revolution' of the sixties. In many ways the economic demise of the IBM of old in the early nineties was a reflection of the inappropriateness of an IBM type of social philosophy in our current period of unravelling. As public and institutional order deteriorates, eventually the enthusiasm cools, having left the old cultural regime discredited.

The third turning – unravelling

An unravelling begins, as we have seen, once a society-wide embrace of the liberating cultural forces is set loose by the awakening. People have had their fill of spiritual rebirth, moral protest and lifestyle experimentation, as was the case in northern California. Eventually cynical alienation hardens into a brooding pessimism. While personal enterprise and satisfaction amongst a distinctive minority in, for example, Silicon Valley is high, together with the earnings that go with it, public trust ebbs within a fragmenting culture of haves and have-nots.

Specifically within an IBM context, today we can see many individuals acquiring wealth and experiencing well-being through their employment within the company. However, overall, the kind of loyalty that the mighty corporation inspired in the seventies and eighties has substantively gone. IBM man, and indeed IBM woman, is becoming a thing of the past as the trust in the paternal company as a former lifetime employer begins to disappear.

The fourth turning – crisis

A crisis arises in response to sudden threats that would previously would have been ignored or deferred, but which are now perceived as dire. Great perils boil off the clutter and complexity of life, leaving behind one simple imperative: the business or society must prevail. This requires a solid public consensus, aggressive institutions and personal sacrifice. As I have indicated, IBM has in one sense already entered the crisis and in another sense has not yet done so. On the one hand, the early nineties heralded a profound threat to the company's survival, as for the first time in its history the company sustained major losses in the face of new and severe competition in the emerging PC market. In the corridors of IBM power, there is a strong focus on survival. However, and on the other hand, no significant cultural revolution has yet taken place in the business. The external economically and technologically laden sense of crisis has not been matched by an internal socially and culturally laden one of equal proportions. The interplay between economy and culture, in that sense, has been a halfhearted one, perhaps even involving a destructive rather than a creative tension between them. The current knowledge intensive awakening, as some of our MBA participants have realized to their cost, is only a glimmer of one, vulnerable to the crisis immediately upon them, the unravelling that is generally in the air, and the memories, albeit fading ones, of hierarchies of authority.

Economy and culture

Overall, for Strauss and Howe, the four turnings have kept the great wheel of time in motion, infusing business specifically and civilization generally with periodic new doses of vitality, propelling the human and commercial adventure ever forward. During a high, earnings and productivity growth is typically smooth and very rapid, while during an awakening a soaring economy, or business enterprise, hits at least one spectacular bust. Amidst an unravelling, activity again accelerates, but now the growth is fitful, as we have recently seen with IBM, and as we also shall see with Sainsbury's in this book. In a crisis, enterprise is rocked by a combination of panic, depression, inflation and loss. Near the end of a crisis, a healthy entity may or may not be reborn. In the realm of ideas, the *saeculum* regularly oscillates from a focus on the spirit (in an awakening) to a focus on the world (in a crisis).

While a crisis totally alters the cultural framework for the expression of thought and feeling, in a high the culture (IBMers in starched white collars and pin-striped suits) optimistically reflects the consensus about the fledgling order. Come the awakening, the new order feels secure and prosperous enough to enable a new culture to erupt. New norms and styles first assault and then embed themselves within the post-crisis order, as the hippies of the sixties become the Steve Jobs of the seventies and eighties. In an unravelling, finally, the new corporate or societal culture flourishes, splinters and diversifies into Apples, Compaqs, Dells, Microsofts, Sun Microsystems, Sequents and Netscapes.

We now turn more specifically to the 'high', set in the context of its associated cast of characters, considering each of the other cycles in turn, this time together with their corresponding archetypes.

FOUR TURNINGS

High

First turnings and archetypal lifecycles

After a winter of devastation as was the case for Thomas Watson in his final NCR days in Ohio, spring is announced and there is a sentiment of relief, of simple pleasures and the planting of things that will grow. Beneath the outward contentment, people ignore what are later deemed to be flagrant injustices. Highs are good times for those who inhabit and accept the predominant culture, societally or organizationally. This was certainly the case for those who, as employees within or as customers without, bought into 'Big Blue' in its heyday.

For Strauss and Howe, as faded 'nomads' or entrepreneurs replace prophets or visionaries like Thomas Watson Senior in maturity, they slow the pace of change. They shun the old crusades in favour of simplicity. As powerful 'heroes' or captains of industry like Thomas Watson Junior replace nomads or entrepreneurs in midlife, they establish an upbeat, constructive ethic of discipline. As conformist artists or scientists like Ben Wood at IBM replace heroes like an Edison in young adulthood, they become sensitive helpmates, lending their research and development expertise and co-operation in an era of growing calm. As prophets or would-be visionaries like the Steve Jobs-to-be replace artists or scientists in childhood they are nurtured with increasing indulgence by optimistic adults in a secure environment.

Awakening

Second turnings and archetypal lifecycles

An awakening is an era of cultural upheaval and spiritual renewal. It begins when the waxing discipline of the high suddenly seems tiresome, unfulfilling, illegitimate and unjust. This was the time for Apple and Microsoft, albeit only temporarily in the former case, to triumph over bureaucratic 'Big Blue'. By now, the core high virtues are regarded as outmoded, even unnecessary. As inner life strengthens, its outer life weakens. People exalt rights over duties, self over society, ideals over institutions, creativity over conformism, Silicon Valley over the American rustbelt. Such awakening eras are memorable for their images of contrasting extremes: the triumph of power, wealth and knowledge side by side with the passionate outcry of the spirit. That outcry, in IBM's case during the fifties and sixties, came more from the liberated intellect than from the freed spirit. The spiritual awakening occurred therefore outside of 'Big Blue' rather than within, from those who went on to try and beat IBM rather than join it, so that its unravelling today misses an important beat. As expansive heroes like the younger Thomas Watson replaced nomads in elderhood, they orchestrated ever grander constructions, like the 360 range. They set the stage, in opposition, for the spiritual goals of the young, who therefore tended to shun the large corporations that represented the establishment. As new-style artists or scientists replace old-time heroes in midlife, meanwhile, they apply expertise to improve things while calming the passions of the young. As self-absorbed prophets replace artists in young adulthood, exemplified by Steve Jobs, like Apple, they challenge the moral failure of elder-built institutions like IBM.

In this way they spark a society-wide spiritual awakening. As nomads or budding entrepreneurs replace prophets in childhood, they are left under-protected at a time of social convulsion and adult self-discovery; acquiring a cynicism about moral crusades, ending, for example, by creating a Microsoft or a Netscape.

Unravelling

Third turnings and archetypal lifecycles

During the eighties, Reagan in America and Thatcher in Britain stood firm against the consciousness revolution and symbolized the primacy of the establishment. Thereafter they both symbolized its defeat and the primacy of the self. Not trusting government, people did trust the individual through the marketplace, cultural diversity, interactive technologies, new age spirituality and born-again evangelism. For Margaret Thatcher, in her own memorable words, 'there is no such thing as society, only individual family units'. As niche groups were strengthened, they began erasing old (universal) worldviews and constructing new (particular) ones, much to the old IBM's chagrin. Unlike in the high there was no such thing any more as 'normal' public, technological or commercial opinion. As each group, like a Compaq or a Microsoft, extolled its own authenticity, it defined its adversary's values as indecent, obscene or evil. Transnational capital rocked the American economy, billion-dollar leveraged buyouts reshuffled entire corporations, the Asian miracle was here today and gone tomorrow as the Sumatran fires burned, and the more long-time workers a company laid off, the more its stock rose.

The awakening complete, people are now fully immersed in their own self-centred purposes. The new social priority is to atomize, not to gather; we have the onset of 'portfolio man', of portable skills and outsourced IT. We would have had the triumph of a Don Estridge over the IBM bureaucracy, if the latter had been willing to unravel.

Finally, management gurus Goshal and Bartlett emerge with the enterprise of our unravelling day, none other than the 'Individualized Corporation'. The heroic corporations that they represent are no longer the American Expresses and the IBMs, the Matsushitas and the Toyotas, the Marks & Spencers and the Shells of this world, but rather the ABBs and the Skandias, the 3Ms and the INTELs, the Canons and the Kaos, all of which have become renowned for their flexibility and for individuality.

As empathetic artists replace heroes in maturity, they quicken the pace of social change, shunning the old order in favour of complexity, pursuing – like Benoit Mandelbrot who departed from the IBM mainstream – theories of 'chaos' to their ultimate limit. As judgemental prophets or born-again evangelists replace artists in midlife, they preach a downbeat, values-fixated ethic of moral conviction. As alienated nomads replace prophets in young adulthood, they become brazen free agents, whizz-kid high-tech entrepreneurs, lending their pragmatism and independence to an era of growing social turmoil, outside IBM rather than within it. As heroes replace nomads in childhood, they are nurtured with increasing protection by pessimistic adults in an insecure environment, urged to be obedient achievers and team players. Finally comes the crisis.

Crisis

Fourth turning – a morphology of crisis

A crisis era begins with a catalyst, a starting event, or sequence of events, that produces a sudden shift in mood. Arguably Apple and Microsoft between them played that role for IBM. Once catalysed, an entity achieves a regeneration, a new counter-entropy that reunifies and re-energizes civic, economic or business life. Paradoxically, within IBM this both has and has not happened, and ambivalence is rife in the business today.

To the extent that a thoroughgoing crisis has taken place, so the now regenerated 'non-entity' is propelled towards a climax, a crucial moment that confirms the death of the old entity and the birth of the new community. The climax culminates in a resolution, a triumphant/tragic conclusion that separates winners from losers, resolves the big questions and establishes the new order. Such a fully fledged crisis is yet to happen to IBM, but may have been anticipated in the interdependent context of the company and the insurance industry by our young MMBA turks.

Every fourth turning starts with a catalytic event that terminates the mood of unravelling and unleashes one of crisis. Whereas sparks in a high reinforce feelings of security, in an awakening they create argument, and in an unravelling anxiety. With the advent of the crisis, sparks of history trigger a fierce new dynamic of group synergy. People stop tolerating the weakening of institutions, the splintering of the culture, the individualizing of behaviour, the fact that it's all right for MBAs, albeit in moderation, to have high-flown ideas.

Collective action is now seen as vital to solving a society's, or indeed IBM's, most fundamental problems. An invigorated business ecosystem starts propelling itself along a trajectory that nobody had foreseen before the catalysing event. Perhaps by fostering the degree of interdependence that hastens IBM becoming a non-entity, our IBMers on the MMBA are wittingly or unwittingly forcing the crisis pace. The crisis climax is human or business history's equivalent to nature's raging typhoon, the kind that sucks all surrounding matter into a single swirl of ferocious energy.

Crisis climax

Normally occurring late in the fourth turning – possibly a full generation after the third – the climax gathers energy from an accumulation of unmet needs, unfulfilled expectations, unresolved problems. It then spends that energy on an upheaval whose direction and dimension were beyond comprehension during the unravelling era. The climax shakes an organization or society to its roots, transforms its institutions, redirects its purposes, and marks its people for life. The climax can end in triumph or in tragedy, or some combination of the two. Whatever the outcome, an entity passes

through a great gate, along the way becoming a non-entity, before fundamentally altering the course of its work and life. Soon afterwards, this great
gate is sealed by the crisis resolution, when, according to Strauss and Howe,
victors are rewarded and enemies punished, when one IBM-like entity dies
and another that we have yet fully to see, is born.

Fourth turnings and archetypal lifecycles

A catalytic agent is a reaction enabler, an ingredient that lowers the energy
threshold required to produce a chain reaction. Imagine a test tube of chemicals whose mass, temperature and pressure remain constant (or rise
gradually) but which cannot alone produce an explosion no matter how
often it is ignited. There must be a slight change in chemical composition,
something that can lower the threshold energy for ignition. Since the dawn
of the modern world, there has been for Strauss and Howe only one fourth
turning archetypal constellation: elder prophets, midlife nomads, young adult
heroes and child artists. The indulged prophet children of highs, born in
the aftermath of one crisis, foment the next crisis upon entering elderhood.
The abandoned nomad children of awakenings become the pragmatic midlife
managers of crisis. The protected hero children of unravellings provide the
powerful young adult soldiers of crisis. The suffocated children of crisis come
of age as artist youths.

A fourth turning prophecy

These crisis events will reflect the tearing of the civic or organizational
fabric at points of vulnerability: problem areas neglected, denied or delayed
during the unravelling. Aggressive individualism, institutional decay and a
short-term orientation can proceed only so far before a business or society
undermines the long-term promises on which a market economy must rest.
Through the unravelling people will have preferred (or, at least tolerated)
the exciting if bewildering trend towards chaos and complexity. As the crisis
mood congeals, people will come to the jarring realization that they have
grown helplessly dependent on a teetering edifice of anonymous transactions and paper guarantees, virtual organizations and portfolio careers.
Indeed we had a foretaste of such a situation, in November 1997, when the
Korean economy in particular, and the Far Eastern Tigers in general, were
badly shaken by financial debacles. The era will have left the financial world
arbitraged and tentacled – debtors won't know who holds their notes, home-
owners who owns their mortgages, shareholders who runs their equities. It
will also have left the world of work atomized and virtualized, outsourced
and re-engineered to the point of unsustainable discontinuity.

People will feel as if a magnet has been passed over society's disk drive,
blanking out the social contract, clearing the books of vast unpayable
promises to which people once felt entitled.

The economy or enterprise could reach a trough that may look to be the start of a depression; from this trough the makings of a new social or economic contract and order may arise. This is a low point that neither IBM nor Sainbury's have yet reached and which, over the long term, may prove to be a disadvantage rather than an advantage.

The course of the fourth turning

In the course of every *saeculum*, the awakening gives birth to a variety of individual and collective ideals that are mutually incompatible within the framework of the social or institutional order. For example, the intellectual freedom demanded by the likes of a Benoit Mandelbrot and the organizational discipline demanded by IBM turned out to be incompatible. Perhaps that is also why the free-spirited Apple could not sustain its social and collective momentum. In the unravelling the gap between desires and responsibilities widens, sours and polarizes. Free market based capitalism, for example in America in the sixties, co-existed with a move towards social responsibility.

The prospect of a heroic Bill Gates remaining and being respected as the richest man on earth, while millions around him are on the poverty line, progressively loses its lustre. In the crisis, and if there is to be a new resolution, a new social or economic contract has to reconcile these competing principles on a new and potentially higher level of civilization or enterprise. In the following high, this contract provides the secure platform on which a new social or economic infrastructure can be hoisted. Come the fourth turning, in the white heat of an entity's rebirth, a grand solution may suddenly snap into place – history is seasonal, but its outcomes are not foreordained. The course of our national and corporate destinies, for Strauss and Howe moreover, will depend in large measure on what we do now, as a society, as IBM, and as individuals, to prepare.

CONCLUSION

Preparing for the future: moving with the seasons

We need, Strauss and Howe say, to participate in seasonal activities, by taking advantage of the current turning.

- The diversity and complexity of the 1990s era is thrilling when intelligently explored; at the same time, there is plenty to guard against.
- Diversity is producing new racial enclaves; the gap between rich and poor is daunting; we should address these problems, while realizing the fourth turning will be addressing them more purposefully still.

We need to avoid post-seasonal behaviour, by terminating habits that were appropriate for the prior turning but are not for the current one:

- The belief in public sector liberalism emerged in the last crisis, rose in the high, crested in the awakening, and is falling out of favour in the unravelling.
- Today's unravelling does not require profane media or endless budget deficits, but it does require individualism and institutional decay.

We now return to the origins of the cycles of history, before going on to the future from where, if not IBM, the Navaho Indian left off in the past.

The eternal return

On the earthen floors of their rounded hogans, according to Strauss and Howe, Navajo artists sift coloured sand to depict the four seasons of life and time. Their ancestors have been doing this for centuries. They draw these sand circles in a counterclockwise progression, one quadrant at a time. When they near the end of the fourth season they stop the circle, leaving a small gap. This signifies the moment of death and rebirth, what the Greeks called *ekpyrosis*. According to Navajo custom, this moment can be provided (and the circle closed) only by god. Like most traditional peoples, the Navajo accept not just the circularity of life but also its perpetuity. Each generation knows its ancestors have drawn similar circles of sand.

IBM at this point in time has lost touch with its own primeval origins, lodged in the hidden depths of time. The cycle of history which has underpinned its own high, suppressed awakening, and manifest unravelling will perhaps return to haunt it unless it recovers its sense of locality amidst its rampant globality. Such a locality, in its own case, is lodged in the indigenous American soils from whence Thomas Watson came. For all the changes that have been rung in some eighty years of its existence it needs to find its source of continuity amidst all the change. In the process, moreover, it needs to reawaken from a pragmatic slumber that has blinded it to the cultural revolution that it helped to spark but then lost sight of. It is time for IBM to recover its most knowledgeable own, that is the fractal theory that was invented by its unsung prophet, the mighty Mandelbrot. While there have been plenty of nomads and heroes in the company, the artists and prophets have been buried in the 'Big Blue' undergrowth. If IBM is to rise again from its potentially crisis-ridden ashes, then the meaning of chaos and complexity for its continued unfolding needs to emerge dynamically.

While our IBM participant Liz Machtynger – even together with Graham Sumner and Brian Foss, Gavin Brown and Graham Parry, as well as her precedessors Axel Kock in Germany and Ivan Doppel in Switzerland, John Moon, Catherine Boardman and Doug Morris in Britain – may find this a tall order, there is help along the way. For it may well be that in order to reinvent themselves they may have to recognize the insurance industry, taking the high knowledge management ground that Liz and her colleagues are attempting to capture. Inevitably, though, such knowledge grounds will lack ultra-stable foundations if they are not cyclically lodged within IBM and indeed Native Indian history. Benoit Mandelbrot's exogenous fractals may have as much to contribute here to IBM's prospective crisis-and-resolution as Lew Gerstner's home truths, autopoiesis set within a business ecosystem may have as much to say for IBM's future as automation set with an information age.

Much of the flavour of Strauss and Howe's cycles of history applies to another of our modern, industrially oriented companies, Sainsbury's in the UK. On this occasion, however, I want to move more wholeheartedly over from the fourth turning to the age of business ecosystems. Such an age in fact forms part of the unravelling in which we are currently engaged.

BIBLIOGRAPHY

1   Sobel, M., *Colossus in Transition*, McGraw-Hill, 1992.
2   Carroll, B., *The Unmaking of IBM*, Pitman, 1994.
3   Ibid.
4   Ibid.
5   Ibid.
6   Strauss, W. and Howe, N., *The Fourth Turning: Cycles in History*, Broadway Books 1997.

8 The age of business ecosystems

From Sainsbury's pioneering to its renewal

THE ORGANIZATION

Sainsbury's is a founder member of our MBA programme, having been involved from the start in 1988. The original motivation for joining, when our programme was in its infancy, was to be involved with a practically based programme of management education that was at the leading edge. In those early days food scientist Jane Gilbert, for example, did some pioneering work bringing together groups of suppliers to enhance the quality of the goods they were selling to Sainsbury's. This approach was picked up five years later by Steve Leng, in logistics, when he worked on the supply chain to establish a much more co-operative approach to running the business as an ecosystem. In the process Jane and Steve each developed their individual managerial knowledge and skills and themselves.

More recently though, particularly since the mid-nineties, Sainsbury has become more aware of the need to manage knowledge purposefully, and of the role that a project based MBA can play in that respect. Alan Mackenna was one of the Sainsbury pioneers, entering our programme when we had become more sensitive to the need to manage knowledge collectively rather than merely to develop individuals. He was a financial controller with Homebase when they took over the Texas stores. He observed, during his first MBA teambuilding project set across the Homebase–Texas divide, that the latter were able to run comparatively small retail outlets profitably. He was intent on taking a leaf out of the Texas book, and in his 'extraordinary' second project set up his own learning community, subsequently sponsored by senior management, to further the cause of small stores.

This pursuit of a service oriented cause fuelled the progress of his second and third projects, and Sainsbury's is now poised to move along that particular, multiple store format road. Meanwhile, and alongside him, two of Alan's colleagues were active on other major projects for their MBA. Warren Scarr took over responsibility for launching Sainsbury's loyalty card, and Colin Rye for project-managing the launch of the new bank. Both have turned out, for Sainsbury, to be very successful ventures within a project based context. In fact, Colin has had a book on Change Management published by Kogan Page. Another member of Alan Mackenna's learning set, Kevin Robbins, has responsibility for upgrading structural capital, i.e. the information technology for all Sainsbury's checkouts.

In Kevin's case, this project spilled over from his third mastery one to become what we have termed a post-MBA legacy project. Not to be outdone by their predecessors, and branching out in a new direction, Robert Moffat, originally from retail, and Ian Williamson, from store formats, have been working on a joint second project to advance the cause of what might become a University of Retailing. Learning from the experiences of fellow MBA students at Anglian and at Lloyd's, the Sainsbury duo are trying to combine the best of two worlds. On the one hand they wish to maximize the opportunities for individual learning in Sainsbury stores, while on the other hand they want to develop ways and means of purposefully managing knowledge, especially given Ian's strategic positioning within the store formats arena.

Colin Rye had joined our programme when Sainsbury was Britain's leading supermarket chain. While its pioneering days were historically over, the firm retained its sense of value – good food costs less at Sainsbury's – which gave it a market edge. In fact, under its charismatic chairman during the course of the eighties, the company had expanded extremely rapidly, throughout England and indeed into New England in the US, so that it had reached critical mass. Such an expansion, both geographically and marketwise, had been enabled, at least in part, by the sophisticated information systems that the company had developed. Colin Rye has played his part, as a middle manager, in that development.

By the time Colin had completed our programme, the tide in Sainsbury's had begun to turn. Although the do-it-yourself part of the whole business, Homebase, had recently taken over its much bigger competitor, Texas, the food supermarket part of the business was being eclipsed by its arch rival Tesco. This had come as a great shock to the rather arrogant Sainsbury system. Moreover, the charismatic if somewhat autocratic Sir John had retired, and had been replaced as Chairman by his nephew David Sainsbury. David was a more reflective person than his uncle, a graduate of the Harvard Business School but less of a 'retail is detail' man.

In the mid-nineties, then, Sainsbury was struggling to gain a new authority in the marketplace, one based more on its brand reputation in general, and on its market presence in particular, than on its reputation as a food retailer. It therefore decided to team up with the Bank of Scotland to offer a banking service to its loyal customers, and Colin was chosen as the person to head up the new project. For him this was a step beyond *Managing Change*,[1] in the conventional sense of the term, for this was not only a step change for the company from retailing food to promoting financial services: it also required a whole different attitude to the way it worked. Sainsbury, and consequently Colin, had to learn how to co-evolve with its partner in a way, and on a scale, that it had never done before.

INTRODUCTION

The death of competition

Britain's leading food retailer J. Sainsbury has, on the one hand, emerged from a 'high', in the seventies and eighties, towards something of a 'crisis' in the nineties, without as yet any explicit evidence of its awakening and unravelling. On the other hand the trend from pure competition to a mix of competition, conservation and most recently catalysation has been apparent for some years now. In fact, in 1997, the company's new managing director set up an internal consultancy unit with such 'catalysation' implicitly if not yet explicitly in mind.

What did come out of the blue, though, was the appearance of a book on the mainstream business scene entitled *The Death of Competition*.[2] It was unexpected because its author, James Moore, is a respected American business consultant, not some fringe operator emerging from the California of the sixties. He draws more, in fact, upon conventional Darwinian evolutionary biology than he does on the less established contemporary ideas on co-evolution that we, together with Stacey and Wheatley, have outlined. Yet his orientation is startling. For Moore, the assumption that there are distinct, immutable businesses within which players scramble for supremacy is a tired idea whose time is past. The new business paradigm, for James Moore as for his compatriot Peter Senge,[3] requires thinking in whole systems. Yet Moore takes a quantum leap beyond Senge's learning organization in inviting us to see our business as part of a wider economic ecosystem. Thus we need to understand the economic systems evolving around us, finding ways to contribute.

Starting with our understanding of the big picture rather than specific products and services, business evolution for Moore therefore beomes a more important concept than simply competition or co-operation. In that sense Sainsbury's, for example, would have to undergo a mindshift from one of competing ever more fiercely with Tesco's to co-evolving with the institutions and individuals that it relates to, including competition like Tesco's!

In essence, with the death of competition as a prevailing ethic, organizations are required to seek out potential centres of innovation where, by orchestrating the contributions of a network of players, they bring powerful benefits to bear for customers and producers alike. In the Sainsbury case mentioned above, the co-producer is the Bank of Scotland, while the customers are both its existing clientele and the new ones that it draws into its new banking network.

Through, the coming together of disparate business elements into new economic wholes, new businesses are established, through which new rules of competition and co-operation, and new industries can emerge. Companies moreover evolve capabilities around such innovation, and work co-operatively and competitively to support new products, satisfy customer needs, and incorporate the next round of innovation. To that extent a joint venture, like that between Sainsbury and the Bank of Scotland, is more than a marriage of convenience, or even a means of risk sharing. It is a means of realizing genuine synergies, and progressively more of them, than were apparent when the co-producers stood independently apart. As companies then become more sophisticated in creating new business ecosystems, they become like the guiding hand of a gardener or forester in an ecological environment, instead of following the course of a hunter, herder, or indeed steward. This is a far cry from what a Sainsbury or a Tesco was like before, in the days when they were competing.

The economic community

As hunters and herders evolve into gardeners so they develop, according to Moore, an eco-community supported by a foundation of interacting organizations and individuals. This economic community produces goods and services that are of value to customers, who are themselves members of the ecosystem; member organisms also include suppliers, lead producers and indeed competitors. While the supermarketeers are not yet co-operating with their competitors, in the fields of automobiles, electronics and telecommunications this has now become almost second nature to the Fords and the Mazdas, the INTELs and the Toshibas, the Siemens and the Alcatels. Over time, they co-evolve their capabilities and roles, and tend to align themselves with the directions set by one or more of the companies (see Figure 10).

The function of ecosystem leader, which INTEL plays, for example, in the world of semiconductors, is valued by the community, for it enables members to move towards shared visions so as to align their investments and to find mutually supportive roles. Companies compete to unite disparate contributors to create powerful total solutions, and then to establish thriving business ecosystems dedicated to providing these solutions to customers, as IBM – as we saw in chapter 7 – is doing within its insurance sector. These solutions, moreover, depend not only on the core product or service but on a variety of complementary offers that enhance the customer experience. Ultimately, as Moore affirms, returns from the core business are also invested in leadership and support for the ecosystem itself, for 'alliance community development' activities.

The eco-strategist

According to Moore, the major factor limiting the spread of realized innovation today is not a lack of good ideas, technology or capital. It is rather an inability to command co-operation across broad, diverse communities of players who must become intimate parts of a far-reaching process of co-evolution (see Figure 10).

In the classical paradigm of industry based competition, products and even product leadership have become comparatively easy to dislodge.

Stage of development	Leader's challenge	Co-operative challenge	Competitive challenge
Pioneering	Value	Work with customers and suppliers to define the new value proposition and the means of proving it dramatically	Protect your ideas from others
Expansion	Critical mass	Bring the offer to a large market by working with suppliers and customers	Dominate key segments, tie up customers, suppliers and channels
Authority	Lead co-evolution	Provide a compelling vision for the future that draws in customers/suppliers	Maintain strong bargaining power
Renewal	Continue improving	Work with innovators to introduce new ideas	Maintain high entry barriers

Figure 10 Stages of development

Newcomers simply clone the required technologies, make the requisite invest-ments in technologies and people, and start production. By contrast, the environment-shaping leader of a business ecosystem like a Microsoft or a Benetton, setting the stage for a co-evolving system, is difficult to dislodge (see Figure 11). As such a leading eco-strategist, it:

- finds better ways to embed contributions into the products and processes of adjacent companies, as well as to shape architectural standards and customer preferences;
- ties together stronghold sub-ecosystems and/or uses them to create new positions in adjacent territories;
- finds some aspect of value creation where the niche is becoming impor-tant and no player has made a strong stand.

Comparative strategy

In summary, then, and comparing and contrasting the more conventional with the more ecosystemic approaches to strategy, Moore comes up with

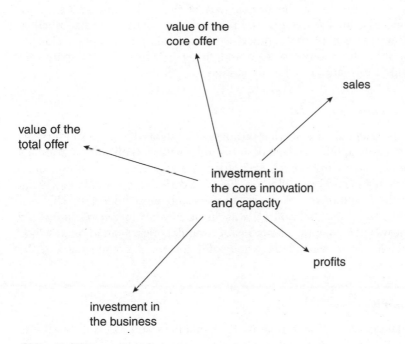

value of the
core offer

sales

value of the
total offer

investment in
the core innovation
and capacity

profits

investment in
the business

Figure 11 The ecosystemic return

the analysis portrayed in Figure 10. The co-evolving system, to the extent that it continues to grow and develop, passes through four stages, which are somewhat analogous to our own. The first of these involves pioneering (colonization), the second one expansion (conservation), the third Moore identifies rather idiosyncratically with 'authority', and the fourth stage with renewal or alternatively with death. Interestingly enough, given his involvement with the 'old paradigm', Darwinian-style evolutionary biology, Moore has not quite caught up with the notion of catalysation though he is familiar with co-creation. He starts with pioneering, which is in our terms colonization.

STAGES OF ECOSYSTEMIC DEVELOPMENT

From pioneering to renewal

1 Pioneering

Entrepreneurs first, then, struggle to form embryonic ecosystems that, while hardly mature, are at least complete enough to fulfil the needs of initial customers. Doing something of dramatic value, compared to what is already available to customers, is the *sine qua non* of the early days of a business ecosystem. The food stores that John and Mary Sainsbury established in London at the turn of the century seemingly offered dramatic value, in terms of value for money, service and hygiene, which the company has endeavoured to retain as it has expanded.

2 Expansion

At a second stage of an emerging business ecosystem, the successful formula is more broadly applied and made more reliable and replicable. Additional waves of customers and other stakeholders are recruited. The overall focus is upon identifying and rounding up the most desirable potential allies available; the best customers, strongest suppliers and most important channels of distribution. While Sainsbury's was in its heyday in the seventies and eighties it was able to apply its successful formula, offering good quality food at affordable prices, across the whole of England, if not throughout the United Kingdom.

3 Authority

To stay successful, a lead company must maintain and fortify its ability to shape the future direction and investments of the ecosystem's key customers and suppliers, thereby maintaining the authority and the uniqueness of its contribution to the community while also encouraging community-wide innovation and co-evolution. In this respect Sainsbury, at least until very recently, has patently failed, which is one of the reasons why it has now been caught up, and even overtaken, by arch rival Tesco. What is important, if the company is to renew its authority, is that it does not regress to its earlier stage of co-ordinated expansion. It needs instead to develop a new approach to co-evolution that, for Sainsbury, encompasses but also extends beyond its alliance with the Bank of Scotland.

In fact it is noticeable that the weight of effort at the moment, as the company attempts to haul itself out of its current crisis, is again in offering renewed value to its customers rather than taking a lead in a process of co-evolution with its customers and suppliers, competitors and collaborators around the world. The banking venture, of course, is the prominent exception to the regressive course it is otherwise taking.

4 Renewal or death

Longevity, for Moore, comes from finding ways of injecting new ideas into the existing ecosystem, thereby establishing a system of symbiotic relationships of lasting value relative to what else is available. Few companies around the world have reached such a stage of development, and Sainsbury's is certainly not yet one of them. In Figure 12 Moore presents, in summary,

EXPANSION

Critical mass

PIONEERING   AUTHORITY
            BUSINESS ECOSYSTEM
Value   Co-evolution

RENEWAL

Continue improving

Figure 12 Sainsbury's business ecosystem

all four stages of ecosystemic development. We now deal with each of these in turn.

Stage 1 – the domain of opportunities

Experimental learning

The challenge for the pioneering innovator, according to James Moore, is to set up a learning cycle, in which the subject is the creation of economic value. Such a cycle should be generated out of the available range of environmental conditions and enabling genetic material facing the business, set within the context of a set of interdependent relationships. This is the challenge now facing Colin Rye, in project managing the joint venture with the Bank of Scotland.

The pioneering goals, then, are primarily to do with learning, that is, learning what value proposition works and discovering how to provide it, through a combination of:

- first intense customer interaction to find out how customers think and to get clues about how they want to use the product;
- second finding sponsor/patron customers committed to helping the core offer evolve fruitfully, as early adopters perceiving the dramatic potential of the innovation at an early stage.

There is a premium, moreover, on inspiration and passion to carry the pioneers though inevitable failures, and on imagination and learning to suggest and implement creative solutions. At the same time, in the core of the offer, as we have intimated, there must be a product or service so valuable to certain customers that they will purchase it even though it is incomplete.

A new ecosystem in fact emerges on the edge of a more established one, or is grafted on to it, or else it comes about through the transformation of some aspect of the existing business. In all cases the community of customers and suppliers must work harmoniously because they are creating something new; moreover, the ability of the network to learn together is crucial. The lead company, in effect, must provide the structure for the alliance, and it must also provide an end-to-end performance overview. At the same time it must make sure that a key portion of the value cannot be replicated by others and is not a likely future target of competitors. Finally, because ecosystems trigger change they inevitably stir up reaction. It is thus crucial for a co-evolutionary strategist like Colin Rye to anticipate and manage these changes so that they are ultimately conducive to the success of the ecosystem.

The ideal stakeholders

The pioneer should first seek out stakeholders, such as suppliers and venture partners, that are what Moore terms real movers and shakers in the broader environment and marketplace. Second, their support must preclude their involvement in competing ecosystems. Third, in their minds, the collaboration should seem central to overall interests. Fourth, amongst themselves, they need to have reasonably complementary rather than competing interests. Finally, they need to have a shared ethic. That brings us on to the expansionary stage 2.

Stage 2 – expansion

The revolution spreads

For an ecosystem to gain distinction, its population and species must expand to the extent that the ecosystem literally teems with life. (This was certainly the case for Sainsbury in the eighties, as it is now for Tesco in the nineties.) Ecological communities mature in at least two ways: first, they expand in biomass, grasslands get denser, trees grow taller, populations of animals multiply. Second, they mature through increased genetic diversity, adding species, elaborating synergistic relationships, becoming ever more artful in turning resources into community life.

The diversity of members in a business ecosystem makes it more robust and resilient, offering greater variety, and a host of creative ideas to help spawn further evolution. Expansion requires a compelling vision of value, and the ability to scale up the ecosystem to provide that value – like Ford cars, McDonald's burgers, INTEL's microchips and Sainsbury's supermarkets. Volume enables companies to anchor huge ecosystems, for scaling and replication require well-designed standard processes. These in turn depend upon well-managed organizations. Expansion, then, is about the race to move from a set of core synergistic relationships to a rich, robust ecosystem.

It is about combining a wide range of value elements, and even aspects of competing ecosystems, into an ecosystem that can capture market territory and defend it against rival ecosystems.

The expanding community

Expansion, for Moore, is fundamentally about getting new partners to join in the economic community. Sainsbury's acquired more customers, more suppliers, and indeed more management consultants. Such expansion of an ecosystem is only secondarily about growing one's firm. Rather, from an ecosystemic perspective that even Sainsbury's in its heyday was probably lacking, and for the lack of which it would later suffer, working with partners provides the wherewithal to grow one's company. Partners rapidly help to fill out and enrich the ecosystem's total package of value. Moreover, having key partners in one's camp may preclude them from assisting other expanding ecosystems, like Tesco's. How fast an ecosystem incorporates new contributions is a function of the openness of the framework. In the best cases the ecosystems become so attractive that organizations ask to join.

The case of IBM

To a large extent, succeeding at leading the growth of a business ecosystem is a matter of shifting the mindset of our leadership from thinking primarily in terms of business entities – companies, people, skills and assets – to seeing business in terms of the frameworks of co-operation and co-evolution within which these entities work together and co-evolve into the future. This requires a cognitive shift from establishing individual companies and helping them to grow to establishing frameworks of co-evolution bringing together the competencies of many firms, from identifying strengths and weaknesses within your own company to looking for creative ways to incorporate resources. Such resources will be resident in companies and industries other than your own.

To Moore, IBM as a whole was a supreme case in point in the seventies and eighties. When the company entered the personal computer business in 1981, it picked up the pieces of another ecosystem that contrasted with its own culture and history of vertical integration. In effect it followed and extended the Apple model of building a community of supporters, taking on partners and opening its computer architecture to outside suppliers. It adopted a microprocessor from INTEL and a software operating system from a then tiny Microsoft, which had purchased MS-DOS from a smaller firm, Seattle Computing, which created a clone of CP/M. IBM then helped Microsoft with management and money, and it provided INTEL with a high-volume micro-processor business. New ecosystems can thus gain a great deal by working with the old. We now turn to stage 3.

Stage 3 – authority

Once its niches become solidified and its species entrenched, a biological ecosystem reaches structural maturity. That is arguably the point that Sainsbury's has recently reached. The amalgamation of the ecosystem has largely taken place and the species have developed a sustainable framework within which to live and co-evolve. The prevailing species have made clear their dominance; the lesser species have accepted the smaller scale that will be their lot, heralding a long period of relative ecological stability. At the same time a new wave of participants begins to thread its way into the mature ecosystem by taking advantage of the fixed structure, and adds vastly to its complexity. When the structure of the ecosystem stabilizes, many new entrants and customers envisage possibilities for themselves and are able to muster power they are eager to test.

Tempted by the promise of joining an ecosystem that is fast expanding and whose potential profits are increasing, they exploit the strategic architecture that another set of firms has built. As fresh participants join the ecosystem, struggles may erupt between the new leadership and the old; companies retreat into their core competencies as new entrants outdo the leaders. The winners in stage 3 are the firms that go beyond rationalizing their own contributions and learn how to influence the structure and evolution of business systems and opportunity environments. The key to becoming a winner and a leader is bargaining power, i.e. becoming absolutely vital to the community as a whole, especially to customers. Today this is clearly the case in the United States for Microsoft in computer software, as it is for INTEL in semiconductors; it is becoming so for Virgin Direct in financial services within the UK, as it has been for Versace in Italy in fashion. We now turn to INTEL.

The case of INTEL

INTEL's systems business and its relationship to the microprocessor business has traditionally been seen in industry, not in ecosystem, terms. In the early nineties the INTEL products group saw the potential for driving new ideas and innovation into the business system in a new way. INTEL used to design circuits. Now, according to Moore, they worry more about the nature of industrial democracy and the design of the interactions among companies, organizations and individuals who shape markets. INTEL's architecture labs are now promoting an open framework for investment, a framework that invites others to bring their innovations to the personal computer platform. The framework is particularly valuable in making a place for smaller, highly creative companies to help co-ordinate the investments of others, rather than make investments themselves. In Moore's terms, as 'chip heads willing to learn', managers starting out with a semiconductor industry orientation became ambassadors to a larger, more diverse community of companies.

Investor relations personnel at INTEL got Wall Street to recognize that the company is not simply a capital intensive producer of a commodity but an important member of the fabric of information industries.

The imperatives of co-evolution

Regardless then, for Moore, of whether stage 3 firms lead or follow, the opportunity environments in which they operate are populated by centres of intense co-evolution. Such enterprises do not necessarily need to be the shapers of the business ecosystem community they join. This is especially the case if they trust and respect its leadership, but they must find a valued contribution to make. Most of all, they need to make a critical and long-lasting contribution to the ecosystem and embed it in the fabric of the community. This brings us to the ultimate stage of either renewal or death.

Stage 4 – renewal or death

Fits and starts

Biological communities, as we have already seen, erupt in fits and starts rather than unfolding in an entirely orderly and incremental fashion. Sainsbury's, for example, appeared to lose its leadership position to Tesco in the UK almost overnight. After protracted periods of stability during which species remain basically the same, sudden bursts of biological change can result in radical transformation or wholesale eclipse of an ecosystem. The collapse of Digital in the early nineties, if not also IBM, has been one of the most noted cases in point.

Biological ecosystems are being transformed constantly, moreover, and in positive ways that enhance capability and/or diversity. The advance of Direct Line and subsequently Virgin Direct in the insurance and financial services markets in Britain are noteworthy cases in point. The means by which this happens include co-evolution among members – in the Virgin Direct case involving Virgin and established insurers Norwich Union – the introduction of new species, and geographically splitting and evolving in parallel. Coping with the threat of obsolescence is the ultimate challenge for a dominant company such as Sainsbury's. In nature, Moore points out, continuous renewal is the order of the day and primary colonization (entrepreneurship in the business case) the rarity. The ability to recognize assets in a dying ecosystem, and re-use them, will be an increasingly vital talent in the twenty-first century.

Bias for action

In stage 4 ecosystems in most cases, Moore asserts, individuals are usually competent and dedicated in their specific contributions. It is the ecosystem as a whole which is underperforming, and not the individual species. Leadership and strategy in the age of business ecosystems must therefore bring several elements together for organizational reform and corporate renewal to have a chance. They must:

• survey the opportunity landscape and understand the current power players and their interests and assets;
• develop valid information about the performance of the whole business ecosystem, and what it means for this ecosystem to succeed. How can this be measured? What factors are required for success? How might these factors be influenced to improve performance?
• organize things to affect the aspects of the business ecosystem that require transformation, taking responsibility for the most important co-evolving factors and actors.

CONCLUSION

James Moore, in heralding the death of competition, has in fact taken off from where his fellow Harvard alumnus Michael Porter left off in his *Competitive Advantage of Nations*.[4] It was Porter, in the early nineties, who alerted us to the importance of what he termed business 'clusters'. For Porter, though, these clusters were still contextualized within the prevailing competitive paradigm which has characterized his particular approach. Moore, on the other hand, has proclaimed that evolution, rather than competition, is the prevailing order of our day. Biology and ecology as underlying disciplines, rather than economics, have captured his imagination, as they have ours. To the extent that a company like Sainsbury's in the UK, or like INTEL in the US, is to evolve, so it needs to assume, at least according to Moore, a co-evolutionary impulse that supplants its former emphasis on competition, conservation and indeed individual customers. The challenge that Colin Rye faces, as he and his colleagues spearhead the company's joint venture into financial services, is to ensure that such an ecosystemic outlook becomes the norm rather than the exception. Britain's former leading supermarketeer has a struggle on its hands which is as much cognitive as it is behavioural.

In other words, leaders and strategists in an age of business ecosystems need to change hearts and minds, from a former emphasis on competition towards a new focus on catalysation, as well as on actions. Sainsbury's, for example, would see their newly formed, so-called internal consultancy unity, in a substantively different light, whereby its protagonists became gardeners rather then herders, co-creators rather conservers, indeed knowledge creators rather than knowledge managers. With such ends in mind there is a need to penetrate even more deeply into the world of ecology, if not also biology and psychology, than James Moore has done. In order to do that Sainbury's may need to discard its modern shackles and enter a more post-modern, knowledge intensive service oriented world.

BIBLIOGRAPHY

1   Rye, C., *Managing Change*, Kogan Page, 1994.
2   Moore, J., *The Death of Competition*, Wiley, 1997.
3   Senge, P., *The Fifth Discipline*, Doubleday, 1992.
4   Porter, M., *The Competitive Advantage of Nations*, Macmillan, 1990.

Part IV

Post-modern

Knowledge intensive services

9 The stories we are

Insuring the poetics of learning

THE ORGANIZATION

Oh to be a mutual, now that the age of finance is here!

What is the future of the private medical insurance industry in Britain, and worldwide? How will it look in ten years' time – after the upheaval of the late 1980s and early 1990s, when large corporate insurers decided to enter a market that was hitherto dominated by Provident Associations – following the election of a new Labour government in 1997? Will this market expand or contract, and what role do mutual societies have in today's global market-place? Will they need to sacrifice their independence and status in order to compete on equal terms with international financial institutions?

These questions have been pondered by many people, but by none more than two individuals who are striving to change the face of the medical insurance industry. Duncan Hopper and Barry Wilding – the one a former coach and the other his graduate student on our MMBA – have both worked in the 'not for profit' medical insurance sector, but have more recently also been responsible for a major commercial insurer's entry into the market. Moreover, not only does Barry have strong views on the future of the industry, but he is intent on leading the way into the brave new world he envisages, having developed his ideas together with Duncan.

In order to develop their view of the new order from Barry's initial ideas, Duncan and he have had to use their immense experience of this market-place, which has traditionally been dominated by Provident Associations. They needed to combine this with an appreciation of the rich history and legacy of the mutuals, and how such organizations have developed and pros-pered over the past two hundred years, alongside strictly commercial companies. At the same time they needed to understand the risks and prob-lems that mutuals now face in today's dynamic and complex market.

Since Victorian times

To appreciate the relative position of mutuals in the insurance market, Barry and Duncan had to consider their history and how and why they had developed alongside commercial companies and charities. Commercial or joint stock companies form the foundation of the world's market-enterprise economy, and work by taking investments from shareholders, using this capital to make profit and distributing it back to shareholders in the form of dividends. Mutuals on the other hand, which flourished in Victorian times, were founded not for profit but for the benefit of their members. Any profit made took the form of a surplus, which goes to make up a reserve, which in turn is used for the overall benefit of their members (who have taken out insurance policies and contracts with the organization) through improved services and facilities. Modern Provident Associations in Britain, however, were largely developed by doctors, concerned about the loss of their private patients around the time of the establishment of the National Health Service. These associations were therefore founded as much to protect the income of doctors in private practice as for any more altruistic reasons. Today over 6 million people in Britain are covered by private medical insurance policies.

Now the consumer is rising . . .

Duncan and Barry understood that the problems, or if you like the opportunities, facing today's companies in medical insurance, stem from a tremendous change in the level of competition for business, and the shift in power that this has provoked. Now the real power, as they see it, rests with the customer. Across the world, barriers such as social class are being broken down and people are becoming more aware of choice. Alongside this shift in power, moreover, is a rise in expectations. It is no longer sufficient to expect the customer to be satisfied with traditional and known needs, as these are continually changing. An acknowledgement of such changes, in the medical insurance field specifically as in knowledge intensive services generally, has become increasingly apparent in the eighties and nineties. It became clear to Barry and Duncan that these new demands had to drive productivity forward in a new way, putting a premium upon information systems, on the one hand, and upon staff involvement, on the other.

. . . and state provision is receding

Another factor that was influencing Duncan is and Barry's thinking, which could have an influence on the advent of a new mutuality, was that state provision in Britain, as in many other countries, is receding. As more and more governments recognize the fact that they are no longer willing or able to fund social benefits, they realize that more and more people will have to develop their own, independent or interdependent, means of supporting their own benefits. Thus, as Duncan and Barry recognized, medical insurance in time will no longer be a luxury purchase. The combination of rising consumer and receding state influence is serving to create new opportunities, and of course more competition.

The need to structure change

At the same time, Barry and Duncan recognized, the insurance industry as a whole within the UK and Europe, within the overall financial services market, was becoming huge. In the UK alone, insurance companies occupy the top six places in the financial services league table. The other four which make up the top ten are all banks, which are now also heavily involved in offering insurance. It was not so long ago, moreover, that banks provided loans, building societies mortgages, and insurance companies insurance, each one exclusive of the others. Specialist companies, such as Providents in the medical insurance field, offered, again exclusively, their niche products. The need for substantial access to capital, while at the same time being fast-moving in responding to changed customer needs, has produced a strange new amalgam of 'big-small is beautiful'. This has led, on the one hand, to an increasing number of mergers, and on the other to demutualization in pursuit of new capital markets. As a result, competition, alongside a new form of co-operation, are both proliferating.

Financial services in the eco-age

Another factor, combined with the increased 'co-opetition', consumer awareness and destablization of traditional business boundaries – which interested Barry in particular – was the emergence of a new breed of 'green' organization. These tended to be commercial enterprises interested in consumer values, of which 'green' ones were an important by-product. The message these companies were giving out was: 'Yes, you must make a profit, but the best way to achieve this is to strike a balance between the needs of customers, stockholders and modern eco-consumer values.' A prime example of this, as is revealed in chapter 13, is Virgin. Virgin Direct, as part of the overall Virgin brand, offers good value for money on the back of integrity and honesty, while substantively involving their staff as well as their customers in the business. If companies like Virgin can provide simple, low cost, mass market products, whilst providing a return for all their stakeholders and acting in a responsible and eco-friendly way, they will not only survive in tomorrow's markets, but thrive.

Entering into the 'jaws' of opportunity

How does this affect health insurance overall, and what did Barry and Duncan see as the implications for them? Provident Associations in Britain are now struggling to compete with their larger commercial rivals. They have little choice but to follow the well-trodden path to demutualization. The larger distributors of financial services, on the other hand, are finding it hard to come to grips with a market where, in the face of proliferating competition, there is so little profit. Why take the risk when you could just as easily buy the service from a dedicated provider – assuming such an animal exists? Which is where the opportunity, identified by Barry and Duncan, exists.

Without the historical baggage of the Providents that they knew so well, and using the lessons learnt from the recent commercial awakening – through Barry's experience at Legal and General – the time was ripe. In fact, back in 1994, Barry had used his second MMBA project to begin to shape his ideas. These then lay fallow while Duncan became involved in setting up a new healthcare division for a major commercial insurer. Once Duncan's appetite had been whetted, though, he was able to broaden the scope of the project substantively – beyond the UK to include Europe – and sound out the prospect with a City contact. The response was warm, but conditional upon the identification of two or three prospective corporate clients. Duncan therefore suggested to Barry that they go together to see the block-buster *Jaws* to get some ideas. Barry then proceeded to use his third MMBA project to take things further. Essentially the opportunity they were now pursuing was that of becoming a manufacturer of healthcare products for third parties. Since completing his MBA Barry, who is continually in touch with Duncan who is now MD with another major insurer, has been positioning himself ever closer to getting his enterprise on the road. He is now installed with a major insurance broker, working out the rhymes and reasons of the new venture, poised for the launch.

INTRODUCTION – STORYING

Self, business and society

Duncan Hopper and Barry Wilding, as we have seen, in recreating themselves are serving to begin to recreate an industry. Up to this point we have concentrated our energies on individual and organizational development, albeit continually taking account of the influence of ecological and cultural diversity on it. We now want to extend the area of creative tension to encompass self and society, starting with William Randall's unique work on *The Stories We Are*, subtitled *The Poetics of Learning*.[1] Randall is a Professor of English Literature at Seneca College in Toronto. His focus therefore is upon storying as a means of developing ourselves as individuals, and in our case we have extended his analysis to incorporate individual managers in the context of whole industries. As we move, then, into this arena of 'reauthorizing' self, organization and society – duly aligned with the notion of 'autopoiesis' – we

NARRATOR

PROTAGONIST   **SELF-CREATION**   READER

RE-AUTHORIZER

Figure 13 Re-authorizing insurance

enter wholeheartedly into post-modernity. Specifically, we shall be illustra-
ting the dynamics of such storying, individually, through the growth and
development of an entrepreneur on our MMBA programme, Barry Wilding,
and industrially through a business developer and colleague of Wilding's,
Managing Director of Pearl Assurance Duncan Hopper. In both cases, the
point of focus will be the insurance industry. For while Barry has been paving
the way for establishing his own health insurance enterprise, Duncan, who
was his coach on our programme, is Managing Director of a major insurer.

Stages of development

Storying for Randall involves four stages, which can be likened to our four
worlds, spread over the course of time. As *protagonists* initially, Barry and
Duncan are basically inside their story, acting and reacting in the present,
unable to see the whole story or even any story. Operating by reflexes, they
do things instinctively on the spur of the moment. To all intents and purposes,
their work and lives therefore are the plot. They are full of anecdotes. In
fact they, like the industry they represent, are as close to raw existence as
one can get. They are hunters, if not also gatherers, colonizing territories.
We call this the preparatory, youthful or primal stage of development.

As *narrators* second, they are more outside their story in psychological and
historical time and space. They thereby have greater control, acting intelligently on their work and lives as premeditated stories. They are thereby
in a position to chart their career and business histories. We call this next
phase the ordinary, adult or rational stage, where herding instincts take over
from hunting ones, and conservation supplants colonization.

Third, as *readers*, they are outside their life-stories and industry-stories even
more, now not controlling them so much as monitoring, recognizing and

intuitively discovering their meaning with hindsight. The tide now turns from anecdotal points and lines of history to a spiralling biography. We call this particular phase the extraordinary, midlife or developmental stage in which the gardener takes precedence over the hunter or herder, and catalysation rather than colonization or conservation rules.

Fourth and finally, as *authorizers*, they imaginatively create their stories, which thereby become their novelty. They are now very much inside the story while at the same time having a strong perspective on the world around them. At this stage their biographies merge with the mythology of the ages, at least in their area. We call this ultimate phase the mastery, mature or metaphysical stage of life. This is a time for co-creation and for stewardship.

Poetry in motion

As protagonist, narrator, reader and re-authorizer, a manager on our programme enters respectively the *p*reparatory, *o*rdinary, *e*xtraordinary and *m*astery grounds of our MBA endeavour, which serve to make up the acronym *poem*. Randall has coined the phrase 'poetics of learning' to describe the progression from protagonist to self-authorization. As such, and as suggested by the etymology, 'autopoiesis' and poetry are, strangely enough, closely aligned. To the extent that Duncan and Barry ultimately become 'masterly', so they will use stories or indeed parables continually to instruct and to provide insight. Moreover, they both are and also will be working within, are constrained by, and contribute to the unfolding stories of particular individuals, organizations and societies.

As motivators and mentors, they are involved in enabling individuals and organizations to create and recreate the stories of their own work and lives through their products. It is here that we, through the MMBA, are involved, indirectly if not directly, in enabling individual companies to become knowledge creating enterprises, whereby the pursuit of self-story and company story, if not also industry story, are intertwined. To entertain a story of how an organization or industry hangs together – past, present and future – is by implication to entertain a theory of how its business comes together within it. Barry and Duncan soak up the plot-lines through their pores, their point of view, their conflicts, their morality, their modes of characterization, their themes, the atmosphere. The more extensive and intensive the need to draw things together, for Randall, i.e. self and world, then the more philosophical, the more scientific, the more innovative.

The novelty of our lives

Should they have the courage to be themselves, the story-world Barry and Duncan create around them differs from everyone else's, in terms of its atmosphere, its openness and its integrity. They live their story, as an embodied novel with its unique vocabulary (fancy rather than plain), plotting (thick rather than thin). The characterization (round rather than flat) is totally distinctive. They carry within them a collection of questions they ask, conflicts they wrestle with, themes to which they continually return. Some people, moreover, typically those who create a new company or industry, are more aware of their collection of questions than others.

Such openness is a function of their compassion, that is the span of their emotional geography and of their childlikeness, that is their ability to live with loose ends. The more complete the story, the more integrated the self, sustaining diversion but maintaining direction. To see the thread running through individual and organizational work and lives, and to honour it, requires a particular discipline. Such a discipline is alert to the role of each event in the working out of the plot of the story as a whole, whatever that plot may be. It is as if each of Duncan's or Barry's life's events could be read as a unique revelation of the movement of a larger, more authoritative reality within which it finds its ultimate source, whatever that reality may be called: the new mutuality, the higher self, or even business mastery. We turn specifically now to what Randall terms 'the poetics of learning'.

THE POETICS OF LEARNING

Autopoiesis

Judaeo-Christian tradition is founded on the conviction that human reality is inherently storied, that all the events of our lives constitute one grand, unfolding plot. In such a context history is somehow purposeful, in that sense 'plotted', so that each event in work and life is novel, and thereby charged actually or potentially with significance. From such a storied perspective, learning is making – making sense, making a life, making ourselves – in that respect it is synonymous with autopoiesis. Learning for Randall, then, in the context of 'the stories we are' is synonymous with self-creation, concerned with how businessmen like Duncan and Barry story and re-story both themselves and their worlds. Such stories are inevitably incomplete. Their lives and careers are still unfolding, mysteries yet unresolved, open books for whose endings they as individuals, like their industry in general, can but wait and see, something 'legendary'.

Towards mastery

Some of us, Randall asserts, are creatures of habit, taking few risks, leaning naturally towards the ways we have behaved in the past, following established patterns to which we have fallen heir. We live unoriginal – or as David Whyte would say 'soulless' – lives, even inauthentic ones, because we are excessively controlled. Others of us, like Duncan Hopper and Barry Wilding, feel the need to walk a road less travelled, even if it means that their lives become more fraught. While people like them approach their work each day as if it were a brand new page or chapter, for other more staid managers it amounts to the same old story, even the same chapter and verse, repeated over and over.

When we speak then of self-creation, or autopoiesis, we raise questions about how Duncan or Barry, or indeed their insurance industry, resolve the tension between the determined and the undetermined dimensions of their existence. In the process both weave their 'soulful' fabric from the warp of the new and the woof of the old. In each case what unfolds is unprecedented and preprogrammed, in relation to what is coming in from the future and from the past. In that context Duncan and Barry develop through themselves what the knowledge creating company or industry – as we shall see in chapter 14 – develops for itself. The proportions in which they blend these elements are among the things that make them unique.

Tension and resolution

Stories represent attempts to tie together the potentials and possibilities implied by beginnings. It is thus the function of endings to bring resolution to problems an individual, organizational, industrial or societal story has raised. Part of the allure of any such story, therefore, and that which the experience of the ending keeps alive, relates to the catharsis that the story provides. The middle is where we encounter the 'agon', the conflict required to move the story along. A story has to have conflict, within or between characters. Such a middle, as we shall see in Anglian Water's case (chapter 15), is the arena of continuous tension between limits and possibilities, dangers and dreams, obstacles and goals, the real and the ideal. In particular it is in the tension – the push and the pull – between the exigencies of the plot and the existence of the characters that we find the central engine of our story. No struggle, no story; no trouble, no tale; no ill, no thrill; no agon, no adventure.

The unfolding plot

As in art generally so in work specifically, according to Randall, people, organizations and whole industries begin at the middle, are thrust into the midst of a particular institutional story, industry story, societal story, world story. Each is suspended in time between a beginning it cannot recall and an end it cannot envisage, constantly having to revise the plot as new events are added to our project. In projecting themselves, as in reading a story, a Duncan or a Barry, an IBM or a Sainsbury, tends to cling to the conviction that they are 'getting somewhere', that the scattered bits of their existence will eventually find their place. Thus a story, their life story, their career story, the industry story, unfolds. The greater the 'energeia' inherent in its beginning moreover, the more pregnant with possibilities the intitial 'germ'.

Narration in fact locates itself in the past in order to allow itself forward movement, as if a story's own future were a vacuum into which it is steadily sucked.

This explains a paradoxical and yet common feature of following any story, be it that of Lloyd's or the Corporation of London, of Ford or of IBM, the sense that how it unfolds is both unexpected and yet, in retrospect, it 'had to be'.

Flat or rounded characters

What work and life are about for Randall – and for organizations and industries – is the continual building of characters out of the incidents of their lives, and the regular testing them by the exigencies of their existence. Flat characters, like an 'organization man' or a 'staid institution' or a 'stagnating industry', are simple, two-dimensional, endowed with very few traits, highly predictable in their behaviour. They are therefore called 'stock' characters, bureaucratic managers, or stagnant sectors of the economy. Their characteristics are steady throughout, their natures fixed, just like a point on the spectrum, like one of Belbin's team roles or of Myers Briggs' types. They are certainly unlike a Barry Wilding or a Duncan Hopper: in Stacey's terms, they are 'ordinary'. However challenging the situations in which the story places them, they undergo little in the way of 'extraordinary' development.

Round personal or institutional characters, on the other hand, are complex, multidimensional, capable of unpredictable behaviour. They develop – dramatically, intellectually, ethically – as the plot unfolds.

FACILITATING RE-STORYING

Co-authoring

Strictly speaking, neither individual nor organization independently author either their work or their lives. Neither do they arbitrarily design the plot from beginning to end. Yet neither do they merely narrate it. Their authority lies rather, which is as much the case for Duncan and Barry individually as it is for the insurance industry generally, somewhere between the two. In fact individuals, organizations and industries, if not also whole societies, co-author or co-create themselves in partnership with authoritative agents: the marketplace or the latest technology, the environment or some moral imperative. Some people and institutions are relatively passive in the matter of self-creation; others more active. Some are less inclined to compose their own life-plot, or vocation, than to adopt one of the packaged ones offered by a family or clan, profession or culture, organization or religion. Others, like Duncan and more particularly Barry, as well as for example the creators of the PC industry, eschew such patterns passionately, doing it their way.

The master story

Re-storying involves a change not merely in an individual or organizational life, but in their master story. When such change happens it is a genuine personal or institutional transformation. The first stage, as we have seen, subject to the individual or industry having undergone the preparatory phase of protagonist, involves *narrating* the story with a new intensity and honesty, thereby conserving its integrity.

A facilitator's, a developer's, or a catalyser's role at this point is primarily that of a listener, affirming the story's novelty. What is the individual, institutional or societal story, they may ask.

The second stage is that of *reading* the story, that is re-viewing and re-cognizing it, including its themes, conflicts, characters, authority, plot-line, genre. What kind of story is it? It can also mean enquiring into the themes and characters of the larger stories, so that the personal leads into the economic and technological, social and cultural. The role of facilitator is to help individuals and organizations, industries and societies, in conjunction with others, expand and deepen their interacting stories, thus releasing the energy bound within them. He or she thereby plays, individually or collectively, the part of an authentic catalyst. Through both narrating and reading, another key question comes – how the story can be 're-genre-ated', or be *re-authored*, or indeed co-created, finding a story big enough to accommodate work and life, industry and society, economy and ecology, as a whole.

Resistance to re-storying

When a person or an industry re-stories, both step out of line, as has often been my own case at the Business School, undermining the authority of the script in which they have previously played their part, and challenging the integrity of their fellow characters and institutions. They now move out of the ordinary into the extraordinary, as Duncan and Barry have been doing, with a possible view to mastery. They in fact overturn whatever apple cart they, and indeed their organizations and industry, have been riding in so far. Their colleagues and co-authors might well not like this. As a creation within a creation, their personal mutiny, their tearing to pieces of the plot of the common larger story – that of both management education and the conventional MBA in my own case – may not be appreciated.

There will consequently be resistance from our selves and from others, both individually and institutionally. We know that we cannot change our stories profoundly overnight. I was at City University for fifteen years before the fundamental re-authorization began. We grow accustomed to the stories we are, we feel cosy inside them. With them we have propped up, in Whyte's terms, a 'work' based image of ourselves that is familiar; thus we, as people and as whole organizations and industries or indeed societies, get in the way of our own 'soulful' re-storying. That is until, in Britain for example, a Tony

Blair comes along and creates, amidst much trial and tribulation, not to mention seventeen years in the old Labour wilderness, a 'New Labour'.

The ultimate art

The more unstoried existence a Duncan Hopper or a Barry Wilding, an insurance industry or a British society, is enabled to transform into new experience, and the more untold experience they are able to express, the more powerfully can self-creation proceed. It is in that light, for example, that Britain's millennium exhibition needs to be seen, as is the case for any society engaged in re-authorizing itself. Moreover, the more artistically coherent and ethically satisfying the story each can live and tell, the more emotionally–socially, intellectually–technologically and practically–commercially fulfilled each may become. The wider our awareness of the stories we are, the more power we have in relation to others, and the more confidently we can critique the larger stories in which our self-telling originates. This is something that, for example, Japan is newly having to come to terms with today. Neither life in general nor work in particular, therefore, are ever purely scientific enterprises; they are always, in their ultimate form according to Randall, aesthetic.

In the end none of us, either individually or collectively, escapes the imperative of making something of our lives as a whole, through our stories, and our world in terms of them. The desire to discern the integrity and connectedness of our inner story over time can be seen as central to our nature, our autobiographical imperative, as people and as cultures, as organizations and as industries, as Barrys or Duncans, or as an entire insurance industry.

CONCLUSION

Storying and knowledge creation

The story of Duncan's or Barry's life and work, then, as is the case for the insurance industry as a whole, can be understood first, according to Randall, as the outside story, the facts of their *existence* that they **combine** together, and conserve. Second, it can be appreciated as the inside story, what they *experience* or **internalize** of the outside story inside themselves, and thereby, as it were, colonize. Third, it can be understood as the inside-out story that each of them *expresses* or **externalizes** to others, with a view to catalysing its development. Fourth and finally, they might perceive it as the outside-in story that they *impress* upon others as they **socialize** with them, with a view to co-creation, individually or institutionally. As we shall see, in chapter 14, this in fact coincides with the unfolding of the knowledge creating company.

A facilitator's, a developer's or a catalyst's – perhaps even an enlightened regulator's – role is to help 'externalize' or catalyse the 'internalized' story, to 'socialize' or co-create an outside one more faithfully, and so 'combine' or conserve more of actual existence into 'internalized' or colonized experience. In fact I increasingly see the functioning of our own MMBA programme, individually and collectively, in that 'storied' light. Moreover, the role is to understand more critically the gaps between that inside story and the stories told inside-out by a Duncan or a Barry, an organization or an industry, and read outside-in by others.

We now turn from the individually oriented west to the institutionally oriented north, and in this case from the Anglo-Saxon world to a central European one. In the process, true to post-modern form, we shall enrich our contact with individual personality set in a developmental context, and with individual culture set within an authentically global one.

BIBLIOGRAPHY

1   Randall, W., *The Stories We Are*, Toronto University Press, 1995.

10 The development spectrum

The Internationales Designcenter

THE ORGANIZATION

When Efthymios (Makis) Warlamis came to Austria from Greece more than thirty years ago, with only a small suitcase in his hand to pursue his architectural studies, he could hardly have foreseen what he and his Austrian wife Heide would create over that period. Starting out in an architect's studio in Vienna in the early eighties, Warlamis teamed up with his wife, who had studied painting, sculpture and pottery. Together with two other colleagues they opened up a pottery workshop in Vienna's first ceramics gallery. The first exhibition in Hamburg was a great success. The Japanese were particularly impressed by the black and white lines.

Although Heide had never been in business before, she took it for granted that she would need to export their products. Many of her ideas emerged from of the necessity of making money. At the same time she and her fellow artists established an artists' collective.

Makis, meanwhile, also a painter, musician and sculptor, besides being an architect, had dedicated himself to the cause of children, with a passionate desire to build Cities for Children, rather than adult wastelands. 'We must in some way give back to the children what we have taken from them.' Makis is currently designing Europe's first children's city. Over the course of the last decade, he has also been putting together an exhibition on the theme of Alexander the Great, first shown in Thessaloniki in 1997, including some 1,000 portraits of Alexander. The exhibition was to be taken on to Egypt, India and China, places where Alexander had lived and fought.

Thirteen years ago the Warlamises couple and their closeknit team decided to move from Vienna to the Waldviertel, 140 miles to the north-west, where they bought a small farm and converted the living space into a manufacturing centre. Living together at close quarters, they anticipated, would promote productivity and creativity. Eight years later this artists' collective took over an old glove factory in Schrems and converted it into a design centre. 'Our design makes use of the physical and cultural resources of a region, and overcomes the gap between art and people, without reducing standards.' In addition to the two Warlamises and their seven partners, twenty people are now employed in the centre today.

The Designcenter, then, shapes ideas by and for people. Makis believes that man is a social animal. Design is a medium of communication and dialogue. Design as metaphor tells a story. Design is also an element of fun in everyday life. It is multifunctional and multicultural because it appeals to a wide range of emotions. From carpet to decorating fabric, from children's furniture to porcelain design, the connection between art and everyday living is manifest. 'The new art has to place the human being at the centre, and it has to be open to other cultures.'

INTRODUCTION

The global businessphere

As we move from the pragmatically oriented Anglo-Saxon world to the rationally and aesthetically refined atmosphere of central Europe, the whole business tone changes. In the process of accommodating it into our paradigm, and as we introduce added conceptual refinements to measure up to our new task, so our four worlds multiply into eight. In effect we enrich the 'four world' polarity through an alternating core and a dual periphery. Having introduced you, moreover, to the 'four worlds' from an ecological perspective, we now want to set the global businessphere in the psychological context of so-called 'spectral theory'. This is an approach to management that we have adapted, over the past fifteen years, from Anglo-Indian Kevin Kingsland's original psychological orientation. In the process we shall be introducing the notion of a 'global' core and periphery, as well as four 'local' poles, all encompassed within the 'global businessphere'.

The 'global' core contains both 'unity-in-variety', which is what melting pot societies like America or Australia have largely achieved, and 'variety-in-unity', which is what Canada, the new European Community and indeed the new South Africa are trying to attain. Whereas a conventional multinational corporation, be it a Ford Motors or an IBM, points in the former direction we, as yet, have no full embodiment of the latter. As we shall be demonstrating, the authentically 'global' enterprise is yet to be born. On the one hand, our supposedly global corporations today lack true variety and, on the other hand, what variety exists has not been truly accommodated.

Though still very small, the Austrian Designcenter that forms the case study for this chapter, and with which we collaborate on our programme, may be more 'global' in its orientation, in the sense described here, than even the mighty IBM. Such an idea centre manufactures, or more usually subcontracts the manufacture of, a diverse range of household products, upon all of which it bestows its own unique design imprint.

Core, polarity and periphery

Such global variety, initially created and subsequently developed at the centre, through creative innovation and harmonic development, needs subsequently to be channelled through 'four poles' that in effect constitute our four worlds. These two sets of polarities, running 'east–west' and 'north–south', provide the basis for deep variations in locality, to complement the globality (setting aside the effects of regionality). The Designcenter's entrepreneurial spirit (western colonization), integration with its environment (eastern catalysation), recycling of resources (northern conservation) and closeknit community (southern co-creation), for example, are four cases in point. While for each there is some combination of regionality, locality and globality, the 'globality' is inevitably tainted by a mixture of regional particularism and American universalism.

Spectrum meets businessphere

These insights into the multifaceted nature of the global businessphere have emerged in one sense over thousands of years, and, in another, over the last twenty years of collaborative endeavour. Such collaboration has taken place between a 'virtual' group of researchers primarily within Africa, Europe and India and secondarily in America, Japan and the Middle East. While one of these, the British psychologist Kevin Kingsland, occupies centre stage in this chapter, two others, Americans Beck and Cowan, are the formative influences in one that follows (see chapter 12). Kingsland, who has drawn upon an ancient Indian source of wisdom, set up a Centre for Human Communication in the English West Country. In the seventies and eighties, some thousands of students joined to participate in, and subsequently form businesses around, so-called 'spectral theory'. The 'spectrum' and the 'businessphere' are in fact two sides of the same coin. For while spectral theory is most strongly oriented towards the individual, the global businessphere is most strongly focused on the enterprise. Both are intimately engaged with the whole society.

A holistic perspective

As managers and as human beings, the Designcenter's founders Makis and Heide Werlamis – ostensibly living and working in a global village – each nevertheless occupies a distinctive world. The one being Greek and the other Austrian, quite apart from their personality differences, each construes their world differently and thereby experiences different realities. It is not possible, therefore, to be truly objective, in management as in life, while remaining anchored within a single culture or language. We therefore have to move around the earth – physically, mentally and emotionally – acquiring new cultural perspectives where the familiar becomes strange. We need to learn to speak with new tongues to discover the constraints of our native language.

As authentically global operators, as indeed the Werlamises have become through their multifaceted designs for living, we need to familiarize ourselves with multiple worlds, culturally and philosophically, psychologically and economically. This has, indeed, been my own reason for being a local management educator and global business consultant, the combination of which is duly orchestrated by an intermediate knowledge creating ecology.

According to Kingsland, our minds hold different models of reality and what is common sense to one group is complete nonsense to another. There is no universally accepted view of human nature, covering what is right and how we can progress. The clash of differing visions, the struggle of competing values, and the failure of people to communicate constitute the essence of the human predicament. An integrated understanding of the whole person, the whole manager, a whole organization or a whole society thus transforms our understanding of the world. Such an integration is dependent, for Kingsland, upon the adoption of a worldview that draws upon an ancient source, the timeless spectrum of light that can be seen just after the sun goes down, and again just before dawn. Between day and night, light and dark, there is a perfect spectrum of deep red at the horizon, gradually changing through orange, yellow, green and blue to indigo and violet at the highest point. Most people are physically aware of these colours from viewing the rainbow, but few civilized people enjoy this perspective between light and dark any more. The Werlamises, with their Designcenter, are doing their fallible best to draw it all together.

It is with that end specifically in mind, moreover, that President Mandela is attempting to turn the new South Africa into a 'rainbow nation'. Such a 'rainbow' individual, organization or society has been able both to differentiate and to integrate their core and periphery together with the two sets of polarities, set within their own context. Within the UK (see Figure 14), these polarities are represented by Wales and England, philosophically if not geographically running east–west, and by Scotland and Ireland, crossing as it were north–south. The core is made up of a combination of Anglo-Saxon, as a source of differentiation, and Celtic, as the force of integration. Finally, the country's southern periphery is made up of the Commonwealth, stretching west–south–east from Canada to Malaysia, while its northern periphery, arching west–north–east from France to Russia is made up of Gorbachev's 'common European home'.

THE GLOBAL BUSINESSPHERE

The central core

The Designcenter

Culture, then, is a persistent and powerful influence. It is difficult, perhaps impractical, for us totally to transcend the culture in which we were raised.

Common European Home

SCOTLAND

CELT

ENGLAND **CELT ANGLO-SAXON CELT** WALES

CELT

IRELAND

British Commonwealth

Figure 14 The United Kingdom in a global context

The way we see the world, our beliefs, assumptions and personal horizons are prescribed in large part by such a cultural inheritance. Makis Werlamis, for example, retains much of his Greekness even though he has now spent the greater part of his life living and working in Austria. Yet few of us, Makis of course being an exception to the rule, know much about the history and development of our culture. Not many Englishmen and women, for example, can readily identify with the fact that they are a mixture of Angle and Saxon, Viking and Norman, if not also Celt. Indeed, many of us have lost touch with our roots, but our roots will not have lost touch with us.

Science, for example, as it is generally understood, is largely a product of 'north-western' culture. However, it is by no means a product of exclusively north-western scientists. People from every cultural background have contributed fundamentally to the development of scientific knowledge, notably for example from the Middle and Far East, so that in this sense it is truly global in its origins. Similarly, while 'management science' has been shaped by this north-western culture, 'business', in the broader sense, is universal. To that extent it is interesting to note that, for instance in German and Japanese, there is no term for management, and indeed no such thing as a homegrown management science, and yet these nationalities 'manage' their businesses pretty well!

Overall, then, from a philosophical perspective, the emergence of the 'west' owes much to the participation of the 'middle east'. For although 'western' or 'northern' science and philosophy is often seen as descending from a Greek heritage, in fact it has done so through the good offices of Islam. It is only with the rise and spread of a Middle Eastern perspective that much of the philosophy, mathematics and science associated with ancient Greece has been

CHANGE AGENT

EXECUTIVE

ENTREPRENEUR   **ENABLER**   ADOPTER
                     INNOVATOR

ANIMATEUR

ADVENTURER

Figure 15 The management spectrum

recovered. This may be one of the reasons why Makis Werlamis is currently building bridges between these two parts of the world by mounting an exhibition on Alexander the Great. When the creative mind of the Greeks reappeared in western Europe, it benefited from knowledge and ideas extending beyond the Greek contribution, as Islam had bridged the gap between India, Africa and Europe. The Designcenter sees itself, via its products, as a contemporary embodiment of such intercultural communication.

Centrifugal and centripetal

Much of our global civilization, then, as Kingsland has indicated, is rooted in two cultures. About 4,000 years ago the primitive Indo-European lived in areas bordering on the Black Sea and Caspian Sea. From there waves of people began to wander south-east to Iran and India, south-west to Greece, Italy and Spain, and westward through central Europe to France and Britain. They also wandered north-west to Scandinavia, and north-east to Russia and Eastern Europe. The culture of the Indo-Europeans was influenced most of all by their belief in many gods.

Sight moreover, as Kingsland has argued, was the most important of their senses, the literature of Indians, Greeks, Persians and Teutons alike being influenced by cosmic visions. Again the Designcenter, through its powerful visual imagination, carries forward that impulse today. Last, the Indo-Europeans had a cyclical view of history, as has been represented by Strauss and Howe in this book.

For the Indo-Europeans there was no beginning and no end. In our global businessphere, residing at the core, the Indo-European culture represents the diffusely 'feminine' centripetal force of unity-in-variety, reflecting what we shall come to refer to as the 'developmental' side of management. In a UK context, as we have seen, it is represented by our more 'feminine' and non-linear Celtish heritage, championed in management by Charles Handy with his *Gods of Management*.[1]

The Semites, on the other hand, originated in the Arabian peninsula. All three western religions – Judaism, Islam and Christianity – share a Semitic background. They were united in their belief in one God. They also had in common a linear interpretation of history. They believed that God intervenes in order to manifest his will in the world, just as he once led Abraham to the Promised Land. Such a linear interpretation is built into the ecological succession that underlies our work, although this work remains connected with the natural cycle already mentioned. The most important of the senses for the Semites is hearing: 'Hear, O Israel.' Religious life is characterized more by extroverted prayer, sermons and the study of the scriptures than by introverted self-communion and meditation. This monotheistic influence, also residing at the core, represents the focused 'masculine' centrifugal force of variety-in-unity, reflecting what we have termed a 'global' intelligence. In the UK it is embodied most particularly in our Protestant, Anglo-Saxon, Christian heritage, championed for example by John Adair, with his action centred leadership, and by John Humble, with his linear-style management by objectives. In our own MMBA context, the project based progression from the 'preparatory' and the 'ordinary' to the 'extraordinary' and ultimately 'mastery' is a case in point.

Unity in variety

Only fifty generations ago, anticipating perhaps our modern transnational corporation, a single Indo-European culture extended from northern India to Eire. From the Tocharians of western China to the Celts of Western Europe the people shared a common root language. The Vedic god of light Mithra, according to Kingsland, was worshipped from Britain to Bharat. In fact the Mithraic doctrine of the soul is intimately linked with Platonic philosophy, whereby the task of man is to liberate his divine part from the shackles of the body. In the same way today, knowledge, rather than physical or financial resources, provides the basis for competitive advantage. Plato, then, espoused a fairly standard version of the dominant Indo-European philosophy of the time.

Philosophy and science, according to Bertrand Russell, were born together at the beginning of the sixth century BC. Thales was not of Greek origin but lived in Asia Minor. He brought with him ideas which were already well developed in Egypt within Africa and Babylon within Asia. This period was an extraordinary one in history when Pythagoras, Isaiah, Zoroaster,

Lao Tsu, Confucius and Buddha each had a fundamental influence. It was also a time when those great world cultures, the Semites and the Indo-Europeans, rubbed shoulders with one another. Whereas the former, as we have seen – Jewish, Islamic and Christian – were monotheistic, the latter believed in a multiplicity of gods. Between these two approaches, there was unity in variety, and variety in unity. In combination, they make up the alternately centrifugal (global and revolutionary) and centripetal (harmonic and evolutionary) core.

The individual polarities

In effect, these two worldviews therefore provide the central 'core', out of which – as we have now seen – subsequently evolved four individual philosophical and cultural systems. Finally these are respectively located within two 'hemispheric' peripheries. Western colonization, to begin with, is embodied in the Designcenter as a business enterprise. Northern conservation is incorporated into the organization as a resourceful system. Eastern catalysation is encompassed within its overall design orientation. Southern co-creation, finally, is embodied within the communal outlook of the institution.

The philosophies of idealism and realism, associated respectively with Plato and Aristotle, have since come to characterize holistic and aesthetic easternness and pragmatic and scientific westernness. Similarly, northern rationalism and southern humanism have been most vividly portrayed through a Teutonic sense of order (the Werlamises' Austrianness), on the one hand, and a Renaissance-style celebration of the human being (the Werlamises' Greekness), on the other. These four worlds, spawned by a creative 'Designcenter' and linked together by an active and interactive periphery, underlie our management spectrum.

West–east

More specifically then, the *pragmatic* mainstem is typically western, most commonly associated with the US and the UK. An action centred approach to learning, a free market approach to economics, and an enterprising approach to 'hunting' for business are all manifestations of this 'local' western mainstem. Therein lies the Werlamises 'colonizing' business acumen. Conversely, the *holistic* mainstem is typically eastern, and is most commonly associated with Japan in Asia, and with Germany in Europe. A reflective approach to learning, a social market approach to economics, and an associative or *kereitsu*-like business orientation are all outcomes of this eastern holism. The Designcenter, as 'gardener' in that eastern respect, serves to catalyse its suppliers and customers, and the societies with which it has become engaged.

North–south

While the west–east polarity is the vitalizing one, associated with enterprise on the one hand, and with consciousness on the other, the north–south one is inherently stabilizing. The *rational* pole, in effect, is typically northern, most commonly associated with Scandinavia on the one hand, and the Benelux countries, northern France, Germany, Austria and Switzerland on the other. A deductive approach to learning, a *dirigiste* or welfarist approach to economics, and an analytical approach to business are all offshoots of this northern focus. The technology based orientation of the Designcenter, furthermore, is a reflection of such rationality. Conversely, the *humanistic* mainstem is typically southern, and is most commonly associated in business terms with Italy, Spain, Portugal and Greece within Europe, and Brazil and the new South Africa outside it. A social orientation towards learning, strongly formed local networks, and a relationship oriented approach contribute to this co-creative southern form of stewardship.

The periphery

Surrounding any business such as the Werlamises, is a physical environment, in their case of granite and limestone, and at the same time a spirit of physical adventure that pervades it. Similarly, and even more particularly today, there is the informational environment that pervades cyberspace.

While the production of information is most prolific in the northern hemisphere, comprising the Triad countries, the mining of physical resources is most common in the southern hemisphere, alongside the proliferation of animal life and nature. We now turn from the global businessphere generally to spectral theory specifically.

SPECTRAL THEORY

The origins of the *chakra* system

While the global businessphere, in conjunction with our knowledge creating ecology, provides the general framework within which this book is set, Kevin Kingsland's spectral theory underpins this particular chapter. The spectral approach, while it can be generally positioned within our businessphere, more specifically originates from the so-called Indian '*chakra*' system. Its founder according to Kingsland, was Gorakhnath, whose aim was to develop a system to enable people to transcend the limits of philosophical argument.

He was originally a Buddhist who lived at a time when Hindu and Buddhist, Zoroastrian and Christian, Confucian and Taoist, Muslim and Jew were vying for philosophical supremacy. More than any great figure to emerge at this time according to Kingsland, Gorakhnath prescribed a holistic approach to life, addressing the full spectrum of human experience and behaviour. Emphasis was placed on the student, or today the manager, carrying out exercises that could lead to direct experience, rather than relying on authoritative sources of knowledge. The school he founded was also a direct challenge to orthodox Hinduism, in that he made its approach accessible to anyone regardless of gender, religion or class. Its members placed great emphasis on the improvement of environmental conditions and on the establishment of a solid economic basis for its activities. Many of its leading exponents, moreover, were accomplished scientists and researchers.

Although Gorakhnath's predecessors in India considered the purpose of their approach as one of transcending material existence, his emphasis was upon embracing the whole of life. While modern philosophy provides arguments about ideas, and classical science provides disciplined exercises for discovering as well as verifying the basis for them, Gorakhnath's approach focused on the development of the philosophical or scientific observer him or herself. Specifically he described our inner constitution in terms of a system of multiple, though interconnected, worlds '*loka*', introducing the notion of the so-called '*chakra*'. Such a *chakra* may be understood as a centre in the human information processing system or, as we shall later see, as a kind of intelligence, a style of management, or a step along the way to turning vision into action. Kingsland attached a colour from the spectrum to each of these seven or eight centres, each of which is made up of different combinations of physical, emotional and mental activity.

The three wise men of psychology

Underlying each of these realms are three basic though interrelated elements called in Hindi *adhyatmika*, *adhibhautic* and *adhidaivka*. More colloquially, we refer to them as 'the three wise men (or women) of psychology'. Eight such differentiations, according to Kingsland, that is different combinations of cognitive, affective and behavioural types, are to be found in management. Some managers are terribly intellectual, others hugely emotional, others markedly visceral. Each flavour of our being, and managing, can be characterized then by a triad indicating the relative emphasis on thinking (cognitive), feeling (affective) or doing (behavioural). Sometimes one component is dominant and is represented by an upper case letter A, B, or C. Sometimes it is recessive and therefore represented by a lower case a, b, or c, yielding eight categories (see Table 7).

In order to be able to communicate with a number of different people, who are themselves functioning at different levels, we need to be able to move around our own managerial personality. The 'other' that we experience, has to be as much part of our own psychological experience as the 'me'. When we as managers interact with other people, therefore, the real interaction is between two aspects of ourselves. To the extent that we successfully interact, therefore, our needs are complementary or 'resonant'. There is ultimately no effective communication at a psychological distance. In the Werlamises' case,

Table 7 The spectral cast of characters

Calibration	Colour	Type	Quality
CAB	Violet	Innovator	Innovative
CAb	Indigo	Enabler	Developmental
CaB	Blue	Executive	Analytical
cAB	Green	Entrepreneur	Enterprising
Cab	Yellow	Change agent	Adaptive
cAb	Orange	Animateur	Sociable
caB	Red	Adventurer	Active
cab	Grey	Adopter	Imitative

Makis is the innovator, while Heide is entrepreneurial but also something of an animateur.

Introquest and extraquest

There are many different ways, as Kingsland indicates, of construing our world, both as a manager and as a human being. We live and work in different worlds of our own making. We need, therefore, to know how and why we value one thing rather than another. If we do not do so we shall not only fail to manage successfully across cultures, within a global context, but will fail to communicate with anyone who is not exactly like us. As scientists and as managers we need continually to explore and discover diversity within our hearts and minds, for it is with them that we try to know, and to manage, the world.

In studying our own nature, as people and as managers, we may turn in two directions. We may look outside or beyond our individuality towards social and economic systems, including business enterprises. This Kingsland terms our 'extraquest', and we refer to as the 'outer businessphere'. Alternatively we may look within, into ourselves, which may be called our 'introquest', or in our terms the 'inner businessphere'. Either quest may be undertaken experientially or experimentally.

While the former is focused on a business or society, the latter is oriented towards our selves as individuals or managers. In that dual context, we might locate the spectrum, as I have now intimated, within the inner-directed (psychological) or outer-directed (commercial) businesspheres.

Psychological types

As far as our 'introquest' is concerned, the best known of all the managerial typologies is the one based on the work of the American psychologist Isobel Myers Briggs who, in turn, drew in the sixties upon the work of Carl Jung. For Jung, there were two ways of looking at the world, sensing or intuiting; two ways of considering things, thinking or feeling; and two ways of apprehending phenomena, perceiving or judging. These six differentiated person-

Table 8 Psychological functions

Function	Attributes
Intuition	CAb
Sensing	caB
Thinking	CaB
Feeling	cAb
Perceiving	Cab
Judging	cAB

ality aspects, or functions, can be linked with the three above-mentioned 'wise men of psychology', that is the cognitive (C), affective (A) and behavioural (B) underpinnings of spectral theory, as indicated in Table 8.

Developmental stages

Apart from Jung's psychological types, the psychological frame of reference most often adopted in management is that of developmental stages. These have most commonly been adapted from the work of the American psycho-analyst Daniel Levinson, who in turn drew on the work of his predecessor, the Danish-American Erik Erikson. While Myers Briggs, then, drew on a Jungian heritage, Levinson via Erikson, who together have also exercised an important influence on our conception of the global businessphere as it unfolds over time, drew on a Freudian one. Erikson proposed, in fact, eight so-called psychosocial stages of development through the course of our lives, which can be spread across the spectrum in the way indicated in Table 9 below. Interestingly enough, the starting point, whereby we either develop an attitude of trust or mistrust, depending on the supportiveness of our upbringing and environment, has recently been identified as the most funda-mental determinant of long-term economic success (see Table 9).

For Francis Fukuyama, the Japanese-American economic historian, the enduring basis for economic development, whether in America, Germany or Japan, is lodged within a civic society founded upon relationships of trust. Contemporary Austria would generally be considered to be such a society. Such reciprocally trusting relationships allied with a sense of control over ourselves and our environment, as has been the case in Austria, provide the socio-political and psychological context for a subsequently economic goal directedness. Such a sense of purpose, thereafter combined with commer-cial and technological, social and psychological competence, provides the preconditions for effective individual, institutional and societal performance.

As such development ensues, a growing intimacy arises between different institutions, both within and across sectors, and the sharing of knowledge supplants the inhibition of such exchange. Ultimately, the concern for the future of our planet, ecologically, and for the well-being of future generations,

Table 9 Developmental spectrum of ages and stages

Colour	Age	Resolution/ Crisis	Optimal outcome
Red	1st year	Trust vs. mistrust	Basic trust and optimism
Orange	2nd year	Autonomy vs. shame	Sense of control over oneself and the environment
Yellow	3rd to 5th year	Initiative vs. guilt	Goal directedness and purpose
Green	6th year/ puberty	Industry vs. inferiority	Sense of competence
Blue	Puberty and adolescence	Identity vs. role confusion	Reintegration of past with present and future
Indigo	Early adulthood	Intimacy vs. isolation	Commitment, sharing, intimacy
Violet	Midlife	Generativity vs. self-absorption	Concern with the world and future generations
Grey	Mature adult	Integrity vs. despair	Perspective, satisfaction, with past, life, wisdom

economically, takes pride of place, to the extent that economic regeneration flows out of spritual renewal, rather than the two being kept segregated.

Spectral psychology

The spectral approach to psychology and to management incorporates the typological and the developmental, but transcends both. The person (and the manager) is located somewhere between the individual and the societal. The mind, like the organization, is multilayered.

We keep ourselves near the edge of chaos in order to maintain a state of optimal health, simultaneously straddling different 'colour bands' or approaches to management. Each type of mind or managerial orientation, whether analytical or innovative, must be developmentally maintained within a range near to the others.

Everything you know about the world, finally, as a human being and as a manager, is a psychological and cultural phenomenon. All observations made in physics and the natural sciences, as in management and the social sciences, are ultimately psychological observations reflecting the organization of your minds, of your institutions and of your cultures. These eight different spectral orientations, in their turn, can be related to the core, polar and peripheral realms of the global businessphere.

CONCLUSION

We have illustrated, up to this point, that a transnationally based manager with a global orientation has to encompass a wide variety of worldviews. We will only be able to do this to the extent that we have located these perspectives within ourselves. Such perspectives, according to Kevin Kingsland, can be subdivided into eight characteristics, each of which carries a particular approach in psychological space and time and thereby to communication. These eight characters and characteristics can be further divided between core and periphery, along with the two sets of polarities. The Designcenter in Austria, by way of a northern example, has a very strong core, given its pan-European orientation, as well as having an especially heavy emphasis on the north–south (Austria–Greece) polarity. That having been said, by virtue of the personalities of Makis and Heide, 'western' entrepreneurship is not in short supply. What is in somewhat shorter supply is an 'eastern' orientation. Halfway towards this orientation is the Middle East.

We therefore turn to Medlabs in Jordan, practically, and to Max Boisot's *Information Space*,[2] theoretically, to cast more light on this eastern matter.

BIBLIOGRAPHY

1   Handy, C., *Gods of Management*, Sovereign, 1978.
2   Boisot, M., *Information Space*, Routledge, 1995.

11 Information space
Medlabs' framework for learning

THE ORGANIZATION

Dr Nabil Nassar was one of the founders of Medlabs in July 1993, through the merger of four leading laboratories in Jordan. Four years later, by 1997, he was contemplating the company's further learning and development within the context of the region as a would-be 'learning society', and our MMBA was to be one of the vehicles for this. For that reason his right hand woman had forged a link, through herself and the company, with our programme. The initial Medlabs merger had come about as a result of many factors, some of them major events. In August 1988 the Jordanian dinar crashed. This happened almost overnight and without prior warning that might have allowed for contingency plans. As a result many business ventures were thwarted, while others, such as the private medical sector, ultimately reaped considerable benefits.

A rescue plan for the economy, adopted by the government and welcomed by the World Bank, required that the public sector shrink, first by reducing the number of its employees and second by transferring many of its services to the private sector. Where the medical sector is concerned, this led to unprecedented growth and upgrading of private hospitals, clinics and ancillary medical services. Centres of medical excellence started to emerge. A landslide in the delivery of private healthcare became imminent.

The beginning of the nineties witnessed another landslide, this time on the political front. Iraq occupied Kuwait. In the wake of the Gulf War, the political and economic constellation had to be reconfigured. Jordan had not only lost a major market because of the UN embargo imposed on Iraq, but was overwhelmed by a flood of refugees and expatriates expelled from Kuwait and other Gulf states.

Dr Nabil Nassar, who established his first medical laboratory in 1980, joined forces with Dr Amid Abdel Noor to establish a second branch in Jordan in 1990. Likewise, Dr Hassib Sahyoun joined up with Dr Jalal Haddadin to open their second Jordanian medical laboratory in the following year. The two groups then, in the light of the above-mentioned economic and political developments, had to decide on their future strategy. The options open to them were either to embark separately on a course of tough competition in the open market or to join forces and create something unprecedented in the Jordanian private medical laboratory sector, a group private practice underpinned by a bureaucratic corporate structure.

What had become obvious to them was that mediocre small operations, run as separate fiefdoms, not only suppressed the advance of laboratory medicine, but, because of their inability to cope with the emerging economic and socio-political challenges, were destined to collapse. The amalgamation of the two groups therefore followed in July 1993. The context out of which this combination of forces had emerged was, first, the rapid development of a medical community, predominantly in the private sector, evolving into a major healthcare provider in Jordan and throughout the Arab world. Second, peace had broken out in the aftermath of the Gulf War, most particularly between the Israelis and the Palestinians, aimed at creating a Middle East free of perpetual belligerency and strife. From the outset, Medlabs established the business concept and social mission that would underpin its efforts: 'To establish diagnostic centers of excellence under total quality management and leading the way, locally and regionally, in the delivery of high standard health care, as well as contributing, through international co-operation, to the advancement of those services.'

To achieve this Medlabs had to overcome at least four formidable obstacles:

1   It had to upgrade the practice and scope of laboratory medicine in Jordan from a rudimentary service into a major diagnostic instrument, which needed to keep pace with the developing, relatively high standards of Jordanian public medicine. Up to that point, medical laboratories had been regarded as the 'underdog' of medicine in that part of the world.

2   It had to define its corporate culture. As a privately owned company, none of Medlab's shareholders had a controlling majority. A compromise 'no boss' solution had therefore to be found. The company therefore had no choice but to go for a consensus based approach, amongst the three if not four previously separate 'fiefdoms', involving balanced participation. This was not easy to achieve, given the different backgrounds of each partner, despite the fact that each had been educated in the 'west'. In fact there were three distinct groups.

   First there was a group of people who were previously employed by the Jordanian Armed Forces, the central 'fieflike' figure here being Dr Haddadin, who was a retired army general. His last commission had been to head up the central department of laboratory medicine at King Hussein Medical City. The military background of this grouping then helped to instil discipline into Medlabs, but at the same time it produced a certain rigidity. Working within the private sector, moreover, was a totally new experience for them. Second, there were the two stakeholders Dr Sahyoun and Dr Nassar, with extensive experience in the free market. Inevitably they became the driving force in the company, seeing it as a continuation of what they had been doing before. Finally, there was a group that previously came from the Ministry of Health and university hospitals. Traditionally, this group looked down on private business, sometimes even to the extent of identifying it with deviousness and with fraud. This public sector group, moreover, tended to have a 'bureaucratic' disregard for subordinate and customer alike. For it management was conceived in terms of rules and regulations, procedures and instructions. Administrative, legal and academic matters surpassed common business sense.

3   Teambuilding and group practice, with a view to building up a new 'Medlabs clan', aligned with open networking in a traditionally closed 'clannish' society, had to be given special attention. Because small-minded clannishness and factionalism could so easily become dominant, failure to mould everyone into an effective team, especially given the geographical dispersion of the group, could have spelled disaster. Fortunately, the ultimate synergy, as opposed to dissipation, of all these forces led to a growth record that attracted not only investment capital but also human resources, thus shifting the balance of power away from the previously separate entities and towards the now corporate one.

4   An image building, and culture forming process had to be instigated, which ran directly counter to the traditionally clannish approaches of most other family based businesses in Jordan. 'Fiefdoms', in Max Boisot's terms, now feeling threatened by the progressive amalgamation of influences, were always ready, especially in the early days, to thwart the progress of the centripetal group practice.

Over the next four years the company structure underwent major successive changes. Based on the 'no boss' ethos, the group organized itself into six scientific and four executive departments. The main partners, in the absence of a central administrative body, took responsibility for all the functions equally. This approach worked well in the early stages but, in the course of the group's expansion, ultimately revealed its organizational weaknesses and inevitable shortcomings. These then had to be addressed.

As the peace process initially served to open up a niche of opportunity, Medlabs identified a future market in the Palestinian territories formerly under Israeli occupation, not least because of the deep affinity that exists between the people of Jordan and Palestine. Although Palestine, both then and now, represented and still represents an area of high investment risk, the board of directors, with little hesitation, decided upon a massive expansion into these Palestinian areas, at the same time as they expanded in Jordan.

It was obvious to them that the maturation and growth of medical services in the Palestinian territories had been arrested by the occupation in 1967, for these services became fully dependent on the Israeli medical services. Moreover, inadequate as these had been, when the occupation forces were withdrawn, a vacuum was created in the delivery of healthcare. A field study subsequently undertaken by a team from Medlabs in 1994 revealed the desperate need of the Palestinians for advanced diagnostic services. The study recommended that Medlabs immediately diversify its activities by introducing radiology and IVF services while also considering the use of telemedical technology at some time in the future. This not only led to a massive expansion of Medlabs but also to its diversification into new fields, which would necessitate the hiring of new expertise. All of this meant that in 1994 the company had to reconsider its structure, following the expansion and diversification strategy, and had to reformulate its vision for the future. To start with, Medlabs also had to cope with complex political difficulties and with volatile security conditions. The across-the-border activities generated their own particular dynamics and demands. In order to lessen the risks involved, a new business entity called Medlabs Holdings International had to be registered as an offshore company in Guernsey, UK. This served to relieve the company of significant pressures, and enabled it to retain impartiality as and when required. Simultaneously a subsidiary management company was also registered offshore. This gave Medlabs the freedom to embark on a wide-ranging number of projects in the region. The holding company, in fact, acquired 99 per cent of the Jordanian and 20 per cent of the Palestinian equity. With the legal status of the company now appropriately defined, focus was shifted, in the latter part of the nineties, to its internal reorganization.

The management subsidiary, still clinging to its 'no boss' approach, subdivided its functions into two equally empowered departments:

- an operations department headed by Dr Nabil Nassar, and
- an executive department headed by Dr Hassib Sahyoun.

At the same time the company retained a certain hierarchy which included its board of directors, chairman, heads of sections, senior personnel and so on. However, the emphasis was on depersonalized functions rather than upon a personally elevating hierarchy, thus retaining the best elements of bureaucracy. While this approach carried with it the need for experimentation from time to time, and thereby some wastage of time and resources, the advantages of such flexibility outweighed the disadvantages, enabling Medlabs to adapt to changing circumstances. Had the company been more rigid in its approach, the challenges it faced would have overwhelmed its capabilities. In the aftermath of Intifada, the cultural and social differences between the varied populations, the rise of fundamentalism on both the Arab and Israeli sides, ethnic intolerance, political tension and insecurity, and economic instabilities would have destroyed the business. In this context, finally, Medlabs is now managing eleven projects in Jordan, as well as seven others in Palestine. The services rendered, moreover, have become highly diversified. In the course of implementing all these projects Medlabs has gained substantial experience in teambuilding, quality assurance, design-technology systems transfer, human resource management and medical consultation at large.

On the basis of this experience the company is expanding into the Gulf, and projects are being considered in the Yemen, Syria, the Lebanon and Egypt. Yara, Dr Nassar's right hand woman, is using our MMBA programme to help determine the best expansion path.

INTRODUCTION

The societal learning cycle

Convergence and divergence

Max Boisot is a quintessential European, yet one who has been very involved in the Euro-Arab Business School based in Granada, Spain. Born in France, and having attended public school in Britain, Max is now a Professor of Management at the Judge Management Institute in Cambridge. Prior to this he spent several years as Director of the EEC sponsored Chinese Business School in Beijing. Max Boisot has devoted his life to developing a concept of economics that is suited to the information age, thereby also building a framework for societal learning. Such a framework transcends the overly simplistic, conventional divide between markets and bureaucracies conceptually, in the same way as the Jordanian based Medlabs transcends it practically.

Eminent European sociologists such as Marx and Durkheim, Boisot points out,[1] have implied that bureaucratic order is what all social evolution ultimately moves towards. On the other hand, Americans such as economic historian Walt Rostow see a market order as the focal point. In effect, by combining the decentralizing power of communications with the rationalizing force of modern technology, Rostow transforms market processes into the solvent of global economic order. Converging cultures, in Boisot's view, whether American or European, Palestinian or Israeli, pay a price for pursuing a common path in their development. For with the resulting loss of cultural variety comes a diminution in their capacity to innovate and evolve.

This is something, as we have seen, that has preoccupied Medlabs in Jordan virtually from the outset of its amalgamated operation.

In the case of Britain, according to Boisot, although market institutions are clearly present, as is the case in the US, the country's cultural centre is arguably much closer to the 'clannish' mode as portrayed in Figure 16. For many institutional procedures, such as the lack of a written constitution, 'establishment' practices, and the famed London Club, proclaim a greater commitment to shared perceptions and values among small groups than to rampant free enterprise.

Similarly Medlabs, having started out as an amalgamation of several medical 'fiefdoms' surrounding each formerly individual practice, has made a concerted attempt to avoid the pitfalls of the undiluted 'clannishness' that is so

CODIFIED

	Market		**Bureaucracy**
	STRUCTURED KNOWLEDGE ARISING FROM IDIOSYNCRATIC CODING		STRUCTURED, TESTED, RECORDED KNOWLEDGE PUBLISHED IN TEXTS
	Proprietary Knowledge		*Public Knowledge*
	4	3	
	1	2	
	Personal Knowledge		*Common-sense Knowledge*
	ARISES FROM FACE-TO-FACE INTERACTIONS IN PRIMARY GROUPS		GRADUALLY ACQUIRED THROUGH PERSONAL LEARNING IN A GIVEN GROUP/CULTURE

UNCODIFIED

Clan   **Fief**

Figure 16 From market to clan

prevalent in the Arab Middle East. While, on the one hand, it operates in a market environment within both Jordan and Palestine, and it recognizes the importance of family clans in both the parts of the Arab world in which it operates, it has attempted to develop a professional – somewhat bureaucratic – culture so as to curb the tendency towards fieflike personality cults.

Centripetal and centrifugal

Centripetal cultures, in Boisot's terms, are those whose institutions are closely bunched together in the 'information space' (see Figure 16), and centrifugal ones are those which are widely dispersed. Centripetalism, for him, expresses a cultural or an ideological bias such as 'clannishness' in the Arab Middle East; conversely, the more centrifugal, the greater is likely to be the part played by configuration rather than by a centre of gravity. The Japanese, for example, have combined some of their own innate tendencies towards 'clans' with elements of markets and bureaucracy. We turn now to each constituent of the information space in turn.

THE INFORMATION SPACE

'Western' markets

Transactional effectiveness, for Boisot, depends on the provision of two items of well-codified, abstract information being available to all members in a given population: quantities and prices. The two core values that underpin market transactions are a belief in individual rationality and in competition as regulating mechanisms. The most fundamental social value underpinning both is the belief that an individual like Dr Sahyoun or Dr Hadaddin must be free to pursue his life's chances as he sees them. Together with this individual orientation towards learning, comes *proprietary knowledge*, owned by someone at some time.

At Medlabs the individual medical practitioners, before they amalgamated their operations, were very much in it for themselves and their families, but more important, for the lasting benefits of their achievements. Knowledge as such was 'proprietary' to one or another, which inhibited the formation of an integrated practice. This is something that Dr Nabil Nassar recognized from the outset as a major business inhibitor, and was determined to overcome such an individualistic tendency in himself and in others. Hunters were a favoured species at the start-up of a business, but such self-centred 'colonizing' was much less appropriate in the phase of consolidation.

'Northern' bureaucracies

Like market transactions, bureaucratic ones depend on the use of well-codified and mostly abstract information such as financial budgets, economic assessments, statistical surveys and medical records. This is evidently the case in a medical laboratory, where such carefully codified information is the *sine qua non* of such an operation.

Not surprisingly, because of the depersonalized and bureaucratic nature of such a laboratory, it has been the 'poor relation' of private medical practice in the Arab world. That is why Medlabs stepped in. From the outset, its orientation was societal as much as individual or indeed professional.

In a pure bureaucracy, though, unlike a marketplace, this abstract information is no longer available to all agents. Rather, it is the authorized possession of a limited number of people like Dr Hadaddin, who thereby stand to gain a legitimate transactional advantage. There is a professional hierarchy, for example, distinguishing doctors from nurses, and an institutional hierarchy ranking medical practitioners above administrators. In the case of the pure bureaucratic transaction, therefore, according to Boisot, we need only to apply two criteria to transactions; competence and accountability. For those who are competent and accountable, in fact, *knowledge becomes public*, and thereby explicitly transferable. This is necessarily the case amongst medical staff in the Amman and West Bank Medlab laboratories.

It provides the basis, not only for the conservation of resources, but also for the expansion of the service along professionally and administratively standardized lines. Managers, become more like herders than hunters.

The competence criterion ensures that only those who know how to use the information they receive do in fact get it, and that those who do not are kept out of the distribution channel. The accountability criterion is required to ensure that the privileged possession of information does not lead to abuse. In a bureaucracy, individuals, whether businessmen or professionals, are no longer free to pursue their own personal objectives – in order to satisfy themselves and their customers – as they are in a market. Objectives are now hierarchically imposed from above, often bypassing the more 'horizontally' based interests of the clientele themselves.

Both markets and bureaucracies, Boisot stresses, are modelled on an equilibrium oriented modern 'Newtonian' view of the world, as opposed to a post-modern 'far-from-equlibrium' one.

Markets and bureaucracies

Defenders of markets believe that an individual like Dr Nassar exercises rationality in the pursuit of his personal goals. Providing that enough of the relevant information is available to all, this atomistic collection of goal-seeking individuals supposedly achieves optimum social outcomes through self-regulation. To that extent each private practitioner, whether in Alabama or Amman, is considered here to have the best interests of his or her patients at heart.

Defenders of bureaucracy, by contrast, challenge this automatic transposition of rationality from the individual to the collective level. They would claim, as Dr Nassar did for example, that private practitioners would tend to be in it more for the money or for their own personal prestige than in the interests of the patients they serve. Conversely, defenders of the market, as recent advocates of privatization have been across the globe, proclaim the virtues of enlightened self-interest, where excesses are curbed by life sustaining competition rather than by the dead hand of 'interfering' authority.

At the same time, however, bureaucracies share with markets a concern for a certain kind of stability. Change in both cases is viewed as an externally generated disturbance of a system wanting to move towards equilibrium. The invisible hand of the market, in the 'western' case, is replaced by the visible hand of an all-knowing administration in the 'northern' one. So, in the Medlabs case, the reputation of the professional administrator is enhanced at the relative expense of the medical practitioner.

While individual freedom in a self-regulating universe remains the dominant value underpinning market transactions, that of subordinating individuals to collective interests becomes the norm in a bureaucratic environment. A belief in the power of orderly and rational planning characterizes the bureaucratic outlook in particular.

'Southern' clans

Things are very different for clans. Small face-to-face groups that operate on the basis of shared but largely uncodified and concrete, that is local, information are identified by Boisot as clans. These proliferate in what we have termed 'southern' climes, including in that respect – to some degree at least – the Arab Middle East. The extensive socialization efforts associated with effective clan governance are specifically geared towards keeping intentions mutually aligned.

Knowledge is personal, and is restricted to an 'in-group' that can be trusted with it. In the Arab world in general, as in the Jordanian context in particular, such alignment tends to be restricted to the immediate family or tribe. In fact, as Dr Nabil Nassar has intimated, the company has deliberately sought to avoid this prevailing Middle Eastern tendency. In such closeknit clans – be they Chinese or Indian, Italian or Mexican – trust turns out to be a required ingredient of all transactions where transactional contingencies cannot be fully specified. Within them, moreover, according to Boisot, learning is a collective process or even a co-creative one; unlike transient market transactions, clan transactions are deeply embedded in, and shaped by, long-term social relationships. Moreover, in the Medlabs case at least, the interests of Palestinain and Jordanian society at least parallel those of the individual founders and their respective families.

While such in-groups are necessarily bound together by feelings of loyalty and mutual obligations, however, they are also sometimes bound by feelings of hostility towards out-groups. Arab–Israeli relations are in fact plagued by such clannish hostility, notwithstanding the political and social initiatives being taken to circumvent it. The same in-group feature characterizes fieflike organizations, although in other respects there are major differences.

Eastern fiefs

Boisot's fourth category, set within his 'information space', is a rather restrictive one when set within the wider context of our 'eastern' worldview. The highly personalized forms of knowledge that characterize his 'fiefs' are most effectively applied when there is little or no codified or abstract information to counterbalance them. *Knowledge* in that context gradually becomes the *common-sense* way of doing things, passed down by, and assimilated from, the all-powerful leader. The wisdom of such 'fieflike' elders, though, is always vulnerable to challenges originating in the growth of structured abstract knowledge visible to all and open to rational criticism. As such abstract knowledge is all-important within a medical laboratory, the fieflike regime which began to emerge in Medlabs' early days had to be purposely broken down.

In other words, it became apparent to practitioners like Nabil Nassar that the reach of such personal power was limited unless it could be amplified by complementary transactional structures operating at a more codified and abstract level. He was thus beginning to operate as a 'gardener' and as a catalyst, serving to bring about a regime change towards a depersonalized bureaucracy. His role in that respect was what may be termed an 'enlightened fief' rather than a progressive bureaucrat or even open-minded entrepreneur.

Under suitable circumstances such personalized knowledge and commitment, in spite of its inherent lack of diffusability when compared to a rule-book, can be selectively imparted to others, albeit slowly and usually interpersonally, as Dr Nassar is currently doing with his closest assistant Yara. The most crucial of these fieflike conditions is a social acceptance of the exercise of personal power by those deemed to possess certain gifts. Doctors in private practice, like power-wielding politicians and entrepreneurs, are often deemed to possess such abilities.

However, fiefs, dependent as they are on the judicious use of individual personal power, often perish with it and thus constitute the least stable of our transactional categories. In fact this is one of the reasons for instability in the Middle East region, as it is in countries ranging from Russia to the Congo today. This cast of four characters, moreover, for Boisot as for us, together with the kind of knowledge they hold, varies as an organization such as Medlabs or Sainsbury's grows and develops over time.

Growth of the firm

Many high-technology firms in the 'west', founded by tough, single-minded entrepreneurs, have an internal culture that for Boisot could be characterized as fieflike. IBM's Thomas Watson and more recently Apple's Steve Jobs are two American examples. In the 'south' this is even more often the case, although such a 'fiefdom' may also incorporate a family based clan. The charismatic and personal power of a founder or founding team pervades the firm in the early years while it is trying to get itself established. Employee loyalty to the firm is intense. These are the pioneering years, in Jim Moore's terms, or the colonizing 'hunting' period in our own.

With the growth of the firm, however, and a subsequent increase in the number of its employees, the founder's charismatic power has to be channelled down through the organization. This is something, as we have indicated, of which Dr Nassar became all too aware, as Medlabs became a consolidated organization. Suddenly, a bureaucratic transactional style is vying with a fief one, as was the case for Medlabs soon after it was established.

In the process, in Boisot's view, the firm shifts from being a purely centripetal culture based on fiefs – this is the way we do things around here – to being more of a centrifugal one. While some of the transactions originate at the top, others – perhaps the majority – are assigned to bureaucratic processes. This is the conservative phase of development, when the herding instinct replaces hunting, and guided expansion ensues. With continued growth, still further structural differentiations take place. In a centrifugal culture, ultimately, a diversity of transactional styles are allowed to co-exist in different parts of the firm and at different levels. Medlabs still has elements of fieflike attributes, combined with bureaucratic procedures, fast-paced market responsiveness, and clanlike loyalty to the Palestinian cause. What is the implication of all this for management in the information age, in Amman or Alabama, Jericho or Johannesburg?

TOWARDS A NEW ECONOMIC PARADIGM

From matter to information

As organizations develop, in the context of our information age, information resources in an ever increasing number of circumstances according to Boisot – Medlabs being a case in point – can be substituted for physical ones. Whatever substitution occurs, moreover, is the fruit of a learning process.

Orthodox economics, Boisot says, cannot convincingly handle such learning since it takes the information environment of economic agents as being a given. It is this 'given'ness, on the one hand, that allows market institutions to be cast in such a favourable light. The information perspective that Boisot has adopted, on the other hand, leads to a need to broaden the economic agenda. Such an agenda needs to accommodate non-market institutional forms as complements rather than as alternatives to markets. What is the real difference, for Boisot, between physically oriented and information based economies?

Creative destruction

The social learning cycle that Boisot cites, composed of not only personal and proprietary knowledge but also public and common-sense knowledge, is a 'creative destroyer'. In other words, in order to accommodate new knowledge it often dislodges existing cognitive investments (mental maps). In so doing it often erodes or weakens the institutional structures that house them. Markets and bureaucracies deal with well-codified and abstract data, differing only with respect to its diffusion. Markets favour information sharing, while bureaucracies do not. Fiefs and clans, on the other hand, work with uncodified and concrete, contextual data (see Figure 16), with fiefs exhibiting a centralizing bias that is much weaker in clans. All social systems of any size, ultimately, will require a mix of these institutional types. Medlabs instinctively seems to have come to that conclusion even if much of the economic and social context in which it operates militates against it.

By making well-codified abstract information a prerequisite for efficient economic transactions, neo-classical economics, typically within the Anglo-Saxon world, confines society exclusively to the market region. It thereby relegates the study of other regions of economic conduct to sociologists or anthropologists.

The efficiency of bureaucracies, fiefs or clans is defined as suboptimal. Thus the kind of bureaucratic government intervention that is commonplace in Korea or Singapore, or the sort of clannishness evident within a Japanese *kereitsu* are ruled out of 'western' court.

'N' and 'S' learning

The belief that development, whether short term or long term, is about ever more codification, abstraction and diffusion of information is labelled by Boisot the 'N' learning hypothesis. Such an 'information space', for him, is a transactional black hole that absorbs all other forms of exchange, and that characterizes, for example, the London or New York stock exchanges. Development in an 'S' learning regime, by way of contrast, requires a continuing evolution and renewal of most existing structures rather than their elimination.

The neo-classical orthodoxy of an exclusively free market regime, by equating capitalism with markets – a single staging post along the social learning cycle – ignores its evolutionary character. For the renowned French historian Fernand Braudel, capitalism is an ancient, multifaceted phenomenon that co-existed with various modes of production, sometimes working in harmony with them and sometimes not. Economic or indeed business models that focus on one economic form to the exclusion of others perform a premature selection on a necessary institutional variety that is never given the opportunity to emerge.

Neither bureaucracies nor markets, in fact, can deal adequately with continuous change. They reduce rather than absorb uncertainty by trying to convert it into calculable, that is codifiable risk. Clans and fiefs confront uncertainty on its own terms, absorbing it through relationships that promote trust and commitment rather than adherence to rules.

Through our own experience in dealings between the City University in Britain and our consultancy based partners in Cairo, this clash between market and bureaucracy on the one hand, and fief and clan on the other has been rife. While revenues, standards and the letter of the law have dominated in the former case, relationships, credentials and the spirit of agreement have prevailed in the latter. Needless to say, as the programme designers and relationship managers, we have been perched in between.

Correcting for this overinvestment in 'the one best way' calls on firms to expand their overall transactional capacities through the internal development of Boisot's centrifugal culture. Within such a context personal and impersonal forms of exchange can mutually invigorate each other. While individual fiefdoms played their significant part in getting the medical practices that preceded the formation of an amalgamated Medlabs off the ground, the clannish nature of family based Arab society, forming much of the client base, could hardly be bypassed. Similarly, the bureaucracy that forms a necessary part of a laboratory operation is of the essence, as is the fact that private healthcare takes place within a market based environment.

CONCLUSION

Ideological and evolutionary order

The prevailing economic paradigm has been fathered, according to Boisot, by two distinct economic orders. One is based on markets, that is, the free enterprise economy, as for example in our case Israel and the United States. The other has been based on hierarchy, the command economy, as, say, in Syria and the former Soviet Union. In spite of important differences between them, they share like siblings certain characteristics. The first is that each in its own way takes information, production and exchange as a given. Information is well codified and readily available where it should be. It resides in economic agents in the market economy, and in the head of a single central co-ordinator in the command economy.

The second characteristic shared by the two economic orders is Boisot's version of centripetalism, that is, 'the one best way', supported hitherto by Thatcherism-Reaganism on the one hand and Marxism-Leninism on the other.

A more penetrating examination of the information phenomenon, of the contingent nature of transactions that feed upon it, and of the evolutionary nature of the knowledge it gives rise to, yields a much more centrifugal concept of the economic order. Such an order is indeed co-extensive with a culture taken as a totality. It is inclusive of its economic and techno-logical, social and cultural activities. The real contest, therefore, for Boisot, is not between the ideology of markets and that of hierarchies as alternative ordering principles for economic action. Rather, the contrast is between a centripetal and a centrifugal cultural and hence economic order, between an ideological and what Boisot terms an evolutionary paradigm. Where Medlabs has scored over many other Arab based companies is in its centrifugal, as opposed to centripetal, nature and scope.

The two Middle Easts

The sadness of the Middle Eastern conflict, as it stands today, is that it is not only politically and socially so profoundly disruptive, but that it is also culturally and economically so. For, on the one hand and for all its sub-regional differences, the Arab world has a strong 'clannish' and 'fieflike' character. In other words, strong family and tribal bonds are combined with powerfully individual personalities. On the other hand, within an Israeli context, notwithstanding the strong clannish element (fiefdoms are not so much in evidence), 'market' and 'bureaucratic' cultures are more prevalent.

While Jews around the world are well known for their entrepreneurial tendencies, set within the context of the marketplace, they are also technocratically inclined and therefore often supporters of bureaucracy. To the extent, then, that the two worlds of Arab and Jew are kept apart, so two actually centripetal regimes – in Boisot's terms – replace one potentially centrifugal one. In fact it is to Medlabs' credit that it has managed to cross such a north-western/south-eastern divide. It is no accident, in fact, that its founders are not only quintessentially Arab, or indeed Palestinian or Jordanian, but that they have also spent long periods in the west and the north. We now turn, finally in this section on post-modern, knowledge intensive services spread around the globe, to the south. In fact we draw upon an approach to community policing that was developed by New Zealand's Maoris, and duly applied in England's Thames Valley. The theory we shall draw upon here is Don Beck's *Spiral Dynamics*.

BIBLIOGRAPHY

1   Boisot, M., *Information Space*, Routledge, 1995.

12 Spiral dynamics

Relational justice at Thames Valley

THE ORGANIZATION

Background to restorative justice

On 1 April 1998, Thames Valley Police in Britain launched a new force-wide initiative based upon restorative justice: any offenders who are eligible for caution (as opposed to court prosecution) will have to come to terms with the impact their behaviour has on their victim and any other relevant parties. This meeting will end with an offer of reparation which may be an apology or a specified action as a means of symbolically repairing the harm done. Restorative justice, adapted from the traditional Maori practice of relational justice in New Zealand, represents a major departure in a traditional British police force's crime strategy. In fact, in October 1997, Home Secretary Jack Straw had attended such an offender–victim 'conference', and, impressed by what he saw, declared to the House of Commons within a few weeks that restorative justice should be written into the Crime and Disorder Bill, making it incumbent on all British police forces to adopt it as common practice.

Restorative justice empowers communities in a process which the formal system normally precludes. Offenders are induced to feel a real sense of shame for what they did. As a result an authentic desire tends to emerge to restore the bonds of community and reintegrate the offender into relationships of mutual support. Victims – as Boyd Rodger, our MMBA from Thames Valley who has had a lot of experience with restorative justice affirms – are part of this form of justice, which as a consequence can help heal a lingering sense of dislocation and fear. Such justice, as Boyd has intimated, is normal to the Maoris. Their traditional sense of community considers everyone to be harmed when a crime is committed.

A crime is not regarded as an offence against the state, therefore the whole community is involved in understanding what happened and agreeing appropriate reparation. Importantly, in the context of restoring meaningful relationships, the offender experiences shame. This may appear to be a world apart from the Home Counties of Thames Valley, but there is an awareness that, when much political debate on crime centres on locking people in prisons, restorative justice presents a more viable human alternative.

From Wagga Wagga to Kidlington

The restorative justice journey from the Maoris to the Thames Valley, has not been a direct one. It came via Wagga Wagga in New South Wales, Australia. In 1990 a local police officer, Senior Sergeant Terry O'Connell, piloted the Maori approach in his own town. Early success in directing young people away from a life of crime convinced Terry that powerful dynamics were at play in restorative conferences. To understand what the Maoris knew tacitly, he worked with leading academic thinkers in the field. Together they developed an explicit model of restorative justice. This played a major role when Terry visited Thames Valley Police in 1994. A pilot scheme was run in the region, and from that point on an organizational momentum developed, which ultimately led to full-scale adoption, as we can see from the Thames Valley 1998 policy statement below.

Introducing restorative justice to Thames Valley

We wish to introduce restorative justice into our working practice because we believe it to be vital to help us, in partnership with our partners and communities, to reduce crime, disorder and fear. This new approach is being developed through the Restorative Justice Consultancy, located at our police headquarters. The overall orientation, moreover, is underpinned by six sets of fundamental principles, involving:

A *balanced approach* – involving victim and offender, their respective families, and the community at large; empowering victims as active participants, leading to mutual agreement through dialogue; seeking to make the victims accountable for the effect of their actions on the community, as well as being in a position to repair the harm; altogether thereby creating safer communities.

A *holistic approach* – working in partnership with other agencies, thereby leading to greater mutual understanding amongst the different parties involved, and of their research and practices; adopting an overall problem solving strategy, of which restorative justice is a part, including extensive consultation internally and externally.

A *positive approach* – all parties involved being restored by the process; using integrative shaming rather than stigmatizing; and requiring professionals to facilitate, not prescribe solutions.

A *tailored approach* – focused upon meeting individual needs, considering all relevant information about each party; seeking a response in proportion to the crime committed; making due use of the pivotal role of conference facilitators.

An *accountable approach* – ensuring the approach is accountable to the public and criminal justice system; making sure the professionals are accountable; safeguarding the interest of all involved in the process.

Finally, a *structured approach* – requiring consistent criteria for staff and training, thereby providing training appropriate to role not rank; providing a consistent system of mentoring; as well as supplying awareness training on how all of this impacts upon organizational culture.

INTRODUCTION

Meme systems

Unlike the indigenous Maoris, with their strongly interpersonal orientation, Max Boisot, as we have already indicated, is the quintessential European, lodged as strongly within his logical-mathematical world as Anglo-Saxon William Randall is steeped in literary and verbal intelligence. Don Beck and Chris Cowan, based at the Centre for the Study of Values in Texas and very much Americans, have played an important part in the development of the new South Africa, covering in their case multiple 'memes' or intelligences. In the process, for the past fifteen years, Don Beck has worked with politicians and businessmen to bring 'spiral dynamics' into that unique part of the world. In fact Beck's first South African book *The Crucible*[1] preceded his subsequent global exposition on *Spiral Dynamics*.[2] For this reason, apart from the fact that Beck himself mentored the coach of the South African world cup rugby team in 1995, we have chosen both 'southern' Africa and also the Maori 'south' – via Britain's Thames Valley – to contextualize Beck and Cowan's work.

Their work draws heavily on the idea of individual and organizational 'memes', or what Harvard educationalist Howard Gardner might have termed 'intelligences',[3] and President Mandela alludes to in the context of his 'rainbow nation'. In all these respects, as was the case for the management spectrum, a richer picture is drawn than previously in this book.

A 'meme', for Beck and Cox who have drawn in turn on evolutionary biologist Richard Dawkins,[4] represents first a core intelligence that forms systems and impacts on human behaviour. Second, it impacts upon all life choices. Third, each meme can manifest itself in both healthy and unhealthy form. Fourth, such a meme is a discrete structure of thinking. Fifth and finally, it can brighten and dim as conditions change. As we can see, then, memes have something in common with the spectrum of intelligences, though Beck and Cowan have done more than Kingsland, in chapter 10, to locate them within a dynamic organizational context.

EXPLOITATION – SURVIVAL

AUTHORITATIVE

	FLEXFLOW	
ACHIEVEMENT		CONSENSUAL
ORIENTED	**GLOBALITY**	ORIENTED

TRIBAL

SURVIVAL – EXPLOITATION

Figure 17 From globality to survival

The core memes

Beck and Cowan divide the eight memes they have identified into two tiers. We call the first tier 'core' memes. They are respectively termed 'yellow' – flexflow, and 'turquoise' – global in their nature and scope.

Flexflow

The 'yellow' meme (a blend of spectral 'yellow' and 'indigo') focuses on competence and functionality, within the context of flexible and open systems. Its worldview is information-rich, and multidimensional, part of a complex interactive system. Thinking is therefore systemic, seeing the world in terms of loosely-bonded parts in constant change, and seeking to understand the flowing processes of being and becoming. Specifically this is the world of a Microsoft, and generally that of a 'high-tech' environment. From a positive perspective, this meme is integrative, evolutionary and accommodating of 'the big picture'; negatively speaking it is unfeeling and distant, and intolerant of incompetence.

Globality

The great questions raised in 'yellow' are answered in this new global order of 'turquoise' (directly equivalent to spectral 'violet') being. Self now becomes part of a larger, conscious whole, both as individual and as organization.

Networking on a global basis now becomes routine as the expanded use of mind, tools and competencies becomes a global reality, focusing on all entities as integrated systems. Positively this meme is conscious of energy fields and holographic connections in all walks of work and life; negatively, there is an arrogance and heavy-handed urge to impose a new orderliness on the world. In fact such globality was anticipated in the 1920s by the South African statesman and philosopher Jan Smuts:

> The apparent retreat to the individual level is merely for the purpose of a greater advance towards wholeness. The new, deeper Self becomes the centre for a fresh ordering and harmony of the Universal. For the Self only comes to realisation and consciousness of itself, not alone and in individual isolation and separateness, but in society, among other selves with whom it interacts in social intercourse. The individual Self is not singular, springing from one root so to say. It combines an infinity of elements growing out of the individual endowment and experience on the one hand, and the social tradition and experience on the other. All of these elements are fused and metabolised into a holistic unity which becomes a unique centre in the universe.[5]

Polar and peripheral memes

We now turn from the first tier to the second tier memes which we, analogously to the spectral intelligences located within the global businessphere, identify as respectively 'polar' (purple and blue, orange and green) and 'peripheral' (beige and red). We start at the periphery.

The peripheral beige meme (uncodified in the spectrum) is structured in loose bands and underpinned by *survival* processes. The polar ('southern') purple meme (approximating to spectral orange) is structured in *tribal* groups and is underpinned by circular processes. These two memes, together, represent much of indigenous Africa, and indeed indigenous New Zealand, as they reflect the orientations of indigenous people around the world. The peripheral red meme (also spectral red) is structured in empires and underpinned by *exploitative*, power seeking attitudes and behaviours. The polar blue ('northern') meme is structured in pyramidal form (directly analogous to spectral blue) and underpinned by *authoritative*, controlling or even authoritarian processes. Conventional police forces, with their strong status orientation and sometimes fear inducing connotations, can fall within these realms. The countervailing orange ('southern') meme is structured in delegative forms, underpinned by *achievement oriented*, strategic processes (exactly equivalent to spectral green). The world of private security forms, and of technology intensive medicine security systems, often fall within this 'orange' meme. In fact the historical divide, in the old South Africa, between the 'First World' and 'Third World' was marked out by the stark division between such high-level 'orange' urban or suburban practice and its low-level rural counterpart.

Finally the polar green ('eastern') meme is structured in egalitarian fashion, underpinned by processes that are both experiential and *consensual* (a mix of spectral indigo, yellow and orange). Such approaches were few and far between in the apartheid days, but are becoming the hallmark of the

Mandela-inspired new South Africa, at least in principle if not yet always in practice. Now we turn from structure to dynamics, with which this book is most particularly concerned.

SPIRAL DYNAMICS

The dynamics of change

OAC

According to Beck and Cowan, people vary in terms of their change potential along an open–arrested–closed (OAC) continuum. If you can discern a person's OAC state on a topic, you know the possibilities for meme change, the amount of energy it will require, and the stress that will result. In an open system it is possible to entertain thinking from new memes on-the-rise and access previous systems when appropriate.

Closed state thinkers, on the other hand, often exhibit a core meme at its peak, shutting the door to the rest of the spiral. As a result, one form of practice, or indeed one centripetal position in Max Boisot's information space, predominates over all others. Beck and Cowan then move on from 'readiness to change' to cumulative 'change states', citing five such stages, which are pertinent to both the new South Africa and also to restorative justice at Thames Valley.

Alpha

In phase 1 to begin with – alpha – memes are healthily *homeostatic*, in equilibrium with surrounding life conditions. This phase can be likened to Strauss and Howe's 'high' (see chapter 8). Within the context of the oppressive apartheid regime, the 'orange' economic orientation for the privileged few went unchallenged. In the Thames Valley case, Boyd Rodger identifies such an *alpha* state with *the prevailing police ethos*, whereby offenders are identified, arrested and then processed through the criminal justice system. They either reform their behaviour or are eventually imprisoned. The police are an independent, isolated professional organization dealing with crime.

The public are not expected to get involved, and the citizen's duty does not extend beyond dialling 999 when the crime is committed. This traditional model was cherished for years at Thames Valley, if not also in times gone by, at Surrey Police.

Beta

In phase 2 – beta – doubt is *aroused* (an 'awakening' for Strauss and Howe) in that a person/company/society enters a new phase of his/her/its life.

It was in this way that the old South African regime gradually came to be eroded. As we leave alpha for beta, we try 'more of the same', refocusing our efforts with a view to working harder and more smartly. Arguably this was the case when the Nationalist regime, in the fifties, replaced the more moderate United Party in South Africa. When Malan and then Verwoerd took over from Smuts, that accelerated movement into deeper beta, in this instance into fully fledged apartheid. In more recent times conversely, for example in South Africa during the eighties, we saw how 'orange' economic achievements began to lose their lustre, and cosmetic reforms were introduced by business, trying once again to work harder and more smartly.

When we turn from South Africa to Britain, throughout the 1980s and 1990s, Thames Valley experienced the national trend of significant rises in recorded crime. Central government and the Audit Commission directed the police service to manage with existing resources, exhorting them to 'try harder'. During this period, *doubting the established model*, Thames introduced many variations on the establishment theme: organizational reforms including total quality, restructuring and teamwork initiatives 'to reduce crime, disorder and fear through being the leading, caring professional public service'. The emphasis at this beta stage was on the professional police service.

Gamma

As we move from turbulent phase 2 into *chaotic* phase 3, which Beck and Gowan term 'gamma', and Strauss and Howe term an 'unravelling', the accessible meme system itself becomes the barrier. The person or company or society knows too much for his, her or its good. In that respect, by way of example, 'blue' separate development goes on a self-righteous crusade, or liberally minded 'green' becomes holier-than-thou.

Thames Valley at this point, according to Rodger, introduced *new thinking*. The Chief Constable, Charles Pollard, together with his senior colleagues, decided that his force needed to deal with the underlying patterns, rather than with isolated events, and thus adopted a problem solving ('northern/rational') approach. Such an approach served to recognize that the police could not achieve the desired results alone, and needed to work in partnership with other agencies. However, and at the same time, the Chief Constable was becoming uncomfortable with the traditional, adversarial system of criminal justice.

Delta

Phase 4 heralds the delta *surge* – a fourth turning 'crisis' – a period of excitement and rapid change where the barriers are overcome and previous restraints drop away. In the macro context this is what happened once F.W. De Klerk began to loosen the apartheid reins. This surge, however, is full of dangers, as we saw during that fraught period when the prospective regime change, in the late eighties, began to become a serious reality. The danger that is run is that people break free of one autocrat to become another's captive. Fortunately, this has not been the case in South Africa but it has unfortunately been rife in other parts of Africa.

The delta phase for Thames Valley represented a *new beginning*. The Chief Constable attended a conference in 1994 where he met Terry O'Connell. He circulated relevant information around Thames Valley and two of his senior colleagues immediately responded positively. It was at this stage that Boyd Rodger, who was then serving as Equal Opportunity Officer, was brought in.

New alpha

The new alpha, for Beck and Cowan in phase 5, brings about the *consolidation* (a new 'high') of the ideas and insights from beta and gamma through the delta surge. Such consolidation, in the Thames case, is being facilitated by Boyd Rodger through his second MMBA project, in explicitly bringing into the public arena the work of American psychiatrist Don Nathanson, who has in turn built on the work of his mentor Silvan Tomkins. In contrast to the behaviourist school, Nathanson has argued that shame 'is the central social regulator which governs our interactions with one another'. As a result the community conference is more likely to motivate offenders to cease offending behaviour patterns than conventional approaches to criminal justice.

Change conditions

What ultimately determines whether individual, organizational or societal change for the better will ensue? Six conditions, according to Beck and Cowan, have to be met if such change is to take place:

- First, the *potential for change* must be there, that is both the necessary degree of openness and also the memes, or intelligences, appropriate to the life conditions (LCs), as we saw specifically with Chief Constable Pollard in the Thames Valley case.

In the South African case generally the openness lay with the newly progressive elements, many of whom were based at the University of Stellenbosch in Cape Town, arising out of the ashes of the former diehard Afrikaner regime. The standards for the appropriate response, in terms of intelligences, were set by Mandela himself, through his spirit of tolerance and reconciliation, specifically embodied in 'The Truth Commission'.

- Second, if there are *unresolved* lower order *problems*, such as high rates of unemployment, you cannot expect to realize change at higher order levels of complexity.

In the South African case, the unresolved 'lower order' problem for the 'green' ANC regime, at the moment, is at the 'red' and 'blue' level, surrounding law and order.

- Third, there needs to be *felt dissonance* within the current meme system before change will be welcomed, as was the case for Thames when they faced up to soaring crime rates.

The dissonance felt politically, in the last days of the old apartheid regime, was between two sides of Afrikanerdom – the old 'red' and 'blue' authoritarian regime epitomized by Verwoerd and Vorster – and the new 'orange' and even 'green' progressive orientation of ex-Prime Minister De Klerk and and former Foreign Minister Pik Botha.

- Fourth, there needs to be *sufficient insight* into the causes of the dissonance, and of alternative approaches to their resolution, as was shown by Chief Constable Pollard.

The insight in the overall, political and economic case was provided by the new and progressive Afrikaner thinkers emerging from Stellenbosch University, on the one hand, and by liberal thinkers in the ANC on the other.

- Fifth, *barriers* to change, such as isolationist attitudes amongst the police, need to be concretely identified, and then *eliminated*, bypassed, neutralized or reframed into something else

De Klerk's famous, risk-laden referendum in the late eighties, when he sought backing for his reforms, was his way of eliminating barriers to progress. Similarly, Mandela identified with, rather than reacting against, white fears of a black takeover.

- Sixth and finally, when significant change occurs you can expect periods of confusion, false starts, *long learning curves* and awkward assimilation, as will undoubtedly be the case for restorative justice in Britain as a whole.

Undoubtedly this is also the case today as the new South Africa struggles to make its way in the world, both internally and also externally, politically and economically. For example, Cyril Ramaphosa, having made the transition from trade unionist to politician to, most recently, business leader, is on such a long learning curve. The new political regime in the country, both economically and socially, is similarly struggling to find its way. Each has been full of false starts, confused periods, coupled with protracted learning curves amidst periods of awkward, if not disrupted, assimilation.

Order of change

In their consideration of the dynamics of change, Beck and Cowan refer to two fundamentally different 'horizontal' and 'vertical' orders. *First order* 'horizontal' changes are the norm when their so-called first tier (polar and peripheral) memes are solidly in control, and when only a few of the conditions of change are being met. Such changes range from fine tuning to progressive enhancement to more fundamental stretch, or oblique change, to Thames Valley's 'problem solving' approach. Altogether they represent the practical limit without second tier (core meme) intervention. Thus P.K. Botha, in the early eighties, introduced nominal changes to apartheid ('fine tuning'), without making any substantive modifications, in the same way as industry, generally in South Africa today, is merely making such 'cosmetic' changes.

Change of the *second order* generally awakens new memes, though it may also resurrect ones that were thought to be buried and gone. This represents, for Beck and Cowan, 'vertical' change through the spiral, which may be either evolutionary or revolutionary, requiring a direct assault on both internal and external barriers, encompassing in our Thames case restorative justice. Such evolutionary change is dependent upon all six change conditions – available potential, realized dissonance, lower order resolution, insight into causes, identified barriers, support for change. However, it is the kind of change that De Klerk might originally have hoped for, which did not involve a fundamental overthrow of his Nationalist regime. When revolutionary change is approaching, though, you will probably recognize beta and gamma signals from several memes at once, when fundamental change is demanded. In the late eighties there was thus not only political violence in the country, and powerful pressure from the international community, but also economic turbulence. Revolutionary change, in the police context in this country, is being adopted, as we shall see in chapter 14, by the Surrey Police, adjacent to Thames Valley. We now turn from spiral dynamics to leadership dynamics.

LEADERSHIP DYNAMICS

Systems, change and spiral wizardry

Systems wizards, so called by Beck and Cowan, understand a given meme thoroughly, knowing intuitively how to 'lead' people. However, they can only do so within a particular meme. Many business entrepreneurs from South Africa or chief constables in Britain, like Kerzner of Sun City fame or Weinberg, who established Allied Dunbar in the UK, are able to lead people on within the context of the 'orange' or 'blue' meme. *Change wizards*, second, also understand the transitional cusps between memes, as is the case for Charles Pollard at Thames. Thus F.W. De Klerk in South Africa was able to link elements of the past, that is 'orange' game playing and 'blue' leadership with the way of the future, that is the 'green' pursuit of consensus through CODESA (the collaborative forum for negotiating an interim government). However, such change wizards tend still to remain colour specialists, De Klerk being restricted to orange, blue and green, and perhaps also red. The ability to encompass a full spectrum of views, third, is the realm of the *spiral wizard*, constructing out of 'second tier' dynamics. This is where President Mandela comes in.

In that wizardlike respect 'turquoise' globality or spectral 'violet' – second tier colours with which Mandela is uniquely endowed – adds a communal/collective perspective that shapes and maintains ordered relationships for the sake of the well-being of the spiral. Living systems, fuzzy concepts, power centres and force fields are blended together in balanced relationships, concerned with the overall life of an individual, a company, or a nation. Conversely, 'yellow' flexflow, more the realm of a Microsoft or an Ian Beckett at Surrey (see chapter 14) than a Mandela, provides the inner-directed, individualistic viewpoint that connects particles and subsystems into natural sequences, focusing on integration. Here linear or more likely systemic process flows create an interlinked value chain. Thus 'yellow' has a decidedly technical, practical, action oriented bent.

Secrets of spiral leadership

Spiral leadership in general for Beck and Cowan, however, first involves establishing positive relationships through *politeness, openness and decisiveness* (POD).

In this context, certainly insofar as politeness and openness are concerned, Mandela has acquired a unique reputation in the world at large. As for decisiveness, especially given his mature age, this might be somewhat less in evidence now. Second, it involves recognizing individual memes at a personal and institutional level, and third fitting different situations to these different memes. *Politeness* is defined simply in terms of civil, friendly, cordial, considerate, genuine, firm but fair, civilized and sensitive behaviour, as indeed exhibited by Mandela. 'Purple' clans thus feel safe and included, 'red' authorities or fiefdoms feel respected, 'blue' institutions or bureaucracies recognize his basic decency, 'orange' businessmen or markets feel challenged, 'green' democrats feel human, 'yellow' knowledge workers appreciate the overall intellectual climate. In these multiple contexts Nelson Mandela has been able to affect positively all walks of South African life, if not also people all over the world.

Openness implies that a leader like Mandela or indeed Pollard be authentic, transparent, sharing, available and emotionally above-board. He thereby fosters a climate that gives others the opportunity to be honest and communicative. 'Purples' as a result can express their fears and attachments, 'reds' can say what they feel without being put down, 'blues' can discuss their grievances through proper channels, 'oranges' can state a case without recriminations, 'greens'' feelings can be acknowledged, and 'yellows' can say what needs to be said. So long as P and O are healthy, *decisiveness* actually feels good because things are happening, and there is clear direction. This is perhaps where Tony Blair in his forties may come into his own even more than Nelson Mandela in his seventies. 'Purple' then relishes a strong chief, 'red' respects toughness, 'blue' welcomes authority, 'orange' thrives on accountability, 'green' accepts decisiveness benefiting all, 'yellow' is most comfortable with functional flexibility and competency driven systems, and 'turquoise' senses the need for unified control on a very large scale.

Recognizing the spiral

The job of leadership, then, whether as a president of a country, as a CEO of a company, or as chief constable of a police force, is to tune the spiral so that the parts resonate with each other rather than cancelling each other out. The opening step is good meme detection by first stepping outside your own meme profile. Second, such spiral leadership needs to recognize the life conditions that surround a particular person, organization or even a whole society. Third, it needs to probe into the whys and wherefores of a particular worldview. Fourth, such leadership needs to be able to identify the different colours a person or group exhibits in different contexts. Fifth, individuals and organizations need to be viewed in terms of their receding and awakening memes. Sixth and finally, memes need to be recognized as living forms that adapt to changes in the milieu, ultimately leading to spiral wizardry.

Flexflow spiral wizardry

A 'flexflow' approach to leadership is becoming ever more the norm, especially within 'high-tech' industries and egalitarian societies, and has been championed by such business gurus as Charles Handy,[6] Tom Peters,[7] Peter Senge[8] and most recently Bartlett and Goshal.[9] A 'yellow wizard' assumes that each employee has individual responsiblity for his or her activities and goals. Contracts are made with individuals for what should be done and when, but not how. As a result, leaders like Ian Beckett empower and facilitate rather than supervise and control. Joint purpose supersedes that of any individual. Diversity of competence and need is taken constructive account of, insofar as people are deemed to be naturally productive if the organization is so designed as to account for their needs and abilities. Conflict should be managed to promote the health of the interactive spiral, not any isolated faction, so that people, technology, procedures are interwoven into the stream of work. Such a 'flexflow' approach is one that will be required if truly effective partnerships between the police, social, educational and health services are to be constituted.

Global spiral wizardy

In the final analysis, though, 'turquoise' spiral wizardry involves management of the whole spectrum: *T*urquoise, *Y*ellow, *G*reen, *O*range, *B*lue, *R*ed, *P*urple and occasionally *B*eige. In a broad South African context this extends from Mandela himself (T), to the impulse behind the new Digital Economy (Y), to the ethos of reconstruction and renewal (G), to the prevailing business community (O), to principles of law and order (B), to 'nature red in tooth and claw' including criminal gangs (R), to traditional communities and healing practices (P).

T   spiritual bonds pull people and organizations together
T   work must be meaningful to the overall health of life

Y   people enjoy doing things that fit who they are naturally
Y   workers need free access to information and materials

G   people want to get along and be accepted by their peers
G   sharing and participating is better than competing

O   people are motivated by the achievement of material rewards
O   competition improves productivity and fosters growth

B   people work best when they do it the right way
B   following their duty, being punished when failing to do so

R   people need to be dominated by strong leadership
R   workers will put up with a lot if their basic needs are met

P   people are 'married' to their group – nepotism is normal
P   workers owe their lives and souls to the organization

ALIGNMENT AND INTEGRATION

Spiral alignment

Beck and Cowan, like many other strategic management thinkers before them, have articulated their own approach to what they term 'spiral alignment' between organization and environment. This involves specifically:

1   *deciding what business you are in*: appreciate why your enterprise exists, what work it does, and what it wants to become (in South Africa's case a 'rainbow nation', or in Thames Valley's case a force for community devlopment);
2   *charting big picture patterns and flows*, through investigating historically 'upstream' via plots/movie scripts; and prospectively 'downstream', through uncovering deep process currents and wellsprings of change;
3   *inventorizing* resources, functional capacities and life-cycle stages
4   *developing* and propagating a *strategic vision*, ensuring that you communicate through the spiral, in all its languages, so as to
5   *establish* a *specific strategy of change*, paying particular attention to the respective memes.

'Purple' will want change to be embodied in rituals, traditions and symbols. 'Red' will require heroic leaders, and storytellers to perpetuate the mythology. 'Blue' strategy will need to be 'carved in stone', in the shape of a mission statement. 'Orange' will be looking for specific signs of 'what's in it for me?' 'Green' will define ends and means in distinctly human terms. 'Yellow' revolves around keeping the whole spiral healthy.

6   Select *the right person for the job*.

If the job is high-risk seek 'orange'. It is in that capacity that Cyril Ramaphosa was chosen to head up South Africa's largest black-owned enterprise. If tough-minded decisions are required choose 'red'. Thus Meyer Kahn, ex-CEO of South African Breweries, was selected to head up the country's troubled police force. If you need to involve people choose 'green', that is Thabo Mbeki, Mandela's heir apparent. If complexity and diversity rule, choose 'yellow' or even 'turquoise', which is where Pollard and Beckett come in. Whereas Mandela himself embodies the latter 'global' role, progressive business leaders today embody the former 'flexflow' orientation.

7   Recognize finally that *change is constant*, requiring continuous movement through alpha, beta, gamma towards a new alpha, and needs integration.

Restorative justice, on its own, will thus only resolve some of the problems facing Thames Valley and, arguably, Surrey's approach to neighbourhood policing (see chapter 14) may serve to resolve some of others.

Spiral templates

Each location along the spiral has its own mental configuration like a radar screen on which the contours of its ideal life are painted. The screen then appears to:

*   'beige' hunter-gatherer societies, such as the indigenous Bushmen of the Kalahari or indigenous Maoris of New Zealand, a *natural order* with which all can *identify*;
*   'purple' clans, such as a traditional 'spirit healer' within a tribal group, a *magic circle* that makes all inside feel *safe;*
*   'red' fiefdoms, an *empire* such as the one established by the indigenous Maoris or the exogenous British, where one feels powerful and in *control*;
*   'blue' bureaucracies, a solid *pyramid* like an entrenched civil service, giving *stability* and permanence;
*   'orange' market players, a *game* such as that promoted by expansive South African or British business entrepreneurs, that promotes *opportunity* and skill;

- 'green' democrats, a supportive *community* that *cares* for its own, typified by the NGOs (non-governmental organizations) that play a prominent part in the new life of South Africa;
- 'yellow' cybercrats, a *flowing stream* crossing shifting natural plates, epitomized by a Microsoft specifically, that exercises its influence around the world, and by the Internet more generally;
- 'turquoise' visionaries, a *living* organism, bringing *order through chaos*, as illustrated hitherto by Jan Smuts' ideas on 'holism and evolution', and more recently in President Mandela's 1994 inaugural speech:

Today all of us confer glory and hope to newborn liberty. We understand that there is no easy road to freedom. We know it well that none of us acting alone can achieve success. We must therefore act together as a united people, for reconciliation, to build together, for the birth of a new world. Let there be justice for all. Let there be peace for all. Let there be work, bread, water and salt for all.

We now turn specifically, with Beck and Cowan, toward the three spiral templates – 'X', 'Y' and 'Z'.

Workflow – the 'X' template

Instead of being rigid and permanent cut-outs, the three spiral plates 'X/Y/Z', for Beck and Cowan, are organic, living layers that fuse together, stretch, adjust and mesh like interdependent layers of our skin. Every variable that influences the job to be done is included in the workflow, through such methodologies as value analysis, enterprise networking and horizontal management. The intent of this 'X' template is to link together all the variables that impinge on the job to be done, so that they are handled in a sequential and logical manner. The payoff is that the ultimate output will be clean, focused, strategic and lean, paving the way for 'Y'-like flexibility.

Such an 'X' template is more likely to be apparent, at a national level, in a systematically oriented country like Denmark or Sweden, or perhaps Austria.

Management – the 'Y' template

People and resources operating the 'Y' template support, facilitate, assist, enhance and improve 'X' template procedures and performance, so that:

- 'beige' is preserved through oneness with *nature*, that is, with animal and plant life, such as Anglian Water becoming 'guardians of the water world';
- 'purple' is nurtured through observing *rituals*, and by expressing a sense of enchantment at life's mystery, as is the case within a traditional, rurally based African or Maori community;

- 'red' is nurtured by preserving stories of company or tribal *heroes*, and by celebrating feats of conquest, as is very much the case amongst the indigenous peoples;
- 'blue' is reinforced through appeals to *traditions*, by honouring length of service and loyalty, as exemplified by colonial regimes, whether English or French;
- 'orange' is exercised by displaying symbols of *success*, individuals being recognized for their achievements, as is very much in evidence amongst the thrusting British, New Zealand, South African business enterprises;
- 'green' is enhanced by stressing the importance of human beings, within a caring, *socially responsible* community, as embodied by the political and social outlook of the current ANC regime;
- 'yellow' is enhanced by conveying a sense of *freedom*, in the context of getting important jobs autonomously done, set within a contemporary 'high-tech' enterprise.

The healthy 'Y' template is flexible, apolitical, demands POA, changes and reconstitutes itself as the 'X' need arises, paving the way for 'Z'-like insight and wisdom.

Command intelligences – the 'Z' template

The unique insight and wisdom of the 'Z' template is the combination, for Beck and Cowan, of *executive core and focused intelligences*:

- specifically the core (EC) – comprising a small group chosen for its competence, experience and maturity – monitors the whole process like the cpu in a computer;
- it represents a microcosm of what is required to co-ordinate 'X' and 'Y' templates, and to maintain a lookout to enable the organization to thrive in the milieu at large.

The second function of the 'Z' template is to bring focused intelligences to bear upon problems through knowledge, know-how and informed perspectives transcending rank in making decisions, for example through what Beck and Cowan have termed:

- a *wild duck pond*, where bright non-conformists can explore off-the-wall ideas;
- a *nursery* or development track where neophytes can be exposed to mainline functions in each of the three templates;
- a *war room* that displays the vital signs of the company, including models of the environment and profiles of competitors;
- a *play pen*, that is, a loose and creative environment;

- a *crisis team* of rapid response experts who can be quickly deployed for damage prevention or control; and
- a *wizard's tree-house*, or periodic convention of spiral wizards, who can scan for new trends and opportunities, and feed them into the command intelligences.

Such spiral wizards are able to span the full meme spectrum, in their awareness and also in their leadership activity, organizationally if not also societally/economically/politically. As for the new South Africa itself, it is too youthful in its own political and economic development to have adopted a template that is not even evident in such relatively mature societies as the United States or Japan. It is now time to conclude this 'spiral dynamic' chapter, set within the post-modern world of knowledge intensive services, extending all the way from medical insurance to restorative justice.

CONCLUSION

The spectral approach taken by Kingsland and the spiral orientation adopted by Beck and Cowan have together added two layers of complexity to our knowledge creating ecology. In the first place the 'four worlds' of hunter and herder, gardener and steward have been turned into eight. In effect, and within the context of what we have termed a global businessphere, these four worlds constitute the polarities, while the remaining four constitute the core and the periphery.

Beck and Cowan's 'first tier', of globality and flexflow, alongside the innovator and the enabler in the management spectrum, constitute what we have termed the core of the global businessphere. It is out of what Nonaka calls (see chapter 14) the arising knowledge vision and enabling conditions that our polar worlds are established. 'Western' colonizing is aligned with entrepreneurship and a 'second tier' achievement orientation. 'Northern'

Table 10 Four worlds revisited

Ecological succession	Ecodynamic character	Management spectrum	Organizational meme
		Innovator	Global
		Enabler	Flexflow
Colonize	Hunter	Entrepreneur	Achievement
Conserve	Herder	Executive	Authority
Catalyse	Gardener	Adopter	Consensus
Co-create	Steward	Animateur	Community
		Change agent	
		Adventurer	Warlike
			Indigenous

CONSERVE

| **High** | **Awakening** |
| *Alpha* | *Beta* |

COLONIZE   CATALYSE

| **Crisis** | **Unravelling** |
| *Delta* | *Gamma* |

CO-CREATE

Figure 18 Dynamic states

conserving goes together with an executive outlook and a disposition towards authority. 'Eastern' catalysation can be aligned with the role of adopter and a consensus orientation. Finally, 'southern' co-creation goes together with the role of animateur and a communal orientation. And on the periphery, we have, for Beck, warlike and indigenous peoples and, for Kingsland, the active adventurer and the interactive change agent.

These altogether provide the very varied but nevertheless static conditions out of which a 'spiral dynamic' still needs to emerge. Such a dynamic Beck and Cowan describe in terms of alpha and beta, gamma and delta conditions, which can be in this case aligned with Strauss and Howe's 'high' (alpha), 'awakening' (beta), 'unraveling' (gamma) and 'crisis' (delta), that is before a new 'high' (new alpha) may be created. In effect, and as is displayed in Figure 17, the ecological successsion can also be aligned with these dynamic states.

We now turn from the post-modern to the perennial, and from knowledge intensive services towards civic reconstruction.

BIBLIOGRAPHY

1   Beck, D. and Lindscott, D., *The Crucible*, New Paradigm Press, 1991.
2   Beck, D. and Cowan, C., *Spiral Dynamics*, Blackwell, 1996.
3   Lazear, D., *Ways of Knowing*, Twilight Publishing, 1994.
4   Dawkins, R., *The Blind Watchmaker*, Longman, 1986.
5   Smuts, J., *Holism and Evolution*, N & S Press, 1987.
6   Handy, C., *The Empty Raincoat*, Hutchinson, 1996.
7   Peters, T., *Liberation Management*, Random House, 1994.
8   Senge, P., *The Fifth Discipline*, Doubleday, 1992.
9   Goshal, S. and Bartlett, C., *The Individualized Corporation*, Butterworth Heinemann, 1998.

Part V

Perennial

Civic reconstruction

13 Freeing up societies

Virgin's simpler way

INTRODUCTION

We are now poised to move out of the realms of the post-modern, lodged in knowledge intensive services around the globe, and into the world of what we have termed the 'perennial', oriented towards civic reconstruction. In that respect, in fact, both Margaret Wheatley's and Kellner Rogers' theoretically 'simpler way', and Richard Branson's practical approach at Virgin constitute something of a 'western' halfway house. Such a freely enterprising approach to exploiting Virgin territory we liken to 'fire'.

Wheatley, like Ralph Stacey, an American management thinker, has been influenced by the sciences of chaos and complexity. The 'simpler way', embedded in such an approach, she says, is a world which we already know – in business as in life in general – without quite realizing it. We may not have seen such a world clearly, but we have been living it all our lives, at home and at work. The world we had generally been taught to see at school was alien to our humanity. We were taught to see the world as if from an accountant's perspective, in Jayne-Anne Gadhia's case, like a great machine. That is why, as we shall illustrate, the young Richard Branson (of Virgin) and Jayne-Anne Gadhia (of Virgin Direct) both rejected this approach: he left school and she left our MMBA course physically (but not in spirit), to get on with life and business. For some of the rest of us, less brave or brazen ('fiery') then Richard and Jayne-Anne, less sensitive or sensible, Wheatley maintains, alienation has spawned the need to dominate. Fear has led to control, in the family, in the community, in the workplace. When we change our image of the world, we leave behind the machine and welcome our free selves back. We recover a world that is supportive of free spirited human endeavour. This free world of the simpler way has a natural and spontaneous tendency towards organization.

It is life's invitation to freedom, creativity and meaning that welcomes us back. From such a 'chaotic' perspective, there are four overriding aspects to life and organization, which apply pre-eminently to Branson and to Gardia, to Virgin and to Virgin Direct. These relate first to the pursuit of self and identity, second to the love of play and recreation, third to the

LIVING
SYSTEMS

SELF AND   **DIVERSITY**   SELF-ORGANIZING
IDENTITY   **UNDERLIES**   NETWORKS
                  STABILITY

PLAY AND
RECREATION

Figure 19 Diversity underlying stability

existence of self-organizing networks, and fourth to the nature of living systems. These four differentiated elements together, are integrated by the ultrastability supplied by diversity. We shall illustrate each of these, first as periphery and second as centre, in the historically unfolding context of the Virgin Group.

PURSUIT OF SELF AND IDENTITY

Life organizes around a self; organizing is always an act of creating an identity.

Inventing yourself

For Wheatley, to begin with, self-organization is the capacity of life to invent itself. This process of invention always takes shape around an identity, like that of Richard Branson, Rowan Gormley or Jayne-Anne Gadhia. In effect it is Virgin Direct, founded by Gormley and Gadhia, that has become involved with our MMBA, initially through two of its staff, Andrew Nicholson and Kirsty Youngman, coached by Jayne-Anne and Rowan.

There is a self according to Wheatley, that seeks to organize, to make its presence known. All living systems have this ability to create themselves, not just initially, but in the continuous process of their lives. For biographer Tim Jackson, there are two Bransons, one behind the other.

> While his father, a lawyer, is a typical if mild-mannered product of a public school his mother was an actress, a dancer, and an air-stewardess. Richard inherited from his father his charm, and an eye for a pretty woman. From his mother he inherited his daring, his aptitude

for sport, and his hyperactive tendency to pursue one madcap scheme after another. The public man is informal, friendly, idealistic, happy-go-lucky, attached to the family, guided by strong principles, and concerned to improve the society in which he lives. The private man is a ruthlessly ambitious workaholic, a hard bargainer, an accountant with an instinctive feel for minimizing the losses on each venture, a gambler who prefers to put his assets at risk every day rather than retire to a life of luxury on what's been made.[1]

I believe this description to be too glib at best, and misguided at worst. The 'chaos' theorists in fact offer a much more interesting and useful interpretation of Branson's approach to becoming something different.

Becoming something different

Life, free to create itself as it will, moves into particular forms, into defined patterns of being. Pathways and habits develop. We engage in change only as we discover that we might be more of who we are, as has decidedly been the case for Branson, by becoming something different.

> Richard's mother had grand ideas for her son, that he would one day be Prime Minister, albeit that he showed little more aptitude for conventionally based scholarship than his father had done. He neither wanted to do his 'A' levels nor to go to university.
>
> Instead he left school early to set up in business. In fact as a child he had already pursued several successful moneymaking ventures, from growing Xmas trees to breeding budgerigars. *Student*, the magazine he started when he left school, was an artistic and literary if not also a commercial success. Its list of contributors and interview subjects reads like a *Who's Who* of the 1960s counterculture. John Le Carré, Vanessa Redgrave, David Hockney, Henry Moore, James Baldwin, as well as Jean-Paul Sartre.[2]

No man is an island

Branson, Le Carré, Redgrave, Sartre, all were freely interlinked spirits. In the world of 'chaos', we misperceive the role of boundaries if we interpret them only as separations. We misperceive ourselves if we think we exist in isolation from others. Richard Branson, for example, had already forged connections with Sartre and with Hockney, with Baldwin and with Redgrave, tenuous as they might have been. According to Wheatley, we misperceive the world if we see it as individuals struggling against one another. Life co-evolves. There are no separated individuals. The co-evolutionary processes of life cannot support isolation. In the case of Virgin Direct, as we shall see later, Branson, Gormley and Gadhia were totally interdependent. From the outset Branson and Powell, moreover, were as one at *Student*. What we create has value only if others find meaning in it. If our system rejects the self or Virgin we have created we are truly valueless. In this respect, self is an opening to connections, not a barrier behind which we fight for survival. When we reach out for a different level of connection, our search for wholeness is rewarded with a world made wholly new.

Letters of support had been solicited from everyone from Peter Sellers to Lyndon Johnson. In fact the *Student* magazine was not an isolated venture. At the same time Branson and his girlfriend established a Student Advisory Centre, a voluntary organization set up to help teenagers solve their problems, and an employment agency which sought to match underemployed nurses with London families who wanted cleaners or babysitters. Branson in fact saw an opportunity to capitalize on the public sympathy for the low pay received by nurses. Personal experience, moreover, had led him to set up the Advisory Centre. For at 17 he had met a girl and made her pregnant, then spent 'three months of hell', not knowing what to do. So together he and his girlfriend set up an advice centre for young people. The Centre to this day, with Branson's financial support, continues to advise on venereal diseases.

In the final analysis though, perhaps because of the way Richard was spreading his wings, *Student* never really made money. New issues could never be produced at the rate of a proper magazine. So Branson diverted himself towards selling records by mail-order. What turned out to be the last edition of *Student* contained the first advert for 'Virgin' records. Richard Branson, at 19, was the senior partner and his friend Nick Powell the junior one. He was also joined in the business by another of his friends, Steve Lewis, who had a passion for pop music, and managed to combine his undergraduate studies with working in the business. After three years moreover Branson came to realize that if he could make money by selling records, he should be able to make even more by manufacturing them. The idea of opening a recording studio was put in his mind by Newman, a guitarist and songwriter who had dabbled in amateur recording for a while. By 1971 Steve Lewis had discovered a kindred spirit. A young South African turned up at the Virgin offices, and announced himself as Simon Draper, Richard's cousin, a literature graduate who had a passion for music. Draper relished the prospect of turning his life's great passion into a way of making a living.[3]

While Draper and Lewis were pursuing their passion for music, and Powell his for management, Branson was pursuing a passion for a particularly playful brand of business. If self and identity provided, the ends of self-organization, play and recreation provide for Branson the means.

PLAY AND RECREATION

The universe is a living, creative, experimenting experience of playfully discovering what's possible at all levels of scale, from microbe to cosmos.

Passion for life

What has kept us, Wheatley enquires, from seeing life as creative, even playful? At least since Darwin, she says, Western culture has harboured some great errors. We have believed that the world is predominantly hostile, that we are in a constant struggle for survival. The environment, or indeed in business the competition, looms over every living thing, ready to challenge, ready to destroy. Get it right or die. These errors of thought have guided most of our decisions. They have kept us from seeing a world, like Virgin's, which continuously explores and creates.

> 'Nik and Richard', Simon Draper would later recall, 'had no particular feel for the music business. They found themselves in it by accident. They were public schoolboys who had dropped out of education'. While the two budding entrepreneurs did what they were good at – Richard sweet-talking the press and striking daring deals, the more introverted Nik reading his management magazines and trying to think of ways in which he could cut costs – they needed some real musical expertise. So there was a vacuum for Draper to step into.
>
> Meanwhile, the new recording studio was preparing for its first formal booking in 1971, an obscure band that was recording there pulled out a demo tape and handed it over to Tom Newman who was in charge of the studio. Simon Draper heard it a whole while later, after the young guitarist had been turned down by almost every record company in Britain, and pronounced it 'incredible'. He decided to tell Richard to sign up Mike Oldfield. *Tubular Bells* put Virgin on the map. It also unleashed a torrent of money into the company's bank account. Virgin Records was now in business as an independent label, and Simon now had enough money to sign the bands he wanted. As the venture grew, Powell and Branson assumed their complementary roles. Powell would produce financial figures for the bank, Branson would take the figures to the meeting and persuade the bank manager to lend a few thousand. It was Branson also whose gusto for life persuaded people that working for Virgin would be fun; it was Powell who stopped the biscuits in the coffee cupboard when times were hard. In common with almost everybody else working for Virgin, Draper, Lewis and Newman were not particularly bothered by money. Music was the passion of their lives.[4]

The logic of play

Life then, for the passionate and the playful, is about invention rather than survival. According to Wheatley[5] we are here to create, not to defend. Out beyond the shadows of Darwinian thought, a wholly different world appears: a world that delights in its explorations; a world that makes it up as it goes along; a world that welcomes us into the exploration as good partners. The key elements of this 'logic of play' are evident in recent work by scientists that explore how life came into being. Everything is at first a constant process of discovery – every organism reinterprets the rules, creates exceptions for itself, creates new rules.

Second, life uses messes to get to well-ordered solutions – using redundancy, fuzziness, dense webs of relationships, and unending trials and errors to find what works. Life as such is intent, third, on finding what works, not what's right – the capacity to keep changing, to find what works now, is what keeps any organism alive.

There are no mere 'windows of opportunity', narrow openings that soon disappear forever. Rather, fourth, possibilities beget more possibilities – they are infinite. Fifth, life is attracted to order. It experiments until it discovers how to form a system that can support diverse members. This system then provides stability for them. Finally, everything participates in the creation and evolution of its neighbours. All of us participate together in creating the conditions of our interdependence.

There were now three key Virgin people.

A pattern seemed to emerge meanwhile whereby Draper could make the artistic decisions about which act to sign, Branson would knock out a broad agreement and then Ken Berry would be left to tie up the details in a formal contract. Later, as Branson withdrew from daily involvement in the label, it would be Berry who carried out the negotiations in all but the biggest deals. Richard, in the interim, devoted much of his time to establishing a network of record companies across Europe, paying attention to an aspect of the business, foreign distribution, that most of the other independents had neglected. At the same time Virgin was willing to hire people who had an enthusiasm and love for music, but no formal experience in other record companies. Once inside, they would find themselves given important jobs to do. Everyone seemed to be friends. And although people took their jobs seriously, they did so as they would take seriously a game of tennis that they passionately wanted to win, rather than as a career.

But it was the company's weekends abroad that did most to cement the team spirit. Starting on a Friday and ending on a Sunday the entire staff of the record company, publishing company and studio management team would decamp to a country house hotel. Business was banned. Instead the guests would spend the weekend playing tennis or golf, swimming and sunning themselves, eating and drinking with great gusto.[6]

All this messy playfulness creates relationships that make available more expression, more variety, more stability, more support. In our exploration of what's possible we are led to search for new and different partners. Who we become together will always be different from who we are alone. We do not parachute into a sea of turbulence, to sink or swim. We and our environments become one system, each co-determining the other.

SELF-ORGANIZING NETWORKS

Networks, patterns and structures emerge without external imposition or direction – organizations want to happen.

Organizations as play

Playful and creative enterprises, like Virgin, are inevitably messy. Errors are expected, explored, welcomed. Yet simultaneity reduces the impact of any one. In other words, more errors matter less if the actors are not linked together sequentially. The space for experimentation increases as we involve more minds in the experiment, as long as they can operate independently, as is so often the case for companies within the Virgin Group. Bacterial colonies successfully locate food by sending out 'random walkers'. Such systems slosh around in the mess, learning all the time, engaging everyone in finding what works. Living in this discovery-focused, messy, parallel-processing world engages us with the world's diversity.

By the spring of 1981 it was ten years since Branson had closed down *Student* magazine to concentrate on selling records by mail order. A great deal had happened since then. Virgin had established a record label, a studio business, a chain of shops, a music publishing house. The record label was the engine of Virgin's growth. Powell parted from the Virgin company and became a Buddhist. Culture Club grew bigger and bigger. Boy George who had signed on for Virgin in the eighties was the world's most successful musician. The sums that flowed into Virgin's bank made the Oldfield's millions seem paltry. The founder of Virgin Atlantic Airlines meanwhile, the company that was to change Richard Branson's life, was a barrister named Randolph Fields. The young barrister realized that Laker's demise left a gap in the lucrative but highly regulated market for air travel between London and New York. He resolved, moreover, to turn in-flight entertainment into the most important selling point of his airline. Flying was to be not merely glamorous but also fun. Meanwhile Fields knew he had to find at least another million, so he approached Branson. Nobody in the Virgin Group knew the first thing about airlines. Branson's most loyal lieutenants were flatly opposed to the idea.

But as far as Branson was concerned, if People's Express could be run by a Wall Street analyst and British Airways by a former executive of Avis rent-a-car, why couldn't a pop tycooon start an airline. In effect Boy George paid for Branson's airline![7]

Co-evolution dances

Branson and Fields came together in extraordinary circumstances, but their very coming together was a part of Virgin's co-evolution. There is an innate striving in all forms of matter, Wheatley stresses, to organize into relationships. There is a great seeking for connections, a desire to organize into more complex systems that include more relationships, more variety. This desire is evident everywhere in the cosmos, at all levels of scale. Everywhere, discrete elements come together, cohere and create new forms. The system maintains itself, moreover, only if change is occurring somewhere in it all the time. New food sources, new neighbours, new talents appear. As conditions change, individuals experiment with new possibilities. Without constant change the system sinks into the death grip of equilibrium. The broad paradox of stability and freedom is the stage on which co-evolution dances. Life for Wheatley leaps forward when it can share its learnings. The dense web of systems allows information to travel in all directions, speeding discovery and adaptation. Access to one another's learning creates resilience and adaptability. All complex organisms evolve through tumultuous co-operative venturing, as has indeed been the case for both Virgin Atlantic and Virgin Retail.

By 1981, Virgin had thirty-five record shops up and down the country ranging from hole-in-the-wall to megastore, and with a bewildering variety of gimmicky sidelines. Clothes had been sold in the record stores for a while, under the name Virgin Rags. By 1984 the retailing side was looking distinctly problematical. While turnoverwise it was the country's third biggest record chain it was not, with the exception of the megastore in Marble Arch, making money. By 1988 it was decided to sell the chain of shops, lock, stock and barrel, and W.H. Smith were approached. In the interim, though, Branson decided to keep the megastores, and see whether they could be turned around. Simon Burke, a trained accountant, took over the balance of the retailing after the core had been sold off to Smith's. After a massive streamlining operation, Virgin Retail proceeded to make a steady recovery, and even opened up a new megastore in the centre of Paris.

By 1992, moreover, Burke had opened up thirty video game stores around the country. Over the course of the next few years, and in collaboration with W.H. Smith's itself, as well as with Chinese and Japanese partners, Virgin opened up megastores in Europe, America and the Far East. For a company then that had merely played at 'shop-keeping' during the first seventeen years of its existence Virgin Retailing was now turning out to be an extraordinary success, with separate management running the American, European and Far Eastern operations.[8]

Mechanism and organisms

Virgin Retail came to the fore during the period that the Virgin Group went public. The move from private to public, and ultimately back again, was a traumatic one for Virgin. The great problem is to find an appropriate balance between the dynamic enterprise of a business organism and the static accountability and responsibility of an organizational mechanism. When, however, we view organizations as machine-like, they unavoidably they become complexities of overly bureaucratic structure, policy and roles.

We build, Wheatley maintains,[9] rigid structures incapable of responding. We box ourselves in behind hard boundaries breached only by hostile forays. We create places of fear. We shrink from one another. We mistrust the elemental organizing forces of life. The struggle and competitiveness that we thought characterized life become the pre-eminent features of our organizations.

> Ten years after the foundation of the record label, Branson had decided to take Virgin public. Knowing that the group would need some tidying up before it could be sold to investors in the stock market, he had resolved to bring in a manager from outside who could groom the company, and reassure the City.
>
> In appointing Cruikshank, as in so many other cases, Branson relied on personal connections. Cruikshank had spent five years with McKinsey before he moved to the Pearson Group, where he was a managing director of the firm's information and entertainment group. The Virgin Group he was brought in to run in 1984 was generating 100 million pounds in turnover, but making remarkably little profit. The record side was minting money but the rest was a rag-bag of different businesses, many of which lost money. What was more shocking to Cruikshank was that the group seemed to have no management structure. The firm was struggling to expand with working capital that was hugely inadequate, and an overdraft facility that was miniscule. Branson, he maintained, should not turn himself into an administrator, but devote his attention to acting as a catalyst, motivating others and enthusing them with his conviction. All that he needed was a couple of people to tidy up behind him, and to help him decide clearly what he was trying to achieve. Trevor Abbott was then brought in as Group Finance Director. Both he and Cruikshank were referred to as 'suits' by the

more creative people. Undeterred by the initial hostility they set about reorganizing Virgin into three divisions: Music, Retail and Vision. The rest were to be got rid of. With that done the next step had to be to ensure that each division had a financial controller with enough experience and authority to handle a growing business. There was also a job to be done in disentangling some of Branson's private interests from the mainstream of the business. In appointing KPMG as the firm's advisors Richard Branson had to say good-bye to the lawyers and accountants who had advised him for years. But Cruikshank was not satisfied with these management changes. Before joining the company, he had wanted assurances from Branson that their agreed mutual goal was to make Virgin public – to have its shares listed on the London stock exchange.

The greater prestige of being a public company would enable Virgin to do bigger business deals. There was, of course, a downside. Once the company's shares were quoted on the stock market Branson would have to exchange the relative freedom of a private limited company, in which his controlling share meant he could do almost anything he wanted, for the more constrained world of a public limited company. Virgin would have to publish a great deal more information than it had done before, and follow more detailed rules. To date Branson had run the Virgin Group with a view to maximizing its value over the long term. If he were to become answerable to shareholders, he would have to achieve the greatest value to shareholders over months.[10]

Our analytical culture, Wheatley maintains, drives us to so many cover-ups that it is hard to see the self-organizing capacity in any of us. We see a need. We join with others. We find the necessary information or resources. We respond creatively. We create a solution that works. How, then, do we support our natural desire to organize and the world's natural desire to assist us? It begins with a change in our beliefs. We give up believing that we design the world into existence and instead take up roles that help it to flourish. We work with what is available and encourage forms to come into existence. We foster tinkering and discovery. We help create connections. We nourish with information. We are clear about what we want to accomplish. We remember that people self-organize and trust them to do so.

PEOPLE AND ORGANIZATIONS ARE LIVING SYSTEMS

People and organizations are living systems; they too are intelligent, creative, adaptive, self-organizing and meaning-seeking.

Symbiosis

Life for Wheatley creates niches, in the world of living 'chaos', not to dominate but to support. Symbiosis is the most favoured path for evolution. Self-definition, through the identification of a niche and the specification of the food required for survival, frees up all other food sources for others in the system. Living systems cannot be explained by competition. Brutal species always destroy themselves, leaving the world to those who have figured out how to co-exist with each other. We are not independent agents fighting for ourselves against all others.

There is no predominantly hostile world out there plotting our demise. There is no 'out there' for anyone. We are utterly intertwined. If we see life as a brutal contest between separate entities, we focus on individual contribution, individual change. This worldview not only makes us feel afraid and isolated but it also causes us to hope for heroes. Yet in a systems-seeking, co-evolving world there is no such thing as a hero. Everything is the result of interdependencies – systems of organization where we support, challenge and create new combinations with others. No one forges ahead wholly independently, not even Branson, moulding the world to his presence while the rest of us trail admiringly behind. We tinker ourselves into existence by unobserved interactions with the players who present themselves to us. Environment, enemies, allies – all are affected by our efforts as we are by theirs. The systems we create are chosen together. They are the result, for Wheatley, of dances not wars, and Branson seems to alternate, willingly or otherwise, between one and the other.

> Branson was bored by finance, by accountancy, and by formal techniques of management. When he had been in partnership with Nik Powell he had pointed gentle fun at the jargon that Powell had picked up from his reading of American business magazines.
>
> Meanwhile Cruikshank saw himself trying to bring to Virgin standards of corporate governance. Branson found it hard not to view this as an obstruction. Too often Cruikshank seemed to wish to scale back his ideas, to bureaucratize his relations with the staff. Whereas Cruikshank seemed to get in the way of Branson's ambitions, Abbott was someone who helped them become a reality. In 1988, Branson reported to the press that Virgin's strategy of investment for long-term growth, with its effect on short-term profitability, had had an adverse affect on the share price. As a result, the benefits of a listing which he anticipated had not been realized. In view of this he was exploring the possibility of a management buyout. A consortium of international banks led by Citibank provided the loan finance required. By 1989, when the buyout was complete, Virgin was twice the size of the company that had gone public in 1985. But the re-privatized Virgin was particularly highly leveraged.

It was against this background that the group began to look for ways of raising capital to pay off debt. It was after all other possibilities had been exhausted that Branson had to face the inevitable: the sale of Virgin Music, the crown jewels of the empire. The decision was a gutrenching one, although the sale to Thorn-EMI ultimately yielded £560 million. At the ceremony marking the sale Branson and his fellow senior management were in tears.[11]

The organizing tendency of life, according to Wheatley, is always a creative act, and that, in its turn, also involves destruction. We reach out to some to create a new being, and sometimes inevitably disconnect from others to destroy the old one. We reach out to grow the world into new possibilities. At the heart of every organization is a self reaching out to new possibilities. We organize always to affirm and enrich our identity. But then we take this vital passion and institutionalize it.

We create too rigid an organization. The people who loved the purpose they served grow to disdain the overly rigid institution that was created to fulfil it. Passion mutates into procedures, into rules and roles. The organization no longer lives. We see its bloated form and resent it for what it stops us from doing.

How, then, do we create organizations that stay alive? We need to trust that we are self-organizing, and we need to create the conditions in which self-organization can flourish. Identity is the source of organization. Every organization is an identity in motion, moving through the world, trying to make a difference. We need to explore first why we have come together. If we took time to ground our work in the deep connections that engage us, we would be overwhelmed by the energy and contributions so willingly given. Virgin, in that respect, still has more than a little way to go, extraverted in nature as it is. Seemingly, notwithstanding the appeals of the simpler way, it will need to organize for greater levels of complexity.

DIVERSITY UNDERLIES STABILITY

Life's natural tendency is to organize into greater levels of complexity to support more diversity and greater sustainability.

Freedom to change

In self-organization structures emerge. They are not imposed. They spring from the process of doing the work. These structures will be useful but temporary. We can expect them to emerge and recede as needed. It is not the design of a specific structure, however, that requires our attention but rather the conditions that will support the emergence of necessary structures. Patterns and structures emerge as we connect to one another.

People support one another with information and nurture one another with trust.

In life, systems create the conditions for both stability and personal discovery. For Wheatley it is a lovely and intricate paradox. We connect with others and gain protection from external turbulence. We become part of something greater and thereby gain more freedom to experiment for ourselves. If we do not exercise that freedom to change, the organization cannot maintain its stability.

From Steve Lewis downwards the staff at Virgin Music were unanimously agreed that Branson had made them feel that they were working together in a cooperative enterprise from whose progress they would all benefit in the longterm. In doing this, he had imbued them with a positive spirit, transmitting as if by telepathy his blind faith that every problem could be surmounted. Behind the jeans and T-shirts, Virgin Music had a clear corporate culture: it could be summed up in the view that it was idle to ask if something could be done. Virgin people would assume that it could and confine themselves to asking how. Branson had not only commanded loyalty but it had given many of the Virgin Music staff – particularly women – grounds for promotion. The mid-nineties heralded Virgin's diversification into soft drinks, via its own brand of Cola, and into financial services.

Rowan Gormley, another South African who had approached Branson with a view to moving into financial services, explained the move by saying that Virgin had become a value-based brand, rather than one dependent on products. Gormley, who had been trained as an accountant, had been working for Electra Trust. Branson had previously engaged Gormley to help him through the innumerable business propositions that landed on his desk. Meanwhile Gormley had become aware of the major revolution taking place in financial services. Essentially two trends were at work. First, consumers were becoming used to the idea of buying products over the telephone. Notable amongst the companies doing it were Direct Line, selling car insurance, and First Direct, a subsidiary of Midland Bank. Second, purveyors of financial products, from mortgages to unit trusts, were under pressure to disclose more clearly the commissions they paid to salesmen and other intermediaries. Gormley's conclusion, according to Tim Jackson, was simple. The first company that devises a way of delivering products that consumers want by eliminating salesmen, he told Branson, will make a bundle. There was just one problem. How would such a company persuade customers to believe its promises, after all the half-truths of the financial industry had been peddled for years? Gormley told Branson then: 'What's required to make this work is not a computer system, nor is it capital. It's a name people will trust. There are only two names in Britain strong enough for this purpose. The one is Marks & Spencer, the other is Virgin.'

Branson took some convincing. He couldn't associate in his mind financial services with the fun image of his company. Once he had eventually become convinced, they had to search for a partner. Branson wanted to team up with a mutual rather than a public company that had the technical knowledge and the capital to launch the new range of financial products. He wanted a company that was big enough to get the project through the regulatory hoops, and that was not too heavily focused on the short term. Soon Virgin settled on Norwich Union as its chosen bride. Recently humbled by a steep regulatory fine for the mismanagement of its pensions operation, Norwich Union was looking for ways of improving its way of dealing with customers. It also had some spare staff and an enthusiastic divisional MD, Phil Scott.

The former venture capitalist Rowan Gormley therefore left Holland Park and decamped to a new office in the suburbs of Norwich, close enough but not too close to Norwich Union itself, where he began to set up a clone of the Direct Line operation. The atmosphere bore little resemblance to the stolid air of the average financial institution. The staff were younger, there were more women, and instead of a sea of polyester suits and drip-dry shirts, the new office was full of gelled hair and comfortable smart-casual clothes.[12]

Life wants to discover itself. Individuals explore possibilities and systems emerge. They self-transcend into new forms of being. Newness appears out of nowhere. Life is on a one-way street to novelty.

Emergence

Such a quality of 'emergence' is the surprising capacity we discover only when we join together, which was as much the case when Fields joined Branson as when Virgin joined Norwich Union. Emergence provides simple evidence that we live in a relational world. Relationships change us, reveal us, evoke more from us. We seek out one another because we want to accomplish something. And then life surprises us with new capacities. Life is playful and life plays with us. A system is fluid relationships that we observe as rigid structure.

What do we do with surprise? What do we do with a world which cannot be known until it is in the process of discovering itself? It requires contant awareness, being present, being vigilant for the newly visible. An emergent world invites us to use the most human of all our capacities, our consciousness. It asks us to be alert in the moment for what is unfolding. An emergent world welcomes us in as conscious participants and surprises us with discovery.

Our plans are nothing compared to what the world so willingly gives us. In classical evolutionary thought, on the other hand, change occurs within individuals. Each of us invents our own survival strategies as we struggle against the environment. When we apply this thinking to organizations, it leads us straight to individuals. If a distasteful situation develops, or we don't like where the system is heading, we just pluck out the bad genes. We look for the mutants in our midst and expel them. Emergent evolution explains systems quite differently. Evolution occurs in many ways, but always from the desire to work out relationships for mutual co-existence. Locale by locale, individuals and groups figure out what works for them. Systems become fluid relationships. They are webby, wandering, nonlinear. Independent 'king' becomes interdependent *kereitsu*.

> By February of 1995, the new Virgin financial services company had sixty employees working at computer terminals. The firm's first product was to be a Personal Equity Plan (PEP), which allowed an individual to invest up to £6,000 a year in approved shares and bonds, and to receive both dividends and profits from rising prices free of tax. Until seven months before the planned launch of the business, according to Jackson, Branson had no idea of what a PEP was, so he was as keen as anyone else in the organization to ensure that the literature was jargon free. The Virgin PEP's selling point, though, would be clear. Its charges would be low – an annual commission of 1 per cent on the portfolio value for both the PEP and its underlying unit trust invest-ment – and it would keep dealing costs to a minimum. Instead of wasting money by buying and selling stocks in a vain attempt to buck the market, the fund would simply put its investors' savings in the blue-chip shares that comprised the stock market index, and leave them there. Gormley explained the move into financial services by saying that Virgin had become a value-based brand, rather than one dependent on products.
>
> While others looked to the Japanese *kereitsu*, a loose industrial group linked by cross-shareholdings that spanned a wide range of industrial sectors, the Virgin Group had its own model. And by 1998, Virgin Direct had moved from PEPs and life insurance into telephone banking, and its staff had grown to 600.[13]

A self-organizing system such as the Virgin Group reveals itself as struc-tures of relationships, patterns of behaviours, habits of belief, methods for accomplishing work. These patterns, structures and methods are visible. We become entranced by their forms. We probe and dissect them down to microscopic levels of detail. Yet efforts directed at exchanging material forms have not given us the results we hoped for. We need to look past these mesmerizing effects of organization and notice the processes that give them shape. Beneath all structures and behaviours lie the real creators – dynamic processes. Structures and behaviours emerge from our relationships. They emerge from decisions about how to belong together. Identity is at the core of every organization, fuelling its creation. In a world of emergence, new systems appear out of nowhere. But the forms they assume originate from dynamic processes set in motion by information, relationships and identity. Organizations for Wheatley spiral into form, cohering into visibility. Like stars on winter nights, they fill our field of vision and enthrall us. But organizations emerge from fiery cores like Virgin's, from richly swirling dynamics. This is where we need to gaze, into the origins that give rise to such diversity of form.

Motions of coherence

Life for Wheatley is motion, 'becoming becoming'. The motions of life swirl inward to the creating of self and outward to the creating of the world. We turn inward to bring forth a self. Then the self extends outward, seeking others, joining together, autopoietically.

Systems arise. Life takes form from such ceaseless motions. Life moves towards life – Virgin Direct. Life in that form accepts only partners, not bosses. Virgin Direct today is thus run by teams of people, with Rowan and Jayne-Anne playing the respective roles of older brother and sister. We cannot stand outside a system as objective, distant directors. There is no objective ground to stand on anywhere in the entire universe. Our disconnection – our alleged objectivity – is an illusion; and even if we fail to realize this, the system will notice it immediately. Systems work with themselves; if we aren't part of the system, we have no potency. Systems do not accept direction, only provocation.

> Small is beautiful is evidently Virgin's guiding principle. Branson believes firmly that people work better in teams that are too compact to be impersonal. Branson has made only a handful of acquisitions in his life. Instead, he builds from scratch. In a business career spanning some twenty-five years he has used this approach to build an international retail chain, an airline, a music business. He is fond of pointing out that while conventional business analysis puts the interests of the shareholders first, followed by the customers and employees, he takes the opposite approach. A good example is Virgin Atlantic. Branson in fact knew little about how airlines present themselves to consumers – and what they knew they did not like. It was therefore necessary to start from scratch, sitting around a table and putting together the myriad of jobs that would need to be done. With Roy Gardner's technical background, the chief engineer from Laker's, and with the people he brought with him, Virgin Atlantic was able to build up a team of expert flyers, plucking them from retirement. The approach with cabin crew was the reverse. Only half had worked on board a plane before. Flying was fun. Flying a new young airline associated with a record was certain to be more fun.[14]

There is no type of a priori intervention that can transform the system or turn it masterfully in a desired direction. The system is spinning itself into existence. It creates itself by exercising its freedom to choose what to notice. It is not volume or quantity that stirs any system. It is interest and meaning. If the system decides that something is meaningful, it absorbs this information into itself. It will display connections we never dreamed of. If we want to work with a system to influence its direction the place for us to work is deep in the dynamics of the system where identity is taking form. Every being, every organization, is an identity in motion, creating itself in the world and creating its world simultaneously. The identity of a system can turn in on itself and become rigid and closed. Or the identity can move out into the world, exploring new ways of being. But always it is the process of self-creation that sets organizing in motion.

A self changes when it changes its consciousness about itself. As the system develops a different awareness, this changed awareness will materialize as new responses. Thus the source of change and growth for an individual or an organization is to develop increased awareness of who it is, now. Although we get terribly distracted by the day-to-day demands of our lives, it is important to keep going back to the deep processes of self-making.

> When opinion pollsters asked young Britons in 1994 who they would most trust to update the Ten Commandments in the modern world, Branson came in a good third after Mother Teresa and the Pope. To the general public then, Richard Branson is the embodiment of all the great modern values, tolerance, informality and human warmth. It is a sobering thought that the very reason he stands out is that business is not usually associated with such values.[15]

Virgin Rail, the most recent of Branson's large-scale ventures in the wake of rail privatization in Britain, consequently has a far stronger identity than all other concessionaires. Indeed, people and organizations with integrity are wholly themselves. No aspect of self is different or stands apart. When they go inside to find themselves there is only one self there. With coherence comes the capacity to create organizations that are both free and effective. They are effective because they support people's ability to self-organize. They are free because they know who they are. Coherent organizations experience the world with less threat and more freedom. In that context Virgin Rail is in it for the long term, thereby making a far larger investment in rolling stock than all of its counterparts.

CONCLUSION

Richard Branson, particularly over recent years in this country, has established himself and his Virgin Group as a kind of British icon, a modern-day Horatio Alger, a latter-day merchant adventurer. In so doing, and in my view, he has done himself and his country both a great service and a great disservice. The great service that he has done is that of creating and maintaining a highly successful business, and brand image, that has not only stood the test of time but also captured the public's trust and imagination. The recent overnight success of Virgin Direct is a clear affirmation of this. Tim Jackson's book entitled *Virgin King* reinforces the individualistic tradition upon which Branson's foundations have been built.

What, then, is the disservice that the public media, perhaps even more than the private Branson, have performed? In essence, the dominance of the extroverted, independent-minded, risk-taking Branson-like adventurer/ entrepreneur has skewed our twenty-first-century image of business. For the successful business of the future is liable to be more interdependently part of a 'business ecosystem' than independently apart from it.

Similarly, the successful business person will be as co-operative as he or she is competitive, as much of a catalyst as an entrepreneur. In fact, as becomes clearly apparent when we see Richard Branson interviewed on the television today, he is as much of an introvert as he is extroverted. It is just that the active and independent side of his personality has been historically overplayed, and the reflective and interdependent side underplayed. Arguably, moreover, the explicitly masculine side of Branson has been reinforced, over and above the tacitly feminine side. In that respect he has been inhibited from expressing, and releasing, his whole personality. Images of enterprising competition have thereby eclipsed those of 'chaotic' co-operation.

In the same way, therefore, as the Norwich Union of which Virgin Direct was originally a part is demutualizing, and thereby rejecting part of its natural birthright, Virgin – in its independently minded, masculine assertions – may be rejecting its own feminine self. To the extent that both fail to become the whole of themselves their ultimate union will be inhibited, or indeed they will already have suffered in that respect. Perhaps the masculine and feminine roles played by Rowan Gormley and Jayne-Anne Gadhia at Virgin Direct may herald a change in the overall field of force within Virgin more generally. Interestingly enough, the first two of Virgin Direct's young managers, Kirsty Youngman and Andrew Nicholson, to participate in our programme bring both female and male perspectives to it, as indeed do Jayne-Anne and Rowan. Perhaps the birth and growth of Direct may herald a new era in Virgin's growth and development as a whole, born out of such relationships. To the extent, then, that we might model ourselves as managers and organizations upon the heroic Branson peronality, we need to look again. For, in its essence, the Virgin Group has been constructed out of Branson's recognition of the universe as a living, creative experience, out of his realization that life in general and business in particular organizes around a self.

Moreover, greater diversity effects sustainability, business life self-organizes into networks and patterns, and successful people and organizations are intelligent and adaptive as opposed to intellectual and inflexible.

This is all a far cry from the orthodoxy of the pioneering entrepreneur, and of his or her pioneering enterprise. It arises, for Jayne-Anne, more out of a search for free expression than for the realization of free enterprise that is Richard Branson's hallmark.

In this way, Virgin generally and Direct specifically bridge the gap between the traditional and the post-modern, with modernity lagging somewhat behind. Moreover, the perennial desire for freedom, as a composite whole, is on the immediate horizon. In fact, and with combined help from Rowan Gormley primarily and Jane-Anne secondarily, Branson's recent ventures into South Africa may turn out to have as much to do with freeing up the society – civic reconstruction – as to do with free enterprise. Moreover, and at the same time as Virgin Direct branches out from investment products and life assurance into fully fledged banking (all telephone based), its reach, in promoting self-sufficiency in individuals and prospectively in nations, is growing. We now fuel the flames, as it were, of our Virgin fire, with the air of knowledge creation.

BIBLIOGRAPHY

1 Jackson, T., *Virgin King*, Harper Collins, 1995.
2 Ibid.
3 Ibid.
4 Ibid.
5 Wheatley, M., *Leadership and the New Science*, Berrett Koehler, 1992.
6 Jackson, *Virgin King*.
7 Ibid.
8 Ibid.
9 Wheatley, M. and Kellner Rogers, M., *A Simpler Way*, Berrett Koehler, 1996.
10 Jackson, *Virgin King*.
11 Ibid.
12 Ibid.
13 Ibid.
14 Ibid.
15 Ibid.

14 Communities at peace
Knowledge creation at Surrey Police

THE ORGANIZATION

In the beginning

It was back in 1829 that England's Home Secretary Sir Robert Peel first declared: 'the principal object to be attained by a police force is the prevention of crime. To this great end their every effort is to be directed.' In revisiting Peel's original concept of preventive policing, a century and a half later, Surrey Police's Deputy Chief Constables Beckett and Hart advanced their notion of 'community policing'. Within such a 'service' based approach, the public assists the police in dealing with and preventing crime, both individually and also institutionally.

To that ultimate end Ian Beckett, in 1996, decided to enlist the support of our project based programme, to help take this concept further. Little did he know at the time, but this would appear later through the mediation of both our Director of MBA programmes at CUBS, Carol Vielba and me, was the fact that Surrey was a trend setting 'knowledge creating organization' in Great Britain. In fact, Beckett and Hart had earlier spent several of their formative young adult years studying at City University, while employed in the force, for their undergraduate and postgraduate degrees. Their communal orientation to policing, then, has led towards a preventative approach which is very different from the reactionary one of responding quickly to emergencies. From this vantage point the police, together with other agencies, stimulate the community itself towards self-policing. Such a proactive orientation moreover is dependent upon the organization 'airing' its newly growing knowledge based competencies, which is perhaps why Surrey Police's former Chief Constable, Peter Matthews, had wanted to encourage Ian Beckett and James Hart to pursue their studies.

While Chief Constable Peter Matthews, and Home Secretary Robert Peel long before him, provided an initial source of inspiration for them, the Surrey Police's unique role in the country since has been to turn a general philosophy into a specifically knowledge based vision. The two major knowledge sources initially identified during their undergraduate studies were general systems theory for Hart, and social psychology for Beckett. For James Hart then: 'the police system itself is composed of sub-systems and elements which are joined in some purposeful way by a series of relationships. Thus the environment is affected by the police system and the police system is affected by the environment.' For Ian Beckett, 'behaviour characterised as pro-social would be expected to produce or maintain the physical and psychological wellbeing and the integrity of those involved'. In fact two modules, one on systems theory and the other on social and community studies, form the police-specific knowledge grounds of the MBA programme upon which a dozen of the Surrey Police have since embarked.

At the same time, when several of the Surrey Police on the programme became aware of Nonaka's work, they realized that they were in effect a knowledge creation organization, with Ian Beckett acting as the so-called knowledge officer and themselves as the 'knowledge engineers'. A leader amongst such 'engineers' was Martin West, whose role it had been during the second 'extraordinary' project to explicitly develop the concept and application of what was known as the 'Blue Knight' programme, which was responsible for delivering community policing in Surrey. At the same time Andrew Neilsen, working alongside Martin, was focusing on the operational issues involved. Interestingly enough Boyd Rodger, who was concentrating on developing restorative justice in Thames Valley Police – a scheme for the communal administration of justice which had been imported from the Maoris via Australia – found that his old boss Ian Blair had now moved on to become Chief Constable at Surrey.

He therefore teamed up with fellow MBA student Mike Ledwidge, based in Surrey, who has been assigned to do the same project in that county. Today's Home Secretary, Jack Straw wanted to see experiments in restorative justice ultimately spread around the country. Straw, in a post-modern context, was thus taking on from where Peel had left off in a modern one. In the course of our programme, finally, it became evident that proactive peace building – alongside reactive peace making and peace keeping – is Surrey's core business. As a result, Glyn Alger and Simon Wilshire, alongside link manager Andy Thompson, have been devoting their third mastery projects to developing the concept of an international peace forum, drawing on their own knowledge based vision of community peace building. We now turn more specifically to review the way in which organizational knowledge creation has emerged, through the seminal influence provided by Deputy Chief Constable Dr Ian Beckett, at Surrey Police.

Classified as a failure – feeling ill at ease with injustice

'Born in Lancashire, I moved when I was a child to Monmouth in Wales, where I attended grammar school. There I was classified as a failure, and so didn't get my "A" levels. Because I was considered to be no good at "proper" school I threw my energies into the school of life, through the scout movement's outdoor activities. Ultimately I became a scout leader, and have thereafter always retained an interest in young people. At the same time I developed a profound sense of unease with any form of injustice, and had a particular problem with bullying. In fact I hated to see strong people damaging kids weaker than themselves.

'When I left school I wanted to go into forestry. I loved scuba diving, walking, and sailing, that is the outdoor life. However, I found out that I had acute hay fever, which made it impossible for me to pursue my nature bound course. So I joined the police, that is the Met, mainly because of the money. Again I had difficulty with the exams. I only passed them second time around. Proper education had seemed unnatural, perhaps even irrelevant to me.

Knowledge bears fruit in works – the enabling conditions

'My reason for wanting to go on to university though, later, was because I had become dissatisfied with the way we were doing things at the Met. The conventional way of going about policing just didn't seem to work. I was a very practical sort of person, so I was looking for an answer to the problem. I was lucky then, at the time, to be awarded a university scholarship. It was pretty generous of the Met to sponsor me. By that time I suppose I was considered to be pretty successful at my job. I had also accumulated experience. It was then that I met James Hart who was based at Surrey Police. Like me he was going to City University, on a scholarship. He was planning to study systems science while I was going into psychology. We were both determined, moreover, to bring something back from our studies into the police force. James was at the time a staff officer working under Surrey's Chief Constable, Peter Matthews. Matthews asked me to see him, together with James. "Why don't you two get some logical basis to policing? Find some way of bringing our village based approach into the city. We need a knowledge base. Perhaps your university studies would help us find one." So I plumped for psychology. Consciously speaking I wasn't sure why. My explicit interest in people, that is in human nature, emerged subsequently, arising out of my undergraduate studies. The psychology course I did had all the right elements to it. Groups. Organizational systems. How to get the best out of people. What motivates us. The more holistic aspect, thanks to James Hart, came from my subsequent exposure to systems.

'Systems and psychology made a good combination. James, through systems, concentrated on the so-called "hard" aspects and I, through psychology, on the supposedly "soft" ones. The police culture was in fact more liberal than people could imagine. For a start they invested in us. I would therefore say it was a benevolent organization at the time rather than a bottom line one. Senior officers like Matthews were very supportive. They mentored us through.

Neighbourhood policing – the knowledge based vision

'In fact we were encouraged, both by our organizations and by City University, to do our final year project together, systemically combining our two disciplines. Peter Herriot, now well known in academic management circles, was my tutor. Our object was then not only to get an undergraduate degree but also to work on what we came to term "neighbourhood policing" '. This whole concept then emerged from the work of two lowly undergraduates, though we inevitably stood on the shoulders of knowledgeable others. We did, though, the usual data-based research to try and understand for ourselves what was going on in policing neighbourhoods.

'Traditionally when you come back from university nothing much happens. But it so happened that the Brixton riots occurred in the summer of 1981. Peter Matthews, cropping up again in our lives, knew what we were up to at university. After the riots the Scarman inquiry took place, and I was taken back into the Metropolitan Police force in London. They thought neighbourhood policing was a soft option. That for me was a real anomaly. Normally the police divided things up, categorically, into hard or soft issues. We obviously didn't see things that way.

'In any case a joint task force was set up between Surrey and the Met, drawing upon – under Matthews' influence – our neighbourhood policing project, which had come to the notice of the Scarman inquiry. The police as a whole took Scarman very seriously. Our project was initially undertaken in a small group of London and Surrey based police stations. By then Kenneth Newman had taken over as Britain's Police Commissioner. He had read about our work. We subsequently expanded the number of experimental sites. James and I then played about with the experimental design. The study was subsequently evaluated by the police foundation. In fact they struggled to understand the systemic nature of it. They found difficulty in relating the outcomes to the inputs. Nevertheless, the work continued in Brixton. I was posted as Chief Inspector there. As our work was theory and hypothesis based, I could see the gaps emerging between theory and practice. So at Brixton I developed the model further. I then got involved in management training, and thereby learnt a lot about management styles. I developed our approach further on my own. It was now 1984. Ultimately, then, the model I developed at Brixton was somewhat different from our original one. I effectively rewired it. Subsequently it looked different on the surface, but it wasn't so in essence. I had changed the tyre, to use an analogy, and put a different ratio into the gearbox, but it remained the same kind of car.

'I then went on to Battersea. They had some of the same problems we had experienced in Brixton. High street robbery, for example. We reduced it, as we had done in Brixton. How I did all of this is in the City University library, as my doctoral thesis. That Ph.D. which I went on to undertake at City University, as did James Hart, served to accelerate my understanding of systems.

'A couple of major implications of our work were that, First, uniformed patrol officers could form the basis for neighbourhood policing – which was of course against traditional police culture – and, second, that they should be given the appropriate systems based support. Battersea, then, was a more refined version of our original model. It involved what came to be called sector policing, based on geographical areas, revolving around multiskilled teams. Because we thought the environment was the most powerful influence on patrol officers' tasks, so we gave them geographical responsibility. Our approach in fact became the model for the Met's subsequent adoption of sector policing, serving, as it did, a collection of adjacent neighbourhoods.

Managing knowledge creation

Introducing chaos and complexity theory

'I came on to Surrey, afterwards, because they had been running with the sector policing concept. Chief Constable Williams there knew of our work. He related to it. So he asked us – James Hart was still at Surrey – to get total geographic policing to work. I started to produce a more refined model, working with far fewer resources. I improved on the outcomes, thereby making small differences. It soon became obvious that it was no longer possible to cope with the work that arose on a paper and pencil basis. We had to invest in an enabling technology. At the same time I had to make use of chaos and complexity theory. It had already come to my notice that policing worked well in the borderlines between chaos and complexity, that is on the edge of chaos. Whereas crime and disorder could be modelled on chaos, community could be modelled along the lines of complexity.

'The "chaotic" nature of crime, moreover, pointed to the need for early intervention. Fewer resources invested early made for a bigger effect. You can't always predict, especially under extraordinary circumstances, but you can get it right 90 per cent of the time with standard, that is ordinary, operating procedures. Humans, it seems, are not quite as chaotic as wind and water.

Self-organizing groups

'The police tend to go for complicated solutions to problems, and therefore often fail. I was looking for simplicity, and I needed some powerful concepts to help me along. For example I'm now trying to create what I call "behavioural fractals". I was looking for a pattern to build up a complex system, using a simple basis for it. First I needed a rule based system. Next are the three levels of policing: reponse, reduction and prevention. We've got a number of little teams working on these issues.

'I'm after simple concepts that can be communicated in an hour or so. I have a problem solving group alongside me, aside from their normal jobs of course, containing a mixture of ability and rank. They're composed of training and performance measurement people as well as superintendents. There are in fact many individuals and groups working with me. I've got inspectors in areas working on projects. I've got CID officers. Gradually more groups are forming, self-generating in nature.

'When I look back on what we've achieved, since I failed at school, it's been quite considerable. Of course I've been lucky to have James alongside me, not to mention Peter Matthews and Chief Constable Williams, and now Ian Blair. As far as the Brixton riots were concerned I was in the right place in the right time.

'Above all, though, ever since those instances of bullying that I observed at school, and my early experiences of the problems of policing neighbourhoods, I've been searching for the true and just approach to policing. This I have since embodied in not only peace making and peace keeping, but also in building up a peaceful community in the first place. Maybe that's been part of my own growing-up process, starting out with my enjoyment of the physical environment when I was young, and turning my heart and mind, over time and with the help of my hay fever allergy, to the social and psychological environment. Of course there's so much more still to do, and I'll be relying on the MBA group, and of course many others, to take the work well on into the twenty-first century.'

INTRODUCTION

From being to becoming

In a previous chapter (chapter 12) we portrayed a complex pattern of individual and organizational activity, in the guise of so-called spiral dynamics, set within the context of the Thames Valley Police. Now we turn to the neighbouring Surrey Police force for an illustration of the workings of a so-called 'knowledge spiral'. For it is Nonaka and Takeuchi's[1] 'knowledge creating company' that adds a dynamic 'eastern' touch to an otherwise north-western organization, albeit set in a 'southern' communal context. Whereas fiery Branson brings the spirit of freedom to the civic community, cerebral Beckett brings the power of intellect to bear upon communal matters, thereby turning merely reactive peace keeping into proactive peace building.

The knowledge core

From reactive to proactive

Faced with a crisis, socio-political in one case and economic in the other, the British police force in the Brixton case, like the global Japanese manufacturers more generally, has turned to knowledge creation as a means of breaking away from the past and moving into the future. Rather than reactively fighting for survival with their backs to the wall, physically and economically, they proactively set out to create a new future. Such a proactive approach, moreover, involves both recognizing and renewing the capability of the enterprise as a whole, be it a Surrey Police or a Sony Corporation, to create new knowledge, disseminate it throughout the organization, and embody it in products, services and systems.

To create new knowledge, for such a Japanese enterprise or indeed our British one, means literally re-creating the institution and everything in it, set within the context of an ongoing process of individual and organizational renewal. Such re-creation is not the responsibility of the few – specialists in development, strategic planning or marketing – but of everyone in the organization. Such a process of thoroughgoing organizational renewal, moreover, is one in which Surrey Police is currently engaged, and in which our MMBA participants are deemed to play a significant part.

COMBINE

KNOWLEDGE   *NETWORK*

ENABLING

KNOWLEDGE
INTERNALIZE   EXTERNALIZE
VISION

CONDITIONS

KNOWLEDGE   *CREW*

SOCIALIZE

Figure 20 From knowledge vision to knowledge creation

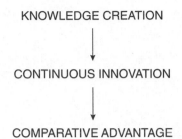

Figure 21 Towards comparative advantage

Japan's comparative advantage, according to Nonaka and Takeuchi, and in the same way Surrey Police's, lies in the 'eastern' way each of them views knowledge. As these two Japanese organizational sociologists see it, in the west (or north) normally, the theory of organization has long been dominated by a paradigm that conceptualizes it as a system that 'processes' information or 'solves' problems. 'Problem solving policing', as practised in the Thames Valley Police adjacent to Surrey, and modelled on an American approach, for example, is a case in point. This paradigm points towards an 'input–process–output' sequence of hierarchical information processing, or even business process re-engineering.

A critical problem with this approach is its rational and pragmatic, as opposed to holistic and humanistic, view of the world. Information processing is viewed as a problem solving activity which centres on what is given to the organization, without due consideration being accorded to what is created by it. Such a 'western' or 'northern' approach thereby emphasizes the absolute, depersonalized, non-human nature of knowledge. As such it is typically expressed in propositions and formal logic. In contrast, Nonaka and Takeuchi, as 'easterners', consider knowledge to be a dynamic human process of justifying personal belief with a view to finding the truth.

Any organization, for them, that dynamically deals with a changing environment ought not only to process information efficiently but also to creatively transform information into knowledge, in support of a profound purpose, indeed like 'peace building'. It is this process of knowlege conversion, into products and services, which is the key to understanding why the Japanese in general, and Surrey Police particularly, have become so successful (see Figure 21).

The path taken by such a knowledge creating organization, whether Mitsubishi or Surrey Police, is to turn knowledge creation into continuous innovation, so as to gain subsequent comparative advantage. For example, Sainsbury's or Anglian Water would not set out to outdo Tesco's or North-West Water, or for that matter to be the customer's first choice or the nation's premier water company. Rather they would set out to create new knowledge for a transcendent purpose, like peace building, whereby new products and services would be the result. Comparative advantage would thus be the outcome rather than the motivating force.

THE KNOWLEDGE CREATING CORE

Developing a knowledge vision

The case of Matsushita – humanware technology

A first step for the knowledge creating enterprise, as we intimated in chapter 10, at core, is to define the 'field' or 'domain' that gives a mental map of the world in which Surrey or Sony lives, and provide a general direction regarding what kind of knowledge they ought to seek to create. Most organizations only have have products and services in mind when formulating strategy, such as preventing crime in the case of a police force. Such products and services have clear boundaries.

In contrast, boundaries for knowledge are more obscure, helping to expand the organization's economic, technological and social scope. A case in point, for example, is Matsushita's knowledge based vision in 1990:

1   We are in the 'human innovation business', a business that creates new lifestyles based on creativity, comfort and joy in addition to efficiency and convenience;
2   We produce 'humanware technology', that is technology based on human studies such as artificial intelligence, fuzzy logic, and neuro-computers as well as chips systems and networking technology;
3   We are an active heterogeneous group, that is a corporate culture based on individuality and diversity;
4   We are engaged in multilocal and global networking management: a corporate structure that enables both localization and global synergy to take place.

Britain, of course, where this book is being written, is a long way from Japan, as is supposedly the Surrey Police from Matsushita Electronics. Yet arguably both enterprises are in the 'human innovation business'.

The case of the Surrey Police

Democratic communal policing

The British police force was founded some 170 years ago, as I have already indicated, by the Home Secretary Sir Robert Peel. One hundred and fifty years later, in 1979, a well-respected modern Chief Constable John Alderson, operating in Devon and Cornwall, amplified considerably upon this strategic intent. For him not only was policing concerned with strengthening the security of property and persons, with investigating as well as detecting, with activating the prosecution of offences within the rule of law, and with facilitating free passage on highways and curbing public disorder. For Alderson a modern police mission was also:

1   to contribute towards liberty, equality and fraternity in human affairs
2   to help reconcile freedom with security;
3   to facilitate human dignity through upholding and protecting human rights and the pursuit of happiness;
4   to provide leadership and participation in dispelling crimogenic social conditions through co-operative social action, as well as, finally,
5   to deal with crises thereby helping and advising those in distress, and where necessary activating other agencies.

These were Alderson's 'value grounds'. As he tacitly implies therefore, and as Acting Chief Chief Constable Ian Beckett and his Assistant Chief James Hart have explicitly pointed out, police organizations are predominantly human activity systems. In that respect they take their place alongside social, educational, health and probation services, not to mention the judicial system and the Home Office.

In revisiting Peel's original concept of preventive policing, now set in the a wider social context, Beckett and Hart advance the notion of 'community policing' picked up from Alderson. In this a 'service' approach leads, reciprocally, to the public assisting the police deal with and prevent crime, both individually and also institutionally.

In referring back to the ideas of John Alderson, they allude specifically to his approach to furthering the 'common good'. For Alderson this:

> would exist in its purest form where all the elements in a community, both official and unofficial, would conceive of the common good and combine to produce a social climate and an environment conducive to good order and the happiness of those living within it.
>
> (Nonaka and Takeuchi 1995)

Such an orientation leads towards a preventive approach to policing which is very different from the reactionary one of responding quickly to emergencies. Such a preventive or proactive approach involves the police in strengthening trust in communities or, where it is lacking, in creating it. From this vantage point the police, together with other agencies, stimulate the community itself towards self-policing. Such a proactive orientation, according to Nonaka and Takeuchi, is dependent upon the organization drawing upon new knowledge, which is perhaps why Surrey Police's former Chief Constable, Peter Matthews, wanted to encourage Beckett's and Hart's studies at university.

Investment in youth

*Peace
building*

| | *Peace
keeping* | SYSTEMS THEORY
CHAOS AND COMPLEXITY
PROSOCIAL PSYCHOLOGY
COMMUNITY HEALTH
URBAN STUDIES | *Peace
making* | **Business
secure** |

**Neighbourhood
secure**   *Peace   SYSTEMS THEORY
                 keeping*   CHAOS AND COMPLEXITY   **Business
                               PROSOCIAL PSYCHOLOGY   secure**
                               COMMUNITY HEALTH   *Peace
                               URBAN STUDIES   making*

*Peace
building*

Investment in youth

Figure 22 Surrey Police's knowledge vision

Systems, psychology and community

GENERAL SYSTEMS THEORY

Whilst Peter Matthews, John Alderson and even Robert Peel long before
them provided an initial source of inspiration for Beckett and Hart, the
Surrey Police's unique role has been to turn a philosophy into a knowledge
based vision. The three major knowledge sources have been general systems
theory for Hart primarily, social psychology for Beckett especially, and the
concept of community for the the two of them together. For the rationally
and holistically oriented James Hart, then:

> In conceptual terms, our concern here is with a police system which
> is defined as a regional police organization interacting with its envi-
> ronment. The police system receives inputs from the environment,
> converts these into outputs in accordance with the system's objectives
> and gives outputs to the environment. The police system itself is
> composed of sub-systems and elements which are joined in some
> purposeful way by a series of relationships. Thus the environment is
> affected by the police system and the police system is affected by the
> environment.

More recently, the general systems orientation has been enriched, by
Surrey, through the addition of chaos and complexity theory to the knowledge repertoire.

PROSOCIAL PSYCHOLOGY

While Hart's orientation, at least initially, was towards the so-called 'hard' systemic knowledge, Beckett's was towards the allegedly 'soft' foundations of social psychology. While Hart was rationally and holistically oriented, Beckett was pragmatically and humanistically inclined. More specifically the latter was oriented, at the outset, towards what has been termed 'prosocial' or positive social behaviours:

> Altruism refers to a regard for the interest of others without concern for one's self-interest. Sympathy refers to a concern with, or a sharing of, the pain or sadness of another person, or even an animal. Co-oper-ation is the willingness and ability to work with others usually, but not always, for a common benefit. Helping refers to the giving of assistance or aid towards a definite object ... Behaviour characterised as proso-cial would be expected to produce or maintain the physical and psychological well-being and the integrity of the other persons involved. This kind of behaviour intends not only the well-being of the other, but also a willingness to share not only the other's ends-in-view, but even his pain, frustration and sorrow. By contrast the kind of behaviour defined as negative social behaviour, if pursued, would circumscribe or destroy the freedom, expression, integrity and physical as well as psycho-logical well-being of the other.

COMMUNITY MENTAL HEALTH

Subsequent to systems and psychology, the third knowledge domain is that of 'community' studies, which Beckett and Hart maintain is the foundation upon which any viable policing strategy stands. They cite a broad definition of such community, expressed as: 'patterned interactions within a domain of individuals seeking to achieve security and physical safety, to derive support in times of stress and to gain selfhood and significance throughout the life-cycle'.

The Deputy Chief Constables go on to identify concepts of urban psychology and ecology, neighbourhood and sense of place, community and social behaviour.

The knowledge based vision, then, in this Surrey case, is based upon systems theory, social psychology and community health, providing the underpinning for creative innovation, leading out of its 'global' impulse (see chapter 10). The enabling conditions, at the same time, provide the 'harmonic' conditions, or the developmental setting for such innovation, on a localized basis. Between the knowledge vision and the enabling condi-tions, then, the 'yang' and 'yin' basis is established for ongoing knowledge creation.

Establishing enabling conditions

Nonaka and Takeuchi identify five 'enabling conditions'[1] for knowledge creation, of which the first three are pivotal:

Intention

The first enabling condition, which in fact overlaps with the need for a knowledge based vision, requires the organization to develop, intentionally, the organizational capability to acquire, create, accumulate and exploit knowledge. In the case cited here such a vision – embodied in peace building, peace making and peace keeping – involves the capability to acquire, create, accumulate and exploit knowledge in general systems, social psychology and community health.

Autonomy

The second condition involves the progressive build-up of autonomous individuals and groups, setting their task boundaries by themselves to pursue the ultimate goal expressed in the higher intention of the organization. Such groups in the Surrey Police, as Ian Beckett has intimated, emerge from training and from performance measurement, and more generally from the police superindendents.

Fluctuation

The third of the fundamental conditions Nonaka and Takeuchi describe is that of top management providing employees with a sense of crisis as well as a lofty ideal. Such so-called 'creative chaos' increases tension within the organization. The crisis, in the police context, is embodied in the so-called 'reactive spiral'. Here, without the restraint of police preventive services, crime and conflict increase to unacceptable levels and the demands on the police spiral out of control.

In the face of such obvious police helplessness there are three characteristic public reactions: apathy and acceptance of random crime, formation of vigilante groups to fight back and the proliferation of organized crime. Conversely, as we have seen, the lofty ideal is lodged within peace building, as well as peace making and peace keeping activities. In fact, very recently, the idea of developing an international peace forum, with which Surrey might be intimately associated, has been mooted.

Redundancy

There are two more significant but relatively less important enabling conditions. The first involves 'redundancy' of a particular kind. Such 'redundant' information enables individuals to invade each other's functional boundaries, bringing about 'learning by intrusion' into each individual's sphere of perception. This is happening in the Surrey Police at the moment, to the extent that the MMBA participants on our programme are engaged in overlapping project based activities.

Requisite variety

Finally, to maximize variety, our two Japanese researchers proclaim, everyone in the organization should be assured of the fastest access to the broadest variety of necessary information. In our police context the 'Blue Knight' project, also involving the systems house Intergraph, is aimed at building up such access. We now turn from the knowledge creating core to the polarities.

THE KNOWLEDGE CREATING POLARITIES

Knowledge as a dynamic process

The knowledge spiral

Our two Japanese sociologists, as we may recall, consider knowledge creation to be sourced by a dynamic human process of justifying personal belief towards the truth. This is a far cry from the pragmatic 'western' or indeed rational 'northern' belief in knowledge accumulation as a depersonalized, information centred process. For the 'eastern' Japanese, and to at least some extent for Beckett and Hart at the Surrey Police, a so-called 'knowledge creating spiral', as opposed to a 'reactive' one, involves four identifiable processes. These, respectively embody the four poles of our global businessphere, and indeed the four discrete elements of our organizational ecology. Each part, finally, of the knowledge creating whole contains a different mix of subjectively based 'tacit' and objectively oriented 'explicit' knowledge (see Figure 23).

Tacit and explicit knowledge

While information in the 'west' may simply be seen as a flow of messages, for the Japanese – as for Acting and Assistant Chief Constables Beckett and Hart – knowledge is created and organized by the flow of information, anchored in the commitment and beliefs of its holder. As a result, as far as Nonaka and Takeuchi are concerned, attention should be focused on the active, subjective nature of knowledge represented by such terms as 'belief' and 'commitment' that are deeply rooted in the value systems of individuals. Therefore knowledge that can be expressed in words and numbers, as

Tacit knowledge to explicit knowledge

Tacit knowledge	SOCIALIZATION	EXTERNALIZATION
from		
Explicit knowledge	INTERNALIZATION	COMBINATION

Figure 23 The knowledge structure

in balance sheets, computer programs or policing menus, only represents the tip of the iceberg of possible knowledge. For Michael Polanyi, the twentieth-century European philosopher on whom the Japanese sociologists draw prolifically, knowledge can be classified into two categories. On the one hand 'explicit' or codified knowledge refers to knowledge that is transmittable in formal, systematic language. On the other hand, 'tacit' knowledge has a personal quality, hard to formalize or communicate. Such tacit knowledge, moreover, is deeply rooted in action, commitment and involvement in a specific context, like policing.

Both tacit and explicit knowledge contain technical and cognitive dimensions. The tacit, cognitive elements centre upon 'mental maps' like 'neighbourhood policing' in which human beings form working models of the world by creating and manipulating analogies in their minds. These working models include metaphors like 'Blue Knight', paradigms, beliefs and viewpoints that provide 'perspectives' that help individuals to perceive and define their world. Surrey Police, through the influence of Beckett and Hart (see Figure 23 for an example), abounds in these. Explicit variations – the traditional grounds of policing – include codified systems of rules and regulations, policies and procedures, trading accounts and software programs. By contrast, the technical element of tacit knowledge covers concrete know-how, crafts and skills that apply to specific contexts as exemplified by 'the bobby-on-the-beat'. Similarly, specialized techniques in problem solving, negotiation, motivation and indeed peace making form the explicit counterparts.

Tacit knowledge, then, is a continuous activity of knowing and embodies an 'analogue' quality that aims to share such knowledge to build mutual understanding. This understanding involves a kind of 'parallel processing' of the complexities of current issues. This is because the different dimensions of a problem are processed simultaneously. An example in the Surrey Police case is the alignment of peace making, peace keeping and peace building aspirations with the core skills of intervention, investigation and problem solving. By contrast, explicit knowledge is discrete or 'digital'. It is captured in records of the past such as libraries, archives and databases, and is accessed on a sequential basis.

Level of social interaction

Nonaka and Takeuchi turn from the nature of knowledge to the scope of knowledge in organizations. At a fundamental level, they maintain that knowledge is created by individuals, be they assistant chief constables, production managers, patrol officers or research assistants. Organizational knowledge creation, therefore, should be understood in terms of a process that institutionally amplifies the knowledge created by its people, and crystallizes it as a part of the knowledge network of the organization. In this context it is possible to distinguish between several types of knowledge creating activity, which correspond with the four poles of our global businessphere, through which the knowledge created by an individual is transformed and legitimized.

Socialization – humanistic – co-creation

In the first instance an informal community of social interaction provides an immediate forum for nurturing the emergent property of knowledge at each organizational level. This is the 'southern' humanistic pole, embodied in what Beckett has identified as 'prosocial' behaviours, incorporating altruism, empathy and a sense of reciprocity. Since the informal community of which such behaviour forms a part might span organizational boundaries, it is important that an enterprise like Surrey Police is able to integrate aspects of emerging knowledge into strategic development. Thus the potential contribution of informal groups to organizational knowledge creation should be related to more formal notions of organization structure, both within the organization and without. This is something that Surrey Police is still struggling to establish, given its highly formalized cultural heritage.

Such *tacit to tacit* socialization, moreover, relies on shared experience that enables members to 'indwell' in others and to grasp their world from the 'inside'. This shared experience also facilitates the co-creation of 'common perspectives', thereby contributing to the 'common good' to which Chief Constable Alderson was so attached. In other words, communication is like a wave that passes through people's bodies and culminates when everyone synchronizes themselves with the wave. In effect, the entire MBA programme, in the Surrey Police context, has been set up, at least in part, to bring about such socialization, which serves as a form of stewardship of the knowledge based vision. To succeed in that respect, it will have to countermand the prevailing individualistic and formalistic culture.

Externalization – holistic – catalysation

Once mutual trust and a common implicit perspective has been formed through shared experience, the team needs to articulate the perspective through continuous dialogue. This process activates what is known as 'externalization', *from tacit to explicit*, whereby participants, acting out of a 'gardening' mentality, engage in the co-development of ideas. This constitutes a holistic 'eastern' orientation. Such a process is seemingly under way between Dr Beckett, at Surrey Police, and some of his training and performance measurement people. Through the use of contradiction and paradox, a dialectical approach can serve to stimulate creative thinking. Such dialogue should not be single faceted and deterministic but multifaceted, providing room for revision or negation. This dialectical thinking, in effect, is a spiral process whereby affirmation and negation are synthesized to form knowledge. Crime prevention and crime detection, peace building and peace making constitute such dialectical notions. While deduction and induction are vertically oriented reasoning processes, what Nonaka terms 'abduction' is the lateral extension of the reasoning process based upon the use of metaphors, extending to analogies and concepts. The emergent concepts then provide a basis of crystallization, or knowledge combination.

Combination – rational – conservation

The third mode of knowledge conversion involves the use of social processes to combine different bodies of *explicit* knowledge held by individuals, through such exchange mechanisms as formal meetings, office memos and codes of conduct that are the stuff of, for example, traditionally oriented policing. The reconfiguring of existing information through 'herding', that is the sorting, adding, recategorizing and recontextualizing of such explicit knowledge can, at the same time, lead to new combinations of knowledge. Modern computer based data processing systems provide a graphic example of such knowledge 'combination'. The 'Blue Knight' project at Surrey, which is geared towards assembling new knowledge through information technology, and the 'menu' policing orientation, constitute such explicit forms of knowledge creation that are 'northern', or rational in focus.

Internalization – pragmatic – colonization

In the conversion of *explicit into tacit* knowledge, finally, that is 'internalization', action is important. We are now in the realm of 'western' pragmatism. Individuals internalize knowledge tacitly, through direct, hands-on experience, thereby both reaching out for and holding on to what they have hunted for. Moreover, for explicit knowledge to become tacit it helps if the knowledge is verbalized or diagrammed into manuals, documents or stories. The quality of that knowledge is influenced by both the variety of the experiences and also the degree to which they are related. It is affected, moreover, by the extent to which the knowledge is embodied through deep personal commitment, thereby transcending the subject–object divide, providing access to 'pure experience'.

It is with a view, for instance, to fostering a more rapid internalization of knowledge that Surrey introduced its neighbourhood policing, whereby multiskilled teams have become attached to particular geographical clusters.

Finally, each of the four knowledge creating modes produces different outputs. Socialization or co-creation yields what the two Japanese term 'sympathized knowledge' such as shared values and technical skills. Externalization or catalysation produces conceptual knowledge, resulting in the new product or organizational designs that proliferate at Surrey. Combination or conservation gives rise to so-called 'systematic knowledge' such as computer programs, financial counts and the management information systems that have been developed by Surrey Police together with Intergraph. Internalization or colonization, finally, yields 'operational knowledge', encompassing project management, production processes and menu policing. We now turn from the knowledge creating core, and the surrounding polarities to the connective elements that serve to link the core with the periphery, i.e. what are known as 'knowledge crew' and the 'knowledge network'.

THE KNOWLEDGE CREATING PERIPHERY

Middle-up-down-management

The practical vehicle for activating the knowledge spiral, releasing the knowledge based vision with the support of the enabling conditions, is for Nonaka and Takeuchi 'middle-up-down-management'. They contrast this with top down and bottom up approaches. In top down management, set within the context of a vertically based organizational hierarchy much favoured by traditionally based institutions such as conventional police forces, the top executives create the basic concepts so that lower members can implement them.

Front-line execution thus becomes largely routine. In a bottom up organization which has a flat and horizontal shape, few orders and instructions are given by top managers, who serve as sponsors of entrepreneurially minded or adventurous frontline employees. Knowledge is created by these employees, who operate as independent and separate actors, preferring to work on their own. Autonomy, not interaction, is the key operating principle. The top down model, therefore, is suitable for dealing with explicit knowledge, neglecting the development of tacit knowledge that can take place on the front line. The bottom up approach is good at dealing with tacit knowledge, but its very emphasis on autonomy means that such knowledge becomes extremely difficult to disseminate and share within the organization.

Table 11   Comparative management

	Top down	Middle up/down	Bottom up
Agent of knowledge creation	Top management	Self-organizing team	Intrapreneur
Management processes	Leaders as commanders	*Leaders as catalysts*	Leaders as sponsors
Accumulated knowledge	Explicit: documented/ computerized	Explicit and tacit shared diversely	Tacit; embodied in individuals

The middle-up-down-management style that Surrey advocates, third and preferably for knowledge creation, establishes bridges between the visionary ideals of the top and the often chaotic realities of work confronted by front-line operators. As such they – exemplified by the MMBA community in Surrey's case – constitute the 'knowledge engineers' in the middle, set within the context of Nonaka's knowledge crew (see Table 11).

Within Surrey Police, while some MMBAs are engaged in building partnerships with community based organizations externally, others are building up the enabling conditions internally. Each is serving as an organizational catalyst. A third group, sponsored by Dr Beckett, is developing new products and services that serve to link enterprise with environment.

The knowledge crew

Knowledge practitioners

Knowledge practitioners consist of 'knowledge operators' who interface with tacit knowledge for the most part, and 'knowledge specialists', who interface primarily with explicit knowledge. The 'bobby on the beat', civilians 'manning' receptions at police stations, and computer programmers setting up the relevant information systems are all examples of such knowledge practitioners. Such practitioners develop a strongly personal *perspective*, a strong degree of *openness* to discussion and debate, as well as a variety of *experience* inside and outside the organization from and through which they are able to learn. They also acquire a high degree of specific skill based *competence*, and functional management knowledge, as well as skill in *interacting* with colleagues and customers.

Knowledge engineers

Knowledge engineers, to whom our MMBA programme is most particularly addressed, are responsible for converting tacit knowledge into explicit and vice versa, thereby facilitating the four modes of knowledge creation. In this way they mediate between the 'what should be' mindset of the senior management and the 'what is' mindset of the frontline employees by creating mid-level business and product concepts. Such middle managers, then, synthesize the tacit knowledge of both frontline employees and executive officers, make it explicit, and incorporate it into new products and technologies.

As knowledge engineers, the participants on our programme become proficient in employing metaphors, and in developing storylines, to help themselves and others *imagine the future*. They become adept at communication by *encouraging dialogue*, and increase their competence in *developing* new strategic *concepts*. They are able to develop *methodologies* for *knowledge creation*, and they become equipped with *project management* capabilities. One such knowledge engineer in the police, for example, Simon Wilshire, is focusing on building up a local partnership with educational, social and probation services, to help in the process of crime prevention.

Knowledge officers

Knowledge officers, like Dr Beckett at Surrey, finally, are responsible for managing the total knowledge creation process at the corporate level. They are therefore expected to give an enterprise's knowledge creating activities a sense of direction by articulating grand concepts of what the organization might be, establishing a knowledge vision in the form of a policy statement, and setting the standards for justifying the value of the knowledge that is being created.

In other words, knowledge officers are responsible for articulating the company's overall concepts, those grand concepts that in highly universal and abstract terms identify the common features linking disparate business activities into a coherent whole. The interrelation of environmental factors, policing products and delivery systems is a case in point in Surrey. More specifically, then, knowledge officers such as Surrey's two acting and Deputy Chief Constables develop the ability to *direct* the entire process of *knowledge creation*, and *articulate* a knowledge *vision* in order to help give an enterprise's knowledge creating activities a sense of direction. They create chaos within the project team, for example, setting *challenging goals*, and they have responsibility for *selecting* the right *project leaders*, or knowledge engineers. Furthermore, and finally, they need to be able to interact with team members in a hands-on way and *solicit commitment* from them. That describes Ian Beckett perfectly. We now turn from the active knowledge crew to the interactive knowledge network.

The knowledge network

The hypertext organization

Nonaka's 'hypertext' organization, so called because of its layered nature and scope, not only serves to accommodate the efforts of the knowledge crew, but also to develop, channel and distribute knowledge through the networks that have been formed. The top stratum of such an enterprise (see Figure 23) then, is composed of the 'project team' layer. Here, as is becoming increasingly the case in Surrey Police as well as in IBM and Sainsbury's, multiple project teams engage in knowledge creating activities such as new product and systems development. In all such cases the team members are brought together from a number of different units across the business system, and are assigned exclusively to a project team until the project is completed.

Alongside this project layer, but occupying a lower order of knowledge creating significance, is the conventionally bureaucratic system, with its normal hierarchy of authority. The project layer, on the one hand, is engaged with developing new knowledge through self-organizing groups. The hierarchical system, on the other, is primarily concerned with categorizing, ordering, distributing and commercializing or operationalizing such knowledge. In effect then, whereas the project layer is primarily focused upon socialization and externalization, the hierarchical system is more engaged with combination and internalization. Underlying both of these, for Nonaka and Takeuchi, is a 'knowledge base'. This third layer does not exist as an actual organizational entity but is embedded in corporate vision, organizational culture or technology. At the moment it is implicit within Surrey Police rather than explicit, embedded in fact within Beckett and Hart's joint research project, undertaken as part of their undergraduate studies at City University!

The corporate vision that arises from it provides the direction in which the enterprise should develop its technology or products, and clarifies the 'field' in which it wants to play. In the case of the Surrey Police, this takes a distinctive shape, given the nature and scope of such a peace building, peace making and peace keeping enterprise. While corporate vision and organizational culture provide the knowledge base to tap tacit knowledge, technology taps the explicit knowledge generated in the other two layers. The ability to switch from one layer to another, so as to form a dynamic cycle of knowledge, is what determines for Nonaka the organizational capability for knowledge creation. A knowledge creating enterprise ultimately must have the organizational ability to acquire, accumulate, exploit and create knowledge continuously and dynamically. Moreover, it must be able to recategorize and recontextualize it strategically for use by others in the organization or by future generations. As we have indicated, a hierarchy is the most efficient structure for the acquisition, accumulation and exploitation of knowledge, while a task force is the most effective for the creation of new knowledge.

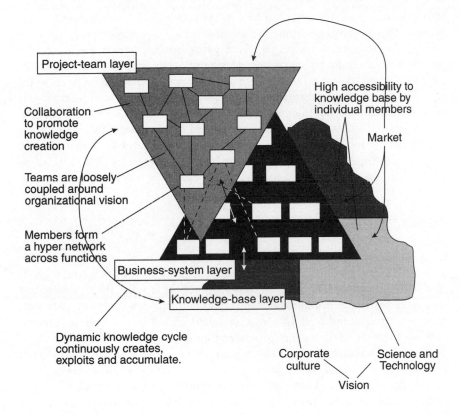

Figure 24 Project based 'Hypertext' organization

Piggybacking on product development

Overall then, managing knowledge creation involves creating a knowledge vision, developing a knowledge crew and thus adopting middle-up-down-management, and switching to a hypertext organization. All of these things Surrey Police have done, though often implicitly rather than explicitly. It also involves purposefully constructing a knowledge network with the outside world, while building up high-density interaction at the front line. Finally, it requires an organization like Surrey Police, or indeed IBM or Sainsbury's or Anglian Water, to piggyback on new product development. Organizational knowledge creation is like a derivative of new product development. How well a public or private enterprise manages it therefore becomes the critical determinant of how successfully organizational knowledge creation can be carried out.

First, then, knowledge creating organizations must maintain a highly adaptive and flexible approach to new product development, which seldom proceeds in a linear manner. In fact it involves continuous trial and error. Second, such enterprises must ensure that a self-organizing team is overseeing new product development. Left to its 'soulful' self in this way, the process will begin to create its own dynamic order, initially like a start-up company, until at some point the team develops its own product concept. Knowledge creating organizations must allow the team autonomy, and tolerate chaos and fluctuation. Third, enterprises need to encourage the participation of non-experts who are willing to challenge the status quo. Surrey Police, for example, has instituted a ritual whereby, at its quarterly ceremonial dinners, such experts are invited into the police fold, and introduced to the corporate family, to ensure that their expert value is internalized.

CONCLUSION

In this chapter on organizational knowledge creation, coupled with the previous ones on spectral theory and spiral dynamics, both set in the context of the global businessphere, we have attempted to do three things, all aimed at fostering organization development through cultural diversity. First, we have introduced you to a so-called global businessphere, serving to bring together under one roof 'western' pragmatism and 'eastern' holism, 'northern' rationalism and 'southern' humanism. Moreover, we have alerted you to the fact that these four polar organizational attributes cannot co-exist in a vacuum. They need both a centrifugal and a centripetal core at the centre of their 'being', and an active and interactive periphery, to project their 'doing'. These eight different attributes can be identified in individuals, as well as organizations and societies, which is where spectral theory has its contribution to make.

Whereas innovators and enablers occupy centre stage, within an authentically global enterprise, change agents and adventurers need to 'man' the periphery. Moreover, whereas the 'western' entrepreneur needs to be complemented by the 'eastern' adopter to form the east–west polarity, the 'northern' executive needs to be complemented by the 'southern' animateur so as to make up the north–south one. Third, then, and in the context of the knowledge creating organization, the knowledge based vision and the enabling conditions need to provide the 'soul' force, while the knowledge crew and the knowledge network serve to make up the active and interactive periphery.

At the same time 'southern'-style socialization or 'co-creation' provides the constantly renewing 'heart' of the knowledge creating enterprise, 'eastern'-style externalization or 'catalysation' the vitalizing 'spirit', 'northern'-style combination or 'conservation' the configuring 'mind', and 'western'-style internalization or 'colonization' the structuring 'body'. Altogether, aligned with an appropriate knowledge vision and the right enabling conditions, they constitute a fully functioning whole. In this way, and to the extent that Surrey

Police becomes a fully fledged knowledge creating enterprise, so it will be composed of heart and mind, body and spirit, encapsulated within what might be termed a 'soul' force.

In fact, Surrey has gone a long way, at least implicitly, towards becoming one of the few knowledge creating enterprises that exist within the 'west', if not also the 'north' and 'south'. The fact that what is implicit has not yet been rendered explicit is partly due to proverbial British understatement, and partly because of the way the police force is constituted. In other words, and in knowledge creating terms, whereas combination and internalization are part of its generalized heritage, socialization is part of the benevolent British policing tradition.

Externalization, though, or the development of new concepts, new products and new processes, fuelled by a knowledge based vision, lies beyond the conventional police ken. The unique role that Deputy Chief Constables Beckett and Hart have played, supported by enabling conditions at City University, was to develop and project their lofty ideals alongside the crisis brought about by the Brixton riots. Moreover, they have stood on the shoulders of visionary giants, most particularly Robert Peel to begin with, John Alderson from the Devon and Cornwall police constabulary, and perhaps Peter Matthews at Surrey.

We now turn from the peaceful community that Surrey Police is attempting to create, through knowledge creating enterprise, to the civic community that Anglian Water is ultimately fostering, through private enterprise in Britain.

BIBLIOGRAPHY

1 Nonaka, I. and Takeuchi, H., *The Knowledge Creating Company*, Oxford University Press, 1995.

15 Enhancing life through water

Anglian Water's paths of change

THE ORGANIZATION

Journey towards transformation

Ian Plover and Dale Evans stood at an Anglian watershed. How were they to transform the two worlds they represented, one focused on people and the other on technology, to Anglian's commercial advantage? Ian was one of the first Anglian Water candidates on our MMBA programme, and had risen from the ranks, as part of the AW 'old breed', to a relatively senior management position. Having started out in Anglian as a physical labourer some twenty years ago, and after steadily making his way up the operational line, he had become, as its Business Manager, right-hand man to the HR Director. As former Employee Relations Manager he had taken a lead in overhauling the company's antiquated, adversarial approach to industrial relations. Dale, one of Anglian's 'new breed', was ostensibly very different: he was a graduate engineer who, having made his way relatively quickly through to Innovation, was then posted to America, for a two-year stint as a Business Development Manager, developing Anglian's international business.

Their respective activities, then, were seemingly poles apart. While one was a 'people person' the other was a 'techie'. While one was involved with the 'core' UK business, the other was engaged with Anglian Water International. While Ian was in people-centred Human Resources, Dale was in product-centred Innovation. Yet in Buffalo the two worlds, teased continually apart by space and time, suddenly seemed to come together. How did this come about? First, and through the Management MBA, both had come across the notion of organizational knowledge creation, which brought people and product together. Second, the transformation that Director of Innovation Peter Matthews had recently undergone, from product developer to taking on the development of the organization as a whole, in addition, had served, via the embryonic University of Water, to set an integrative example. Third, and most importantly, Ian and Dale had a desire to take themselves and their organization on an authentic Transformation Journey. Such a journey, from the outset, would link together the technical and the social – embodied respectively in Dale and in Ian – with the commercial and the environmental. How then could they turn such a prospect into a fullblown reality, together with the author as learning strategist and with Sudhanshu Palsule, who was responsible for the University of Water?

Dale and Ian first met, as fellow MMBAs, soon after Anglian had taken over a water utility in Buffalo, New York. Together – Dale from a technical and commercial (product-market) angle and Ian other from a social and environmental (employee relations) one – they had come up with an imaginative scheme. In the wake of privatizing the local Buffalo water utility, they devised a novel approach to saving jobs, through allocating otherwise surplus employees to a newly devised metering programme.

It then occurred to Dale and Ian that they had a new socio-technical product in the making, which they aligned to 'transition management'. The question was where they could take it from there. They decided, with a truly transformative purpose in mind, that they had to do three things. First they needed to link back (*re-ligere*) in time to the company's roots. Second, they needed to align themselves in space with Peter Matthews' knowledge based vision that Anglian had consistently ignored, and which was set in aquatic, technical and socio-political grounds. Third, as good MBA students, they felt they needed to draw upon some relevant theory.

To begin with, they solicited the help of fellow MMBA graduates Mark Driver and Richard Sage. Mark and Richard's wife Nina – employed by Anglian as a conservation officer – were both passionately concerned about the environmental issues. In fact, whereas Mark's first MBA project had been dedicated to cost savings, in his second he attempted to link up business process re-engineering with the notion of ecological succession. This was not unrelated to the early work I did with Sudhanshu Palsule, on developing a knowledge creating ecology. For his third project, Mark set out to recontextualize his work, (which was based in customer services) ecologically and historically, in an evolving civic community.

Becoming guardians of the water world

Mark has since become a production manager, together with Richard Sage, who had previously been his coach. Richard started out on our programme by establishing an architecture for Anglian's emerging information services, which was subsequently, however, outsourced, and thereby indeed hangs a tale. He then took up a new position as a customer services manager, from where he and his team did some pioneering work on building a learning organization. In fact his so-called 'Transformation Journey' group gained fame, or notoriety, as the 'Circus' – of which John Newall (see below) was part – that set out to entertain as well as to inform Anglians in and outside of Milton Keynes where they were based.

For his third project, building on Mark Driver's earlier work, Richard set out to reconfigure the customer services organization, so as to better integrate its activities with production. Julie O'Connell, a fellow learning set member of Mark Driver's, also focused on customer service both psychologically and economically, from the commercial end of the UK business. Events then overtook them as another restructuring took place, and customer services was split into two parts. In many ways, though, Richard's work anticipated a more fundamental reconfiguration – 'Workforce 2000', championed by Director of Production Roy Pointer. Roy's commitment to upgrade the skills of his production based workforce was subsequently actualized by MMBA graduates Phil Samways and Paul Blantern, as well as by Richard and Mark.

All of them – and others – had by this time been promoted to production managers. On the MBA course they had also gained considerable psychological and social insight into people and organizations. While Paul Blantern, became an archetypal 'knowledge engineer', Phil Samways became something of a prodigal son. For it was Phil who, having devoted his first project to building up a self-managed team, alongside fellow learning set member Chris Royce – under the mentorship of Engineering Director (now IS Director) Mike Biss – subsequently spearheaded Anglian's business development efforts in New Zealand. Here he followed in the footsteps of engineer Phil Butler, another MMBA who had played a leading role in winning the New Zealand bid.

These efforts by Phil Samways and Phil Butler brought in hundreds of millions of pounds' worth of prospective business, arising out of the way in which Phil Samways adapted to local needs. He studied the indigenous Maori culture intensively, in the context of his third 'mastery' project, with a view to Anglian becoming 'guardian of their water world'. It was with that end in mind that David Edge, a fellow MBA, concentrated his first and second projects on the environment, before focusing, in his third, on the insourcing of sludge removal in Anglian. This ultimately led to cost savings of around a million pounds within the company. A similar significant saving was also achieved by another MMBA, Martin Joiner in engineering, when he democratized the capital budgeting process, before setting out to join Dale Evans in America.

While Phil Samways was in New Zealand, fellow learning set member Chris Royce was in Australia, bidding for a contract that incorporated local economic development with water and waste water treatment. To Chris's chagrin Anglian did not win this contract but the company certainly won many friends in South Australia, for the sincerity of their intentions and the seriousness of their efforts.

Towards the University of Water

For his final project Chris devoted himself to establishing a conceptual framework for the emergent University of Water, which is now being further worked upon by the Transition Management Group. One of the group, also including Dale and Ian, Sudhanshu and me, was Steve Kaye, an engineer like Dale Evans who had moved into Innovation, and ultimately took that world by storm. Not only did he actively build bridges between engineering and product development but by his third project he was building strong connections between Anglian Water in Britain and Purac in Scandinavia, through his Innovation based efforts. While Steve had originally worked closely with Dale, Ian Plover had been in close conact with Dave Revitt, both as customer services managers. Having spent his first two MMBA projects converting himself from a 'techie' into a people oriented manager, Dave has subsequently become involved in community economic development within East Anglian, as an AW secondee working with small businesses in the local area. In this way Dave has found his vocation, linking up the technical and social with the economic.

Similarly Graham Whitby at Purac, a subsidiary of Anglian's, also spent his first project looking over the engineer's bridge towards the worlds of business and management, as has been the case for his colleague Paul Botrill. By the third 'mastery' project Graham felt he had made a complete conversion, and had become a whole business manager. Something similar had happened to Ian Turner, also from Purac (UK) in Kidderminster, who having started out as a mechanical engineer, ended up not only becoming a customer services manager but also taking a lead in managing across cultures, between Britain and China. Shaun Carroll, another engineer based in Northampton, has also ended up as a client manager, with a markedly different outlook on life and business from the one he had started with in his first MMBA project.

Role evolution and business development

As Dale and Ian pondered the immediate situation, individually and collectively, they wondered how they could fundamentally transform themselves and the Anglian organization in the light of the trajectory that they and their fellow MMBAs had been following. They were also conscious of the fact that there were several other students who had made remarkable breakthroughs within themselves and yet were not able to translate these adequately into ongoing business and managerial performance. Dale Evans, meanwhile, in 1998, was being promoted to Network Manager, back in the UK, and Ian Plover had become HR's Business Manager. But it was not quite enough for them, and for Anglian. Something transformative for both was missing.

The vital clue to what was missing came when Ian reflected, as coach, upon student Richard Boucher's third project. Richard was another MMBA who had emerged out of the operational backwoods to play a leading part – now positioned within the planning function – in formulating Anglian Water's new Vision and Values. Yet, as good as such a vision was in body and mind, Ian felt that it was lacking in heart and spirit. And then he thought of the Transformation Journey, which, after all, was some kind of spin-off from the MMBA. It was faltering badly – too much heart and spirit and too little body and mind – and there was a need for a global phoenix to rise from out of the local Journey ashes.

For an instant he thought to himself that perhaps a Transformation Directorate should be established, but that, on second thoughts, involved a mere restructuring rather than also a reconfiguring, a revitalizing or a renewing. Ian then wondered about the fate of other fellow MBAs like Bob Bates and John Herring, who had engaged in varying degrees of self-transformation, within the worlds of information services and of water quality respectively, and yet had not markedly linked their own development with that of the organization. That having been said, when Mike Biss took over the IS Directorate, he turned to John and Bob's projects for vital background information. What was that underlying and transformative process though, Ian and Dale wondered, that could serve to evolve if not transform their roles, as well as those of their kindred spirits? How could they ensure, moreover, that the earliest of the MMBA graduates, like Dave Pouncey who now worked in the outsourced information services, and Dave Hellier, who had turned from being an engineer into a commercial manager, were not left behind? At this point, towards the end of 1997, fate intervened. Alan Smith decided to retire from the business, on the grounds of ill health, and the reins were handed over to Finance Director Chris Mellor. Chris had a good relationship with me and asked me to have a look at the range of learning and change initiatives at Anglian, with a view to integrating them better. At this point I turned for practical help to Ian Plover, to his colleagues at City University Business School for research guidance, and for theoretical assistance to California's Will McWhinney. The rest, as they say, is AW/CUBS history. This chapter is indeed written in the narrative form that underlay the 'emergent' approach to change, in which we engaged with Anglian Water, in the spring of 1998, now under the sponsorship of its newly installed CEO, Chris Mellor.

INTRODUCTION – WHY CHANGE?

Beyond initiative overload

Anglian Water has undergone a profound transition in less than a decade, from a public bureaucracy to a private enterprise, from a local East Anglian institution to a somewhat global enterprise, and from an autocratically run to an empowered organization. For half of that period I have been privileged to be Anglian's learning strategist, albeit from an external vantage point. Early in 1998, moreover, as part of the action research Professor Chris Hendry, researcher Sally Woodward and I had been commissioned to do for AW, I was asked by the new CEO, Chris Mellor, to help him assimilate and bring together the myriad learning and change initiatives that had sprung up in AW, despite the fact that a Learning Review group was also officially in place.

Chris wanted to ensure that the ownership of these initiatives would be spread around, rather than being held by one individual or another. For separate development had hitherto led to a singular lack of coherence in the way that change was being managed. From my perspective, drawing upon the information that Sally Woodward generated through her interviews with key initiative holders, I wanted to develop an emergent learning strategy from out of the maelstrom of what had occurred over the previous five years. Conceptually speaking, and apart from my own approach – and that of Sudhanshu Palsule – to *Managing in Four Worlds*,[1] I was generally helped by by *The Stories We Are*,[2], and specifically by Will McWhinney's *Paths of Change*,[3] upon which this chapter is focused.

A map of realities

Four realities

Will McWhinney, an organization developer currently based in Los Angeles, who, interestingly, helped establish Leeds Business School in England, has developed his own 'map of reality', which is in fact complementary to my own. Changes take place, for McWhinney, when boundaries between the logics of the four alternative realities (in *italics* below) are transgressed.

Plurality and agency

The first horizontal axis, running from left to right, stretches from the extremes of pluralism to monism. It separates, on the one hand, realistic change agents from idealistic ones, and the empiricists from the theorists. It thereby distinguishes agents of change who hold the universe to be a multiplicity from those who hold it to be a unity. The second vertical axis extends from change agents who hold a deterministic worldview to those who believe that they have free will to create their own worlds.

There are four extreme, archetypal perspectives for McWhinney: first pluralistic-deterministic or *sensory* ones, and second monistic-deterministic or *unitary*; third pluralistic-volitional or *social* perspectives and fourth monistic-volitional or *mythic* ones. Sensory reality is based on belief in a pluralistic/deterministic world in which change agents – like AW's Technical Director John Green as we shall see – touch, smell and see.

That which is practically sensed, for them therefore, is real. *Social* reality, which is partly where CEO Chris Mellor is coming from, is a more humanistic view of the world, an acceptance of different viewpoints, histories and moral codes as well as the conflicts which such acceptances engender. *Unitary* reality, for an agent of change, is reflected in responsibility and authority,

ANALYTIC

Sensory   *Unitary*

PARTICIPATIVE   ASSERTIVE

Social   *Mythic*

EMERGENT

Figure 25 From analytic to emergent realities

consistency and conservation, which is the other part of Chris Mellor's orientation. Finally, whereas a unitary reality is a world of abstract law, *mythic*
reality, is a world of the 'story'. As we shall now see, my own approach to
change, together with that of my colleague Terry Cook, as illustrated in the
Anglian Water case, was such a mythically based one.

Orders of learning

To understand what is involved in making such a change, we need a language
to describe degrees of such 'orders of consciousness'. McWhinney, amongst
many others in the field, cites Gregory Bateson as having provided such a
change continuum, analogously, through his approach to learning. His
models, or orders of learning and change, are:

- *first order* change, arising out of simple habit formation, without any
  reformulation or conceptualization, involving experiential learning and
  the development of practical, change skills through trial and error;
- *second order* change, assimilating explicitly new concepts of change
  management, for example by forming classes or organizing acts of
  change agency, using mental constructs based on a sense of reality;
- *third order* change management, driven by contraries, and by anomalies
  between practice and theory, at levels one and two, involving 'learning
  to work in spaces beyond our habitual bondage';

- *fourth order* change agency, involving active and reflective transformations in the evolutionary processes of human – or in our case also organizational or societal – species.

In my own role, as learning strategist, I have been focusing on levels three and four. These lend themselves to an emergent, storied approach to change. How then, does this fit in with McWhinney's alternative paths?

WHAT IS CHANGE?

From analytical to emergent

The *analytical* path to change, first (see Anglian's Technical Director John Green below), might be termed planned action. A design is created that solves a problem. In the mind of the analytic the plan produces its execution. A critical element of the authority of this mode is measurement. The *participative* path, second (Anglian CEO Mellor in the storyline), differs from the analytic in that alternative allocations are established by the participants' values rather than being deduced from theoretical premises. The *assertive* path (ex-CEO Alan Smith) involves authority, exercised through personal or institutional expression, that is meaning making. Finally the *emergent* path – the one taken by us here, and by AW consultant Terry Cook in the storyline – operates through the co-creation of ideas, and the opportunities of the people involved, making possible alternative actions and outcomes, through discovering, enabling, empowering. We now turn to the 'emergent' approach to change which was adopted, in this instance, within Anglian Water, and to the 'storying' approach we have deployed here.

The emergent path – storying

The stories that guide change

For McWhinney, as within my own Anglian context, we need a source of guidance, a plot to manage the change from one reality to another. In our case such a plot covered the path of resolution (see below) from the 'crisis of transition' to 'transition management'. Guidance for such change was to be found in narrative forms, in histories, biographies, epic tales, metaphorically in flow forms (e.g. water) and simply in the stories we tell about how we get to where we are (transition management). Such narrative is central to the resolution of issues and conflicts, to the extent that:

- the resolution of conflicts requires involvement of *multiple worldviews*;
- making changes that call on *different realities* will invoke new conflicts, and perhaps introduce new messes;

- to *achieve resolution* we have to work with different realities in ways empathic with the various individuals and groups involved;
- the necessary freedom and support for working with different realities comes in '*storied space*' – that is, in 'retreats' from secular threats;
- we can operate beyond the familiarity of our worldviews only in the consciousness of narratives, the stories, myths and histories we have come to trust;
- like the paths of resolution, there are an infinite variety of stories, but the vast majority follow a *few great plots* that serve as general guidelines to managing change – departure and return in this instance.

The summary proposition is that issues can only be resolved, and change thereby successfully negotiated, in storied contexts. But the concept of 'storied' is not so easily operationalized, for it arises in two realms that are not part of the scientific paradigm, the 'sacred' and the 'unconscious'. The 'sacred' storied context as such, enables an individual like the current CEO Chris Mellor to transcend his secular wordview. We can then present the course of change, as I have attempted to do here, in a way that integrates the histories and visions of the people involved with the new realities that must be encountered. The intended outcome of greatest importance is the adoption and 'sacred' awareness of a path of resolution that is necessary for revitalization or rebirth. It is not expected that all the participants will move beyond their familiar territories, but with sufficient 'vesseling' (see McWhinney's description below) a group can identify what a core story is.

The sacred and the profane

Most leadership and change efforts, for McWhinney, follow primarily from the joint effort of one who commands resources, former CEO Alan Smith or current CEO Chris Mellor in the Anglian case, and one who is the 'sanctified' source of ideas, Terry Cook and me in this instance. I have been given the titles adviser, counsel, guide, mentor or consultant, and even learning strategist! The category 'sacred' indicates that the latter role is denied substantial involvement in the enterprise. That is, the sanctified cannot get significant power or wealth through their work! In contrast, another form of consultant contributes to changes of the secular 'first order', wherein advice is limited by the dominance of a unifying ethos such as total quality or empowerment, represented in Anglian Water by Peter Hillman, who is MD of TQI, and by DDI, who are empowerment consultants. Here advisers speak from a single truth system as experts or technical advisers helping to train others in the use of a skill. The next secular form of consultant creates 'second order' change, incorporating concepts like 'knowledge management' that have been used elsewhere. Steve Gatley in fact, a consultant in knowledge management and external MMBA graduate, plays such a 'second order' role. A learning strategist like me and to some extent Terry

Cook, working with 'third order' and possibly even 'fourth order' change, provides secular leaders with contact with the 'sacred'.

Such 'sacredness' is achieved, for McWhinney in two ways: by vesseling, that is providing the psychological setting for the leaders (and members) to explore their concepts of reality, by being companions to these seekers, and by locating the essential stories, paths and myths for them to traverse.

Such 'third' and 'fourth' order agents of change identify the paths in stories evoked from the participants, or call them up from the so-called collective conscious (or unconscious) of the community. That path becomes the essential core of the resolutionary work. Whereas problem solving is defined by the realities of a situation, the path of resolution is a narrative, the 'stage play' as we shall see. This was essentially the exercise in which a cast of key protagonists became engaged one February day, in the early part of 1998, at the Graffham water treatment works' training centre in East Anglia.

HOW – THE STAGED PLAY

Prologue

Pursuing Anglian novelty

By February of 1998, Chris Mellor had taken over the role of group managing director from Alan Smith. Alan, until recently, had been the prime instigator of Anglian Water's programme of organizational change. As Chris paused to reflect upon what had happened since privatization, he was faced with a fundamental dilemma. For over this period, in order to outgrow its public sector origins, AW had been spurred on by an extraordinary number of changes. Yet these very initiatives, as well as promoting some exciting developments, were beginning to stop some of the ordinary business in its tracks. The way out of such a dilemma, Chris realized as a student of the latest management theory, was not to solve it, but to resolve it at a higher level of complexity.

As a result, by uncovering and amplifying *The Stories We Are* – in William Randall's terms – Anglian would ultimately be able to re-authorize itself. Once the stories of the lead protagonists had been 'narrated', and once meaning had been 'read' into them, in the light of the emergent pattern of change – if the passion to create was there – we could imaginatively release Anglian's novel-ty. By this means we would sustain and enhance the lives of its people and its customers around the world. For Chris Mellor realized that the Vision and Values statement that he had recently been responsible for devising would remain a lifeless document unless it was woven into the fabric of Anglian's unfolding transition story, locally and globally. So who were the key players' To help him resolve that question Chris, via Innovation

Director Peter Matthews, had asked us at City University to discover which of his fellow Anglians, irrespective of their position in the hierarchy, had the seminal stories to tell. The object, initially, was to uncover the story so far, locally and globally, with a view to taking the story further.

Act 1 – In the beginning – the crisis of transition

Reaching for the top – vision and values

(Time goes back to December 1997. CEO-designate Chris Mellor, in his last month before officially taking over as Group MD, is describing to Sally Woodward, to Ronnie Lessem and to Chris Hendry, the recent Anglian context out of which the new Vision and Values statement has emerged.)*

RL   Chris, you're the chief protagonist as far as the newly forged Vision and Values are concerned, so can you please set the context for us?

CM   Be glad to. You see, the business, of late, has been crying out for some aspiring vision to take it forward. What, people have been asking, might such a vision be? What could it be? Such a vision needs to realize Anglian's international ambitions whilst enabling AW to continue to move forward in the UK. With both these ends in mind we've come up with this pretty ambitious aim to become the top UK water utility by the year 2002, and one of the foremost companies in the world by 2007. The challenge now is to turn that vision into action. In the process we need to hang on to the best of where we've come from – that public sector ethos, and genuine sense of public service – while simultaneously turning ourselves into a customer focused business, consistently delivering good returns for each of its stakeholders.

RL   That does sound pretty ambitious, Chris. Are you, individually and organizationally, driven by crisis or opportunity'

CM   We have in fact recently been voted the best water utility in the UK you know, so we don't have an external crisis in any obvious sense. Rather there is a motivational crisis, internally, what you might call a crisis of transition.

RL   What kind of internal crisis?

CM   Since 1993, we've been through a succession of so-called downsizings, and cost cutting. So some people have become very cynical of our supposedly forward looking initiatives, because they see them as a device we invented to take people's minds off the real agenda to cut

*   In preparation for this staged play, Sally Woodward through her interviews under Chris Hendry's guidance, I through my emergent storyline and facilitation, and Ian Plover as implementer had jointly paved the way. The storyline, except for my own points of linkage, is based verbatim on what was said by those interviewed. Moreover, on the actual day of staging at Graffham, the extent to which they wished to follow their edited interview text was left to the characters' discretion.

costs, not to enhance our global brand. So while, on the one hand, some people have literally had their lives transformed through their individual Journey (more of that to come), on the other hand, there's plenty of collective cynicism around. We need therefore to expand our international horizons, where the real growth potential lies, by at least fourfold over the next five years, to make that business viable. If you take the US for example, four years ago we had nothing, and now we supply over a million people with water. In fact if you compare our level of efficiency with companies in America we're ten to fifteen years ahead. Look around the rest of the world, moreover, and you'll find that water services are atrocious, and can only get worse because of increased urbanization.

You have a history of public sector neglect, uneconomic public sector prices, rising environmental awareness, and middle-class populations in developing countries no longer willing to put up with the high levels of pollution.

RL   So the global water crisis is Anglian's local opportunity'

CM   If we are able to grasp it. If we do, then, in ten years' time, the UK will only be a small part of Anglian Water's business. To achieve that end we need to be effectively harnessing our people's potential, and also the market's. You see, for the moment, at best I reckon we're only using 30 per cent of the potential of our people. As a result, over the last four years, we've set up this plethora of initiatives to do something about it. I guess that's because there's no one club in the bag that's bound to work. But, overall and when it comes to people, we haven't been that good at managing change, from start to finish.

RL   So we're in a time of transition, and, at least in 'emergent' terms, we're finding difficulty in finding the right storyline, to take us through it. To succeed in that respect, and having set the opening context for the story so far now Chris, we need to cover more ground. Specifically we need to find those creative tensions, in the middle of our story, that need to be resolved or dissolved, to arrive at a resolution.

Act 2 – The middle – creative tension

Scene 1: Executive Stretch vs. the Transformation Journey

(The scene changes from Chris's office in Huntingdon to Whitwell Training Centre, by beautiful Rutland Water. Chris and Ronnie are now joined by Technical Director John Green and consultant Terry Cook initially, with Alan Smith hovering benignly behind Terry. Subsequently, the University of Water project team John Newall, Chris Holden, Sheila Linklater, David Taylor, join Innovation Director Peter Matthews, leaning heavily on David's shoulder.)

The Journey in context – tapping human potential

CM   What we set out to do then was to alter the mindsets of people, to focus on the customer, to break down hierarchical barriers, to raise people's confidence levels to take decisions, to be more flexible and productive, and overall to develop ourselves individually and as teams. In that latter respect we have developed this very unique concept – I would say – of the Journey, and of course we all have very different views on it. Where it's worked the transformation of the individual has been incredible. So we've stumbled on something there, but of course, it's difficult to assess what it's worth, and it is certainly one of the most controversial things we have ever done.

RL   What do you reckon as Technical Director John [Green]? I imagine the way you see it, there're other priorities, over and above Journeying.

From SSR to Executive Stretch – efficiency, quality and service

JG   That's no maybe. You can talk about both the Journey and the University of Water till the cows come home, but that's missing the fundamental point. Privatization in 1989 is the most significant thing that has happened to this business, not the Journey or our so-called University. Down the line, and for the past eight years, a lot of things we have done have been as a result of our now being in the private sector, where we have new commercial objectives, goals and drivers. That's the nub of the matter. We're now supposed to be profit driven. Post-privatization, the next significant thing that happened to us is that our Group MD Alan Smith, in 1992, went to Harvard. When he came back we all expected a puff of white smoke to come out the chimney, but it took about six months before we saw the impact. Specifically he introduced the concept of the Strategic Systems Review, or SSR as we call it, to try and do three things. First, you may remember, the intention was to take costs out of the business. In actual fact it served initially to take £20 million out of the operating base. Second, SSR set out to flatten the organization, so that we'd become more flexible and responsive. Third, the intention was for Anglian to become more customer focused. Along with these three primary intentions – and entirely secondary to my mind – went all the clichés about empowerment, the removing of command and control, the freeing up of people, and all that sort of thing.

   So we embarked on a culture change in the way we managed the business, in order to improve efficiency, quality and service. Altogether, and over four years as a result, we took £50 million cost out of AW. Let's not forget that.

RL   You've made sure that we shouldn't, John, and that's a very good thing too. I'm all for creative tension, you know, between 'yin' and 'yang'.

JG Whatever that may mean. In 1993 meanwhile, while SSR was in full swing, you may remember I became MD within AW of what we then called Engineering and Business Systems, which included the technical, financial and support functions. As we were grappling with the SSR initiative I was becoming enormously frustrated with the people I was having to work with at a senior level. They really had a silo mentality and there was no common ownership of the problems we had to tackle. At this point I bumped into you, Ronnie. We had dinner together and I told you about my problems, including those I had with a senior colleague (I won't mention the name) who was very 'command and control' oriented. I said 'I feel totally frustrated by all this'. Your response, you may remember, was 'Aren't you the MD?' I said 'yes'. So you asked 'How many people do you have working for you?' I said 'a thousand'. Your reply was: 'If you can't change anything then nobody can. You're responsible for a quarter of the people in AW.'

RL What happened then?

JG As you know, we started this thing which Terry Cook and the Training Manager Debbie Dyson [now Smith], at Whitwell, had called Executive Stretch. It was all about encouraging us executives to think differently. The programme you people ultimately devised, as I recall, extended over six months. Altogether, within it we spent a couple of days together, as a management team, on three successive occasions. We went through your personality spectrum, we went back to our roots, we took a bike ride, we exposed our individual selves.

RL I remember you saw yourself, John, as a 'Travelling Broadcaster'.

JG We gradually got to know, then, where we were all coming from.

RL You know, John, that Exec Stretch was modelled on our project based MMBA, a kind of mini version of it, so to speak.

JG Whatever the origins, our first project arose out of a real crisis in the billing team, a crisis of transition you might now say. In any case we actually rolled our sleeves up around the table to address this problem. As a result we got a colleague out of the mess that he and his work group were in. That demonstrated that the whole Executive Stretch process worked. For it changed a team of individuals who couldn't give a bugger for what was going on the other side of their business – even if they were supposed to be part of a team – to a 'we're all in it together chaps'. So the programme began to cascade. Other executives started to say 'that looks like a good idea'.

Some took their teams away, others took theirs, and all, including Alan's, worked very well. So the whole process began to gain a lot of credence.

The rise of the Journey and the fall of Executive Stretch

JG   And then it was sort of grabbed away from us, and Whitwell Training Centre said 'thanks very much it's wonderful'. HR and Whitwell and one or two other enthusiasts grabbed the change process, and became enthused by it all. Yet there was no ownership back in the business. I'm not against change. I am very supportive of it, bearing in mind my experience with Executive Stretch. I am just very much against these endless 'initiatives', and we get one new one every week! What the business hasn't done is to impose some discipline on it and say 'well great initiative but where does it fit within the plan?'. That's my view.

RL   And it's a pretty compelling, if 'masculine', one at that. I guess, Terry, you have a somewhat different, perhaps more 'feminine' perspective.

TC   Thanks for the cue, Ronnie. I've been waiting very patiently in the wings. John's Executive Stretch programme had originally begun, you know, because, as part of my initial work as a freelancer at Whitwell, I had to do the course calendar. I thereby discovered that the courses that were being offered were predominantly technical (masculine). So I had this idea that we should do this more managerially and socially (feminine) oriented 'Executive Stretch' thing. I therefore put a one-page description together.

Most of what I'd written was in fact wishful thinking. But lo and behold! no sooner had I sent it out than John Green gave us a call. 'This Executive Stretch thing,' he said. ' I think I need something like it for my team.'

Well I have to say all hell broke loose at Whitwell. 'My god, somebody wants me,' I said to Debbie Dyson. There were sharp intakes of breath as I reflected on the naïveté of my thinking. 'No, no it couldn't possibly be me running it; it will have to be some heavyweight, some sort of learned person who's got more street cred than I have.' And so, Ronnie, you were wheeled in because you got involved with Anglian – via the then HR Director – through your project based MMBA. So you and I were thrown together to run this thing, and you kind of picked it up and made something of it. Up to that time it had been merely a thought transcribed on to one sheet of paper.

You brought in your worldly wisdom and said, 'Yes, I can see how it might emerge.' There we were, myself as the archetypal practitioner – 'ground control' as I called myself, on one side. You as the heavyweight academic – 'Confucius he say', as I termed you, were on the other. We'd never worked together before, and I didn't know where you'd be coming from. But, curiously enough, as things panned out, we blended very well together. Arising out of it all ultimately, and thanks to the kind of experience we had built up with John Green and his team, was a kind of Executive Stretch blueprint.

RL   I well remember first sharing with you Alan's amazing challenge that we should develop an Executive Stretch for all Anglian employees.

TC   That, you may recall, was on a Monday evening. Tuesday morning I woke up early and started drawing. And from that came the Transformation Model. I subsequently went away and wrote up some more stuff with you, Ronnie. Three months later Customer Services Director John Sansby and I presented the model to a group of people at Anglian. It was met with derision, I have to say. But they were too gentlemanly to be unpleasant. I remember sitting down at one point and Alan Smith passing a note to me saying 'chin up, people were never destined to like this'. I was probably on the verge of tears. Alan's sponsorhip at the time was crucial. For in spite of the fact that 130 out of 150 people didn't like it, the Journey still went ahead.

RL   Pretty good intentions those. I guess the problem, with the current benefit of hindsight, is that the Journey would need modification if it was to achieve results, commercially as well as individually.

TC   Maybe yes, maybe no. Overall for me, and perhaps where I parted company from John [Green], the Journey was not a process that promised a specific solution. In that sense it was probabilistic rather than deterministic in its orientation. It set a broadly based stage across which the best-possible-solution of the time might be proposed. True to probabilistic form, in fact, there was no strategy developed for the promotion of the Journey. It just leaked out here and there, and people started responding.

     There was a lot of word of mouth and a great deal of mystery attached to it. When people phoned in they were asked who they would want to bring with them on the Journey. So in the first year there was a lot of momentum. It became relatively fashionable to do it.

RL   Sounds like your approach, Terry, was more feminine, playful and diffuse, whereas John's was more masculine, serious and focused.

TC   Yes and no. The trouble, as I see it, is to this day, we've never had significant buy-in from a lot of the key decision makers. So the one thing that's been sadly missing is what we termed 'the navigation compass'. If you like, this is the group that would be destined to take the Journey along profitably 'westwards' and purposefully 'eastwards', effectively 'northwards' and communally 'southwards', to be the mentors, the sponsors of the Journey, based on the business context.

JN   Can I come in here, Ron and Terry? I reckon you're failing to see the University phoenix, rising out of the Journey ashes, before your eyes.

RL   You may well be right, John [Newall]. Please do come in.

From Journey to University – the phoenix rising from the ashes

JN I came on to the Journey, personally, because I felt there was this vague, undefinable need to find out a bit more about myself.

CH All I wanted was a nice night at a hotel, and that was the only reason I signed up for the Journey. It took me away from the workplace, and I got together with a group of other guys who were fairly likeminded. So it started out as a good excuse to get away for a day, and have a good time, and ended up changing six guys' lives completely! In fact the business has ended up with a group of people who want to make the most of themselves. If you like, the carrot was the night out, but what Anglian got back in the end was much more than it put in.

JN So what actually happened, Chris, to make that shift?

CH I'd never looked into me before to discover why I did certain things. Why hadn't I gone to university? Why had I joined Anglian? Neither myself nor others in the group had ever asked ourselves such questions. So, for our first expedition, we got to know our Directors by physically journeying, with them, to the four corners of our East Anglian region. For the second one, in fact, we went along to schools and talked about the Journey, about Anglian Water, about where water came from and where it went to, and what happened in between.

JN So, all in all Chris, you think the Journey gave you guys the opportunity to reflect on who and what both AW and yourselves are, and to spread that awareness and activity through the local community?

CH Yes, yes. But whether you'd have got me on to the journey by setting that expectation to begin with I very much doubt.

    If you'd have said to me, 'I'd like you to do the Journey so that you can reflect on your work and life', I'd have thought 'Oh, err'. The result of the journey for me now, though, is that I've started to work on what has come to be called the University of Water. I have continually, along the way, exchanged views with its champion Peter Matthews.

RL So what is your role, altogether?

CH Now we're facilitators of the University of Water, in that we are bringing Peter's initial blueprint to life, making sure that whatever happens is applicable to the whole workforce, and it's not elitist.

SL And from within the business we try and pick the best expertise. 'That guy is our best hole digger, so we need him to show others how to go about it.' When we leave we don't want the business to fall apart. So people must share with each other whatever they know, and that will be done through the University of Water.

JN That's absolutely right, and if you take into account preferred styles of learning, part of our role would be to give people some insights into what these are. Also we have to decide how much knowledge should be imparted through courses, or through people sharing with each other, or through benchmarking, or through coaching and mentoring, or through books and tapes.

CH   Exactly. Exactly. We're also developing our own Intranet, capturing the implicit knowledge people have in their heads and spreading it around.

Scene 2: The University of Water vs Aqua Universitas

(The scene changes from the rural beauty of Rutland to the fenlands of Cambridgeshire. At the Innovation Centre, Chris, Ronnie and now Ian Plover are joined by Keith Edwards, Peter Matthews, Pat Green and Dale Evans, all connected with innovation. The emphasis now shifts from business and people to include, more particularly, technology and the environment.)

The organizational journey – from the old to the new world

KE   I was one of the very few people in this organization, in fact, Chris [Holden], who knew where the University of Water came from. For I was actually there when it was invented, with Peter Matthews, John Sansby, yourself Ronnie and some others from our Executive Stretch group. We were in the refectory at Whitwell talking about various things, what was wrong with our organization and what was right with it, and out came the concept of the University of Water. It was to become a centre of AW excellence, and a fount of knowledge.

RL   Which I reckon is somewhat different from where Chris Holden and his people are coming from. Their version is more individually oriented, albeit in the context of the business. What do you reckon, Peter?

A window on the soul of the company

PM   My current role as Innovation Director in the organization, as you know Ronnie, is a reflection of my calling. In fact we created the role, you and I, in discussion together on our Exec Stretch. Subsequently, and in an evolving context, wisdom creation is becoming my vocation. It is with such an emerging end in mind, as I can now see retrospectively, that I have spent most of my adult life in Anglian Water, in the process developing myself and the company through science and technology, ultimately now spreading out internationally.

RL   Through the University of Water?

PM   My portfolio of responsibilities has extended from technology and innovation to knowledge management and knowledge creation. Now I am championing the University of Water while acting as ambassador to the Anglian Water Group, internationally. As such I do a lot of professional and commercial networking around the world, and sit on the

Board of many of our overseas operations. Overall I view my port-folio as representing 'the window on the soul of the company'. Through that window people see, on the one hand, learned people and on the other hand knowledge as a driver. Both together serve to create new technology and a clean environment, all of which gives us our repu-tation as Anglian Water, nationally and internationally.

RL   It seems to me then, Peter, that while the University of Water serves to individually develop the 'learned people' explicitly, in the way that John Newall and Chris Holden have described, 'Aqua Universitas' – which I believe to be the registered name of the University in this country – implicitly serves as the collective 'knowledge driver'. What do you reckon, Pat [Green], as Anglian's most significant innovator?

From individual training to organizational learning

PG   I can't say I'm surprised, Ronnie, by the conflict that still reigns between explictly individual training and implicitly organizational knowledge creation. You see, what we are best at in Anglian, given our mecha-nistic orientation, is individual training. That's what Whitwell has conventionally been about. Individual learning, however, is a little more difficult than training. In fact, team learning, which is what Steve Gatley claims the Journey is ultimately supposed to be about, is very difficult to pin down. Organizational learning, if not also knowledge creation, is of course the most difficult of all. Indeed, the organization seems not to want to learn, at least that's the feeling you get at times.

RL   You say the organization actually doesn't want to learn?

PG   You have got to remember the roots of the organization, Ronnie. There have been loads of people, layers and layers checking each other. They have been more interested in finding the spelling mistakes in a document than in finding out what's been written about. And when you have got that kind of critical approach you don't feel trusted. Anglian, moreover, and partly as a result, has previously had a crisis culture. What we have therefore been very adept at is letting every-thing fall totally apart and, because we're good in a crisis, pulling it all back together again. Historically we've never proactively, and purposefully, managed transition. What we're only beginning to realize now is that teams, for example on a Journey, should be effective without such a crisis. Conventionally then, if you're seen rushing about, thun-dering along, getting red in the face, with also a thousand miles on the clock of the car – while also being armed with reams of paper – then people think 'crikey that person is doing something well'. Maybe you'd be more productive if you spent some time sitting down listening to Louis Armstrong or Wolfgang Mozart. You might do more work that way! I think we are now just about breaking away from that. We are a company, in 1998, in transition. We're at a flux point.

RL You're more bullish, then, about the effect of the Transformation Journey, say, than your namesake John Green is?

PG Well yes and no. Where John and I might well agree is that the biggest and most noticeable change in Anglian Water today has not been achieved directly through the Journey or the University of Water. Rather it has been accomplished through what we call 'Workforce 2000'. What Production Director Roy Pointer, his HR Facilitator Trish Brocklebank, and some other production people have achieved is to model the ideal employee in production where, I suppose, most people are employed in water and sewage works. They set up this kind of specification, which is a sort of mixture of academic achievement – including for people who are pushing brooms as manual workers – and other experientially based matters. So there is some NVQ-type thing that they can achieve plus they need to have a willingness to change as well. This leaves the production people with two choices. They either leave or else they undergo training and culture change till they sit in the right corner. Someone who has a good level of education, but doesn't want to fit into the ideals of the company, will have as much difficulty as somebody without the right qualifications.

RL So, Pat, you've taken us on a journey, so to speak, from individual training to organizational learning that incorporates 'Workforce 2000'. Along the way you yourself have mentored some key agents of change in this business, like Steve Kaye in Innovation and Dale Evans, next in our storyline. Dale brings an international, environmental perspective.

Act 3 – In the end is the beginning

Scene 1 – Transition management

(The scene finally changes from East Anglia to North America, to an office inside a water treatment works by the Niagara Falls, where Dale Evans from Innovation and Ian Plover from Human Resources are engaged in an unusual partnership with the Americans. Glyn Eastman of AWI (Americas) and Tony Eckford (Director of Anglian Water International) look on encouragingly as Dale Evans and Ian Plover exchange perspectives.)

RL Dale, in following your MMBA progress I have come to believe that you, together with Ian, may have *the* heroic tale to tell.

A heroic journey – gathering momentum

DE Until two years ago, I was parochially Anglian, notwithstanding my Welsh background. When I started the City University MMBA programme I had been in engineering for seven years, occupying a variety of posts that enabled me to progress up the technical structure. My development in Anglian had seemed to be in steps, following routes that had been determined by those who went before. Come the new structure, in 1995, my name did not appear in the Project Manager's box. I was disappointed, and yet in a way felt released. This was the catalytic event to invite me to do something different, to respond to a call to adventure. So I secured a post in Innovation. In fact, I worked for Pat Green, who was to become a kind of role model, having already been a major source of inspiration for me when I was in engineering. Soon afterwards, I spent two short periods supporting international projects in Brazil and New Zealand. While in Brazil, in November 1995, I applied for a job in a joint venture recently formed between American and Anglian Water.

When I was offered the position I discussed it with my wife Sarah, who said, 'Let's go for it and take things as they come.' We needed to immerse ourselves in our new environment, to become an integral part of it. Only in that way did I develop the inner sense that drove me forward on my 'road of trials'. My second 'extraordinary' MMBA project – the first one was geared towards teambuilding – was therefore aimed at using our interaction with our environment to create new perceptions and products, not to conform. Whilst this project then established a behaviour and a culture that responded to our environment, the third one involved embedding that creation, thus continuously changing our products and processes.

RL   Do you feel your approach, then, was representative of that of AWI?

DE   Most of our success in America has been achieved through medium-sized enterprises set up in the Midwest, the Mid-Atlantic and Pennsylvania. Yet this is an approach to our business that has hitherto been officially recognized as nothing but a stop-gap. As the patience of the parent company and the shareholders is tested, the pressure to win the big high profile contracts increases. In responding to this pressure, I feel, there is a real danger that we move further away from creating our own market, and our own projects. If we do, we will return to compete in areas where we see others, like the French, being successful, through big bids for big projects. Yet, if we are exploring the unknown, if our environment is chaotic, then we should be prepared to follow a strategy and a philosophy that recognizes this. This means continuously creating new products, perceptions and knowledge, and making them part of what we are about – and doing it as quickly as possible. It is as if old AWI (big bids, big projects), mimicking our competition, needs to die, so we may be reborn, our selves.

RL   So are you saying that AW needs to re-invent itself.

DE   As a local part of a global whole. It is such a simple and basic notion: the recognition that any living entity exists within its own ecology. As such it picks up on changes within its environment, using these changes to renew its existence. Trees and plants grow and shed leaves with the seasons. They use the living environment around them to seek new opportunities for growth. Whether we have been creating new knowledge through people, recognizing the nature of emergent strategy, understanding the chaotic nature of natural systems, or recognizing that personal creativity arises out of our ability to exist in a state of surrender, all of these things rely on us being part of a totality. I understand it through my reality, when in the midst of the valleys of Abergwesyn, surrounded by the immense presence of nature; to be amongst the black rocks, rushing streams and damp forbidding moors.

Reinventing ourselves – from utility company to utility product

RL So you, and AEET, are entering into a brave new world together?

DE We have reconceived of ourselves at AEET productwise, in terms of what Ikijiro Nonaka would identify as knowledge 'combination', after much dialogue and debate between us, in terms of four dimensions. We needed to respond, first, to the local nature of our environment, and to be more commercially responsive in our approach. The two aligned dimensions, *local* and *dealing*, are comparatively alien to us. On any project, which I have have engaged in here in America, I have systematically identified and involved the local stakeholders. We have committed to becoming an active part of the community, both during the product development stage and throughout the project. The ability to package, sell and negotiate a project – *dealing* – is one where we are necessarily short of the requisite skills. As a utility company in the UK, we have not yet had to compete, and are consequently not experienced. It is vital, as I'm sure we all acknowledge, that we learn as much as we can, as quickly as we can. In AAET it is also important that we recognize that the dimensions of 'local' and 'dealing' are linked.

    As far as *technology* and *delivery* are concerned, this is the strongest link between AAET and the utility parents. While the overall product we offer differs for each locality and deal, the ability to integrate and deliver a wide range of knowledge and skills in the provision of quality service remains constant. The current industry in the US is fragmented, with little co-ordination between water, wastewater and customer services. So our theme, our product, has become a 'one stop shop' for water services. It connects the development of our product with our roots, and gives us a framework against which we can leverage our utility skills and competencies. In fact, over the past twelve months, AAET has won ten-year, full service contracts in Evansville, Indiana, New York and now Buffalo.

RL It's interesting, Dale, if we step back into history, we will find that the Buffalo workforce have served as a kind of 'evolutionary catalyst', to help take AW on to the next stage in its own development. For, as a novice like me sees it, the first initiating vision of civic reconstruction had served in the nineteenth century to create a publicly, though parochially based, water industry that served to advance the public health of this nation. Historically and nationally, the second differentiating stage in the industry's development late in the twentieth century had been from a locally and socially oriented public enterprise (the 'old Labour' thesis) to a regionally and economically oriented East Anglian private one (the 'new Tory' antithesis). The third transnationally based integrating stage to come, towards the twenty-first century (the 'New Labour' synthesis), is now upon us. It would need to create a community oriented business that combined, regionally and nationally as well as now globally, the best of both Anglian's worlds. That seems to be what's happening in 'Buffalo' – in indigenous American tradition the symbol for wisdom (Peter Matthews would love to know that!)?

This must all be music to your ears Ian [Plover] as a fellow MMBA, especially as I know you have got intimately involved with the Buffalo project. I guess the difference between you and Dale, though, is that you are an AW person, 'man and boy'. Also, whereas he is a technologist by profession, your intrinsic orientation is towards people.

Scene 2 – From adversaries to partners

(*The water treatment works fades into the background as a dark, smoke filled room appears in the foreground. Ian and Dale are sitting there, waiting to be joined by the union officials who have formed part and parcel of Ian's life.*)

From Biggleswade to Buffalo

IP   I always felt that my success was based on the fact that I was supported by the people I worked with.

RL   How did you find the transition, then, between rural East Anglia, Anglo-Saxon to the hilt, and urban New York State, which is a mix between Afro-American and Italian Mafia I believe!?

IP   Our American colleagues had planned that we would say little when we first met up with the workforce. 'Just go through the motions,' they advised me. They were therefore more than a little surprised when I proposed that we share with the unions our plans. They immediately told me that I didn't understand American culture. Fortunately for me, my MMBA colleague Dale here, who was leading the team, took a leap of faith in me. We met the 'Mafia'-like union representatives in a dark windowless room. They had names like Scardino, Panarro, Botticello. I have to admit I began to get more than a little nervous. We broke the ice, though, by telling them our plans and concerns, and 'the man from England' (that is me) even spoke of Partnership. After meeting together for two hours, we agreed to get together again three days later, to openly share their concerns with us. One of the American managers previously so opposed to what I wanted to do, in fact, then came up to me and said, 'We could never have gone about things the way you did, 'cause it's not the way we do things around here.' In any case, we met again with the union three days later, after which we agreed that all future meetings would be conducted in the same partnership spirit. As I left the meeting one of the key union players, Larry Panarro, came up to me in the yard and said, 'I think we can do business with you guys.' We may be 3,000 miles apart but people are people the world over. Needless to say, we signed the contract a few days later. So, as an Employee Relations Manager – who had for the past year been working with the local unions to establish a social Partnership in Anglian Water (UK) – I was able to play my role in securing the contract in the USA, based on the same values of how to deal with people.

My role in both contexts has therefore been to create environments where catharsis can take place, given the atmosphere of mistrust which previously existed, followed by a rebuilding of relationships, to help manage our transition.

RL   And transition management is what is now bringing yourself and Dale, Steve Kaye and Sudhanshu, together with myself together here and now. I guess Chris Mellor has great hopes that the lessons of Buffalo specifically, and Transition Management generally, can be spread far and wide. That will have to be the next part of our story.

CONCLUSION – WHEREUPON – RETROSPECTIVE MEANING

The vast majority of stories follow a few great plots

In effect, the 'great plot' of AW's transition followed the perennial storyline of 'departure and return'. In that respect, the University of Water, as represented by John Newall's project team, became the synthesis arising out of the TQ/Executive Stretch (thesis) and the MMBA/Transformation Journey (antithesis). Similarly, the University of Water oriented towards individual learning as thesis – out of which organizational knowledge creation through Innovation arose as the antithesis – were both subsequently subsumed under a Transition Management synthesis. Moreover, and as can be inferred from the Figure 26, as we dissolve levels towards progressive resolution – from the crisis of transition to transition management – so Bateson's orders of learning, or change, are progressively transformed.

They evolve from first and second order competition and core competence, to third and fourth order catalysation and co-creation. Ultimately, civic reconstruction and our knowledge creating ecology serve to realize

Thesis	Synthesis	Antithesis

VISION AND VALUES

C o - c r e a t i o n

Civic   Knowledge
reconstruction   creating ecology

TRANSITION MANAGEMENT

C a t a l y s a t i o n

Aqua Universities/   Innovation/
individual learning   knowledge creation

UNIVERSITY OF WATER

C o m p e t e n c e

Executive stretch/   MMBA/transformation
total quality   journey

STRATEGIC SYSTEMS REVIEW

C o m p e t i t i o n

Figure 26 Departure and return

AW's vision and values. For McWhinney, in the final analysis, a path of change is a sequence of steps directed by an overall sense of direction through a space of alternative realities; it is the plot of a story. The paths are not simply problem-solving activities strung together opportunistically but the elements of a narrative that have a distinctive foundation, a path and a resolution. Traversing the multiple realities co-evolves our sensory and unitary, participatory and mythical worlds. We now turn from 'water' to 'earth', that is to Anita Roddick's Body Shop, that is 'Body and Soul'.

BIBLIOGRAPHY

1   Lessem, R. and Palsule, S., *Managing in Four Worlds*, Blackwell, 1997.
2   Randall, W., *The Stories We Are*, Toronto University Press, '1994.
3   McWhinney, W., *Paths of Change*, Sage, 1997.

16 Sustainable development

Body Shop meets the MMBA

THE ORGANIZATION

Managing naturally

Anita Roddick and the Body Shop in general, have become something of a 'natural' icon in Britain, if not also around the globe. Interestingly enough, I have discovered, much of their perennial management ethos, we shall see, applies to our knowledge creating ecology.

'One of the great challenges for entrepreneurs is to identify a simple need. People tend not to trust their gut instincts enough, especially about those things that irritate them, but the fact is that if something irritates you it is a pretty good indication that there are other people who feel the same. Irritation is a great source of energy and creativity. It leads to dissatisfaction and prompts people like me to ask questions. Why couldn't I buy cosmetics by weight or bulk, like I could if I wanted groceries or vegetables? Why couldn't I buy a small size of cream or lotion, so I could try it out before buying a big bottle?

'The other half of the equation was that I wanted to try to find products made from natural ingredients. At that time in the early seventies, no one was talking much about the advantages or potential of natural products – the green movement had yet to get started – but I knew that for centuries women in "underdeveloped" areas of the world had been using organic potions to care for their skin with extraordinary success. I knew this to be true because I had seen it with my own eyes, initially in the Polynesian islands. When I had first arrived in Tahiti the first thing that struck me was the women. I was mesmerized by them. They were straight out of a Gauguin painting, with a wonderfully liquid quality. Later in my travels I kept coming across further examples of women using local natural ingredients for skin and haircare. Whenever I could I adopted local practices – caring for my body and hair in the same way as the native women, and using the same ingredients. So when I started to look for products for my shop I already knew of some twelve natural ingredients that I had seen working in various parts of the world. I had meanwhile been doing a lot of research on do-it-youself cosmetics in the local public library and mixing ingredients in the kitchen. In the end I went through Yellow Pages and found, under 'Herbalists', a small manufacturing chemist in Littlehampton, Sussex, where we lived. I told the herablist what I wanted – things like cocoa butter, jojoba oil, almond oil and aloe vera. At the same time I was looking for a suitable site for my shop, and had clearly in mind the look I wanted to create, something like a spaghetti western.

Spirited business

'Talking about the products was never a chore. Passion persuades, and by God I was passionate about what I was selling. I loved to tell people where the ingredients had come from, how they were used in their original state and what they could do. The names of the products themselves generated endless questions – Honey and Oatmeal Scrub Mask, Cucumber Cleansing Milk, Seaweed and Birch Shampoo, Avocado Moisture Cream. I read everything I could lay my hands on about the use of natural ingredients for skin and haircare.

'The Body Shop succeeded for two principal reasons. First, I simply had to succeed while my husband Gordon was away, on a Latin American adventure. The underlying drive that kept me going was that I had to eat and our two daughters had to be fed and clothed. Second, to succeed you have to believe in something with such a passion that it becomes a reality. I had total faith in the idea of the shop and I had a zest for trading. Mark, my herbalist, turned out to be as manic a herbalist as I was a trader. His creative contribution to our product range since the beginning has been immense – his company has grown with us and is the Body Shop's major supplier.

'Gordon's return from his travels was providential, because after a year's absence he brought with him fresh vision. He saw the potential of the business and saw a way to expand, even though we had no more money and the banks wouldn't lend us any more. He saw the way ahead as lying in "self-financing", which is now called franchising. All the early franchisees were women, and that pleased me. I could see that men were good at the science and vocabulary of business, at talking about economic theory and profit and loss figures. But I could see that women were better at dealing with people, caring and being passionate about what they were doing. Here we were then, a poet (Gordon) and a teacher (Anita), running what was fast becoming an international business that was growing at an unbelievable rate. I handled the product development, design and public relations; Gordon dealt with all the legal and financial matters. In the early eighties, as expansion gathered pace and our financial resources were ever more stretched, Gordon felt it was time to go public.

A force for social change

'The very notion of using a business as a crusader, of harnessing success to ideals, set my imagination on fire. From that moment in the eighties the Body Shop ceased to exist, at least in my eyes, as just another trading business. It became a force for social change. It became a lobby group to campaign on environmental and human rights issues. It became a communicator and an educator. To use the vernacular of the sixties, we entered into the consciousness-raising business.

'In the following year we used the shops directly for the first time as a platform to protest against the slaughter of whales. Such environmental campaigning, in fact, raised the profile of the company considerably, attracted a great deal of media attention and brought more potential customers into our shops. But much more important, in my view, was the spin-off for our staff, enabling them to get involved with things that really matter – pushing for social change, improving the lot of the underprivileged, helping to save the world. Retailing now became integrally involved with community.

'In fact the Body Shop agreed to become the first corporate sponsor in 1989 for a Canadian television series, *Millennium*, which aimed to record the wisdom and culture of endangered tribes around the globe. I had always regarded these people as the natural caretakers of the earth and was more than happy, where possible, to combine my "Trade not Aid" trips with reconnaissance for *Millennium*. I subsequently made extended visits to Nepal and to the Sahara. To meet the primitive peoples there, and to see how they survive with such dignity against the odds, was very nourishing for the soul.

'I subsequently began talking with Sony about prospectively fitting video cameras powered with solar batteries so that such indigenous peoples, including those resident in the Amazon rainforests, could record their collected customs and wisdom about their lands, its animals and plants. The Paiakan Indians in Brazil, specifically, were anxious that we find ways of assessing what applications of their plant material might be useful in the West.

'People ultimately talk of the Body Shop as a multinational company because we trade in forty-seven countries. I prefer to describe us as global. The magic of the word is that it is responsible, it is multicultural, it has an anthropological and spiritual tone. Global companies have values; multinationals just trade. I have said for years that the responsibility of business is not to create profits but to create live, vibrant, honourable organizations.'[1]

INTRODUCTION

Elemental knowledge

Duly informed about the ethos of the Body Shop, we now enter the penultimate chapter of this book through the 'indigenous people's' door, via 'mother earth'. Here a perennial approach to life in general, and to scientific and managerial activity in particular, prevails. We shall start the theoretical section of this chapter by referring to indigenous science, and then proceed to management. The context, as we have seen, is that of the Body Shop.

For Anita Roddick, the Body Shop's founder, business is a 'Renaissance concept', where the human spirit comes fully into play. How, she asks, do you enable the release of spirit, when, for example, you are selling something as inconsequential as a cosmetic cream? The answer, for her, lies in creating a sense of holism, of spiritual development, of feeling connected to the workplace, to the environment, and to relationships. Such a connectedness takes us back to the indigenous world which quantum scientist David Peat has recently uncovered. David Peat is an English physicist who has spent much of his life in America, where he has become preoccupied with the emergence of the new physics. Most recently, he has taken an interest in indigenous cultures[2] most particularly those in North America, with a view to uncovering their indigenous, 'scientific worldview'. 'Western' education, he says, which we also term 'northern', predisposes us to think of knowledge in terms of factual information, information that can be structured and passed on through books, lectures and programmed courses. Knowledge is seen as something that can be acquired and accumulated, rather like stocks and bonds. By contrast, within the indigenous world, the act of coming-to-know, for Peat as indeed for me, involves nothing short of personal transformation. Paradoxically, though, 'western' scientists who have been struggling at the cutting edges of their fields this century have come up with concepts that resonate with the indigenous 'southern' world. For example, quantum theory stresses the irreducible link between observer and observed. Indigenous science also holds that there is no separation between individual and society, between matter and spirit, between each one of us and the whole of nature.

Indigenous science teaches that all that exists is an expression of relationships, alliances and balances between 'energies, powers or spirits'. For Roddick, as we have seen, business is a focus for spirit. Indigenous knowing, for David Peat, could no more encompass matter in isolation than the theory of relativity could separate space from time. Indigenous science, and hence management, as we shall see, does not seek to found its knowledge and action, as we do in the 'west' and 'north', at the level of some elementary particle, theory or process. Rather it involves harmony and compassion, dream and vision, earth and cosmos, hunting and growing, technology and spirit, song and dance, colour and number, cycle and balance, death and renewal. It thus represents an overall ackowledgement of the elemental powers that animate the world around us. In turning now from science to management, we draw upon American consultant Emmett Murphy.

Cangleska Wakan

Two Americans, one a management consultant, Emmett Murphy, the other a literary agent, Michael Snell, recently brought out their unusual treatise *Forging the Heroic Organization.*[3] Murphy, who is the author of an earlier book on *The Genius of Sitting Bull,*[4] evidently feels that the worldview of the indigenous American Indian has much to offer contemporary American managers, particularly from the point of view of creating unity out of diversity. The necessary vision, according to Murphy and Snell, comes not from a contemplation of the present or the future, but from a return to a neglected or forgotten past. It is for this reason, perhaps, that Anita Roddick insists on going back to the source, whether in Sarawak or the Sahara, to find new ideas.

Systems theorists remind us, Murphy and Snell say, that mature and adaptive life forms can always find ways of survival in the rich resources of their intellectual and physical history. 'Cangleska Wakan', the Native American concept of the Sacred Medicine Circle or Hoop, provides just that, showing business leaders how to integrate the needs of the organizational stakeholders and how to focus everyone's energies to fulfil them.

Over a century ago, the two Americans maintain, the Sioux of the Great Plains lived by the tenets of 'Cangleska Wakan', which represented a practical as well as a philosophical model of organization. The so-called 'Sacred Hoop' encompassed the relationships, priorities, values and processes for managing life in a world prone to rapid and often unpredictable changes in the economics, politics and physical fates of tribal units.

The Sioux Indians understood that their existence depended on a practical understanding of the full continuum of relationships in the world, and the Hoop afforded a simple yet powerful tool for keeping these relationships in mind. So today, Murphy and Snell argue, as American leaders come to grips with the consequences of recent failures and struggle to regain the concepts of reciprocity and integration, they can use the Native American concept of the Hoop as a practical tool for re-establishing balance amongst all the synergistic relationships in organizational life. For the Body Shop, such social and environmental dimensions are woven into the fabric of the company itself.

COMING TO KNOWING

Knowledge as process

In such a perennial, native world as for example Anita Roddick's, according to scientist David Peat, you cannot 'give' a person knowledge in the way that a doctor gives a person a shot for measles. Rather, each person learns for himself or herself through the processes of growing up in contact with nature and society: by observing, watching, listening and dreaming. This is precisely the way in which Anita functions. Coming-to-knowing, Peat maintains, means entering into relationships with the spirits of knowledge, with giants and animals, with beings that animate dreams and visions, and with the spirit of the people, whether Nepalese or Paiakan.

Within an indigenous society, moreover, while knowledge as a process transforms, it also brings with it obligations and responsibilities. Knowledge, on the one hand, for people in the 'west' and 'north' is an abstraction with no independent existence. Its only manifestation is its existence as a physical record in a book, as chemical and electronic signals in a human brain, or as encoded within muscular skills in the human body. When, on the other hand, Peat listens to Native people, he gets the impression that knowledge for them is profoundly different. It is a living thing that has an existence independent of human beings. A person, or indeed a manager like Anita Roddick, comes to knowing by specifically entering into a relationship with the living spirit of that knowledge, or that organization.

Learning by observation

In an indigenous society, therefore, children learn by watching and hanging around rather than through structured teaching, questioning or experimenting. Having developed the necessary skills and confidence, they then return to the group and perform the new task in public. Coming-to-knowing through a 'tacit' combination of watchfulness and direct experience is the antithesis of our 'explicit' programmed learning that first structures knowledge and then imparts it in 'bite sized chunks'. Native children, are trained in this tacit method of observation from childhood. It is not an active, grasping, controlling sort of knowledge pursuit that drives them to want to pick up the world and put it in their pocket. Neither does indigenous science want to hold on to and retain what is 'picturesque', 'beautiful' or 'striking'; rather it is part of the general flux and process of physical or human nature.

The quality of silence

Learning from nature and from an Elder, as Anita Roddick has so often done through her travels across indigenous worlds, involves a special quality of silence and alert watchfulness. The respect one shows to the Elder serves to create the area of quietness and receptivity into which such a wise person can speak. Coming-to-knowing arises out of silence. Native people love to gossip, but at the same time each person has a quality of silence, the silence of action suspended in potential.

Likewise, Peat asserts, the Big Bang began as a tiny fluctuation within an ocean of absolute silence. Such a silence is like the surface of a calm pond: throw in a pebble and you can watch the ripples expand right to the pond's edge and reflect back inward again. Drop a pebble into a pond that is ruffled by the wind and its disturbances are lost in the general agitation of the water. Out of this power of silence, moreover, great oratory like that of Martin Luther King is born. When Native people, including of course their leaders, speak, they are not talking from the head, relating some theory, mentioning what they read in a book, or what someone else has told them. Rather they, like the Kayapo Indians of Brazil, speak from the heart, from the traditions of their people, and from the knowledge of their land; they speak of what they have seen and heard and touched, and of what has been passed on to them by their forefathers, otherwise referred to as the 'spirits' of their ancestors. It is that inner silence that allows them to listen to the promptings of their hearts and to the subtle resonances that lie within each word of a language and which, when uttered, reverberate through the world.

Stories of origin

An indigenous orientation, Peat stresses, is a science, or management, of reality and place, such as those in which the the Body Shop's products originate. It is never abstract because it is always firmly rooted in the concrete, in the history of a people, in a journey they have taken and in their daily obligation to renew the compacts they have made with the world around them. The same applies, as we shall soon see, to 'indigenous' management.

Western or northern science – the science of analytical chemistry, elementary particle physics, or business management – can be carried out in a well-equipped physical, economic or social laboratory. Such activity can take place anywhere in the world, for the knowledge it gives about the world is assumed to be objective, independent of the individual who discovers or applies it, and the location in which it is.

Indigenous science or by analogy management, however, refers to the particular landscape, or 'organization-scape', that people such as the Wodaabe of the Sahara occupy. The memory of this desert landscape transcends anything we have in the modern world, for its rocks, animals, plants and people are also imbued with energies, powers and spirits. The whole of the land or enterprise is alive and each person is related to it. The land or indeed society sustains it and, in turn, the ceremonies and sacrifices of the people aid in its renewal. Peat alludes to the fact that many Native people, say that they have 'a map in the head'. The map, he asserts, is an expression of the relationship of the land, or society, to the people, or organization. Moreover, it transcends any geographical representation, for in it are enfolded the songs, ceremonies and histories of a people. With such a 'map in the head' you are never lost. Not only can you find your way through the bush, along a river system, or sail the ocean out of sight of land, but you know where you are in another sense. You know where your people have been for hundreds and thousands of years.

Within such stories can be found the origins of space, time and causality. Just as the human body is kept healthy and in harmony by its immune system – a field of active meaning that permeates the body – so too, an indigenous people and the land they care for are sustained by the relationships and renewals contained within these maps and stories, which are being continually re-created through the Body Shop's products. For Native people the land is their body and their flesh, and its landscape can be found with the map in the head. To deny a people's origins is to cut them off not simply from the land they physically occupy but also internally – from the very sense of their bodies. For that reason the Body Shop feels deeply obligated to those from whom its skin and haircare products originate.

Healing, wholeness and meaning

Native American people, moreover, invariably speak of obligations rather than of rights, and of the importance of their ceremonies of renewal. For they say nothing persists: all is flux, and unless a society is willing to renew itself through sacrifice it will pass away. Thus in America a 'southern' people who had obligations to renew the land met a 'northern' people who believed in land ownership. A people who believed in balance and the renewal of time met those who believed in progress, control, accumulation and linear time. Those who had based their lives on consensus met treaties and hierarchical government. Those to whom justice was the return of harmony to the whole group met adversarial trial and punishment.

Indigenous societies locate their being in the power of spirit, not in 'original sin' but in their 'origin story'. It is the source of their existence, the meaning that lives within them, and the basis for the dynamic balance they must maintain throughout the circles of their time. In turn this spirit is a part of the land that people occupy and care for. The traumas of forcible displacement and the requisitioning of lands, the disruption of traditional ways and forms of governance, the importation of alcohol and drugs, the loss of education, and the education of children in an alien world have all contributed to the breaking apart of such indigenous societies and a fragmentation of their meaning.

When spirit departs, the relationship with the powers, energies and Keepers of the Land, like the corporate culture, are weakened. Without them the people will die. Exogenous structures overtake the indigenous process. Our 'western' or 'northern' minds attempt to categorize and to compartmentalize so that the subtle is distinguished from the manifest. It is interesting that the scientific revolutions of this century have all demonstrated the errors of such compartmentalization; thus matter has been conjoined with energy, and space with time. David Peat's experience of indigenous science has been that Native people do not differentiate and categorize in the same way. The whole notion of relationship is central. While we in the 'West' emphasize objects and categories, the Native 'southern' mind deals with processes and relations. It is not so much that there is a world of stones and trees and another one of spirits, powers and energies, but rather that they are all one, and it is our particular human way of seeing, or the limitations to our seeing, that causes us to elevate one particular aspect over another. This is why the Body Shop seeks to initiate conversations with its customers rather than browbeating them into buying. Such custom is more than a number on the proft and loss account.

THE SACRED ORDER

Sacred number

Within Native America specifically and within the indigenous world gener-ally, number is seen in a profoundly different way from how it is seen in the 'west': not as dry, abstract and dehumanizing but as alive, real and immediate. Mathematics is a sacred practice related to the dynamics of the whole cosmos. Numbers are the manifestation of beings. Tally marks made on a stone, for example, refer to a journey that is connected with a land and its people.

As we saw in chapter 8, for the ancient Greeks and Indians, as for the Native Americans if not all other indigenous peoples, the number 4 expresses, on the one hand, a state of balance and harmony, and, on the other, a dynamic movement of spiritual forces within the cyclical nature of time. The number 4 then, represents the four elements, the four directions and indeed four seasons. It is embodied within powerful concrete devices, images or algorithms.

Through Four Winds the cycles of the seasons are manifest on earth, and the animating powers or spirits or energies that bring about maturity, contin-uation, renewal and refreshment are brought into being. The Four Directions are pictured as spokes on a 'Medicine Wheel' or 'Sacred Hoop', and refer not only to the transformation of the seasons but also to the movement from birth to death; to health and healing; to the dynamics of the individual psyche; to the concept of justice; to the meaning of the sacred colours; to the history of a group; to the tasks that must be carried out by the different peoples of this earth. For Emmett Murphy, moreover, as we shall see, they allude to organizational roles and functions.

Within indigenous science, and by implication for management therefore, the number 4 is not a thing, it is not a mental abstraction, but a living spirit; likewise the so-called Sacred Hoop is not a static diagram on a piece of paper, but an unfolding process. The Hoop is a movement in which each of the sacred directions gives way to the next, for it is always in rotation. And so within the number 4 stands each of the sacred directions, each one being at the same time a point of arrival and departure. Each number, in fact, also contains its neighbour, for it gives birth to and dies away from it. In the language of the great Swiss psychotherapist Carl Jung, and his friend the American physicist Wolfgang Pauli, ultimately, the centre is the speculum. It is the mystical mirror that stands between two worlds and reflects each into the other, yet belongs to neither. The essential processes of sacred mathematics are dynamic: the number 5 is born out of the number 4, standing at the heart of the hoop. Out of this the number 5 acknowledges the four directions and also the land and the sky. So out of the four directions emerge seven.

The dynamics of the sacred numbers are always rotating, unfolding one out of the other, folding back into each other. Each number is a starting point and an ending point. Number is no longer an abstract object. It is a process, a dynamic, a moving alliance of spirit and energy, as well as quintessentially an 'open system'. For the Blackfoot Indian, the circle is always left open so that the new may enter. Nothing is permanent, no situation is ever fixed, and no category is ever closed.

The sacred vibration

When the Native American has to speak English rather than Mic Maq he feels that he is being forced to interact with the world of objects, things, boundaries and categories in place of a more familiar world of flows, processes, transformations and energies. While the surface world of objects and material things can easily be identified by the eye, it is the ear that must deal with the more subtle levels of flux, transformation and reality behind appearances. Algonquin language, for instance, being for the ear, deals in vibrations in which each word is related directly not only to a process of thought, but also to the animating energies of the universe.

What is therefore needed, quantum physicist David Bohm has argued in his book *Wholeness and the Implicate Order*,[5] is a new sort of language. Such a language needs to be based on processes and activities, on transformation and change, rather than upon the interaction of stable objects. It would be based on verbs and on grammatical structures deriving from verbs. Such a language, Bohm argued, is perfectly adapted to an order of enfolding and unfolding matter and thought. What to Bohm had been a major breakthrough in human thought – quantum theory, relativity theory – was part of the everyday speech of the Blackfoot.

COMPARATIVE SCIENCE AND MANAGEMENT

The power of observation

Indigenous science, as Peat has illustrated, like indigenous management, is a disciplined approach to understanding and knowing, or rather, to the process of coming to understanding and knowing, as well as ultimately doing. It has a supporting view of the nature of reality, deals in systems of relationship, is concerned with the energies and processes within the universe, while also providing a coherent scheme and basis for action. At the same time, it is not possible to separate indigenous science or management, as we saw for the Body Shop, from other areas of life such as spirituality and social order.

'Western' science, or scientific management, is generally characterized by careful, repeated observation and the collection of data, and by rational 'masculine' action taken on the basis of it. Such an approach, in turn, requires a high degree of technology and the development of a conceptual framework that allows scientists, and scientific managers, to identify and isolate what is to be observed, studied and acted upon.

Very careful and painstaking observation, is also emphasized in Native science and is part of the coming-to-knowing process of every indigenous person. A study of rocks, crystals, wood and other materials has enabled indigenous people to use them in the construction of various tools and objects. For observations to be of use, they must be recorded and passed on. In the case of 'western' science this is done through textbooks, scientific papers, lectures and student apprenticeships. In contrast, for indigenous peoples, and 'symbolic' managers, 'feminine' knowledge about the world or organization is embodied in traditional or proverbial stories.

The nature of experiment

In physical or management science in the 'West', experiments are designed to exclude or control external influences, and to emphasize a few key variables and conditions, which can then be studied, or acted upon, in a repeatable fashion. In its extreme form the dictum is held, in science as in management, that 'if it cannot be measured it does not exist'. While indigenous science, according to Peat, does not imply experiment in the western or northern, scientific sense, it does employ a disciplined approach to merging horizons with the inner reality of the world, physically and managerially, revealing its different levels of process. In this way it enters into direct relationships with animals and plants, and of course with people, as Anita Roddick has so often done.

Prediction and control

According to the renowned Anglo-Austrian scientist and philosopher Karl Popper, to be called scientific a theory must be constructed in such a way that its predictions are capable of being falsified in a crucial experiment.

Native scientists have concerned themselves with prediction, but through an approach that is different from the Popperian one. What we take for prediction could, in the case of indigenous science or management, be closer to an expression of the harmonies and relations between things. The idea of prediction within the 'West' is based upon the linear flow of time. But in a society that views time as a circle there is never that sense of separation between present and future. Thus, prediction would not so much mean the ability to see into the future from the past, but rather a concern with the liminal, where things pass from one world to another, or when a product is translated from an indigenous context into a modern one.

Prediction, of course, in science as in management, is closely linked with control. If a scientist or a manager can describe a system according to some theory or model, and if he or she can predict the outcome of particular effects, then it becomes possible to control people or things. Similarly in indigenous science or management, in order for a person to move within a world of powers, spirits and energies, it is very important to have a map, to be able to enter into relationships with surrounding energies and to have knowledge of sources of power. But it is a different map from that of the scientific manager.

Objectivity, uniformity and modelling

'Western' science, as well as management, is strongly associated with the search for objective, independent thought or explicit action. In Native science, however, stress is laid upon direct subjective or tacit experience and upon closeness to nature.

A 'western' approach, for Peat moreover, rests on the notion of the uniformity of physical or human nature and its laws. While indigenous science also stresses unity and balance, it at the same time gives importance to diversity, as the Body Shop does, as well as to the particular event.

The 'western' or 'northern' orientation in fact emphasizes thoretical models, that is, simplified conceptual frameworks, in which one particular aspect of natural phenomena can be studied, and acted upon, through reason and experiment. Although an indigenous approach is not normally concerned with abstraction and simplification, it nevertheless possesses a strong component of representation. A particular symbol for it is not an abstraction or a reflection of reality, in the way that a model within a 'western' orientation is, but something that permits direct connection with the spirits, energies and animating power of physical and human nature. There is the sense that, like a holograph, a symbol can enfold the whole of reality. Thus the Sacred Hoop or the Fourfold Way, as we have seen, reflects a multiplicity of meanings, rather than just one.

A 'north-western' approach, then, seeks ultimate truth, believing in a rational universe that can be understood through experimentation and reason set within the context of particular theories and hypotheses, using the methods of induction and deduction. Truth in Native science, or in Body Shop's approach to management, is of a very different order. Truths are not value-free but depend upon tradition and social and spiritual sanctions. Dreams and visions are systems of validation. Truth, moreover, is contained within origin and migration stories, songs and ceremonies, natural skin and haircare products.

Surfaces and depths

The 'western' way, in fact, is a triumph of understanding the surfaces of things. The prehensile power of eye, hand and mind gives us the sense of reaching to, and acting upon, the inner essence of things by breaking them apart, dissecting the parts, exposing ever smaller entities and ever more detailed surfaces. At the same time, theories and abstract models of these new domains are created in the mind and are served by beautiful and powerful mathematical systems.

By contrast, indigenous people do not seem to live with such a visually apprehended surface orientation. The people rather rely upon the ear to reveal a world of energies and vibrations. While 'north-western' thought and action grasps at the surface, the indigenous heart, mind and being seek the 'inscape', that inner voice and authenticity that lies within each experience and aspect of nature. In engaging the inscape a person is not preoccupied with measuring, comparing, classifying, categorizing or fitting things into a logical scheme, but rather with seeking a relationship that involves the whole of their being.

A Native person, for Peat, like a business enterprise for Anita Roddick and an educational one for me, is always part of a much greater entity, and can never truly be separated from it. Each is an individual expression of the collective, and, in turn, the group comes together in ceremonies to draw upon a much greater energy. Something analogous happens with a super-conductor. In a superconductor, it is possible for an electrical current to flow past obstructions without experiencing any resistance at all. This happens because the various excitations in the metal – the photons and the dressed electrons – act in a coherent and co-operative fashion. It is as if there was a consensus to the movements so that all conspire to move in a co-ordinated dance. Rather than seeking control, change and progress, an indigenous society prefers to live in harmony with the world. Power certainly exists but it lies more within alliances and the ability to call upon external energies than it does in the human will or the release of mechanical force.

We now turn from David Peat's primarily scientific orientation to Murphy and Snell's primarily managerial emphasis upon 'forging a heroic organization'.

FORGING THE HEROIC ORGANIZATION

Principles of Cangleska Wakan

In Sioux culture, the Sacred Hoop, as we have seen, encompasses all things, animate and inanimate, that make up the universe. The Hoop is a state of being, an understanding of the universe that connects all things to a common destiny. The Hoop explicitly depicts the interrelationships among all elements of life, humans, animals, spirits, air, water, earth and sky. In the Sioux world, no element acts alone; all components act in concert to create harmony or disharmony. The circle, then, symbolizes the Sioux belief that all things participate in one ordered whole, sharing the same physical and spiritual space. It embraces, for Murphy and Snell, the idea of inclusion and the potential for everything within the Hoop to grow and change. Each point in the circle represents the interrelationships that comprise the organizational universe, as is the case for the Body Shop, and the knowledge creating ecology for ourselves. In the Hoop, moreover, humans act in concert with nature, not just existing within the universe but also contributing to its co-creation. Each individual element influences all the others.

The Sioux would never have invented a 'manifest destiny' moreover, the two authors maintain, that might claim for themselves, as the founders of the 'new world' did, a god-given right to conquer and dominate all within their reach. Instead the Sioux saw themselves as woven into the fabric of the world, sharing their needs and purposes with those around them. They respected the world within which they lived to such a degree that, to their ultimate misfortune, they did not ever comprehend the white man's concept of owning the land. They were the land, in the same way as the Body Shop is at one with nature.

These beliefs, for Murphy and Snell, stand in direct contrast to the organizational or national mindset of modern business or education (such as conventional cosmetics companies or MBA programmes) or society, in the same way as for Peat they contrast with classical science. Where the Sioux perceive existence as a circle, 'north-western' business people, or indeed business academics, tend to perceive it as a hierarchy of relationships and a linear progression, typically envisaging their world in terms of segmented hierarchies or curricula, and time lines: in the same way as events in the past and future bear little relationship to the present, individuals occupy positions on the rungs of a ladder that, for Murphy and Snell, in practice allow few to excel.

Where the Sioux classified themselves as part of the world – on a par with nature and the other stakeholders in the Hoop – managers in American organizations typically see themselves as separate from the community, their environment and all other stakeholders, be they domestic customers or foreign competitors. In contrast, a 'Heroic Organization' such as the Body Shop, as characterized by Murphy and Snell, deals with the process of change in terms of 'walking in a sacred manner', which they consider to be a richer and more comprehensive version of the common expression 'walking the talk'. For the leaders of such an organization, exemplified by the Roddicks, walk in the sacred manner along a path of potential, reciprocity and balance. In the table below we summarize Murphy and Snell's view of what they term their 'Heroic Organization', reflecting indigenous wisdom.

Table 12 Cangleska Wakan and the Heroic Organization

Cangleska Wakan	*The Heroic Organization*
Individuals take from and contribute to the whole: 'The Universe'	All stakeholders, from managers to the community, contribute to the whole: 'The Organization'
The Universe consists of all the entities that contribute to it, from people to the stars	The Organization consists of all its stakeholders, what they contribute and what they take
The term 'sacred' means filled with intangible power, that is the potential for shared creation	The potential of each stakeholder to innovate, create or destroy provides the key to an organization's power
The circular concept of the Hoop requires all 'points' of the circle to possess a significant identity	In the Heroic Organization the chain becomes a circle: in it the CEO and frontline workers possess equal power
In the Hoop all movement depends on all other movement to create continuous, harmonious, unified motion	The Heroic Organization encourages stakeholders to evolve, assume new responsibilities, share power and information and to fulfil potential
The concept of time specifies that any event results from a multitude of forces – past and present, direct and indirect	The Heroic Organization evaluates its status in terms of all its stakeholders, past achievements and its future goals
The Sioux view all elements of the universe as 'alive', with the power to grow and change, hence being 'sacred'	'Walking in a sacred manner' means adherence to a protocol for tapping the potential for growth, change and improvement amongst all stakeholders
Chiefs wield no coercive power – they can only lead individuals on a shared path	Leaders wield power only in the sense that they tap all stakeholders' potential to recreate the organization
For the Sioux, the nonlinear nature of time means that people must maintain a heightened sense of their environment, watching for signals	The Heroic Organization focuses on all its stakeholders' experiences and watches for signals that allow it to anticipate and avert crises before they unbalance the organization

Such an 'indigenous' view of reality, then, is very much the one we have adopted in the context of our knowledge creating ecology, a view that so clearly serves to differentiate our approach from that of a conventional MBA programme, on the one hand, and management consultancy, on the other.

The heroic process

Viewing the organization as the sum of all its relationships, according to Murphy and Snell, and building on the strengths of those relationships with all stakeholders – leaders, employees, customers, suppliers, competitors, the community, regulatory agencies – affords an organization like the Body Shop the self-awareness it needs to act with confidence in a changing world. The tenets of the Hoop suggest three steps any organization can take, as far as the two Americans are concerned, to tap the full potential of all its stakeholders:

1   leading through strategic humility
2   building heroic partnerships
3   walking in a sacred manner

Lead through strategic humility

Cangleska Wakan, then, defines a protocol for leadership behaviour diametrically opposed to most contemporary 'north-western' thinking on the subject of leadership. Americans, Murphy and Snell point out, have tended to laud their leaders as individual heroes singlehandedly accomplishing corporate miracles. To build heroic partnerships with stakeholders and to walk in a sacred manner, heroic leaders must first harmonize their own needs with those of everyone in the organization and the larger community – as is the case for the Body Shop and hopefully for ourselves – in which they function. Doing so does not signal weakness, but rather emotional security.

Walk in a sacred manner

Every organization or society, following from the above, needs to function within a context for action that aligns its resouces and activities with the underlying economic, social and technological forces that create the market and define the needs of its stakeholders. This is quintessentially the case for the Roddicks. In the Sioux world, like theirs, the everyday experience of living close to the natural world dominated people's lives. Whether the day's events chronicled a victory on the battlefield or success in the hunt, the Sioux examined the impact of these events on their vision of community.

Such an assessment makes it possible to walk in a sacred manner, as was the case when the Body Shop championed the cause of the Egoni people in Nigeria or the whales in the Pacific Ocean, and is indeed also the case when I champion the cause of the student against the 'power hierarchy' of conventional academe.

Build heroic partnerships

Ironically, Murphy and Snell maintain, the absence of a contemporary 'Medicine Circle' of stakeholders has meant that otherwise interesting and creative organizational or leadership techniques have tended to exacerbate rather than resolve the disconnection between them. Instead of connecting and uniting at a fundamental level, most organizations, unlike the Body Shop, have used a fragmented approach, relying on virtual alliances, team learning, quality improvement and business process engineering by isolated individuals or groups without paying sufficient attention to the overall impact of these efforts on the whole circle of stakeholders. Not surprisingly, these fragmented efforts have generally produced fragmented results, for a Heroic Organization gains strength from a spiderweb of relationships, where strands of reliance connect each stakeholder to all the others. Weaken one strand and you weaken the entire web. Strengthen each strand and you strengthen the whole web. Like the strong strands of the spiderweb, strong bonds among all stakeholders – including in our case hunters and herders, gardeners and stewards – afford the organization flexibility in the face of change, enabling it to capture the results that benefit each and every stakeholder.

During the early nineties the Body Shop combined with Friends of the Earth, Survival International and Greenpeace to run joint campaigns on acid rain, recycling, the ozone layer and the genocide of indigenous tribes. We are doing our best to develop intimate relationships with both our organizational clients and our Anglo-Saxon and Middle Eastern societies. The Hoop defines an organization as a network of relationships and partnerships among all the persons involved in it and encourages them to act in concert inside and outside the organization. Organizations thus learn about themselves by learning about their relationships with all their stakeholders.

CEO
Heroic leader

MANAGERS	CUSTOMERS	FRONT LINES
Heroic advocate	**Heroic partner**	

BOARD
Heroic guardian

Figure 27 The organizational Medicine Circle

Each of these contributes in a special way towards the organization's success, and each poses unique risks and opportunities to it.

The customer

The organizational Medicine Wheel, for Murphy and Snell, revolves around the customer (for us Anglian or Ford, Sainsbury or Surrey Police), the central concern that binds the efforts, the interests and the aspirations of everyone in the circle.

In Sioux culture on the plains, the customer represented the obligation of each member of the tribe to serve and protect every other member. Shamans, for example, such as in our case Anita Roddick, chose their vocation for personal reasons, but were obligated to fulfil that vocation in support of the 'tribal' community, as caretakers of our global environment.

Frontline workers

Frontline workers (for us the individual student and faculty), such as those within each Body Shop franchise, live and work daily as *heroic partners* with the customer. This constant frontline contact affords them a dual allegiance: first to serve as the voice of the customer for the organization, and then to speak on behalf of the organization to the customer. The Heroic Organization heeds both allegiances in order to develop responsiveness to customer needs, always respecting both directions of the feedback loop.

Managers

In the organizational Medicine Circle, managers function as *heroic advocates* for the customer, as I myself act as a champion for our corporate clients, a major shift in perspective from decades past, where managers operated as dictators of company policy. This transforms middle managers, in Murphy's view, from 'bodyguards' who separate upper leadership from the front lines into customer advocates, who bring the front lines to the leaders. Such frontline concerns, for Body Shop, are not only the individual preferences of consumers, but also the collective rights of civilizations, whether those of the Paiakan of Brazil or the Egoni peoples of Nigeria. Today's managers, then, can accomplish this transformation by redefining their roles as active problem solvers on behalf of the customer.

The CEO

Within the organizational Medicine Circle, a CEO like Anita Roddick becomes a *heroic leader*, exhibiting such leadership through service. Instead therefore of presiding at the top of the organization, such a leader works in its midst, on behalf of the individual customer and of society as a whole, recognizing the value of all stakeholders in their organization's success, and seeking harmony among all of them, as is indeed my own natural and indigenous bent. Having set forth on a quest, in Anita's case on behalf of the indigenous peoples and natural environment of the world, the hero or heroine returns home to share the fruits of the quest. The return-and-share decision makes the leader truly heroic.

The board

Finally and ideally, the Board should serve as both the *heroic guardian* of the customer's interests and as a balancing force within the circle of stakeholders. As such its role is to protect the organization's superordinate value structure, the overriding values of the Hoop: commitment to the welfare of all stakeholders and dedication to harmony among them. In the Body Shop case this includes not only individual customers and employees, suppliers and subcontractors around the world but also the natural environment as a collective whole. In our own case we serve individual, organization and society – in reverse order!

The Sioux, of course, held nothing more sacred than the natural world because the land, or in our case knowledge set within the context of a knowledge creating ecology, gave them all the prerequisites of life, as is ultimately the case for the Body Shop .

CONCLUSION

The Body Shop in the commercial world and we in the educational, in conclusion, partake of the indigenous wisdom embodied in the Paiakan or Sioux people that happens to resonate with much of what is contained in quantum physics. This wisdom is what we have termed perennial, rather then merely indigenous or even traditional. In terms of Murphy and Snell's 'organizational medicine cycle', Anita Roddick is a 'heroic CEO', the franchisees act as 'heroic partners' to both customer and community, many of the Body Shop managers are 'heroic advocates' of social change, and the Board is a 'heroic guardian' of the enviromental cause. In our own terms, then, I have a visionary part to play in our overall enterprise, together with our sponsoring companies as would-be 'heroic partners'. Indeed, in at least one or two instances, our 'link managers' and even our CEOs act in company as advocates for knowledge creation and civic reconstruction, as opposed to mere management education.

That having been said, the 'Heroic Organization', and the holistic philosophy that it purportedly represents, actually falls short of the Body Shop's, and indeed our own, ultimate aspirations. For at the centre of both of our beings is not the local customer in isolation but also the global environment as a composite whole. In context, both of us are as much concerned with civic reconstruction as a whole, albeit through 'trade-not-aid' in the Body Shop case, as we are with serving the individual customer (or student). We now turn, finally, to Ken Wilber, who is concerned, like Anita Roddick and us, with *Sense and Soul*.

BIBLIOGRAPHY

1   Roddick, A., *Body and Soul*, Ebury Press, 1990.
2   Peat, D., *Blackfoot Physics*, Penguin, 1994.
3   Murphy, E. and Snell, M., *Forging the Heroic Organization*, Prentice-Hall, 1994.
4   Murphy, E., *The Genius of Sitting Bull*, Prentice-Hall, 1992.
5   Bohm, D., *Wholeness and the Implicate Order*, Ark Publishing, 1980.

Part VI

Conclusion

Catalytic zone

17 Entering the catalytic zone

Becoming worldcentric

INTRODUCTION

Cosmic consciousness

In this concluding chapter, in drawing together the threads of the traditional and the modern, the post-modern and the perennial, I want to draw upon the work of that extraordinary American social philosopher, Ken Wilber.[1-3] Wilber's most recent book, *Sense and Soul*, a culmination of his work to date, serves to integrate philosophically, what we have presented here managerially and organizationally. In a sense, in journeying from Lloyd's set within the City of London, to the Body Shop and seeing it in the context of our own knowledge creating ecology, we have indeed moved from common sense to civic soul. In the process, moreover, we have aligned ourselves ecologically with Diana the huntress, the conserver, the gardener, and the steward, as we intimated at the outset of this book.

For Wilber, the point of a genuine environmental ethics, such as that ostensibly followed by the Body Shop and by us, is that we are supposed to transcend and include the whole of life and organization in a genuine embrace. Because human and business beings, whether engaged in manufacturing automobiles like Ford or providing insurance like Virgin, contain matter and life and mind as components in their make-up, then of course we must honour all of them, not only for their own intrinsic worth, which is the most important, but also because they are components in our own being, and destroying them is literally suicidal for us. It is not that harming the ecosphere, or our businessphere, will eventually catch up with us and hurt us from the outside. It is that the ecosphere for Wilber, and the businessphere for me, is literally inside us, is part of our being, our compound individuality – harming either sphere, as he and we put it, is internal suicide, not just some sort of external problem.

The basic drive of evolution, individually as well as institutionally, is to increase depth from (in our terms) individual education to civic reconstruction via knowledge creation, through the development of an appropriately catalytic process. This involves harnessing the self-transcending drive of the

Cosmos – to go beyond what went before (in our case in terms of management education) and yet include it, and thus increase its own depth (towards civic reconstruction). There is in effect a spectrum of individual, organizational and societal consciousness, and evolution catalytically unfolds that spectrum.

All too human

So there is an overall continuity as well as discontinuity to evolution, which can be aligned, as in our catalytic programme, with traditional (primal), modern (rational), post-modern (developmental) and perennial (metaphysical) eras.[4] Every stage of evolution eventually reaches its own limitations, and these may act as triggers to the self-transcending drive. The inherent limitations create a type of turmoil, even chaos, as we saw with Lloyd's for example, through its so-called 'reconstruction and renewal'. The system either breaks down (self-dissolution) or escapes this chaos by evolving to a higher degree of order (self-transcendence), as for example Surrey Police has done, through creating order out of chaos.

This new and higher personal and institutional order escapes the limitations of its predecessor, but then introduces its own limitations and problems that cannot be solved at its own level. In other words, there is a price to be paid for every evolutionary step forward, as IBM today may or may not have quite realized. Old problems are solved or defused, for example IBM reorienting itself away from selling hardware towards promoting business solutions through 'knowledge management', but only by introducing new and more complex difficulties, related to newly established organizational dynamics which have tended to go unrecognized. Hence the continued loss of valued personnel. We are all, for Wilber, tomorrow's food. The process continues, and momentum is found in the process itself, not in any particular epoch or time or place. In that context, to take another example, Anglian Water is intent now upon 'enhancing life through water' generally, rather than merely being concerned simply with water treatment, and this has brought about its own problems as well as opportunities.

Modernity, in the form of the Enlightenment follows the traditional agrarian commercial epoch. The concomitant technical developments served to transform the traditional – for example prospectively but not yet actually at Lloyd's – into that of industrialization and a rational perspective. Industrialization, for all its Fordist horrors, was first and foremost a technological means of securing subsistence not from human muscle working on nature but from machine power working on it, as the original Henry Ford was at pains to point out. As long as traditional societies demanded physical labour and commercial acumen for subsistence, those societies inevitably and unavoidably placed a premium on male physical strength and mobility.

They also fostered exploitative commercial enterprise. But within a century of industrialization – which replaced male physical and commercial strength with gender-neutral machines and depersonalized bureaucracies – the women's movement emerged. Social structures had emerged for the first time to a point at which physical and financial strength did not overwhelmingly determine power in culture. Biology was no longer destiny. So companies like Sainsbury now employ a woman as the Finance Director, if not yet their retail one! Within one or two centuries – a blip in evolutionary time – women have acted with lightning speed to secure legal rights to own property, to vote and to be their own persons, though this is still more evident in post-modern companies like Virgin rather than in modern corporations like Ford.

The great post-modern revolution

The fundamental Enlightenment paradigm, Wilber informs us, is known as the representational paradigm. This is the idea that you have the self or subject, on the one hand, and the empirical or sensory world, on the other. All valid knowledge therefore consists in making maps of the empirical world, such as Lord Sainsbury's or the conventional MBA's single and simple 'pre-given' world. And such a mass distribution or mass education map is accurate. If it correctly represents the empirical world, then it is 'truth'. As such, and in the latter case, hundreds of thousands of MBA students around the world continue to clamber after this truly wonderful qualification! The problem with maps, of business administration or of mass distribution, is that they leave out the mapmaker, whether it is Frenchman Henri Fayol in the first instance or Englishman Lord John Sainsbury in the second. However, beginning particularly with the German philosopher Kant, and running through his nineteenth-century compatriots Hegel and Nietzsche, and French philosopher Foucault – all great post-modern theorists – we find an attack on the mapping paradigm. For it fails to take into account the self that is making the maps in the first place. The self indeed, like the corporate self of a Tesco's today, as Sainsbury may have discovered, did not just parachute to earth. It has its own characteristics, its own structures, its own development, its own history – and all of these influence and govern what it can see, what it will see in the supposedly 'single' world around it.

The parachutist, as Wilber puts it, be it a Ford or a Sainsbury, is up to its neck in, for example, Fordist contexts, which determine what it can see in the first place. The self in general, and the manager and organization in this case, does not have an unchanging essence so much as it has a history, and the mapmaker will make quite different maps at different stages in his or her growth and development. In Kant's 'Copernican Revolution', the mind of for example Lord John forms the world more than the world of Sainsbury forms the mind of Lord John. And Hegel then added the crucial point that, in one way or another, defined all post-modern theories: the mind, the subject, can only be conceived as one that has developed. Each worldview then gives way to its successor, as Lord John gave way to his nephew David Sainsbury, because of certain inherent limitations in the earlier worldview.

This generates a great deal of disruption and chaos, as we have seen for instance at Sainsbury's recently. The system, if it does not collapse, escapes this chaos by evolving to a more highly organized pattern, which our MMBAs at Sainsbury have been struggling to find. At each stage of development – traditional, modern, post-modern, perennial – the world looks different because the world is different. Modernity, for Ford as for IBM as for Sainsbury, has to give way, kicking and screaming, to post-modernity. In our own case this involves the advent of the post-modern, or even perennial, catalytic zone in place of modern management education and business administration. Wherever there is the possibility of transcendence, moreover, there is by the same token the possibility of repression. Sainsbury, for example, strives today to get 'closer to its customer', harking back to tradition rather than forward to the post-modern, and thereby becoming a leading player in a business ecosystem.

The higher, however, might not only transcend and include: it might transcend and exclude, repress, alienate, dissociate. IBM, for example, has dissociated itself from its formerly traditional communal as well as modern bureaucratic heritage, to some great cost as well as benefit. Body Shop has tended to repress a similarly modern impulse towards mass marketing and distribution, also to its cost as well as benefit. So this theme – transcendence versus repression – is an altogether crucial theme of historical development. So Wilber urges us to watch carefully for signs of repression at each stage of personal evolution, as we do in relation to organization development, individual and collective. Such repression, in a case like that of Sainsbury, includes a suppression of the feminine and intuitive spirit of one of the two founders, not the rational co-founder John but his wife and other co-founder Mary.

Societally speaking then, the phase-specific, phase-appropriate modern worldview, having served its conventional, organizationally and managerially MBA-like purposes, is now for Wilber living in its own fumes. We are breathing our own overly rational exhaust, in Tom Peters' and in Henry Mintzberg's terms. And how we collectively handle this will determine whether a new or more adequate worldview emerges to defuse these problems, or whether we are buried in our own wastes. Hopefully, and to the extent that our own knowledge creating ecology serves to turn a modern masters in business administration towards both a post-modern and perennially based catalytic zone, we will be able to help ourselves move along Wilber's evolutionary way, within 'the four corners of the Cosmos'.

THE FOUR CORNERS OF THE COSMOS

The four points of the compass

For Wilber, as for ourselves, the process of life, individually and collectively as well as subjectively and collectively, manifests itself as four quadrants. Through this book these have been preceded by:

- Stacey's division between 'ordinary' and 'extraordinary' management, and Whyte's differentiation between 'work' and 'soul', as well as
- Goshal and Barlett's threefold differentiation between entrepreneurship, integration and renewal, both set against the backdrop of

the traditionally and commercially based Corporation and Lloyd's of London. Subsequently these four quadrants have continually re-presented themselves, second, in terms of:

- James Moore's evolving business ecosystem and
- Strauss and Howe's societal turnings,

reflected in Ford, Sainsbury and IBM-like mass producing and consuming, product oriented modernity, and then third in:

- William Randall's stories that we are, our own global businessphere,
- Max Boisot's information space and
- Beck and Cowan's organizational memes,

reflected in the emerging insurance industry in the UK, within a Designcenter in Austria, Medlabs in the Arab Middle East, and an approach to community policing in Britain modelled on the Maoris, each of which is oriented towards a post-modern era of knowledge intensive services, finally succeeded by:

- Margaret Wheatley's simpler way,
- Ikijiro Nonaka's knowledge spiral,
- Will McWhinney's paths of change and
- Emmet Murphy's grounds of being,

reflecting those perennial elements of fire, air, water and earth respectively within the Virgin Group, Surrey Police, Anglian Water and Body Shop.

These four quadrants, then, in their different manifestations representing the four compass points of the known Cosmos, are all needed to navigate accurately through personal, organizational and societal worlds. Specifically, for Wilber, these quadrants are represented as behavioural (pragmatic), socio-technical (rational), cultural (humanistic) and intentional (holistic). Objective

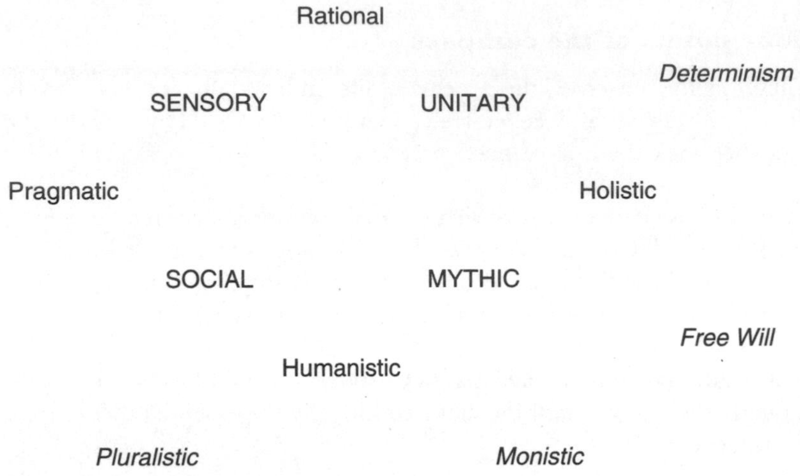

Rational

Determinism

SENSORY   UNITARY

Pragmatic   Holistic

SOCIAL   MYTHIC

Free Will

Humanistic

Pluralistic   *Monistic*

Figure 28 Alternative realities

scientific and 'behavioural' (economic) descriptions, that have traditionally predominated, for example, within Lloyd's are seldom oriented towards an interior consciousness. 'Cultural' refers to all the interior meanings that we share with similar communities – the shared collective worldview that so preoccupies, for example, the Body Shop . 'Social' refers to all the exterior, material, institutional IBM-like forms of the community, from its socio-technical base to its written codes. An individual or organization can only 'intentionally' (socio-psychologically) respond, finally, to those stimuli that fall within its interior worldspace, or worldview.

The four quadrants, for Wilber, then, are the interior and exterior of the individual and the collective. If we, as a nation in Britain, or elsewhere, do not take all of them into account, we will go limping into the future. The wider currents will not be activated in our own managerial and organizational, if not also societal, being. We will, in effect, be ordinary local driftwood on the shore of this extraordinary global stream. We will mistake our crutches for liberation, our management education for our civic reconstruction, we will offer our wounds to the world, we will bleed into the future all smiles and glory. Knowledge for Wilber – and for ourselves (see Figure 28) individually, organizationally, societally – will never bear fruit in works.

Two hands – Left and Right

The downside of the rational Enlightenment paradigm for Wilber was that, in its rush to be empirical, it collapsed interior depths into observable surfaces, and it thought that a simple mapping of these empirical exteriors was all the knowledge that was worth knowing. This conventional MBA-like approach left out the mapmaker himself – the self, the interiors. Surfaces must be seen, while depth must be interpreted. Right Hand paths are always asking 'What does it do?', whereas Left Hand paths are asking 'What does it mean?' We are dealing, Wilber maintains, with the Right and Left Hands of consciousness, of how life processes actually manifest themselves in the world, and we definitely need both hands.

If we listen carefully, Wilber maintains, we can hear each voice whispering gently its truth, and finally joining in a harmonious chorus that quietly calls us home.

Attuned to the Cosmos

The crucial point is that the subjective world, in our terms the 'psycho-social' of the manager him or herself, is situated in an intersubjective cultural space, 'western' or 'eastern', 'northern' or 'southern'. It is the collective, 'cultural' space, whether a Body Shop or a Britain, that allows the subjective individual space, you and me, to arise in the first place. Without this cultural background, my own individual thoughts as a manager would have no meaning at all. In other words, the psycho-social space is inseparable from the cultural one, as is Makis Werlamis from both Greece and the Designcenter. This kind of background, as Anglian Water, for example, is internationally coming to recognize, provides the common context within which one's own thoughts and interpretations, as well as one's company's commercial prospects, will have some sort of meaning. The socio-technical space, in contrast, describes the system in purely objective and exterior terms. It does not want to know how collective values are intersubjectively shared, as is currently the case, for example, within modern Ford, IBM or Sainsbury. Rather it wants to know how their objective correlates fit functionally in the overall socio-techical system. The subjective, like an Anglian Water or a Body Shop, uses interpretation of interior depth; the objective, like a Ford or an IBM, uses empirical-analytic observation of behaviour. Both have partial validity; they are correlates of each other. We now turn, more specifically, to the evolution of individual, organizational and societal consciousness.

FROM BREADTH TO DEPTH

Evolution of consciousness

Every individual, organization or society, for Wilber as for us, has a certain centre of gravity, around which norms, rules, basic institutional forms are organized. This centre of gravity provides the underlying cultural cohesion and social integration for the business or society. This centre, moreover, acts like a magnet on individual and organizational development, pulling each towards whatever level of consciousness is accessible. Beyond that, according to Wilber, the magnet will drag the individual or organization down. How then does such a centre of gravity acquire weight and depth?

Navigation first for the individual or organization, in such a context, involves four drives – personal agency (part), which is strong for example at Lloyd's, and social communion (whole), which prevails for example at Surrey Police), self-actualization (progression), which underlies Anglian Water's Transformation Journey, and self-dissolution (regression), which an IBM or a Sainsbury may be prone to, as each attempts to evolve. At each stage in the manager's or organization's (or indeed society's) growth and development, these four basic choices are available. Too much or too little of any of these four drives, and the self or society, public or private enterprise, according to Wilber, gets into pathological trouble. IBM, with its currently exaggerated personal agency, beware!

A *fulcrum*, second, is a crucial fork in the developmental road. How does the individual or institutional self deals with that fork decides their or its subsequent fate. Every fulcrum has a 1-2-3 structure. (1) The self or organization evolves or develops or steps up to a new level of awareness, as with Barry Wilding's aspiration within medical insurance. It identifies, or is at one with, that level. (2) It then begins to move beyond that level, or differentiate from it, dis-identify with it, or transcend it, as Anglian Water, for example, is attempting to do. (3) The organization identifies with the new and higher level and centres itself there, which is Ian Beckett's aspiration for knowledge creating Surrey Police. Identify, dis-identify, integrate; or fusion, differentiation, integration; or embed, transcend, include. So we have a ladder and its basic rungs. At each rung there is a different type of self-identify, self-need and moral stance. In our own case, we are struggling to dis-identify with management education, so that we can enter, instead, whole-heartedly into the catalytic zone. That, for Wilber, is a thumbnail sketch of development. The ladder with its basic rungs of awareness, for us pragmatic and rational, holistic and humanistic; the climbers – us within and alongside City University, with our fulcrums; and the different view of the world from each rung of the ladder, say from management education to civic reconstruction. The self at any given point in its indivdual or organizational development will tend to give around 50 per cent of its responses from one level, 25 per cent from the level above it and 25 per cent from the level below. No self is ever simply 'at a particular stage'. Furthermore, there are all sorts of regressions, spirals, temporary leaps forward, peak experiences, and so on, as we have seen amongst our MMBA students and within our sponsoring organizations.

In summary then, and to reiterate, all individuals and enterprises have four capacities – agency and communion, self-transcendence and self-dissolution. Because of the self-transcending drive, new entities emerge. As they emerge, they emerge 'holarchically'. They transcend and include. Entities not only have an inside and an outside, they also exist as individuals and collectives. This means that everyone has four facets: intentional-psychological (inside, individual), behavioural-economic (outside, individual), cultural-epistemological (inside, collective) and socio-technical (outside, collective). Humanity, through long and painful experimentation, learnt to ground knowledge in the realities of each quadrant, that is in each of these four worlds. Each one potentially evolves through ladder, climber and view: the ladder or basic structures or nested holarchy of development; the climber or self with a fulcrum at every stage – fusion/differentiation/integration; and the changing worldviews – traditional/modern/post-modern/perennial – each of which produces a different orientation to management education.

THE BIG THREE – I, WE, IT

The collapse of the Cosmos

In the modern MBA world, the science of business administration has been freed from traditional, commercial instinct; each functional domain has been set loose with its own power, its own truth and its own approach to business management, each of which has something equally important to say. But by the end of the twentieth century for management, and indeed already by the end of the eighteenth century in a more general sense, the extraordinary development of science began to throw the whole system off balance. For Wilber, the advances of the 'it' domains (behavioural-economic and socio-technical) began to eclipse, and then actually deny, the values and truth of the I (intentional-psychological) and we (cultural-epistemological) domains.

Wilber's so-called 'Big Three' (I, We, It) began to collapse into the Big MBA as a single entity. Empirical science, just like the Case Clearinghouse, and science alone, could pronounce on ultimate destiny. When only objective 'its' (behaviourally-economically or socio-technically oriented) are considered real – production and IT, marketing and corporate strategy, human resources and organizational behaviour, accounting and finance – then the mind itself becomes a *tabula* that is totally *rasa*. As such it is utterly blank until filled with pictures or representations of the only reality there is: objective and sensory business administration. Within the techno-economic base, a culture unfolds its possibilities. And within the industrial base, an altogether productive, technical and instrumental 'it' mentality unfolds. That is the power of industrialization, joined with the accomplishments of empirically based physical, social or management science, to select for a world where objective 'its' alone are real. Everything else stems from that selection.

The 'it' domain grew through modernity according to Wilber, as the conventional MBA was set within company based education and the training of individuals, like a cancer – a pathological growth – invading, colonizing and dominating the 'I' and the 'we' domains. The moral decisions of the culture were therefore handed over to scientific, technical or administrative solutions. Science, business administration, management education or corporate strategy would solve everything. All problems in the 'I' and 'we' domains were converted to technical, administrative or 'training' problems in the 'it' domain. And thus science or administration, HR or management development, would not only solve all problems, it would decide what was a problem in the first place – it would decide what was real and what was not.

Human beings, like everything else, were studied only in their empirical and objective dimensions, and thus were reduced to mere depersonalized 'its' in the great intwerwoven web – witness the rise of conventionally based human resource management theory and practice – with no significant depth and no profound intentionality and no personhood to speak of. No wonder the human resources seem to be fading, practically speaking, into a somewhat impotent background. If ever there was a phoenix waiting to rise from out of the flatland ashes, here is one, and yet, it has not yet found its place. For, on the one hand, the differentiation of the Big Three – 'I', 'we' and 'it' – brought enormous gains – in the liberation movements, in the democracies, in the knowledge quest, in scientific management and bureaucratic organization and, in its day, in human resource management. On the other hand, Wilber maintains, it inadvertently allowed the fundamental collapse of the human and managerial Cosmos, into flat and faded traditional exteriors and modern surfaces, bereft of post-modern individuality, and perennial community, embodied indeed in a conventional MBA. This is ironic.

For the very rationality that had freed humanity – and business through the MBA – from its overly primal way of being, was in the process of destroying it. Anybody, in business or otherwise, can say they are thinking globally, but very few can take an authentic, four-worldly perspective. To actually live from a 'worldcentric' or universal perspective requires – and this is the key for Wilber, as it is for ourselves – several major interior stages of transformation to take place. In this book these have been alternatively represented as autopoietic self-making in the person, stages of ecological succession in the organization, and societal turnings in the nation.

These all culminate in our own knowledge creating ecology, facilitated through our catalytic zone. If we ignore such interiors of personal, institutional or cultural transformation, and just fix our eyes on an objective 'global' map of business administration or of management education, we will ignore the actual path of getting people and institutions to a global or worldcentric stance. We will have a goal with no developmental path. And we will have a map that denies and condemns transcendence or transformation, which for Wilber is the actual path itself.

The ego and the eco

That having been said, rational modernity, at its best, does represent a worldcentric morality, a universal pluralism. I am certainly struck every year, when I first meet up with students from all over the world, gathered together for our conventional MBA at City, that such a universal pluralism is being engendered through their meeting with one another. Such a curriculum of study, however, that serves to bring them together in a world-centric setting, does not exist in the same purposeful vein in the traditional, transactional, commercial world of sensory reality.

The great advance of modernity was to differentiate the Big Three, and this can be found admirably set out in the writings of Kant – his great critiques deal with science, ethics and art in the same way as modern business administration distinguishes the economic, technical and social functions from each other. But the great failure of modernity was its incapacity to integrate the Big Three, as critics such as Hegel would point out. In the same vein no course in Integrating Studies, Corporate Strategy or Organizational Behaviour in which I have participated within an MBA, has ever managed to achieve such generality. For the rational ego – that great autonomous master of its universe – had simply sealed over its pre-personal (primal) roots. It had cut off its subconscious urges as well as its super-conscious inspiration, as is the case in modern corporations and business education today. I will never forget the protestations of an illustrious Professor of Economics at our university, when he was alerted to the fact that I was encouraging our undergraduate students to set up mini-business enterprises. 'What business do you have teaching your Business Studies students how to set up in business?' he complained vociferously to our Course Board.

What MBA programmes on the one hand and modern computer technology (and the Information Age) on the other mean is that the techno-base of a CUBS or an IBM can support a worldcentric perspective, a global consciousness, but that it does not in any way guarantee it. As we have seen, cognitive advances are necessary but not sufficient for moral advances, and the cognitive means usually run way ahead of the willingness to actually expand the realms of expanding awareness. The Net offers the worldcentric possibility but does not guarantee it. The flatland idea is that the Internet is global, so the consciousness using it must be global. For Wilber, as for ourselves, that's not even close to the truth. Most people are still at the egocentric and ethnocentric, traditional modes of awareness that predominate, for example, within the Lloyd's market. And no systems map, no Internet, will automatically change this. No such maps in themselves, in other words, will foster the interior transformation required to become, individually and institutionally, truly worldcentric. Education for managers, knowledge management for industry, is not enough. It tends to remain within flatlands. That is why we need to enter our catalytic zone, where the knowledge creating ecology unfolds.

The unpacking of self

That having been said, many individuals misguidedly intuit the 'World Soul' or 'Spirit in Business' solely in terms of the Higher Self or Inner Voice, that is, in our terms, 'manager self-development'. However true that aspect of self-realization may be it seriously diminishes the 'we' and the 'it' dimensions. It fails to give a decent account of the types of business acumen, socio-technical systems and cultural awareness needed overall. It centres on the intentional-psychological self, but it ignores the behavioural/economic, cultural and socio-technical. The totality of business and management, at any level, manifests as a self in a community with social and cultural foundations as well as objective correlates.

Thus any higher managerial self will inextricably involve a wider business community existing in a deeper objective state of affairs. Contacting the Higher Self is not the end of all problems but the beginning of immense and difficult work, for Wilber, to be done in all quadrants. This involves not just realizing such a higher self (intentional), but seeing it embraced in culture, embodied in nature (behavioural/economic) and embedded in socio-technical institutions. Processes within a knowledge creating ecology manifest themselves in all four quadrants: pragmatically realized, rationally embraced, holistically embodied and humanistically embedded.

CONCLUSION

Towards globality

We have been seeing, approximately since the Second World War, the slow shift from modern rational-industrial society to what Wilber terms a 'vision-logic', post-modern informational society. This transformation is being driven by a new techno-economic base (informational).

But it also brings with it a novel worldview, with a new mode of self as well as novel intentional/psychological and behavioural/economic patterns, set in a new cultural worldspace with new socio-technical institutions as anchors. This post-modern vision/logic information based enterprise, needs a knowledge creating worldview, set in a techno-economic base of digital information transfer, and a self-actualizing orientation – if ultimately its economic behaviour is to fit functionally in the new worldspace. So Lloyd's or Corporation of London, Ford, Sainsbury or IBM, as well as Anglian Water, Body Shop or Virgin, beware. There is no salvation to be found in flatlands.

The transformation actually required, according to Wilber, as we have experienced over ten years through the agonies and ecstasies of our own development within and around the MMBA, places a new and terrible burden. For the greater the depth of transcendence, the greater the burden of inclusion. In other words, civic reconstruction is dependent upon knowledge creating institutions, which in turn require an upgrading of intellectual capital, which in turn is dependent on good quality education and training. Every human being or business enterprise still has to start its own development at square one. Even a person or institution born into a grand vision-information culture nevertheless begins development on what we have termed a primal (sociocentric) and rational (conventional) level, before moving to a developmental (post-conventional) then metaphysical (world-centric) level. As a society's, or an organization's, or indeed our MMBA programme's centre of gravity puts on more and more weight – as more individuals and institutions move from egocentric or sociocentric to world-centric – this places a huge burden on the need to inegrate these individuals vertically. This needs to take place, moreover, at different depths in their own development. And the greater the depth of an individual, corporate or societal culture's centre of gravity, as for example Body Shop knows all too well, the greater the demand and the burden of this vertical integration.

Alleviating the depth gap

Thus the 'economic gap' between rich and poor, for Wilber, is bad enough, but much more crucial – and much more hidden – is the 'culture gap', the 'depth gap', the 'values gap'. This is the gap between the depth offered as a potential by the culture, or for example by our knowledge creating ecology, and those (managers and organizations in our case) who can actually explore that depth. And as our centre of gravity puts on more and more weight, there are more and more individuals and organizations who can be left behind, marginalized, excluded from their own intrinsic unfolding, disadvantaged for Wilber in the cruellest way of all: in their own interior consciousness, value and worth. And since other programmes recognize no depth in their conventionally based MBA flatland, they cannot even begin to recognize the depth gap, the culture gap, the consciousness gap. Such a gap, for Wilber, will therefore continue to wreak havoc, until this most crucial of all problems is first recognized, then framed in ways that allow us to begin to work with it.

The egocentric and sociocentric (primal in our terms) could not care less about global civilization, or for that matter about our knowledge creating ecology, unless you scare them into seeing how it affects just their personal or corporate existence. In doing that, you have simply reinforced exactly the self-centric survival motives that are the cause of the problem in the first place. It is only at a global, so-called post-conventional, worldcentric stance that individual managers can recognize the actual dimensions of our environmental crisis, and, more important, develop the moral vision and fortitude to proceed on a global, four-worldly basis. Obviously, then, a significant number of individuals must reach a worldcentric level of development in order to be a significant force in global community building, duly engaging then in civic reconstruction.

We have had our fair quota of these on our MMBA, but we have not yet sufficiently advanced the force of our catalytic zone for them to exert as much knowledge creating impact on the evolution of civic community as we would have liked. Our retreat in Austria, a month after this chapter is being written, is oriented towards a higher resolution of such a force. Because human beings have relatively more depth than, say, an amoeba, we have more rights. As a result there are more conditions necessary to sustain the wholeness of a human being like Barry Wilding or an organization like Medlabs. But we also have many more responsibilities, not only to the human societies of which we are parts, but to all the communities of which we are a part. We exist in networks of relationships with other entities in the physiosphere, the biosphere and the noosphere. Our relatively greater rights absolutely demand relatively greater responsibilities in all those dimensions. Failure to meet these, Wilber maintains, will lead to our self-destruction, whether in Paris or in Palestine, in Thames Valley or in Toronto. Wilber's first pragmatic rule for environmental ethics therefore is: in pursuit of your vital needs, consume or destroy as little depth as possible. Do the least amount of harm to consciousness you possibly can. Destroy as little intrinsic worth as possible. Protect and promote as much depth as possible. Hunters (students) need herders (link managers), as much as gardeners (facilitators) are in need of stewards (vision-logic leaders). In fact it is important to promote the different levels of our ecology, from knowledge vision to knowledge practice.

A developing individual, organization and society will have to evolve in a way that therefore integrates consciousness, culture and nature, and thus finds room for art, morals and science – for personal value, for collective wisdom and for technical know-how. Only by rejecting flatland can the good and the true and the beautiful be integrated. Only by rejecting flatlanders, Wilber urges, can a family of nations emerge, committed to the vigorous protection of worldcentric space, glorious in its compassionate embrace. Attention to Gaia *per se* might lead to sustainable material growth, but not to sustainable spritual progress. And, for Wilber as for ourselves in the final analysis, we desperately need both.

For it is only in being able to transcend our own limited and mortal egos that we can find that common source and ground of all sentient beings. In the process the education of the individual will need to be supplemented by the upgrading of intellectual capital, knowledge creating companies will manage to emerge, and civic reconstruction will thereby have to ensue. In this way a Steve Kaye alongside an Anglian Water or an Ian Williamson alongside a Sainsbury, a Terry Heyday alongside a Lloyd's or a Glyn Alger or a Boyd Rodger alongside a Surrey or a Thames Valley police, will jointly become all that it or they can be: a source that bestows new splendour on the setting sun and radiates grace in every gesture, in our case a knowledge creating organization explicitly engaged in civic reconstruction, a catalytic zone, a place to engage individually and collectively in one's 'soul practice'.

BIBLIOGRAPHY

1   Wilber, K., *Sense and Soul*, Simon and Schuster, 1998.
2   Wilber, K., *The Eye of the Spirit*, Shambala Press, 1997.
3   Wilber, K., *A Theory of Everything*, Gill Macmillan, 1996.
4   Lessem, R., *Management Development and Cultural Diversity*, Routledge, 1998.

Epilogue: Transition Management

Two cultures

In the fifties C.P. Snow wrote his famous book on the 'Two Cultures' in Britain, that is, the arts and the sciences. In the context of our own work, the other two cultures that have remained all too long apart are those of business and academia. In fact the supposed reconciliation of their two orientations, through for example in-company MBAs and executive development programmes, we believe to be at best only halfway houses to integration.

In fact, and based on our ten-year experience of running a project based 'in-company' MBA, we have come to the conclusion that such a conventionally based approach to linking up business and business school (while having some invaluable features to it), ultimately – and in relation to the development of the organization – can only work partially. The reason is that, at the end of the day, while the corporate output is collectively oriented towards profitability, crime prevention or social welfare, the academic output is individually oriented towards a personally awarded, academic qualification in business administration, change management, organization development or what have you. This individual–organizational divide, even more so now we believe than the difference between theory and practice, prises apart these two business and academic cultures.

What then are the features of the in-company MBA, such as the one we have run for ten years at City University, that do work for the organization?

First, the project based approach we have adopted does serve to ensure that, at least to some extent, the knowledge acquired 'bears fruit in works'. Second, the rounded curriculum undoubtedly enables the individual to acquire a wide-ranging perspective on management, which a shorter executive programme would not quite provide. Third, and in fact for us the most significant feature of this conventionally based, in-company MBA, is the prolonged two-year 'Transformation Journey' upon which the individual embarks. For without the incentive provided by the prospective master's degree, the practising manager would not be prepared to set out on what is generally a profoundly reflective as well as intensely active journey. That is the case especially if the programme has as strong an emphasis on manager self development as ours at City has done, as well as upon the development of managerial knowledge and skills. In effect, such a journey enables the individual to advance from what may have hitherto been a mere job, into a more meaningful role or even, especially in midlife, a calling.

Arguably then, a tailor-made, in-company master's programme can go up to half of the way towards delivering corporate, as well as individual, benefits. How then can that other half be filled? The Four Worlds Institute has been established, in co-operation with corporate others, explicitly to fill the gaps left over by the conventional wisdom. As a result of this corporate shift in our orientation, the directorship of the more explicitly individually oriented Management MBA, at City University, has recently changed hands. In parallel, our major focus of attention has shifted then, via the Four Worlds Institute, from the individual to the organization, towards business ecosystems, as well as towards societies at large.

Moreover, we have supplemented the relatively static notion of an MA in business administration with a more dynamic orientation towards managing individual (mastery) and more so organizational (transformation) transition.

Individual Mastery and Organizational Transition

World 1: Pragmatic – Action Learning – City University's MMBA

The Institute then, co-operatively sets out to address Four Worlds, that is, firstly the 'western' world of the Individual, secondly the 'northern' world of the Organization, thirdly the so-called 'eastern' world of the 'Business Ecosystem' or 'Kereitsu', and ultimately what we term the 'southern' world of Society as a whole. As far as the individual manager is concerned, and in conjunction with a progressively and practically minded business school such as City University, the Institute sets out to supplement project-based management education with purposefully oriented individual and organizational learning. To that extent, Reg Revans' approach to Action Learning is of 'preparatory' or 'primal' significance in that it provides a pragmatic, experiential base to individual and group learning. Such an individual and practical starting point is not surprising, given the Institute's base in the 'West', and it has arguably been most expressly fulfilled through Sainsbury's (one of Britain's leading supermarketeers) long-standing involvement, as founder members, of individual managers on City's MMBA programme. Such involvement was originally guided by Management Development Manager Judith Evans as Learning Facilitator.

World 2: Rational – Knowledge Management – University of Water

As far as the organization as a whole is concerned, and most actively in cooperation with the University of Water at the Anglo-Swedish utility Anglian Water, we have set out, over the past five years, to help the corporation enhance its core competence. Focussed on Transition Management, Anglian Water is explicitly engaging in 'flow management'. Its University of Water has in fact thereby emerged, with our due assistance, as a symbol of Anglian Water's transition from a parochially based public bureaucracy into a privately constituted global enterprise. In the process, it has become internationally renowned for its learning and knowledge oriented activities, and as such has recently been written up in a Harvard Case Study. In its 'University' prospectus, then, Anglian declares its commitment to learning at work, thereby improving customer service, enriching the quality of life of its employees, developing the organization as well as new technology, and in the process extending and applying its knowledge through business and academic alliances.

The University's 'faculties', drawing again upon our four knowledge domains, have thereby been constituted in terms of business development, engineering and technology, environment and planning as well as human and social sciences. Each of these faculties is intended to champion a relevant, overall area of knowledge in the business, duly focussing on the core competencies, and sources of intellectual capital, identified by the Company as underlying its future success. In that context, Leif Edvinsson's rationally based approach – which we therefore term 'ordinary' – to 'Intellectual Capital', emerging out of Sweden's Skandia Finanical Services, is seminal.

In the final analysis then, and in order to embody its vision in the wider business world – as well as within its own company – Anglian Water, led by its new Chief Executive Chris Mellor, is establishing a long-term Transition Management programme, aimed organizationally at corporate transformation, and individually at global leadership. Such a programme will not only serve to develop and consolidate the knowledge base for its global thrust but also to align itself with actually and potentially linked public and private enterprises, locally and globally, so as to become a world leader by 2007. The University's efforts, finally, are guided by Sudhanhsu Palsule, as its Knowledge Manager.

World 3: Developmental – Knowledge Creation – Neighbourhood Policing

The development of a 'business ecosystem', that is, a cluster of related enterprises, has been most expressly illustrated by the Surrey Police with whom we have been closely associated for the past two years, in conjunction with local communities around the world. In revisiting Robert Peel's original nineteenth-century concept of preventative policing, now set in the wider social context, Deputy Chief Constable Dr Ian Beckett has advanced the notion of 'Community Policing', whereby a 'service'-oriented approach leads, reciprocally, to the public assisting the police to deal with and prevent crime. Such a preventative or proactive approach involves the police in strengthening trust in communities or, where it is lacking, to creating it. From this vantage point, the police, together with other agencies, stimulate the community itself towards self-policing.

Such a proactive orientation moreover for Nonaka and Takeuchi, who are the 'extraordinary', developmentally oriented Japanese theorists in this knowledge creating organizational respect, is dependent upon Surrey Police, in conjunction with ourselves, as well as other knowledge based institutions.

Surrey Police, in fact, have been richly endowed, even before Ian Blair took over as its new Chief Constable, with a Visionary Leader in Ian Beckett, a Learning Facilitator in Andy Thompson positioned at the edge of human resources, and several Organization Developers such as Glyn Alger and Martin West. The latter have both shared responsibility for the so-called 'Blue Knight' programme, incorporating the technology based end of the 'Neigbourhood Policing', together with the American systems house, Intergraph. Moreover, Surrey finally, through their peace building orientation, have been playing a part in what we have termed 'civic reconstruction', whereby we are working together, both actually and also prospectively, in Palestine and in South Africa.

World 4: Metaphysical – Civic Reconstruction – Rebuilding Palestine

The culmination of our 'Four Worlds' orientation, embodying so-called 'mastery', is represented by our work – like Surrey Police's – with whole communities, to help reconstruct them root and branch, and in the process serve to create, in Max Boisot's terms, a veritable framework for a learning society. Working with City University Business School, and our partners in the Arab Middle East, TEAM – the largest engineering and management consultancy in the area – we have evolved from running an MBA programme.

As such we have engaged with our individual and organizational participants in societal learning, and thereby in civic reconstruction. A notable organizational case in point has been Medlabs, based both in Jordan's Amman and also on the Palestinian West Bank, who are building up the local health services and with whom we have worked closely. In fact, health and education has featured heavily in the context of our Middle Eastern Management MBA in the region, and we are currently seeking to evolve the programme, explicitly, from individual and organizational learning towards inter-organizational knowledge creation and civic reconstruction. Our orientation towards peace building, together with Surrey Police's, provides a focal point for this.

Towards a University of Life

Four Worlds: Integral – Towards a University of Life

All that is now left for us, by way of this epilogue to our book, is the hope, if not also the opportunity, of bringing all Four Worlds together. For, this our final port of call, we enter Richard Branson's Virgin, and into what has generally been called Virgin Direct, and specifically their One Account. For it is in that context that all four worlds are being brought together into just one.

In Richard Branson's recent autobiography, where he extols the process of 'Losing My Virginity',[1] he claims in the opening lines that 'I always had an urge to live life to the full'. As a quintessential westerner, cast in the guise of the merchant-adventurer of old, Branson has an uncanny affinity with the 'east'.

In fact Virgin does substantive business with Japan, and he likens the Virgin Group, philosophically, with its long-term orientation. At the same time Richard, if not overtly 'northern' or rational in orientation, has always been an avowed European, and has Virgin megastores operating success-fully in France and Germany. Ultimately, moreover, Virgin generally and Virgin Direct specifically are very much 'family' businesses, with a strongly 'southern' community feel to them.

Interestingly enough in fact, in 1998, Virgin Direct, under the influence of Jayne-Anne Gadhia who now runs the One Account, and supported by the company's founder and managing director, Rowan Gormley, established 'Development Destinations' for all its staff. The keynote for this, drawing upon our own frame of reference, was the Four Worlds. 'If we could only harness the best features of the four corners of the world', its promotional material intimated, 'what a force we would be!' Thereafter the brochure, given to all the company's employees, described the features of the West (profit and organizational effectiveness), the East (empathy as self aware-ness), the North (systems and procedures), and the South (strengthening the community), and how to get there.

The challenge that the One Account faces is how it can turn a home-grown year of development, located within its own neck of the Virgin woods, into a veritable University of Life, embraced perhaps by Virgin as a whole, aimed at making individuals and organizations, industries and societies more worldy wise. So where would Richard Branson himself fit in?

Interestingly enough, when Branson turned 40, after the great leap into setting up Virgin Atlantic, he began to wonder whether he should change the pattern of his life, from one that was fundamentally outer-directed to one that would become manifestly inner-directed. Specifically, and at that time, he thought of going to university and studying history. Alternatively, he contemplated venturing into politics, studying some major issues such as healthcare and homelessness, and then fighting hard for political change to implement them. Arguably, and in our worldly terms, he was intending to turn from the active West towards the reflective East, or ultimately towards the communal South. All of these thoughts, in fact though, were pushed out of his mind by Saddam's invasion of Kuwait.

Now that Virgin has ventured into so many different walks of life, commercial and technological, social and cultural, and that Richard Branson has entered the inner-directed phase of his own life, it may be time for that active embodiment of life, the Virgin Group, to become at the same time its reflective embodiment – that is, a Virgin University of commerce and community, of art and technology. As for that lover of freedom Richard Branson, so for Rowan Gormley: 'Possibly a great moment in my life, as a young man, was reading a pirate copy of Mandela's speech at the Rivonia trial. I had been led, by the white community, to believe that he was a raving terrorist. But this wasn't the language that I came across in his speech. It was a call for life and liberty.' To the extent that we are able to align life and liberty – individually and organizationally, industrially and society – with what has hitherto been identified with management education, so we will have genuinely served the cause of civic reconstruction, across the world.

We end this story, then, of what we have termed an 'evolving organizational ecology', through the four worlds, with the mythology of the Holy Grail, and of the knights of King Arthur, so strongly a part of our English heritage.

The end to this story is being told at a time when the East, in the latter part of the 1990s, is going through a turbulent time and the global economy, as a result, is bursting at the seams.

'The orient thereby looks expectantly towards the West. It is waiting for the West to discover a form of social organization which will be a moral one, yet able at the same time to incorporate within itself the mechanical civilization of the Western world. If the West succeeds in creating such a world, then the East will recognize that the West also possesses a light; that a new light is able to approach the 'ex Oriente Lux'. If this does not take place, then the Eastern problem will remain unsolved. This social order will need to reckon with certain demands which are a necessity of our age. The first of these demands is: Industry, by virtue of its own natural legitimacy, must become a unity over the face of the whole earth. The second demand is: On the basis of the life of rights, all men are equal. And the third is: Every individual must choose his nationality with the same freedom that he chooses his religion. A brotherhood of states then, of more or less equal standing, is taking the place of the British Empire. The spiritual history of mankind demands that this transformation be undertaken and carried further in full consciousness of the goal to be attained. For evolution leaves open only two ways. Either the Voice of the Spirit of the Age will remain unheard and unheeded, and in that case the East will determine to destroy Western civilization, economically if not politically or militarily. This will arise because the West is immoral.

But the East will then be unable to put up a better social organization in its place of the old, and will lead the way back to primitive industrial conditions.

Or the call of the Spirit of the Age will be heard, and heard in that place where there is not only the possibility of knowledge, but where action is also undertaken. This is the tremendous question which today emerges from the theme of King Arthur, and from the quest for the Grail.'[2]

To that extent, and through the Four Worlds Institute, in association with Buckingham University in England generally, and our Indian colleague V.S. Mahesh specifically, we have now established a Masters programme in Transformation Management, taking on from where our Management MBA has left off.

BIBLIOGRAPHY

1 Branson, R., *Losing My Virginity*, Virgin Publishing, 1998.
2 Stein, W., *The Death of Merlin*, Floris Books, 1990.

Index